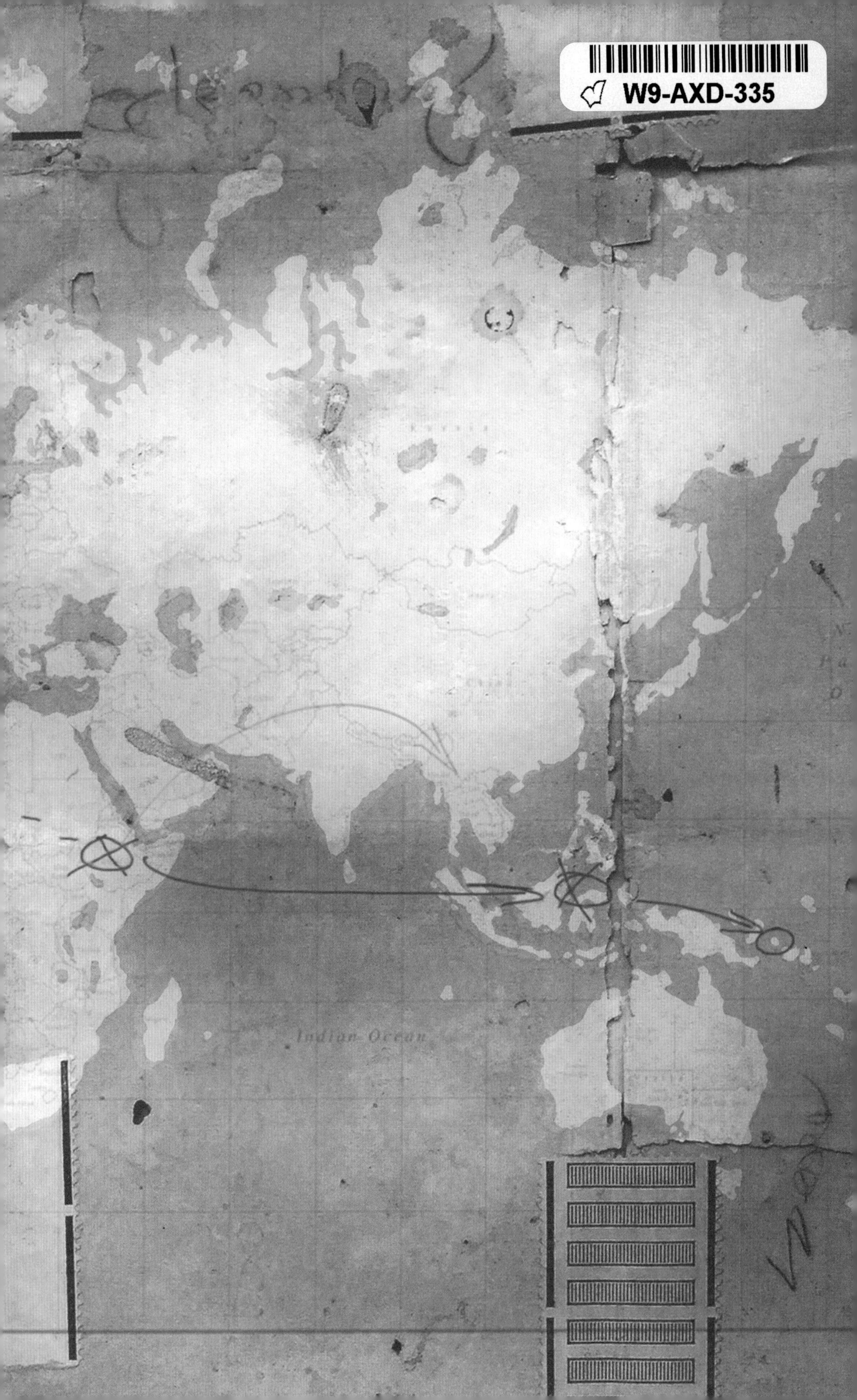
Indian Ocean

*For my dad, Dermot Mooney,
who took me to the movies.*

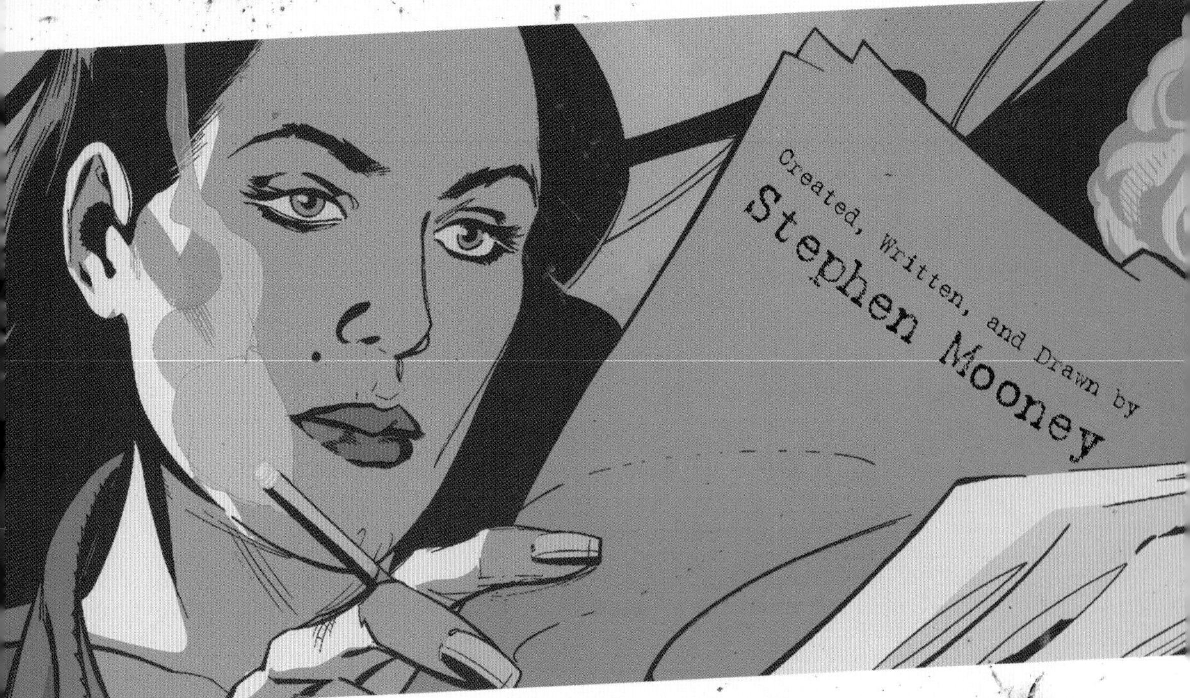
Created, Written, and Drawn by
Stephen Mooney

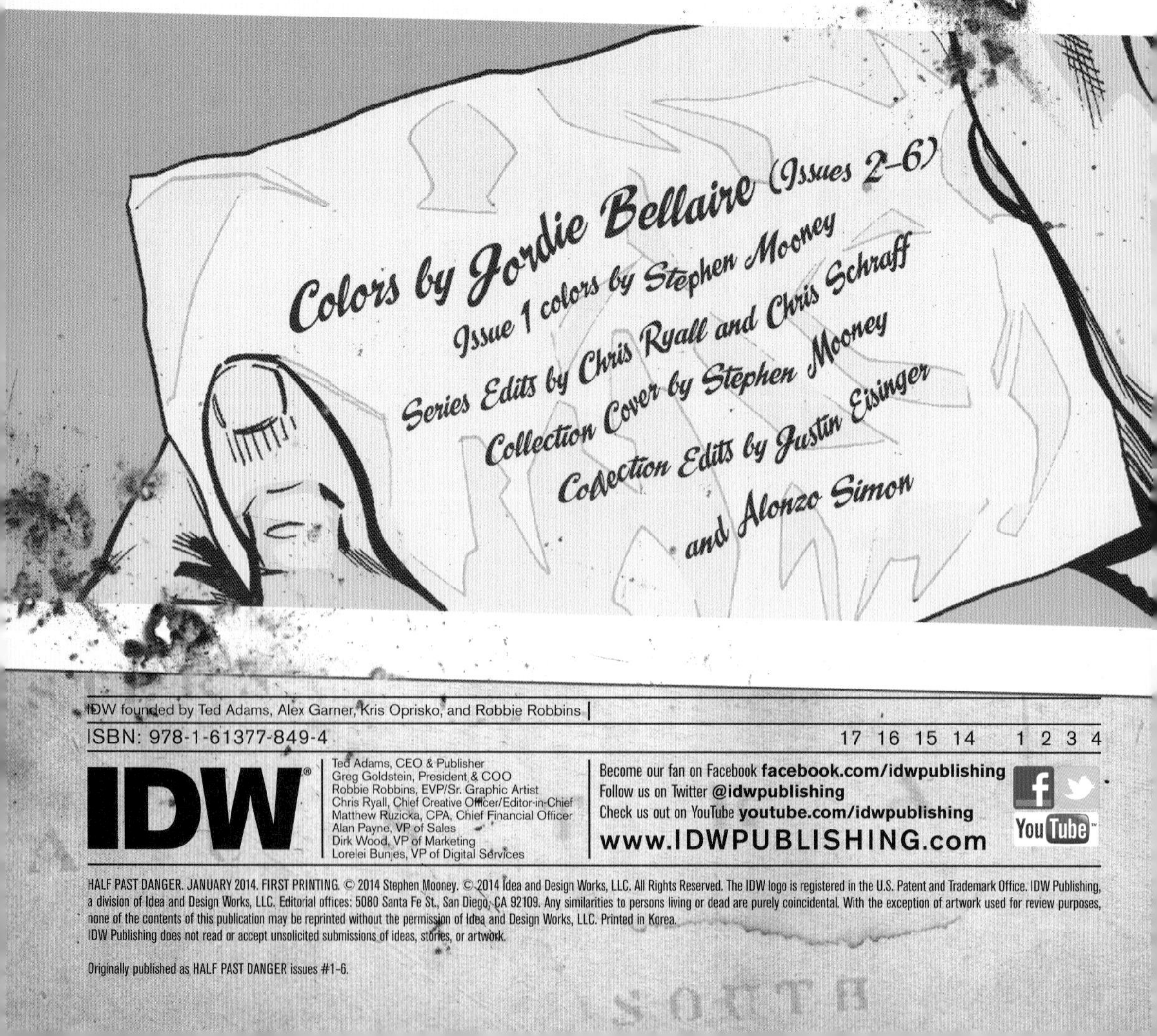
Colors by Jordie Bellaire (Issues 2-6)
Issue 1 colors by Stephen Mooney
Series Edits by Chris Ryall and Chris Schraff
Collection Cover by Stephen Mooney
Collection Edits by Justin Eisinger
and Alonzo Simon

IDW founded by Ted Adams, Alex Garner, Kris Oprisko, and Robbie Robbins

ISBN: 978-1-61377-849-4

17 16 15 14 1 2 3 4

IDW

Ted Adams, CEO & Publisher
Greg Goldstein, President & COO
Robbie Robbins, EVP/Sr. Graphic Artist
Chris Ryall, Chief Creative Officer/Editor-in-Chief
Matthew Ruzicka, CPA, Chief Financial Officer
Alan Payne, VP of Sales
Dirk Wood, VP of Marketing
Lorelei Bunjes, VP of Digital Services

Become our fan on Facebook **facebook.com/idwpublishing**
Follow us on Twitter **@idwpublishing**
Check us out on YouTube **youtube.com/idwpublishing**
www.IDWPUBLISHING.com

Originally published as HALF PAST DANGER issues #1–6.

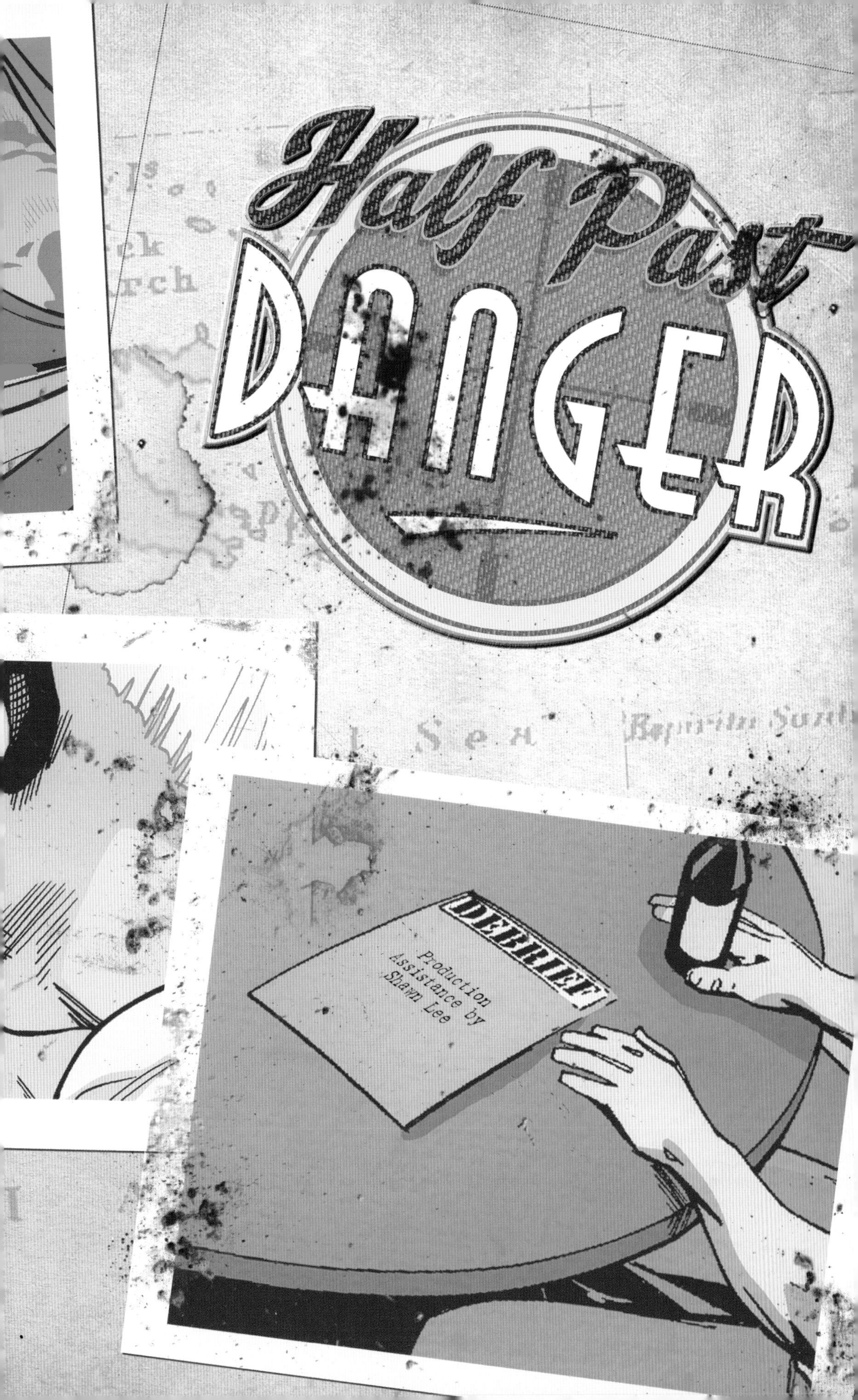
Half Past
DANGER
DEBRIEF
Production
Assistance by
Shawn Lee

Chapter One

BITE THE BULLET

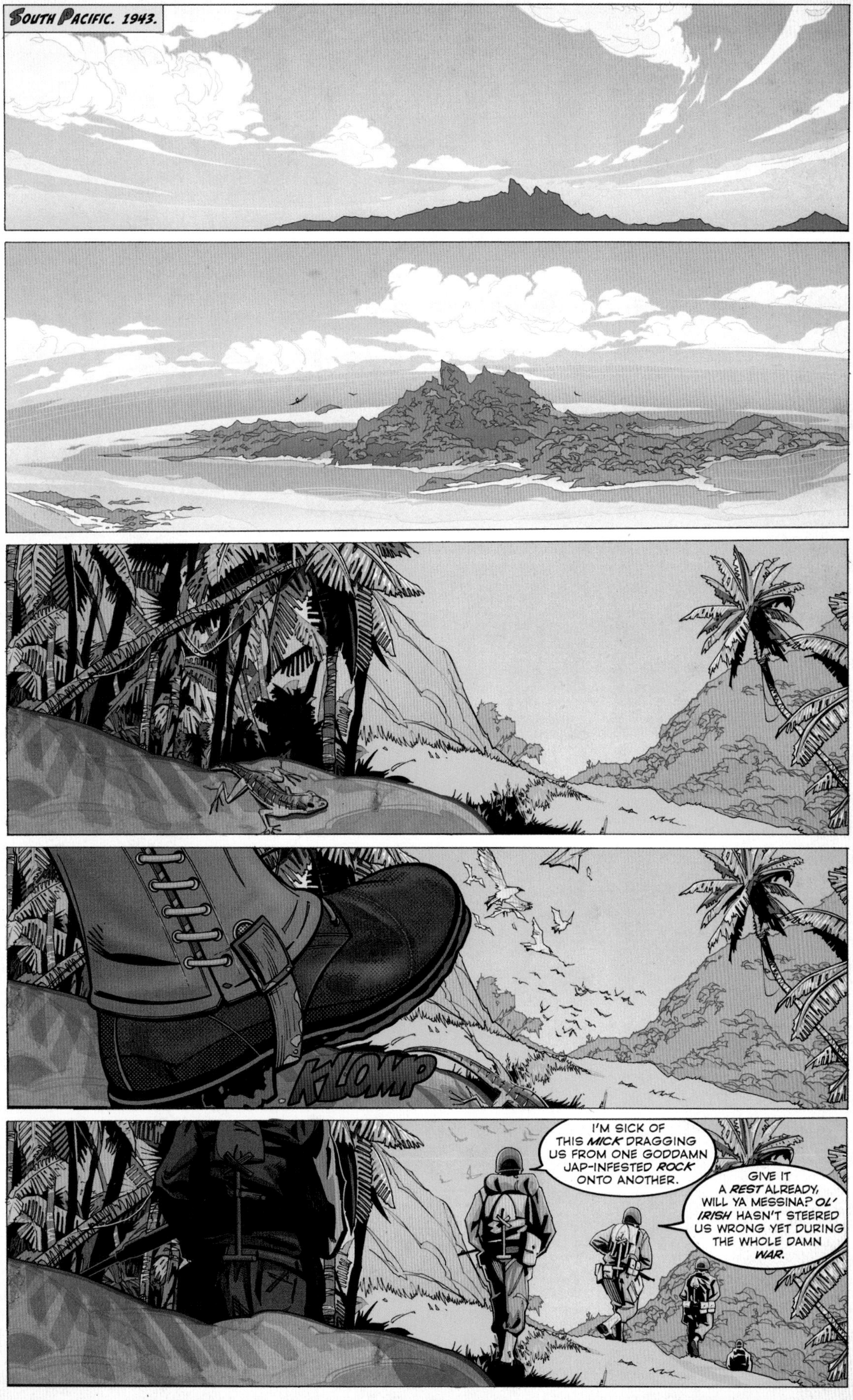
SOUTH PACIFIC. 1943.
KLOMP
I'M SICK OF THIS MICK DRAGGING US FROM ONE GODDAMN JAP-INFESTED ROCK ONTO ANOTHER.
GIVE IT A REST ALREADY, WILL YA MESSINA? OL' IRISH HASN'T STEERED US WRONG YET DURING THE WHOLE DAMN WAR.

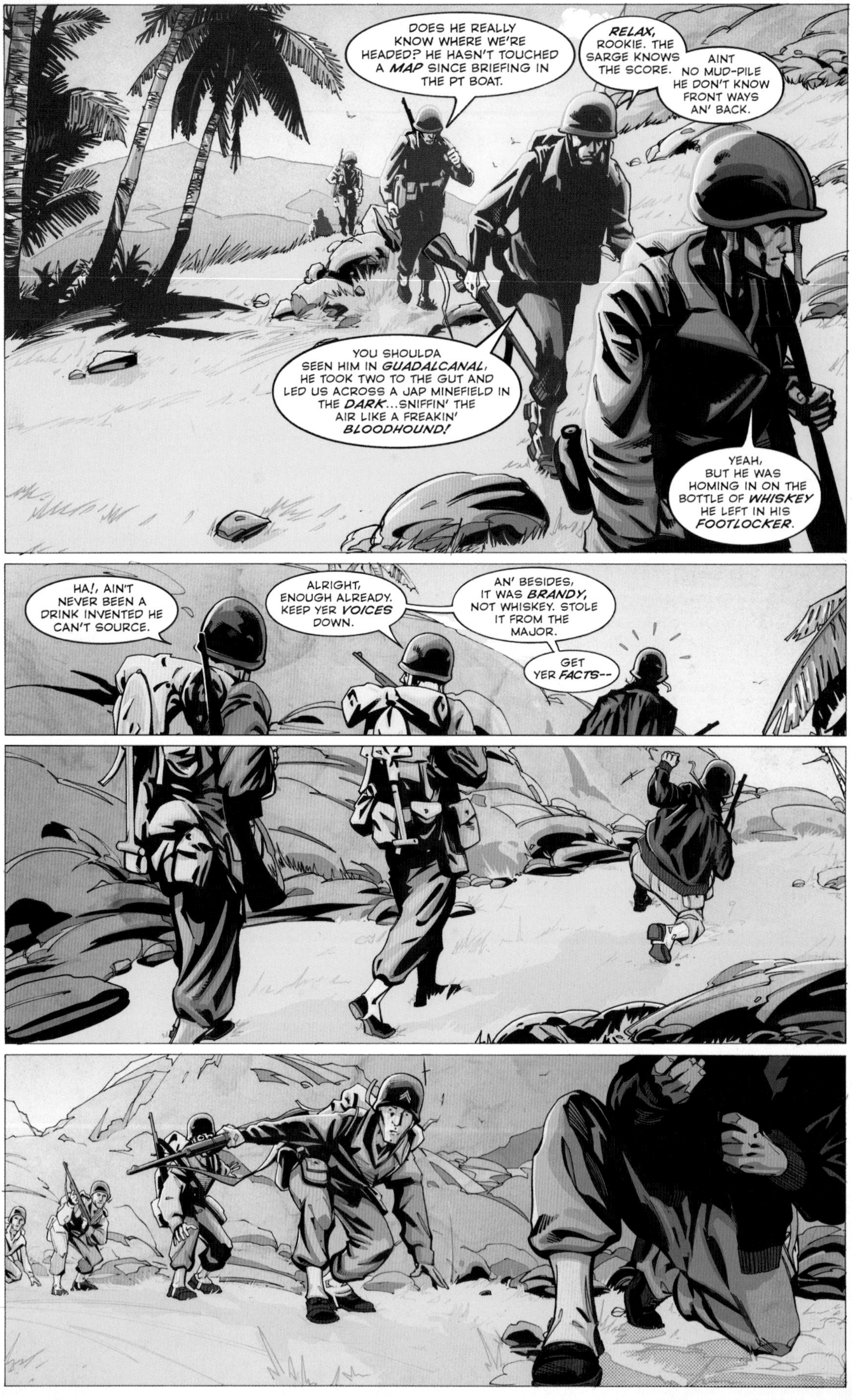
DOES HE REALLY KNOW WHERE WE'RE HEADED? HE HASN'T TOUCHED A MAP SINCE BRIEFING IN THE PT BOAT.
RELAX, ROOKIE. THE SARGE KNOWS THE SCORE.
AINT NO MUD-PILE HE DON'T KNOW FRONT WAYS AN' BACK.
YOU SHOULDA SEEN HIM IN GUADALCANAL, HE TOOK TWO TO THE GUT AND LED US ACROSS A JAP MINEFIELD IN THE DARK...SNIFFIN' THE AIR LIKE A FREAKIN' BLOODHOUND!
YEAH, BUT HE WAS HOMING IN ON THE BOTTLE OF WHISKEY HE LEFT IN HIS FOOTLOCKER.
HA!, AIN'T NEVER BEEN A DRINK INVENTED HE CAN'T SOURCE.
ALRIGHT, ENOUGH ALREADY. KEEP YER VOICES DOWN.
AN' BESIDES, IT WAS BRANDY, NOT WHISKEY. STOLE IT FROM THE MAJOR.
GET YER FACTS--

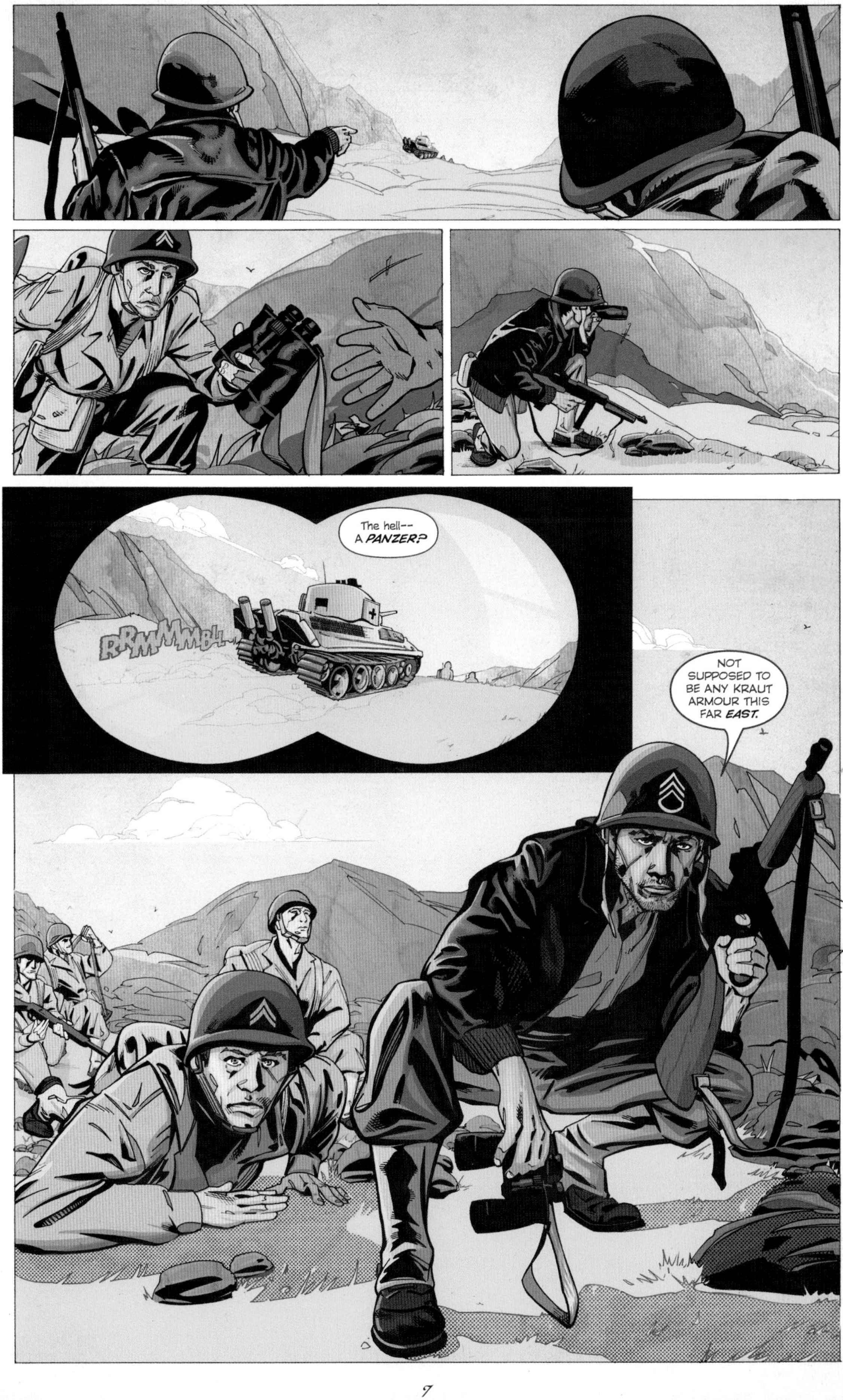
The hell--
A PANZER?
RRMMMBL
NOT SUPPOSED TO BE ANY KRAUT ARMOUR THIS FAR EAST.

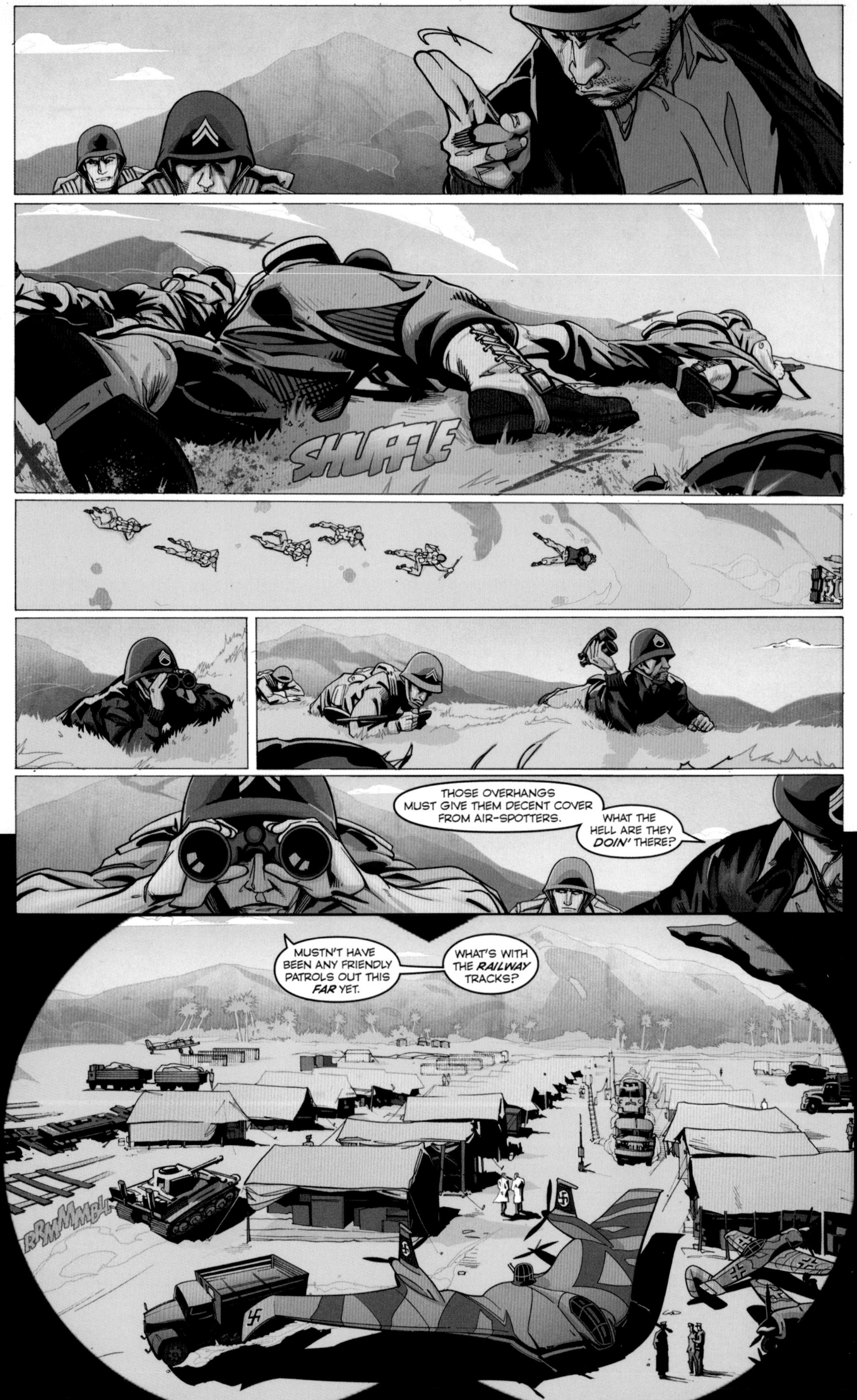
SHUFFLE
THOSE OVERHANGS MUST GIVE THEM DECENT COVER FROM AIR-SPOTTERS.
WHAT THE HELL ARE THEY DOIN' THERE?
MUSTN'T HAVE BEEN ANY FRIENDLY PATROLS OUT THIS FAR YET.
WHAT'S WITH THE RAILWAY TRACKS?
RRMMMBL

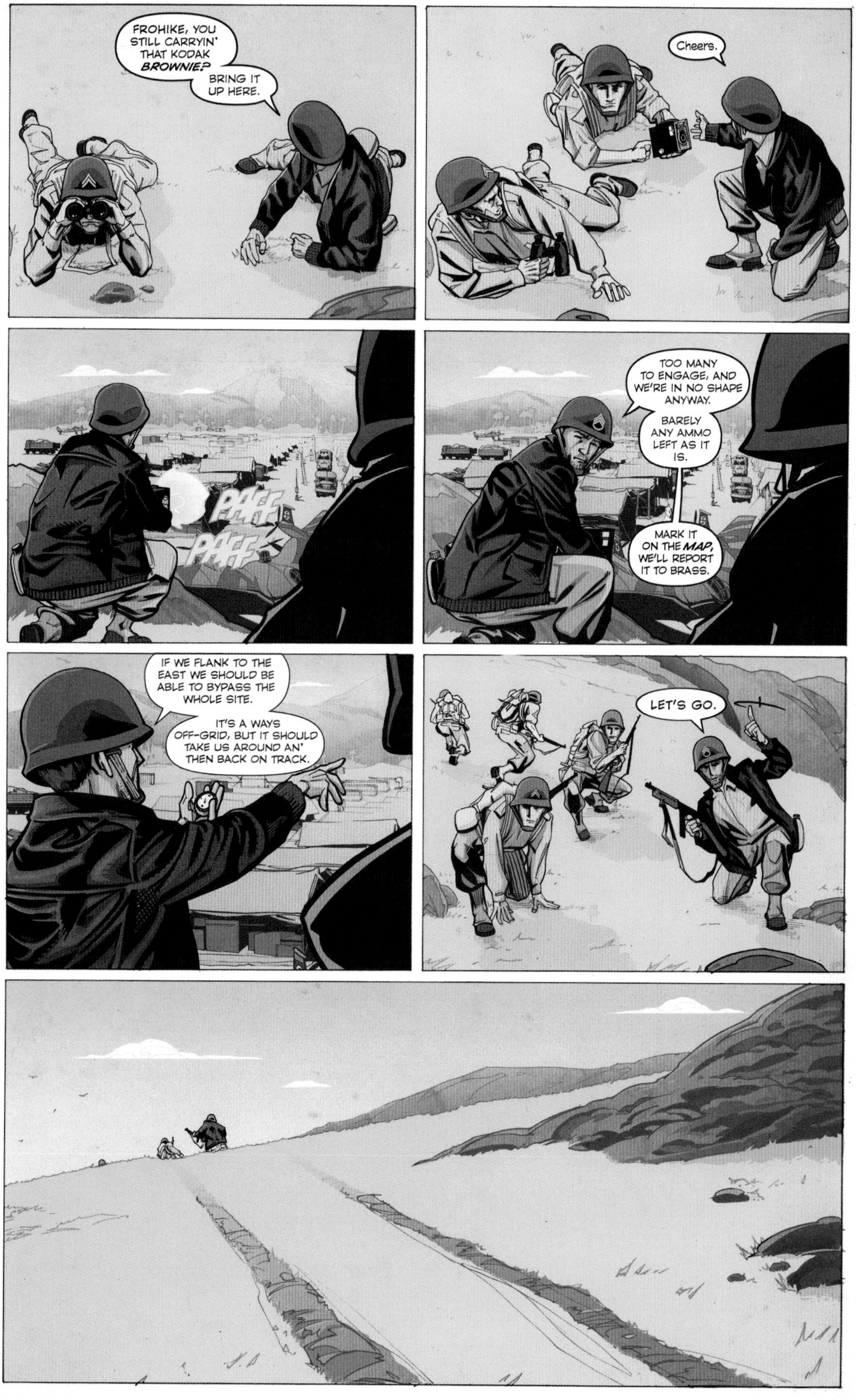
FROHIKE, YOU STILL CARRYIN' THAT KODAK BROWNIE?
BRING IT UP HERE.
Cheers.
PAFF
PAFF
TOO MANY TO ENGAGE, AND WE'RE IN NO SHAPE ANYWAY.
BARELY ANY AMMO LEFT AS IT IS.
MARK IT ON THE MAP, WE'LL REPORT IT TO BRASS.
IF WE FLANK TO THE EAST WE SHOULD BE ABLE TO BYPASS THE WHOLE SITE.
IT'S A WAYS OFF-GRID, BUT IT SHOULD TAKE US AROUND AN' THEN BACK ON TRACK.
LET'S GO.

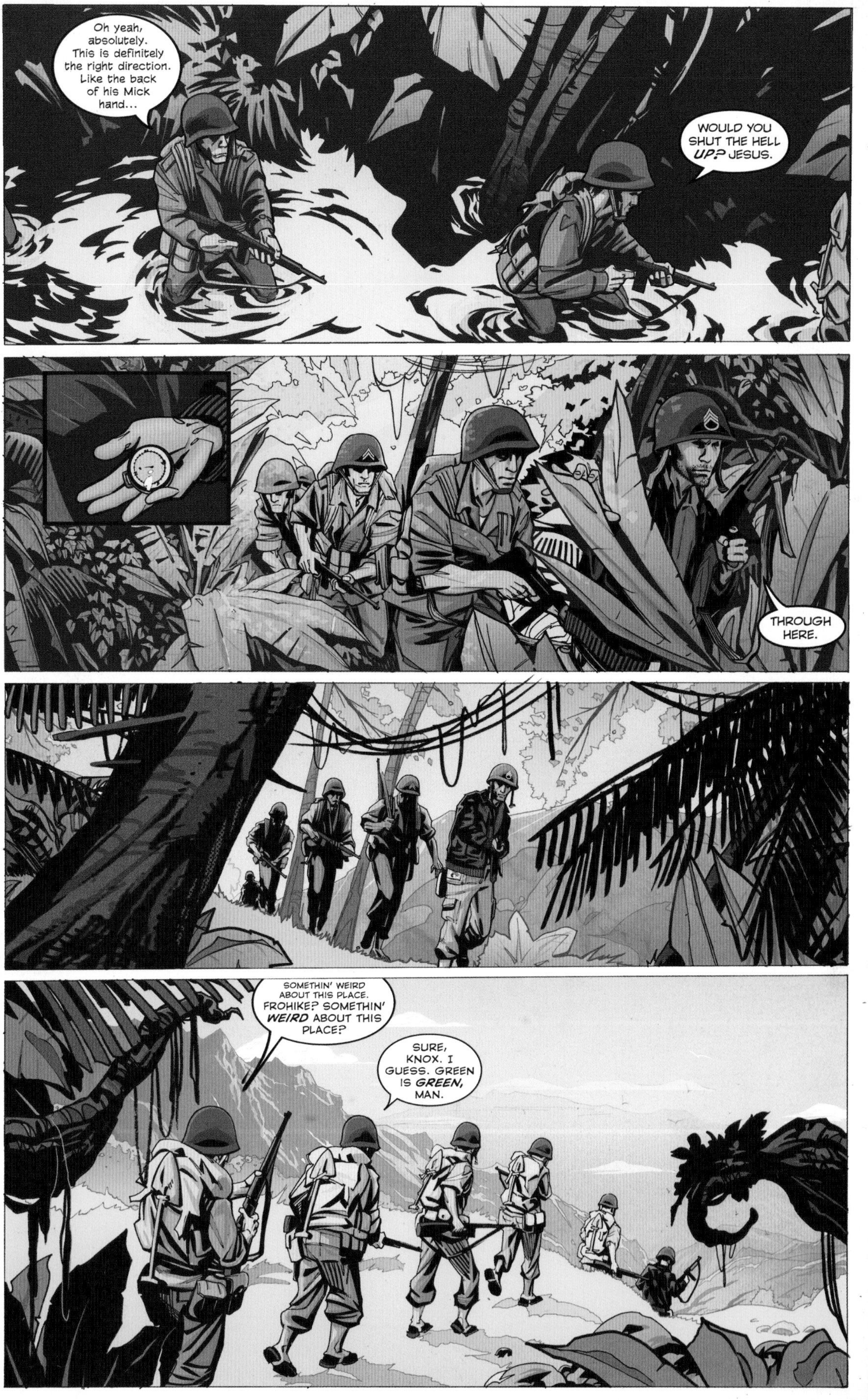
Oh yeah, absolutely. This is definitely the right direction. Like the back of his Mick hand...
WOULD YOU SHUT THE HELL UP? JESUS.
THROUGH HERE.
SOMETHIN' WEIRD ABOUT THIS PLACE. FROHIKE? SOMETHIN' WEIRD ABOUT THIS PLACE?
SURE, KNOX. I GUESS. GREEN IS GREEN, MAN.

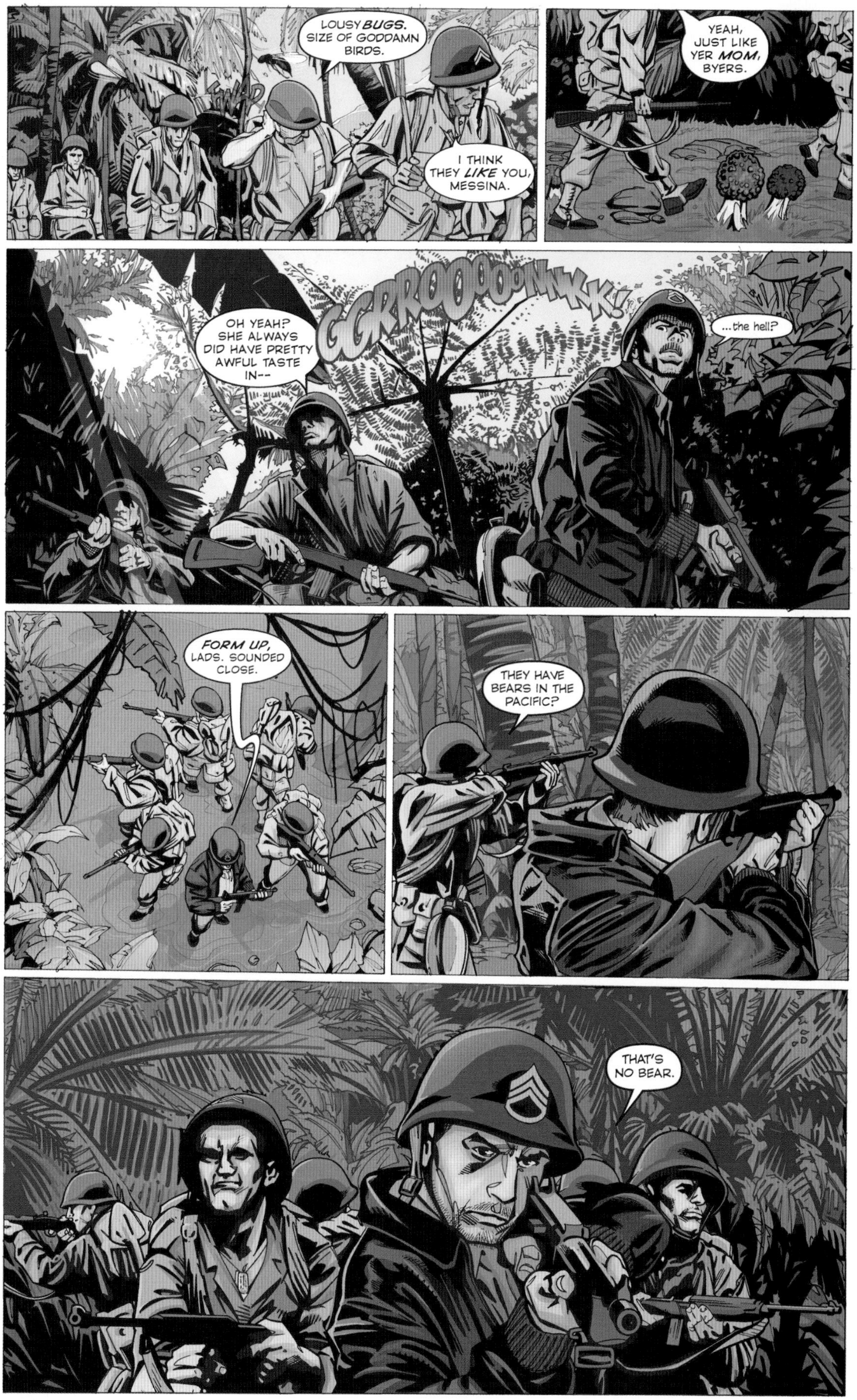
LOUSY BUGS. SIZE OF GODDAMN BIRDS.
I THINK THEY LIKE YOU, MESSINA.
YEAH, JUST LIKE YER MOM, BYERS.
OH YEAH? SHE ALWAYS DID HAVE PRETTY AWFUL TASTE IN--
GGRROOOOONNKK!
...the hell?
FORM UP, LADS. SOUNDED CLOSE.
THEY HAVE BEARS IN THE PACIFIC?
THAT'S NO BEAR.

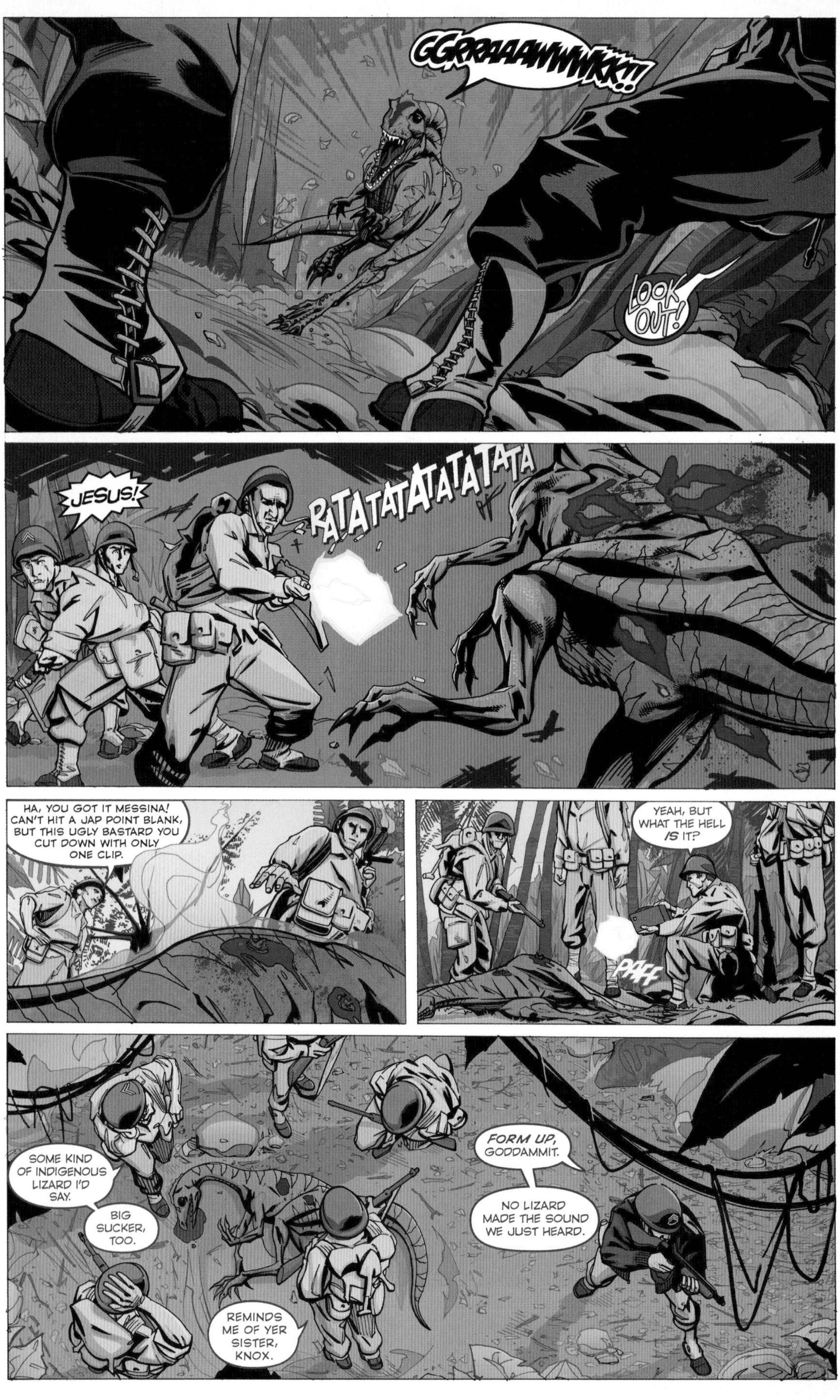
GGRRAAAWWKK!!
LOOK OUT!
JESUS!
RATATATATATATATA
HA, YOU GOT IT MESSINA! CAN'T HIT A JAP POINT BLANK, BUT THIS UGLY BASTARD YOU CUT DOWN WITH ONLY ONE CLIP.
YEAH, BUT WHAT THE HELL *IS* IT?
PFFF
SOME KIND OF INDIGENOUS LIZARD I'D SAY.
BIG SUCKER, TOO.
REMINDS ME OF YER SISTER, KNOX.
FORM UP, GODDAMMIT.
NO LIZARD MADE THE SOUND WE JUST HEARD.

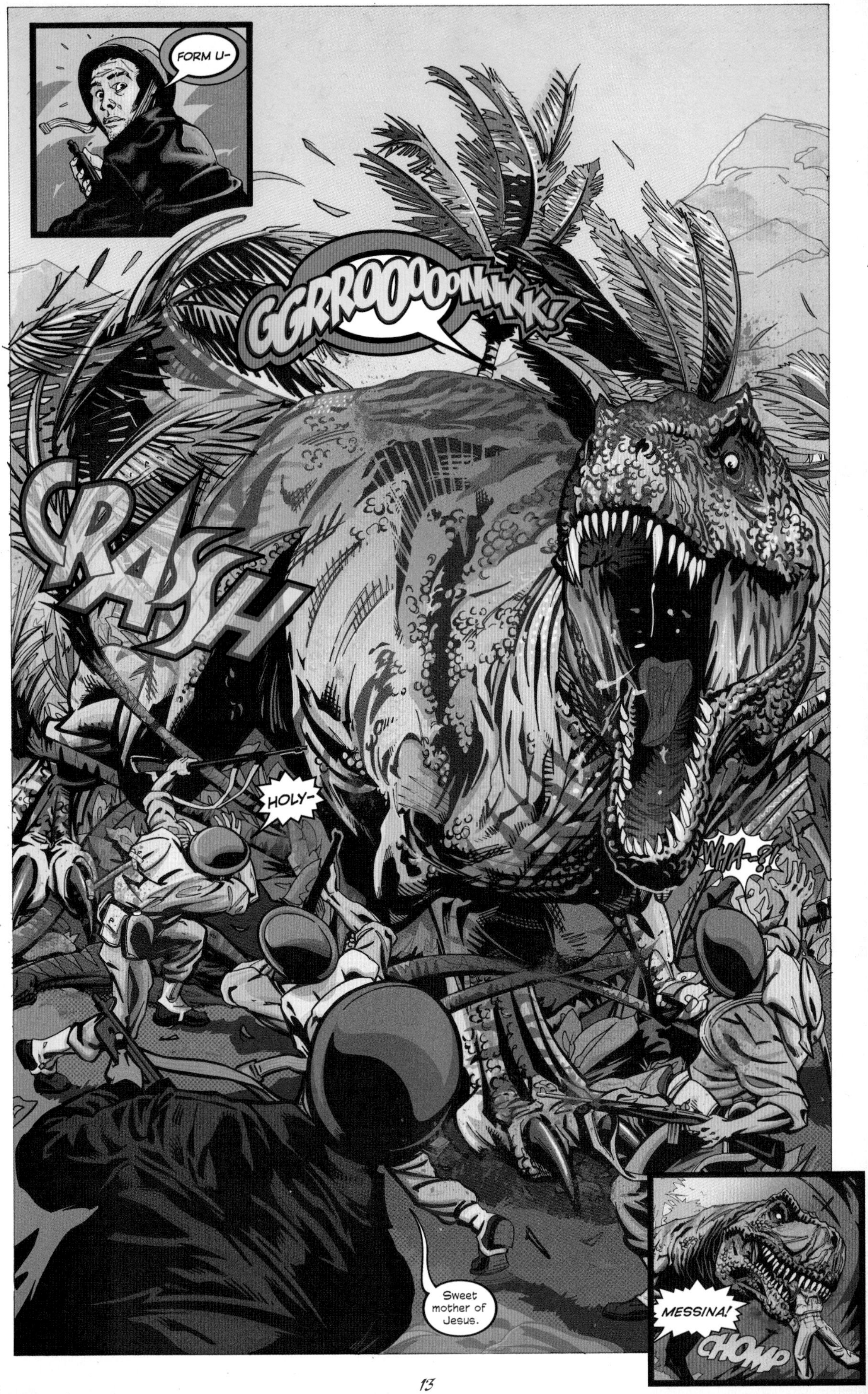
FORM U-
GGRROOOOONNKK!
CRASH
HOLY-
WHA-?!
Sweet mother of Jesus.
MESSINA!
CHOMP

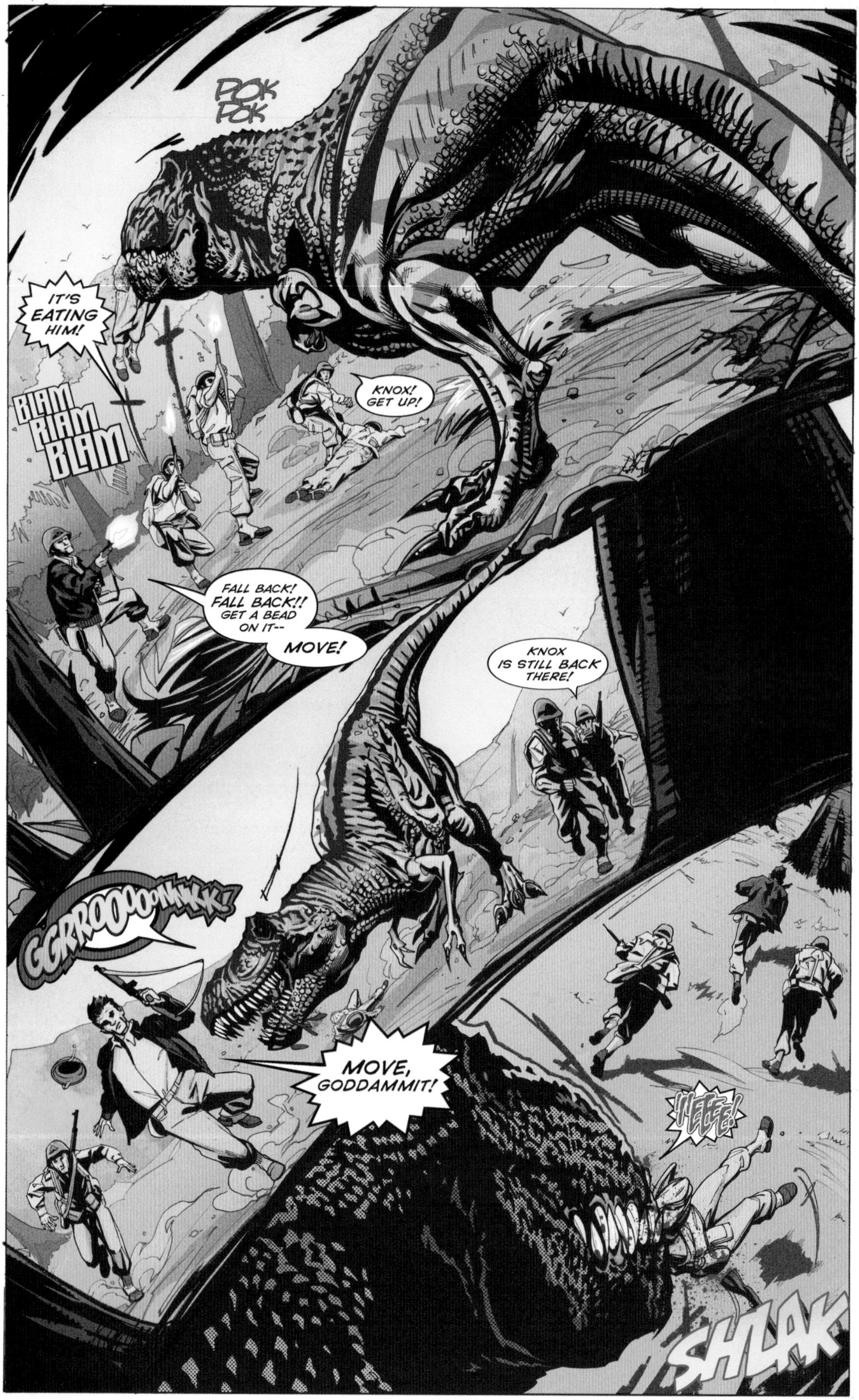
POK POK
IT'S EATING HIM!
BLAM BLAM BLAM
KNOX! GET UP!
FALL BACK! FALL BACK!! GET A BEAD ON IT--
MOVE!
KNOX IS STILL BACK THERE!
MOVE, GODDAMMIT!
SHLAK

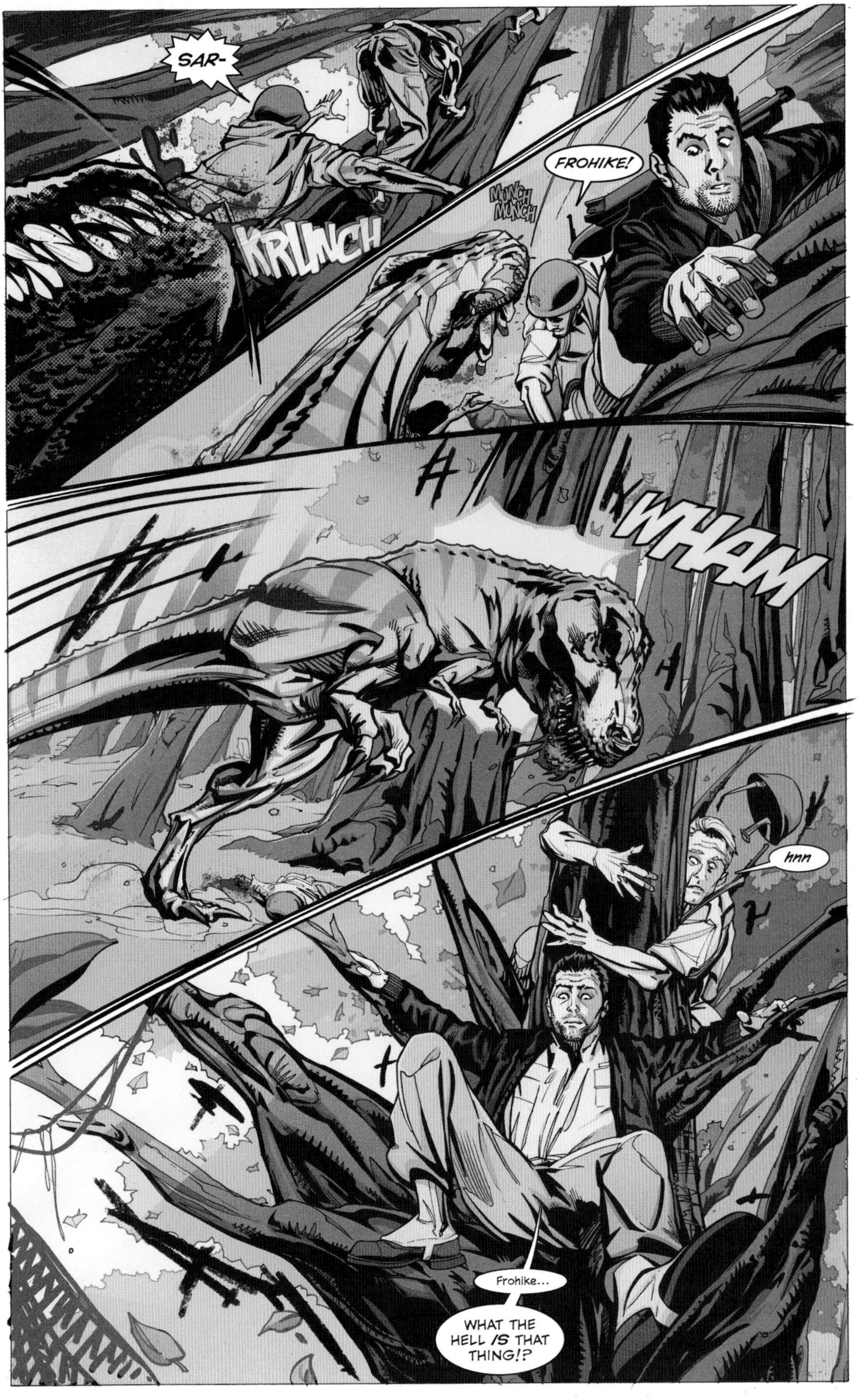
SAR-
KRUNCH
FROHIKE!
MUNCH MUNCH
WHAM
hnn
Frohike...
WHAT THE HELL *IS* THAT THING!?

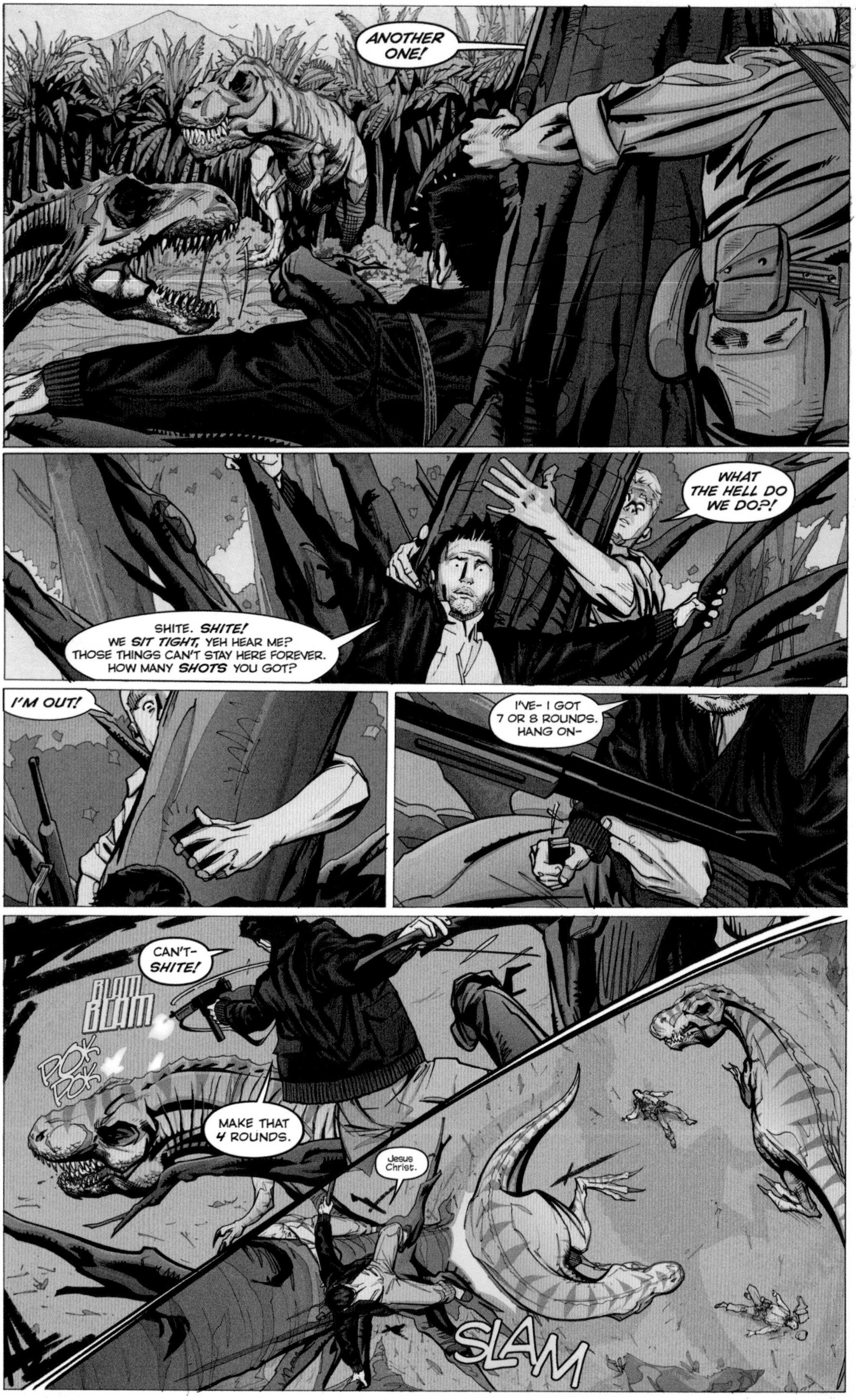
ANOTHER ONE!
WHAT THE HELL DO WE DO?!
SHITE. SHITE! WE SIT TIGHT, YEH HEAR ME? THOSE THINGS CAN'T STAY HERE FOREVER. HOW MANY SHOTS YOU GOT?
I'M OUT!
I'VE- I GOT 7 OR 8 ROUNDS. HANG ON-
CAN'T- SHITE!
BLAM BLAM
POK POK
MAKE THAT 4 ROUNDS.
Jesus Christ.
SLAM

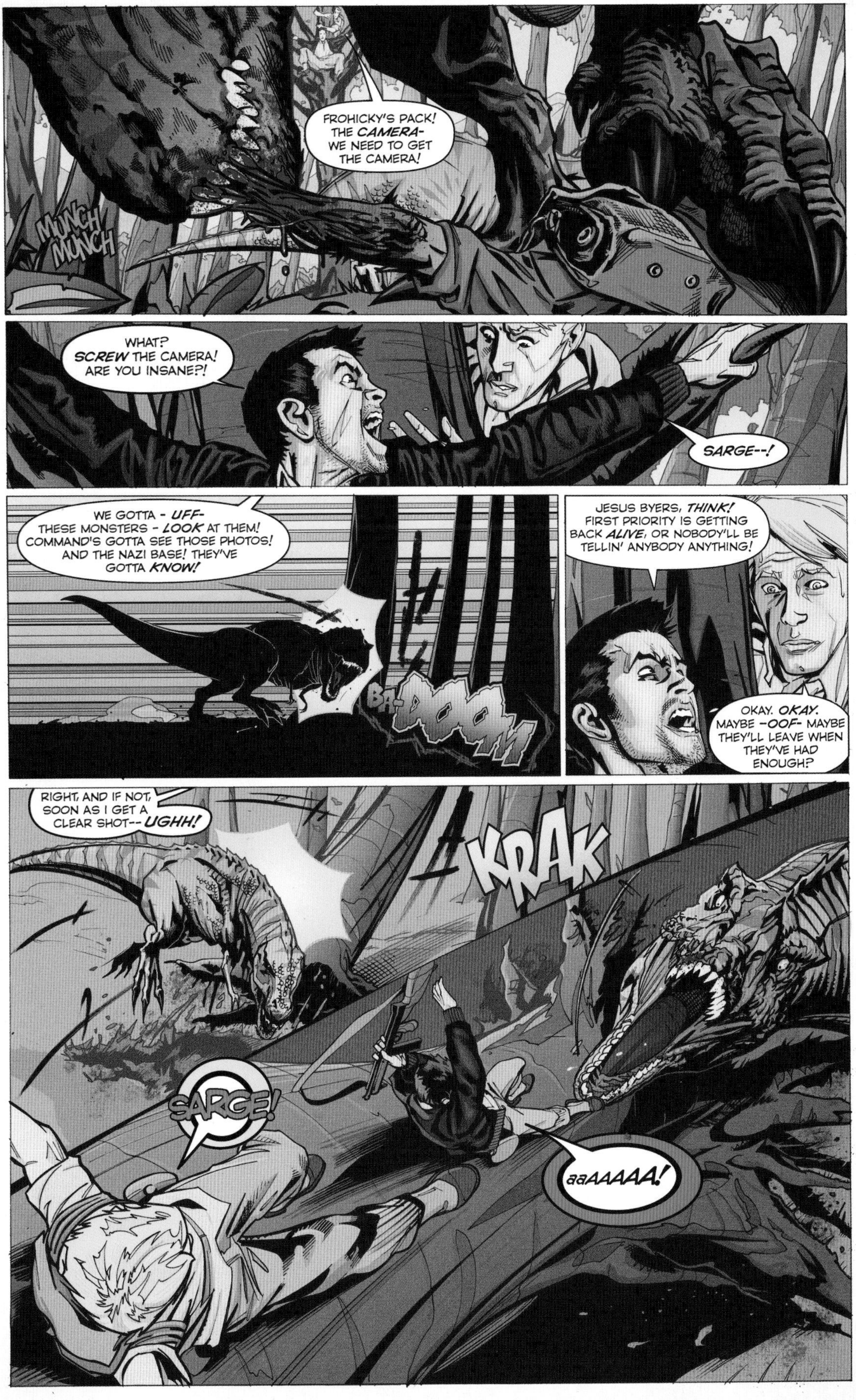
FROHICKY'S PACK! THE CAMERA- WE NEED TO GET THE CAMERA!
MUNCH MUNCH
WHAT? SCREW THE CAMERA! ARE YOU INSANE?!
SARGE--!
WE GOTTA - UFF- THESE MONSTERS - LOOK AT THEM! COMMAND'S GOTTA SEE THOSE PHOTOS! AND THE NAZI BASE! THEY'VE GOTTA KNOW!
BA-DOOM
JESUS BYERS, THINK! FIRST PRIORITY IS GETTING BACK ALIVE, OR NOBODY'LL BE TELLIN' ANYBODY ANYTHING!
OKAY. OKAY. MAYBE -OOF- MAYBE THEY'LL LEAVE WHEN THEY'VE HAD ENOUGH?
RIGHT, AND IF NOT, SOON AS I GET A CLEAR SHOT--UGHH!
KRAK
SARGE!
aaAAAAA!

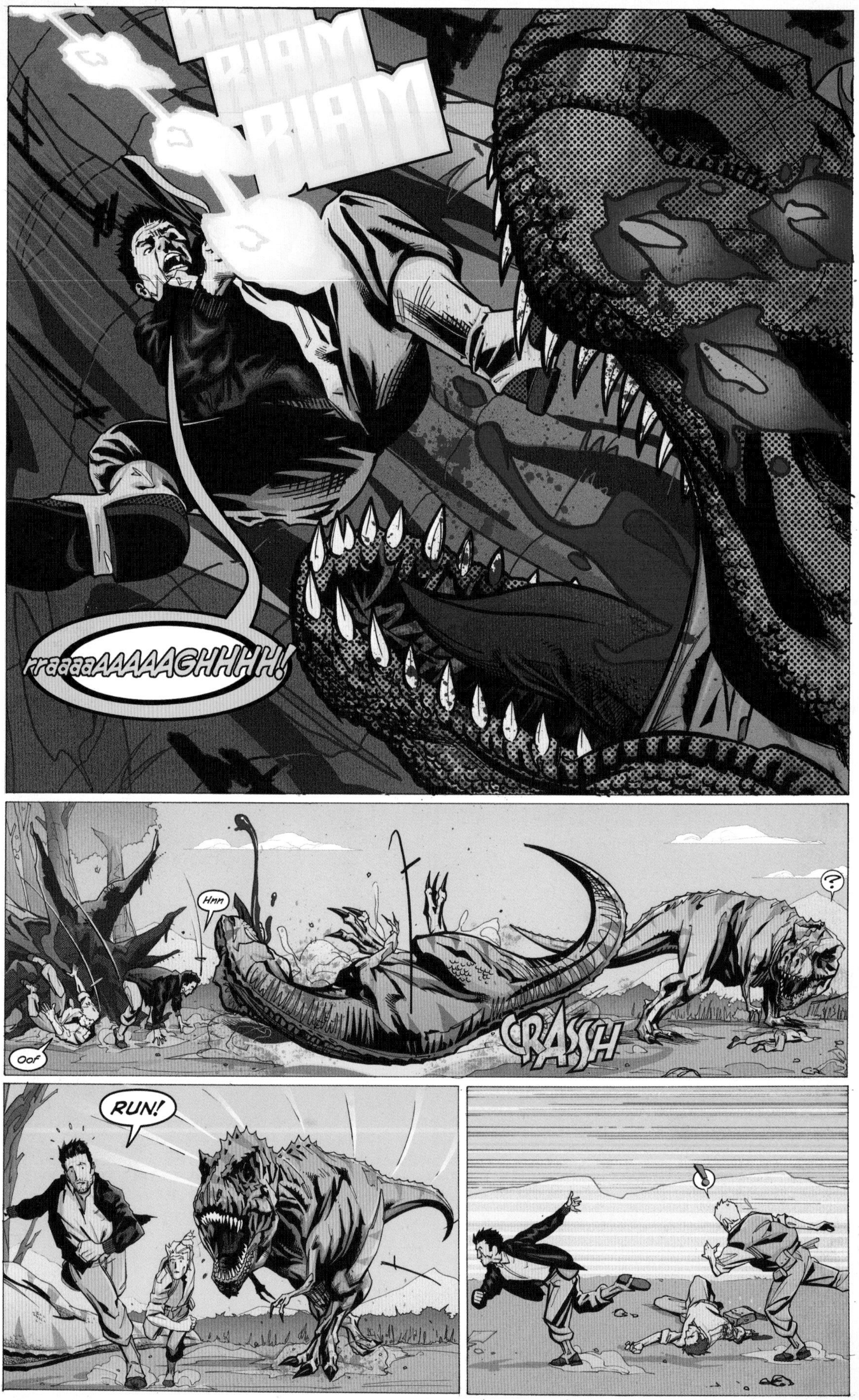
BLAM
BLAM
rraaaaAAAAAGHHHH!
Hmn
?
Oof
CRASSH
RUN!
!

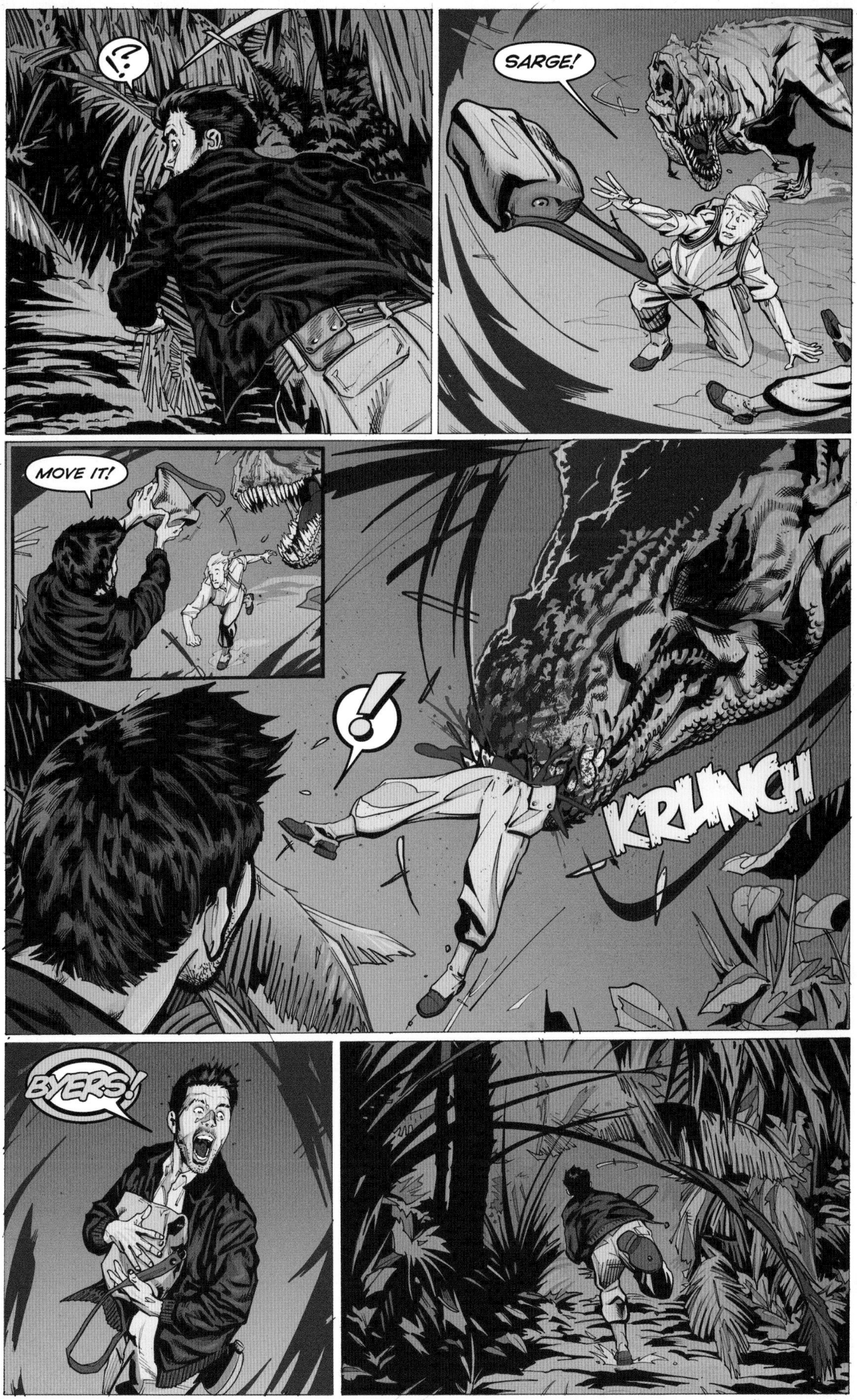
!?
SARGE!
MOVE IT!
!
KRUNCH
BYERS!

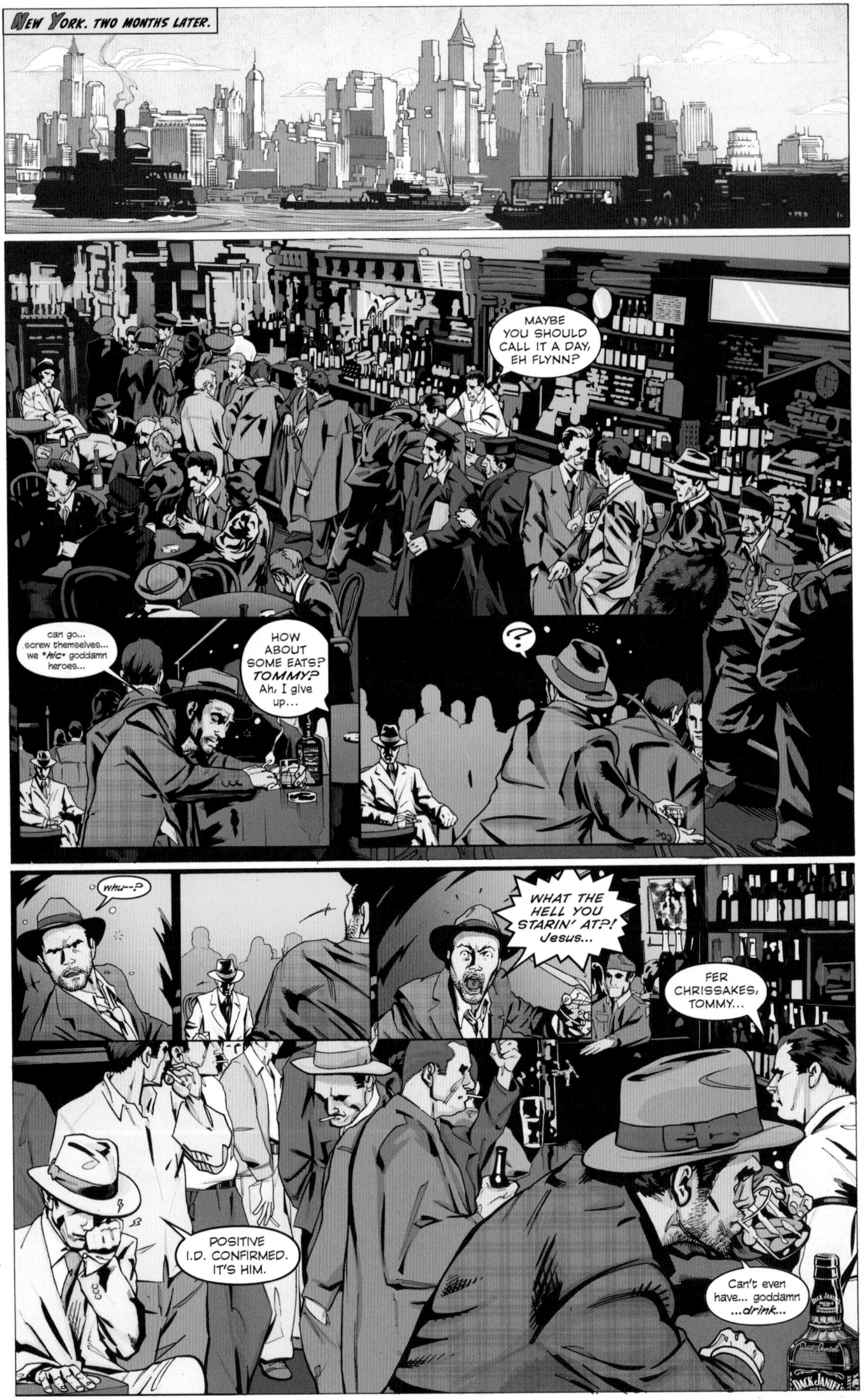
NEW YORK. TWO MONTHS LATER.
MAYBE YOU SHOULD CALL IT A DAY, EH FLYNN?
can go... screw themselves... we *hic* goddamn heroes...
HOW ABOUT SOME EATS? TOMMY? Ah, I give up...
?
whu--?
WHAT THE HELL YOU STARIN' AT?! Jesus...
FER CHRISSAKES, TOMMY...
POSITIVE I.D. CONFIRMED. IT'S HIM.
Can't even have... goddamn ...drink...

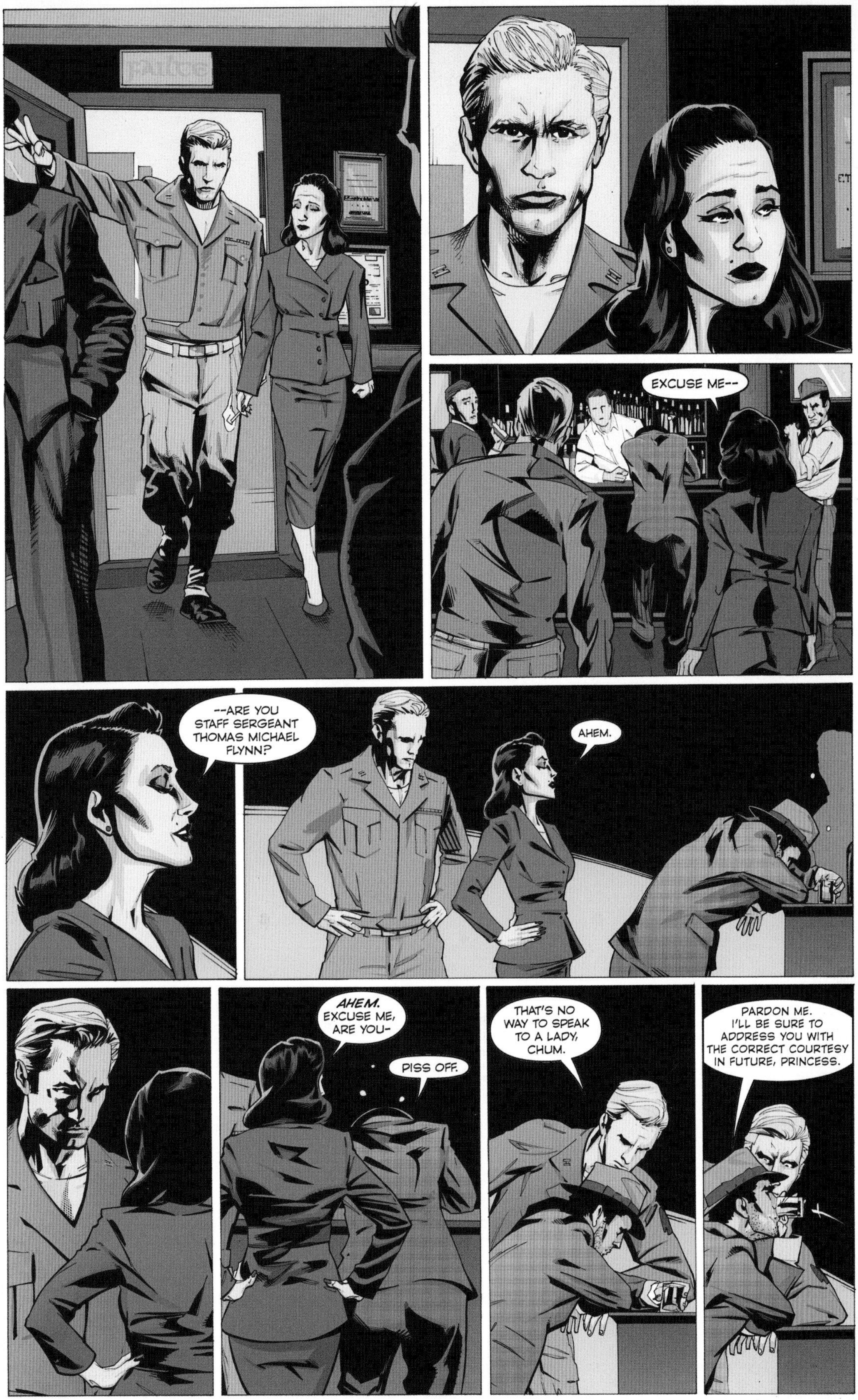
EXCUSE ME--
--ARE YOU STAFF SERGEANT THOMAS MICHAEL FLYNN?
AHEM.
AHEM. EXCUSE ME, ARE YOU-
PISS OFF.
THAT'S NO WAY TO SPEAK TO A LADY, CHUM.
PARDON ME. I'LL BE SURE TO ADDRESS YOU WITH THE CORRECT COURTESY IN FUTURE, PRINCESS.

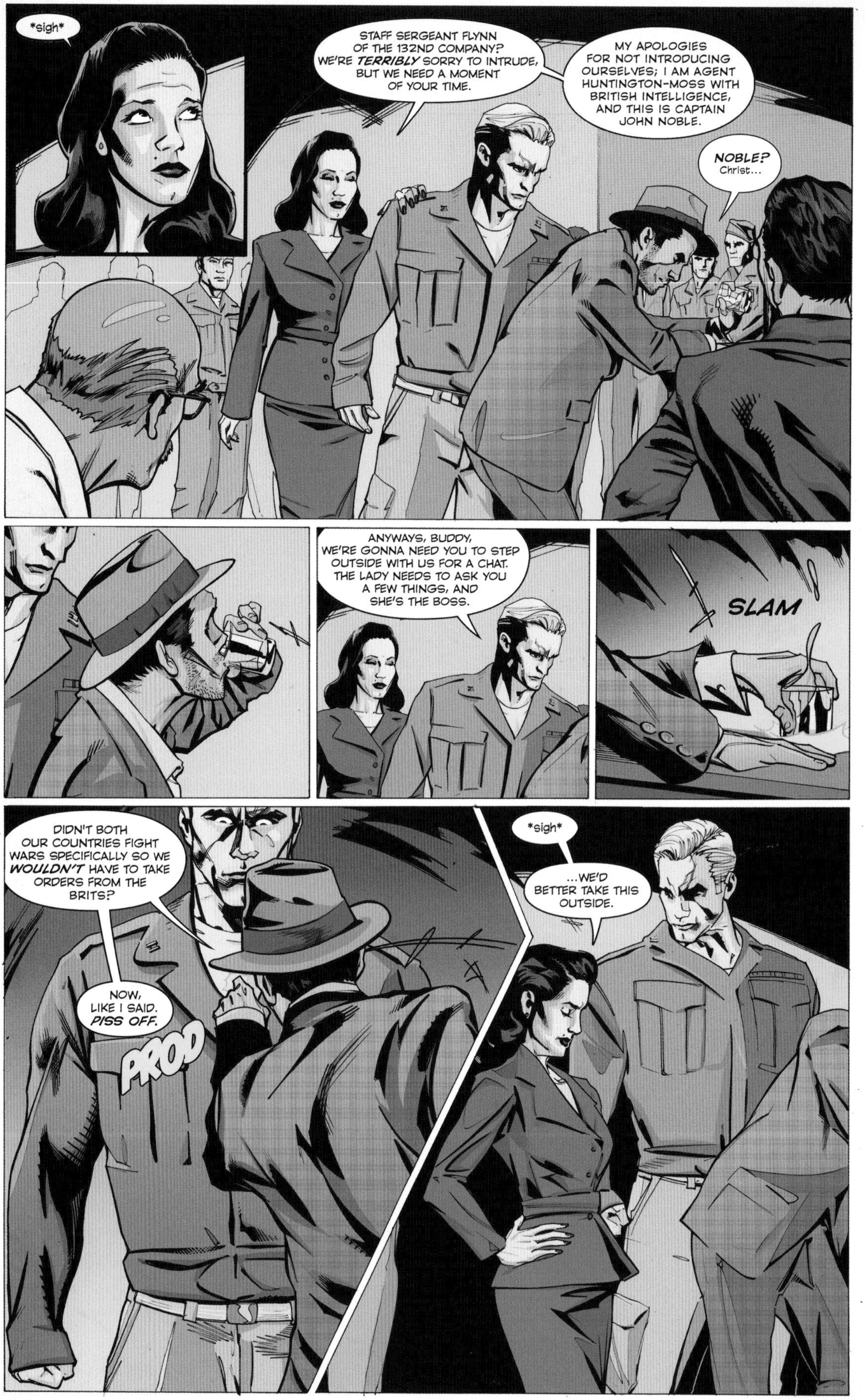

sigh
STAFF SERGEANT FLYNN OF THE 132ND COMPANY? WE'RE *TERRIBLY* SORRY TO INTRUDE, BUT WE NEED A MOMENT OF YOUR TIME.
MY APOLOGIES FOR NOT INTRODUCING OURSELVES; I AM AGENT HUNTINGTON-MOSS WITH BRITISH INTELLIGENCE, AND THIS IS CAPTAIN JOHN NOBLE.
NOBLE? Christ...
ANYWAYS, BUDDY, WE'RE GONNA NEED YOU TO STEP OUTSIDE WITH US FOR A CHAT. THE LADY NEEDS TO ASK YOU A FEW THINGS, AND SHE'S THE BOSS.
SLAM
DIDN'T BOTH OUR COUNTRIES FIGHT WARS SPECIFICALLY SO WE *WOULDN'T* HAVE TO TAKE ORDERS FROM THE BRITS?
NOW, LIKE I SAID. *PISS OFF.*
PROD
sigh
...WE'D BETTER TAKE THIS OUTSIDE.

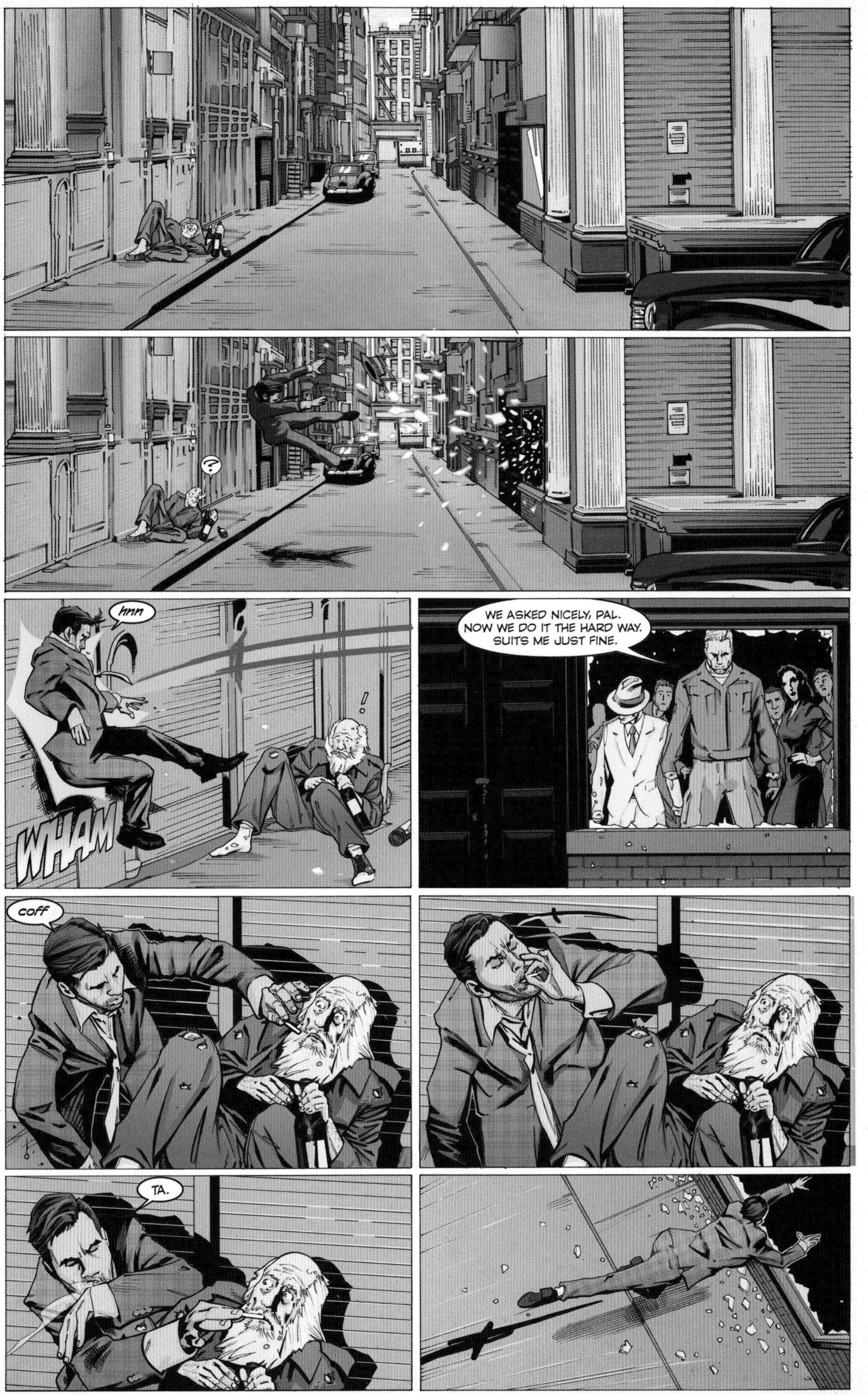
?
hnn
!
WHAM
WE ASKED NICELY, PAL.
NOW WE DO IT THE HARD WAY.
SUITS ME JUST FINE.
coff
TA.

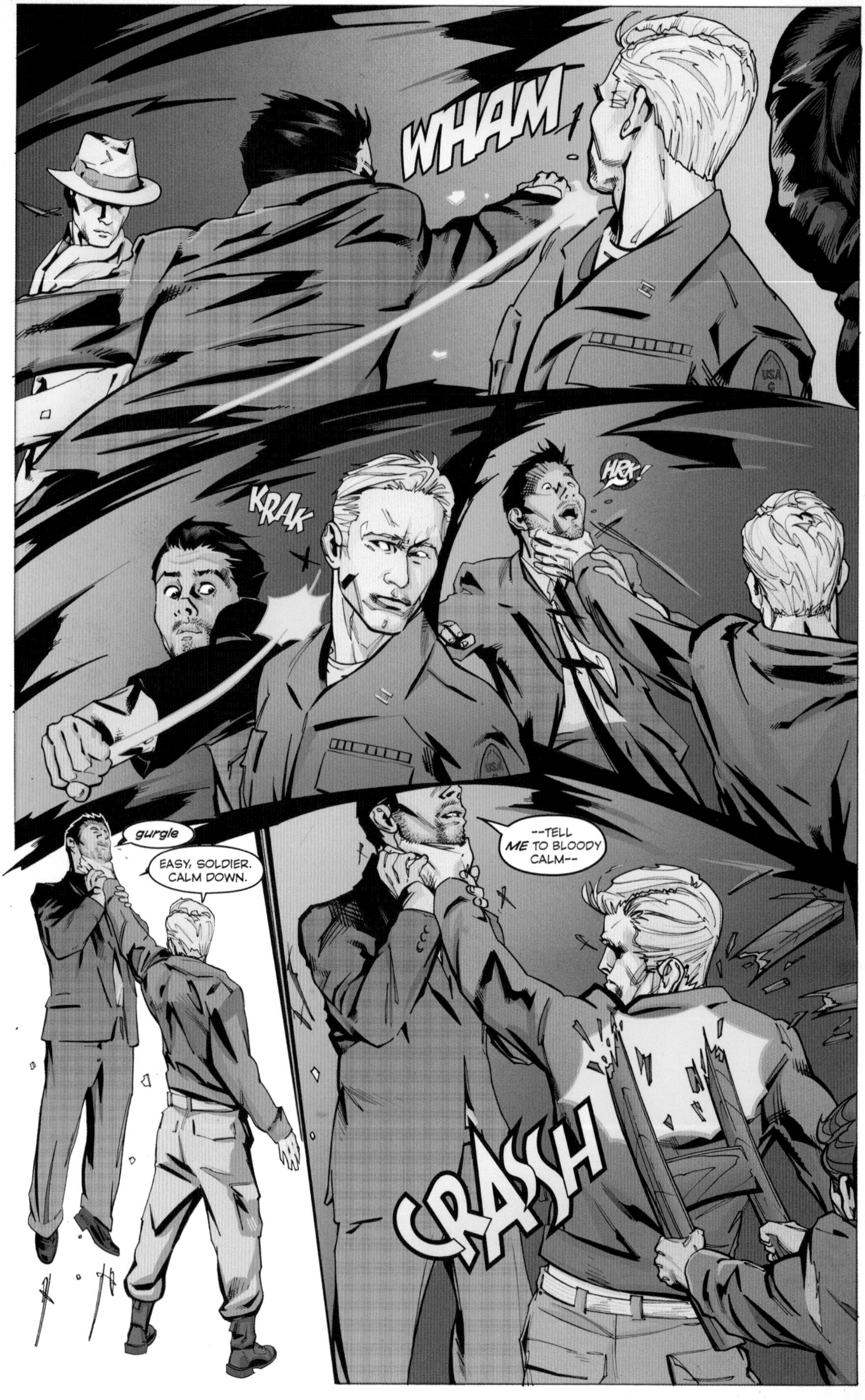
WHAM
KRAK
HRK!
gurgle
EASY, SOLDIER. CALM DOWN.
--TELL *ME* TO BLOODY CALM--
CRASH

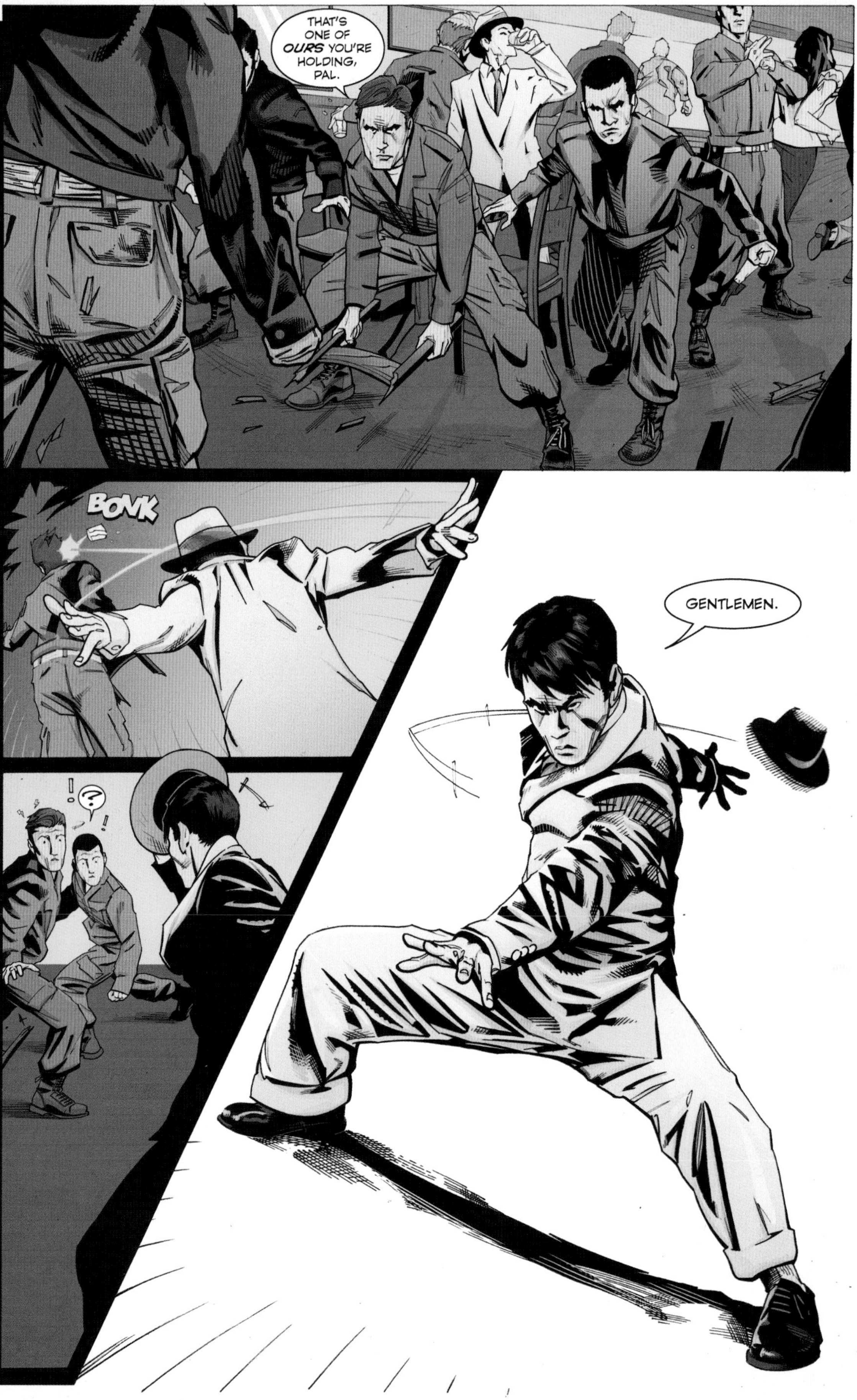
THAT'S ONE OF OURS YOU'RE HOLDING, PAL.
BONK
!
?
!
GENTLEMEN.

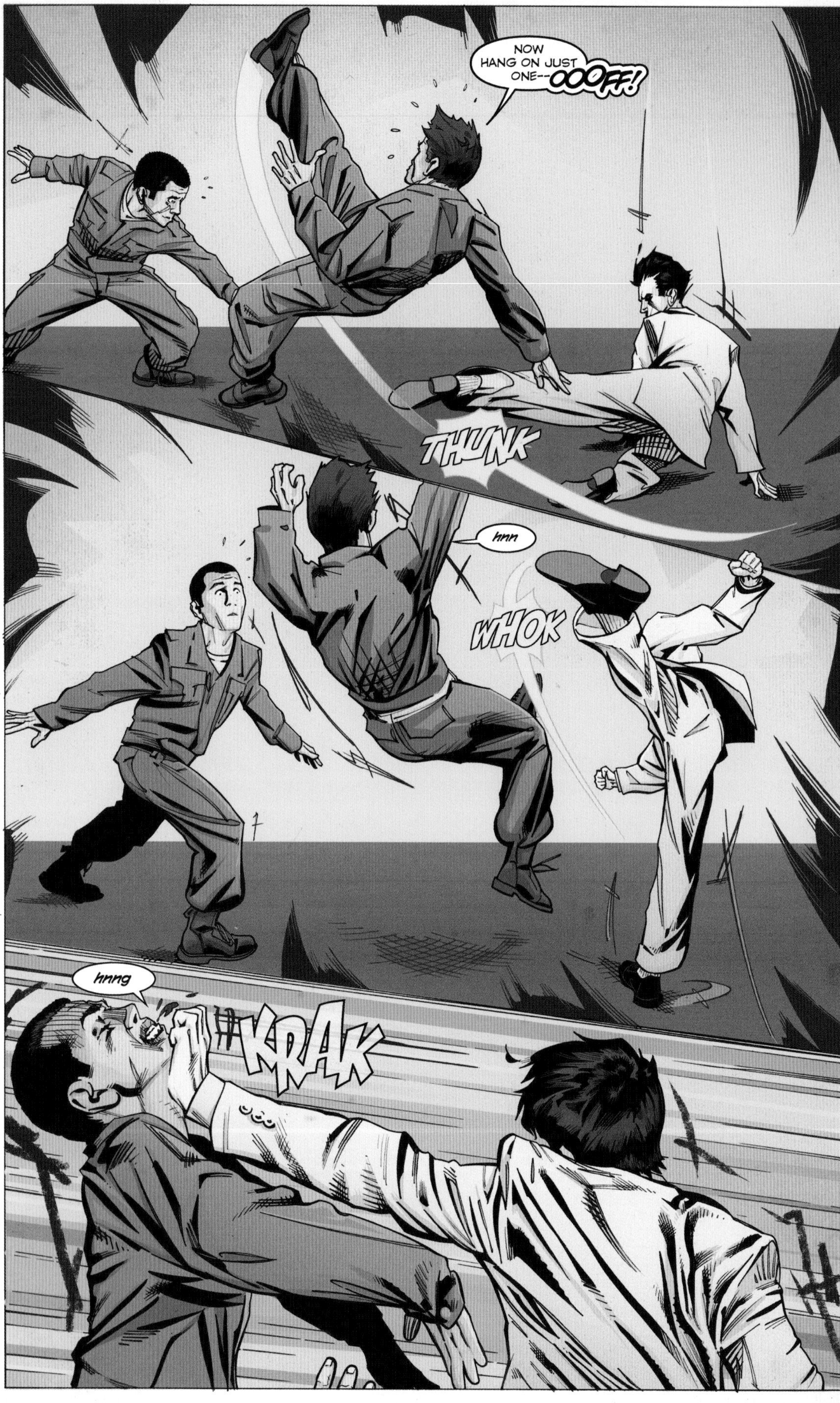
NOW HANG ON JUST ONE--OOOFF!
THUNK
hnn
WHOK
hnng
KRAK

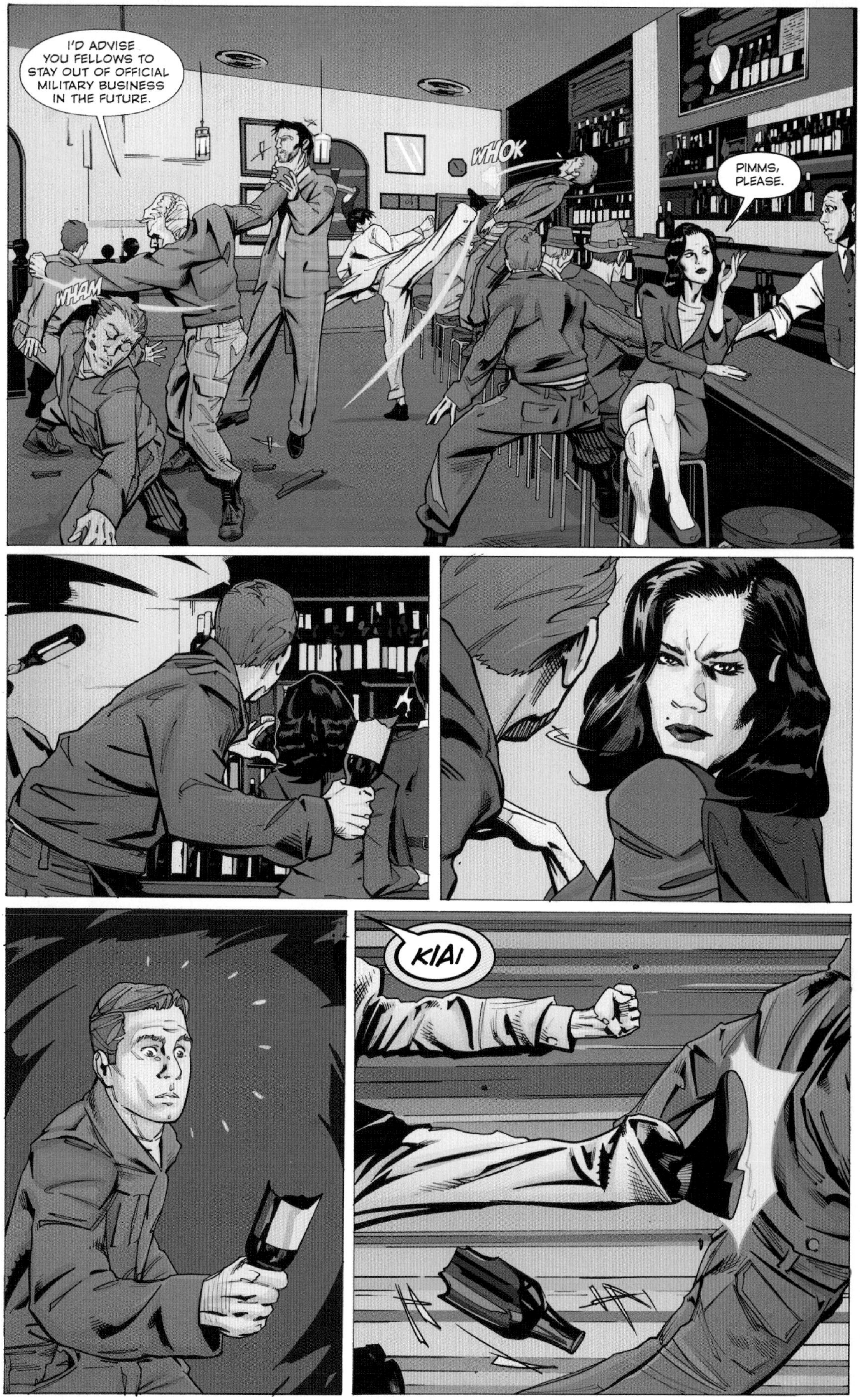
I'D ADVISE YOU FELLOWS TO STAY OUT OF OFFICIAL MILITARY BUSINESS IN THE FUTURE.
WHAM
WHOK
PIMMS, PLEASE.
KIAI

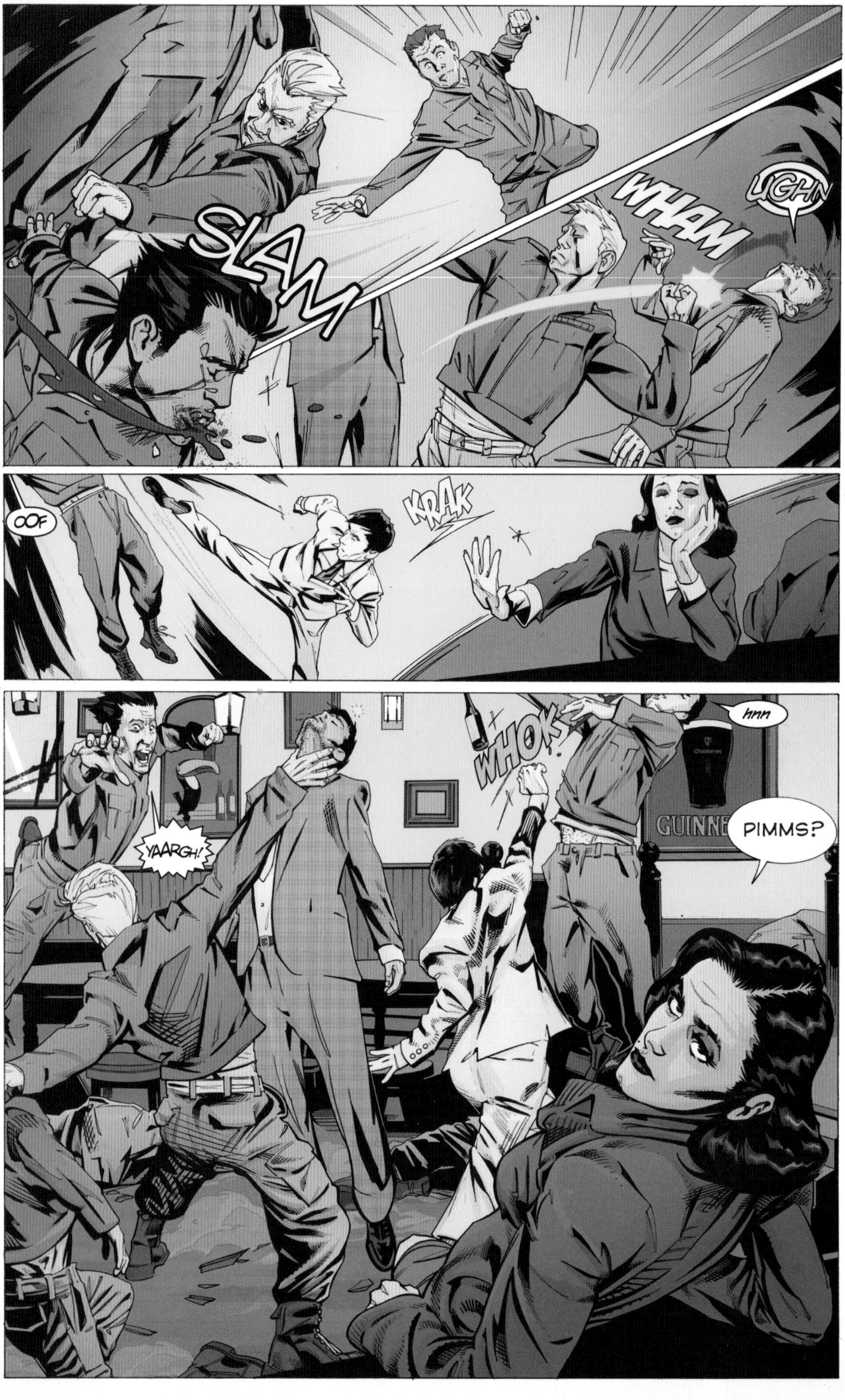
SLAM
WHAM
UGHN
OOF
KRAK
WHOK!
hnn
YAARGH!
GUINNE
PIMMS?

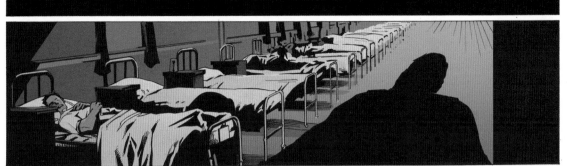

hnn

--the hell?

YOU'RE AWAKE. GOOD. *UP AND AT 'EM*, CHUM. TIME TO GET YOU BACK IN THE WAR.

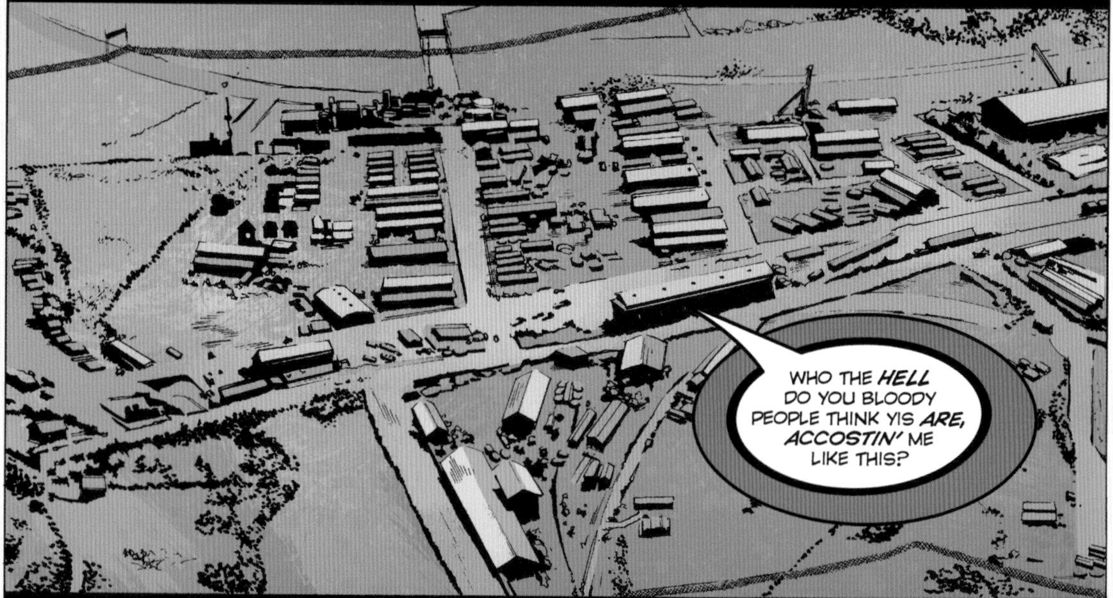
WHO THE HELL DO YOU BLOODY PEOPLE THINK YIS ARE, ACCOSTIN' ME LIKE THIS?

Chapter Two

IN LIKE FLYNN

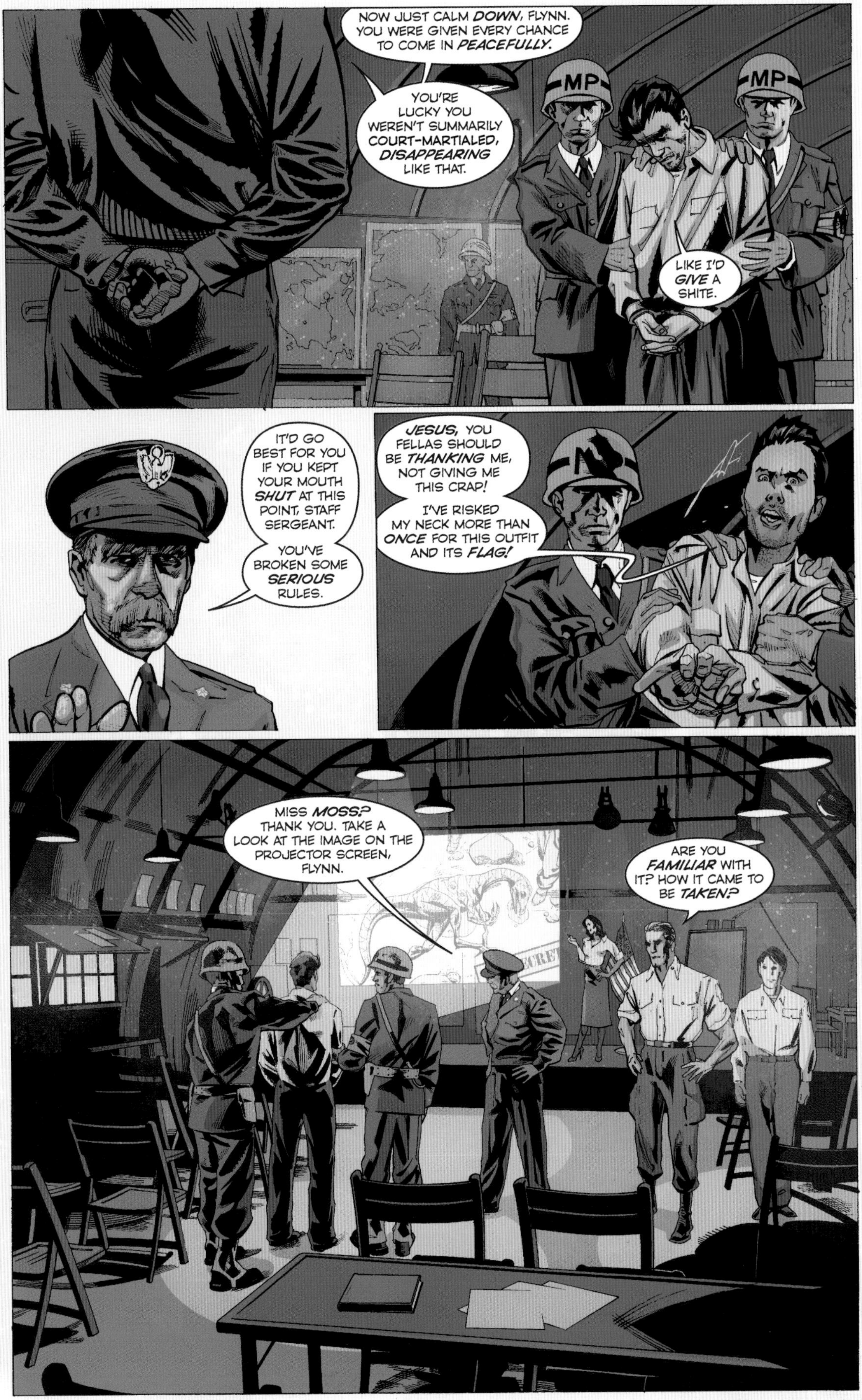
NOW JUST CALM DOWN, FLYNN. YOU WERE GIVEN EVERY CHANCE TO COME IN PEACEFULLY.
YOU'RE LUCKY YOU WEREN'T SUMMARILY COURT-MARTIALED, DISAPPEARING LIKE THAT.
LIKE I'D GIVE A SHITE.
IT'D GO BEST FOR YOU IF YOU KEPT YOUR MOUTH SHUT AT THIS POINT, STAFF SERGEANT.
YOU'VE BROKEN SOME SERIOUS RULES.
JESUS, YOU FELLAS SHOULD BE THANKING ME, NOT GIVING ME THIS CRAP!
I'VE RISKED MY NECK MORE THAN ONCE FOR THIS OUTFIT AND ITS FLAG!
MISS MOSS? THANK YOU. TAKE A LOOK AT THE IMAGE ON THE PROJECTOR SCREEN, FLYNN.
ARE YOU FAMILIAR WITH IT? HOW IT CAME TO BE TAKEN?
SECRET

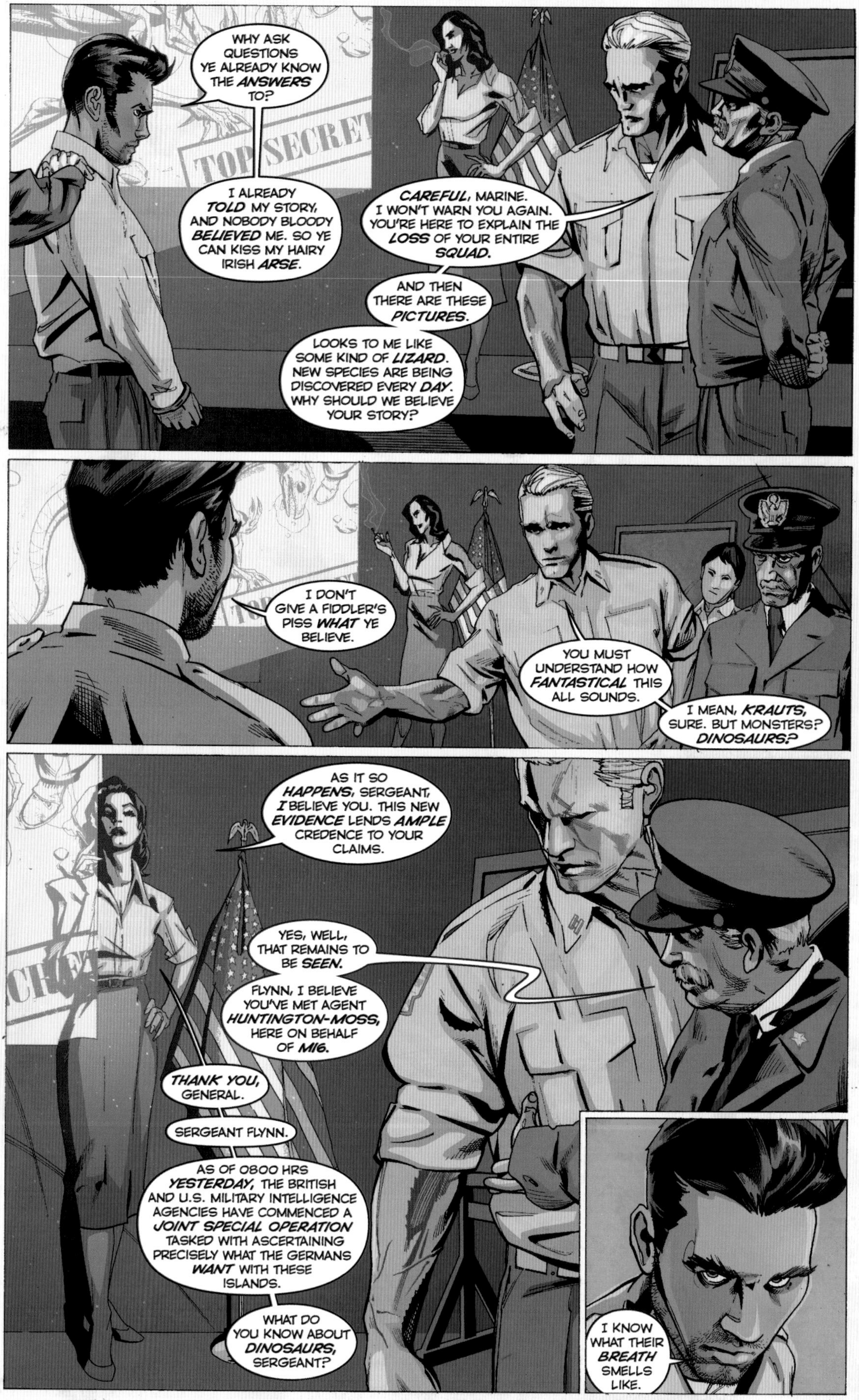
WHY ASK QUESTIONS YE ALREADY KNOW THE ANSWERS TO?
TOP SECRET
I ALREADY TOLD MY STORY, AND NOBODY BLOODY BELIEVED ME. SO YE CAN KISS MY HAIRY IRISH ARSE.
CAREFUL, MARINE. I WON'T WARN YOU AGAIN. YOU'RE HERE TO EXPLAIN THE LOSS OF YOUR ENTIRE SQUAD.
AND THEN THERE ARE THESE PICTURES.
LOOKS TO ME LIKE SOME KIND OF LIZARD. NEW SPECIES ARE BEING DISCOVERED EVERY DAY. WHY SHOULD WE BELIEVE YOUR STORY?
I DON'T GIVE A FIDDLER'S PISS WHAT YE BELIEVE.
YOU MUST UNDERSTAND HOW FANTASTICAL THIS ALL SOUNDS.
I MEAN, KRAUTS, SURE. BUT MONSTERS? DINOSAURS?
AS IT SO HAPPENS, SERGEANT, I BELIEVE YOU. THIS NEW EVIDENCE LENDS AMPLE CREDENCE TO YOUR CLAIMS.
YES, WELL, THAT REMAINS TO BE SEEN.
FLYNN, I BELIEVE YOU'VE MET AGENT HUNTINGTON-MOSS, HERE ON BEHALF OF MI6.
THANK YOU, GENERAL.
SERGEANT FLYNN.
AS OF 0800 HRS YESTERDAY, THE BRITISH AND U.S. MILITARY INTELLIGENCE AGENCIES HAVE COMMENCED A JOINT SPECIAL OPERATION TASKED WITH ASCERTAINING PRECISELY WHAT THE GERMANS WANT WITH THESE ISLANDS.
WHAT DO YOU KNOW ABOUT DINOSAURS, SERGEANT?
I KNOW WHAT THEIR BREATH SMELLS LIKE.

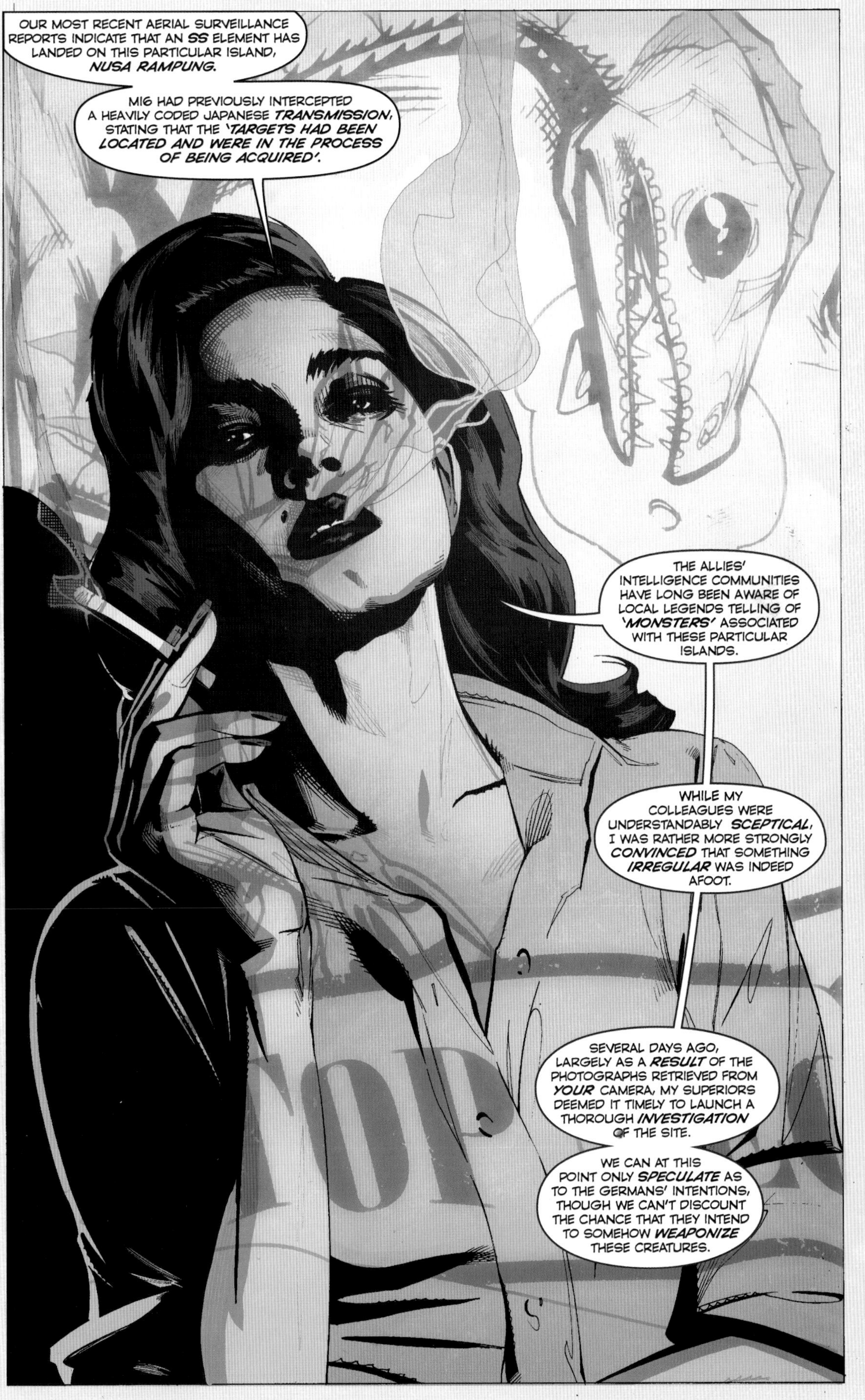
OUR MOST RECENT AERIAL SURVEILLANCE REPORTS INDICATE THAT AN SS ELEMENT HAS LANDED ON THIS PARTICULAR ISLAND, NUSA RAMPUNG.
MI6 HAD PREVIOUSLY INTERCEPTED A HEAVILY CODED JAPANESE TRANSMISSION, STATING THAT THE 'TARGETS HAD BEEN LOCATED AND WERE IN THE PROCESS OF BEING ACQUIRED'.
THE ALLIES' INTELLIGENCE COMMUNITIES HAVE LONG BEEN AWARE OF LOCAL LEGENDS TELLING OF 'MONSTERS' ASSOCIATED WITH THESE PARTICULAR ISLANDS.
WHILE MY COLLEAGUES WERE UNDERSTANDABLY SCEPTICAL, I WAS RATHER MORE STRONGLY CONVINCED THAT SOMETHING IRREGULAR WAS INDEED AFOOT.
SEVERAL DAYS AGO, LARGELY AS A RESULT OF THE PHOTOGRAPHS RETRIEVED FROM YOUR CAMERA, MY SUPERIORS DEEMED IT TIMELY TO LAUNCH A THOROUGH INVESTIGATION OF THE SITE.
WE CAN AT THIS POINT ONLY SPECULATE AS TO THE GERMANS' INTENTIONS, THOUGH WE CAN'T DISCOUNT THE CHANCE THAT THEY INTEND TO SOMEHOW WEAPONIZE THESE CREATURES.

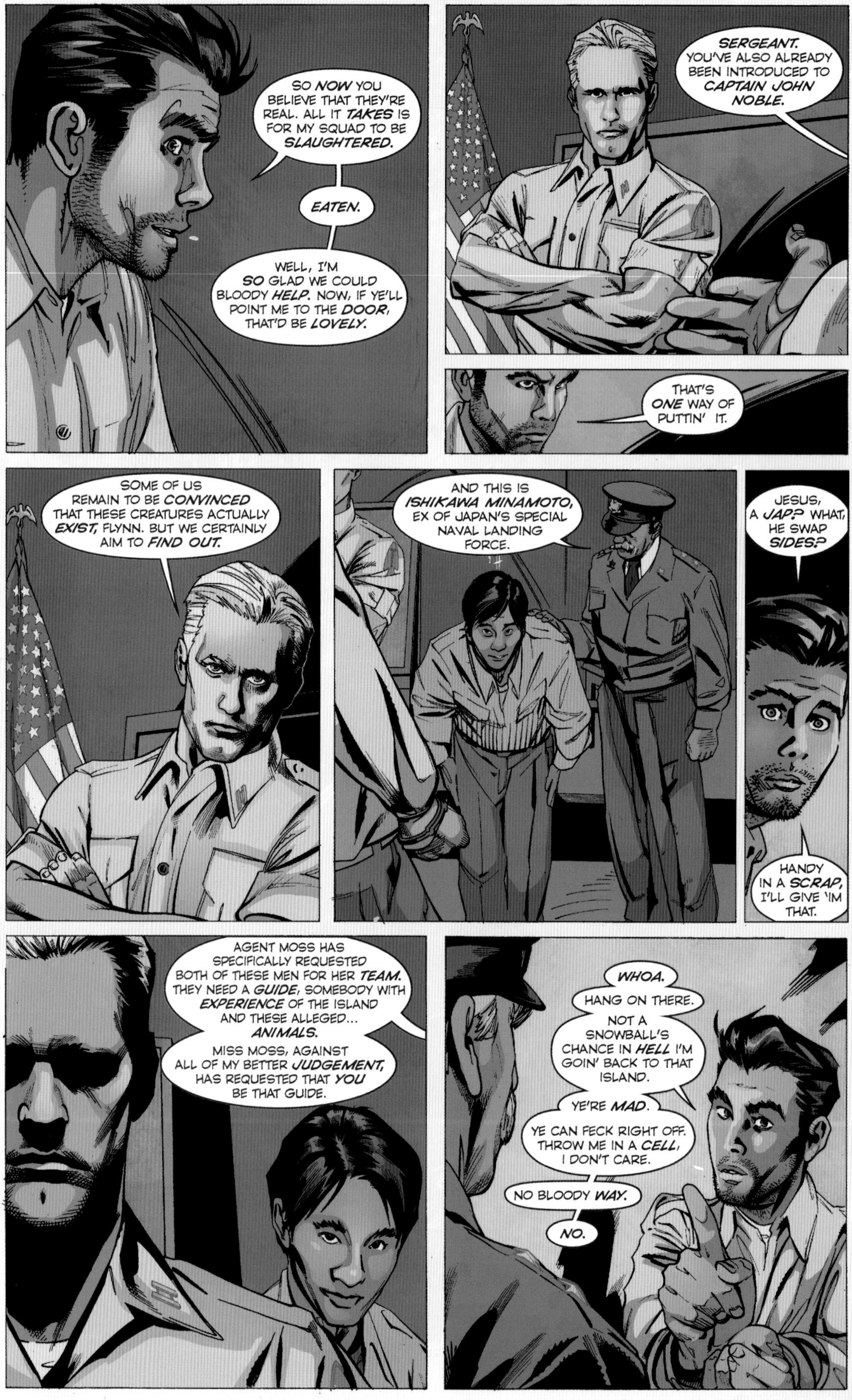
SO NOW YOU BELIEVE THAT THEY'RE REAL. ALL IT TAKES IS FOR MY SQUAD TO BE SLAUGHTERED.
EATEN.
WELL, I'M SO GLAD WE COULD BLOODY HELP. NOW, IF YE'LL POINT ME TO THE DOOR, THAT'D BE LOVELY.
SERGEANT. YOU'VE ALSO ALREADY BEEN INTRODUCED TO CAPTAIN JOHN NOBLE.
THAT'S ONE WAY OF PUTTIN' IT.
SOME OF US REMAIN TO BE CONVINCED THAT THESE CREATURES ACTUALLY EXIST, FLYNN. BUT WE CERTAINLY AIM TO FIND OUT.
AND THIS IS ISHIKAWA MINAMOTO, EX OF JAPAN'S SPECIAL NAVAL LANDING FORCE.
JESUS, A JAP? WHAT, HE SWAP SIDES?
HANDY IN A SCRAP, I'LL GIVE 'IM THAT.
AGENT MOSS HAS SPECIFICALLY REQUESTED BOTH OF THESE MEN FOR HER TEAM. THEY NEED A GUIDE, SOMEBODY WITH EXPERIENCE OF THE ISLAND AND THESE ALLEGED... ANIMALS.
MISS MOSS, AGAINST ALL OF MY BETTER JUDGEMENT, HAS REQUESTED THAT YOU BE THAT GUIDE.
WHOA.
HANG ON THERE.
NOT A SNOWBALL'S CHANCE IN HELL I'M GOIN' BACK TO THAT ISLAND.
YE'RE MAD.
YE CAN FECK RIGHT OFF. THROW ME IN A CELL, I DON'T CARE.
NO BLOODY WAY.
NO.

KNOCK KNOCK

COME ON IN, IT'S OPEN.

FLYNN.

MORNIN'.

WHAT SAY WE TAKE A WALK, STRETCH THOSE *LEGS.*

ONLY IF YER *BUYING.*

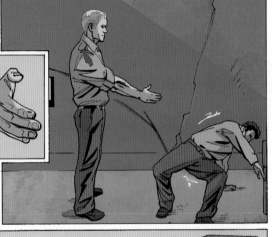

ALRIGHT.

I'M NOT YER *DOG,* SO WHY ARE YEH *WALKING* ME?

INFORMATION. I NEED TO KNOW WHAT IT WAS LIKE.

SOMETHING KILLED YOUR MEN.

SOMETHING RIPPED THEM APART. AND I BELIEVE YOU'RE VERY *ANGRY* ABOUT THAT.

WOW. A REGULAR *SAM SPADE.* I'M ANGRY. BUT I'M NOT *CRAZY.*

YOU DIDN'T *SEE* THOSE THINGS.

THEY TORE UP MY SQUAD LIKE A LOSING TICKET AT *BELMONT.*

FIVE MEN *DEAD,* JUST LIKE *THAT.* YOU WANT ME TO GO *BACK.*

SAVE YOUR *BREATH.*

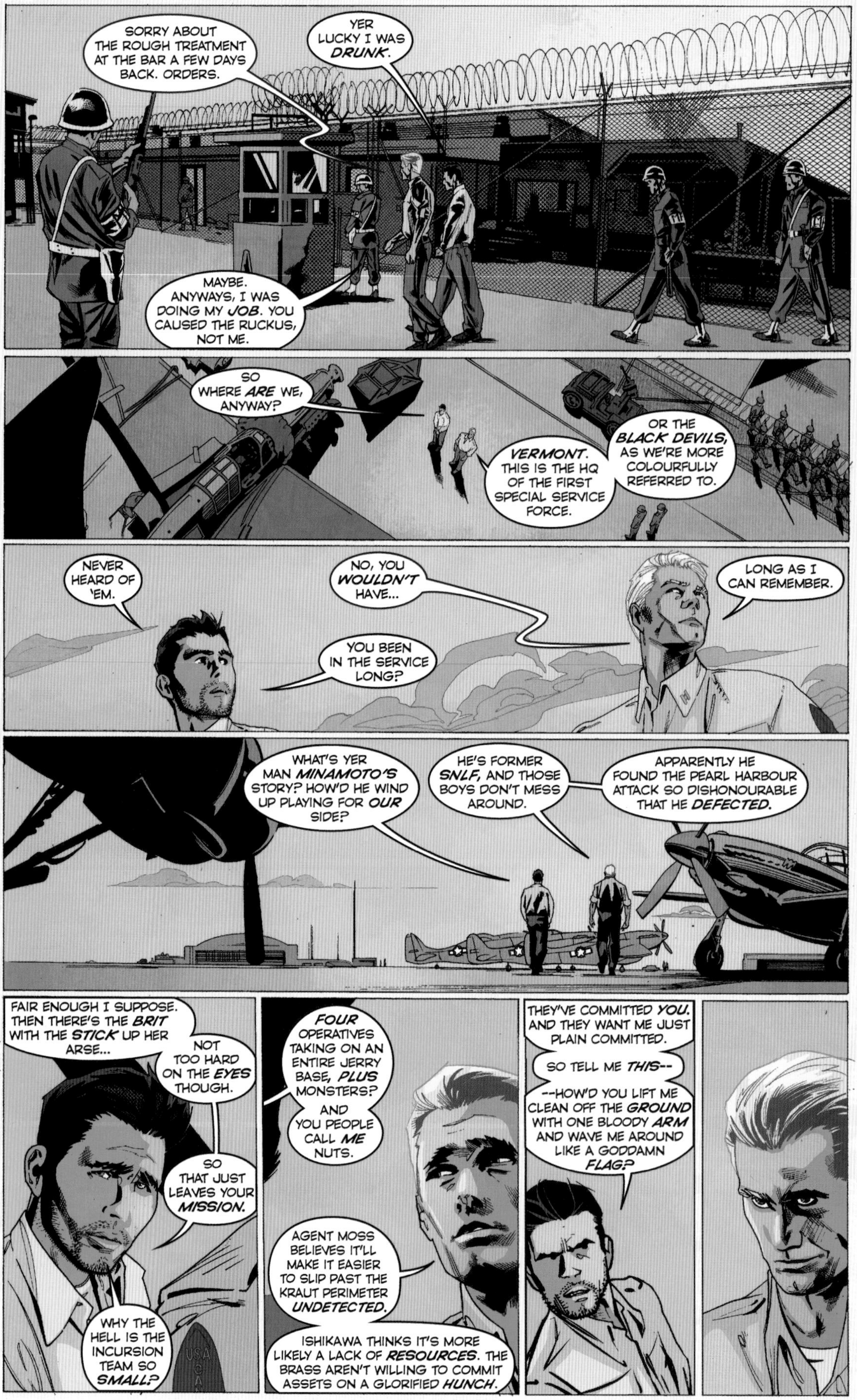
SORRY ABOUT THE ROUGH TREATMENT AT THE BAR A FEW DAYS BACK. ORDERS.
YER LUCKY I WAS DRUNK.
MAYBE. ANYWAYS, I WAS DOING MY JOB. YOU CAUSED THE RUCKUS, NOT ME.
SO WHERE ARE WE, ANYWAY?
VERMONT. THIS IS THE HQ OF THE FIRST SPECIAL SERVICE FORCE.
OR THE BLACK DEVILS, AS WE'RE MORE COLOURFULLY REFERRED TO.
NEVER HEARD OF 'EM.
NO, YOU WOULDN'T HAVE...
YOU BEEN IN THE SERVICE LONG?
LONG AS I CAN REMEMBER.
WHAT'S YER MAN MINAMOTO'S STORY? HOW'D HE WIND UP PLAYING FOR OUR SIDE?
HE'S FORMER SNLF, AND THOSE BOYS DON'T MESS AROUND.
APPARENTLY HE FOUND THE PEARL HARBOUR ATTACK SO DISHONOURABLE THAT HE DEFECTED.
FAIR ENOUGH I SUPPOSE. THEN THERE'S THE BRIT WITH THE STICK UP HER ARSE...
NOT TOO HARD ON THE EYES THOUGH.
SO THAT JUST LEAVES YOUR MISSION.
WHY THE HELL IS THE INCURSION TEAM SO SMALL?
FOUR OPERATIVES TAKING ON AN ENTIRE JERRY BASE, PLUS MONSTERS?
AND YOU PEOPLE CALL ME NUTS.
AGENT MOSS BELIEVES IT'LL MAKE IT EASIER TO SLIP PAST THE KRAUT PERIMETER UNDETECTED.
ISHIKAWA THINKS IT'S MORE LIKELY A LACK OF RESOURCES. THE BRASS AREN'T WILLING TO COMMIT ASSETS ON A GLORIFIED HUNCH.
THEY'VE COMMITTED YOU. AND THEY WANT ME JUST PLAIN COMMITTED.
SO TELL ME THIS--
--HOW'D YOU LIFT ME CLEAN OFF THE GROUND WITH ONE BLOODY ARM AND WAVE ME AROUND LIKE A GODDAMN FLAG?
USA

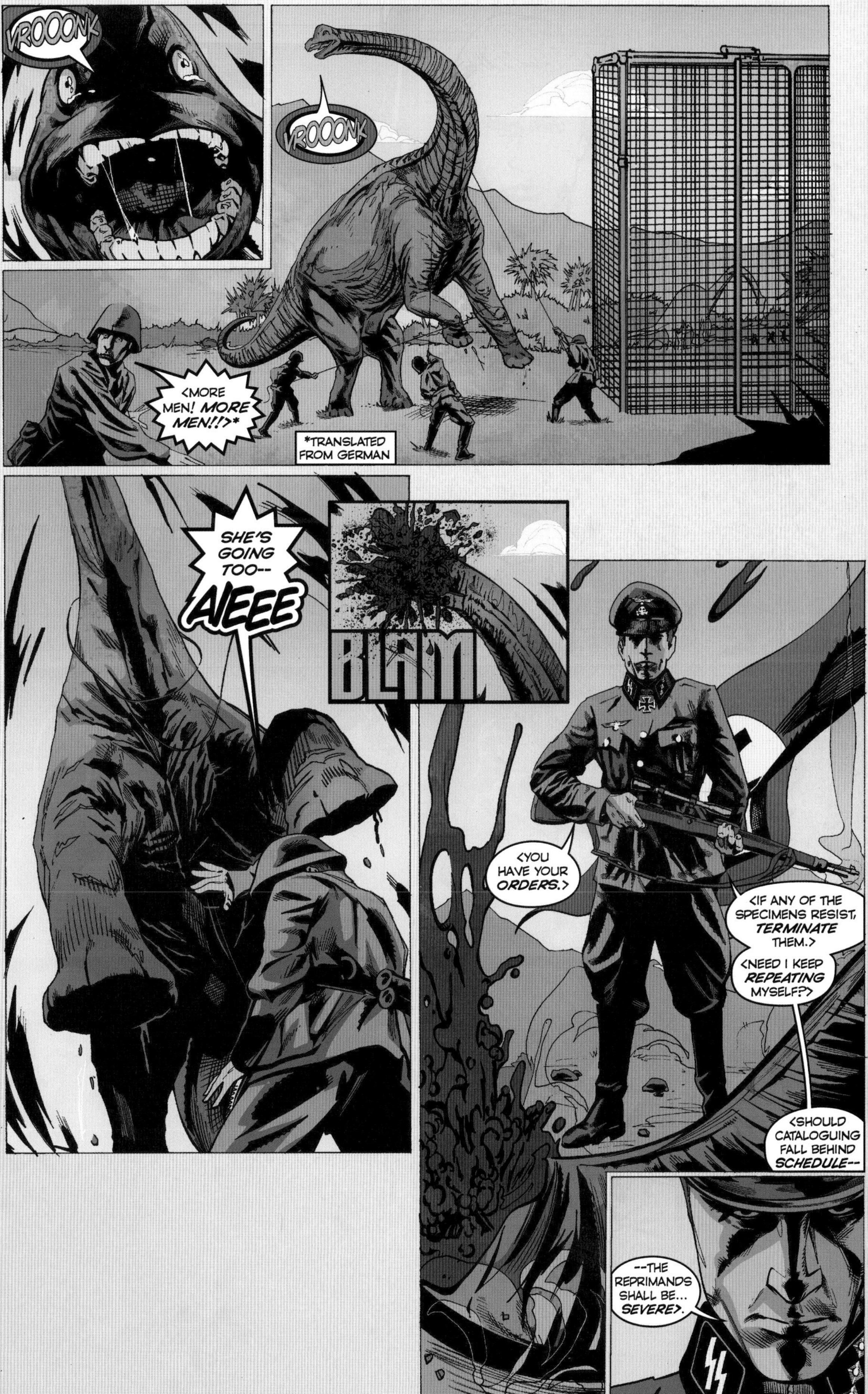
VROOONK
VROOONK
<MORE MEN! MORE MEN!!>*
*TRANSLATED FROM GERMAN
SHE'S GOING TOO--
AIEEE
BLAM
<YOU HAVE YOUR ORDERS.>
<IF ANY OF THE SPECIMENS RESIST, TERMINATE THEM.>
<NEED I KEEP REPEATING MYSELF?>
<SHOULD CATALOGUING FALL BEHIND SCHEDULE--
--THE REPRIMANDS SHALL BE... SEVERE>.

KNOCK
KNOCK

READY FOR ANOTHER WALK?

ENOUGH. I'M NOT *GOING*.

TAKE A *BREAK*.

WHY'D YOU JOIN UP, FLYNN?

THE GLAMOUROUS *LIVING* ARRANGEMENTS.

WHY DOES *ANYBODY* JOIN? TO STOP THE *JERRIES*.

IRELAND WASN'T GETTING *INVOLVED*. COULDN'T JUST SIT THERE ON THE SIDELINES AND LET OTHER FOLKS DO ALL THE *FIGHTING*.

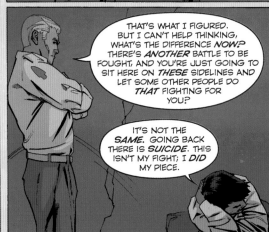

THAT'S WHAT I FIGURED. BUT I CAN'T HELP THINKING, WHAT'S THE DIFFERENCE *NOW?* THERE'S *ANOTHER* BATTLE TO BE FOUGHT, AND YOU'RE JUST GOING TO SIT HERE ON *THESE* SIDELINES AND LET SOME OTHER PEOPLE DO *THAT* FIGHTING FOR YOU?

IT'S NOT THE *SAME*. GOING BACK THERE IS *SUICIDE*. THIS ISN'T MY FIGHT; I *DID* MY PIECE.

THOSE WERE *YOUR* MEN! MAKE THEIR DEATHS *MEAN* SOMETHING! DON'T YOU WANT *PAYBACK?*

LOOK, *ENOUGH* WITH THE COD-*PSYCHOLOGY*, ALRIGHT?

I WOULDN'T BE OF MUCH HELP OVER THERE ANYWAY. *JESUS*.

YOU'RE A GODDAMN *COWARD*.

ORDERS ARE IN. WE SHIP OUT AT *06:00* TOMORROW. *HIM?*

HE'S *OUT*.

38

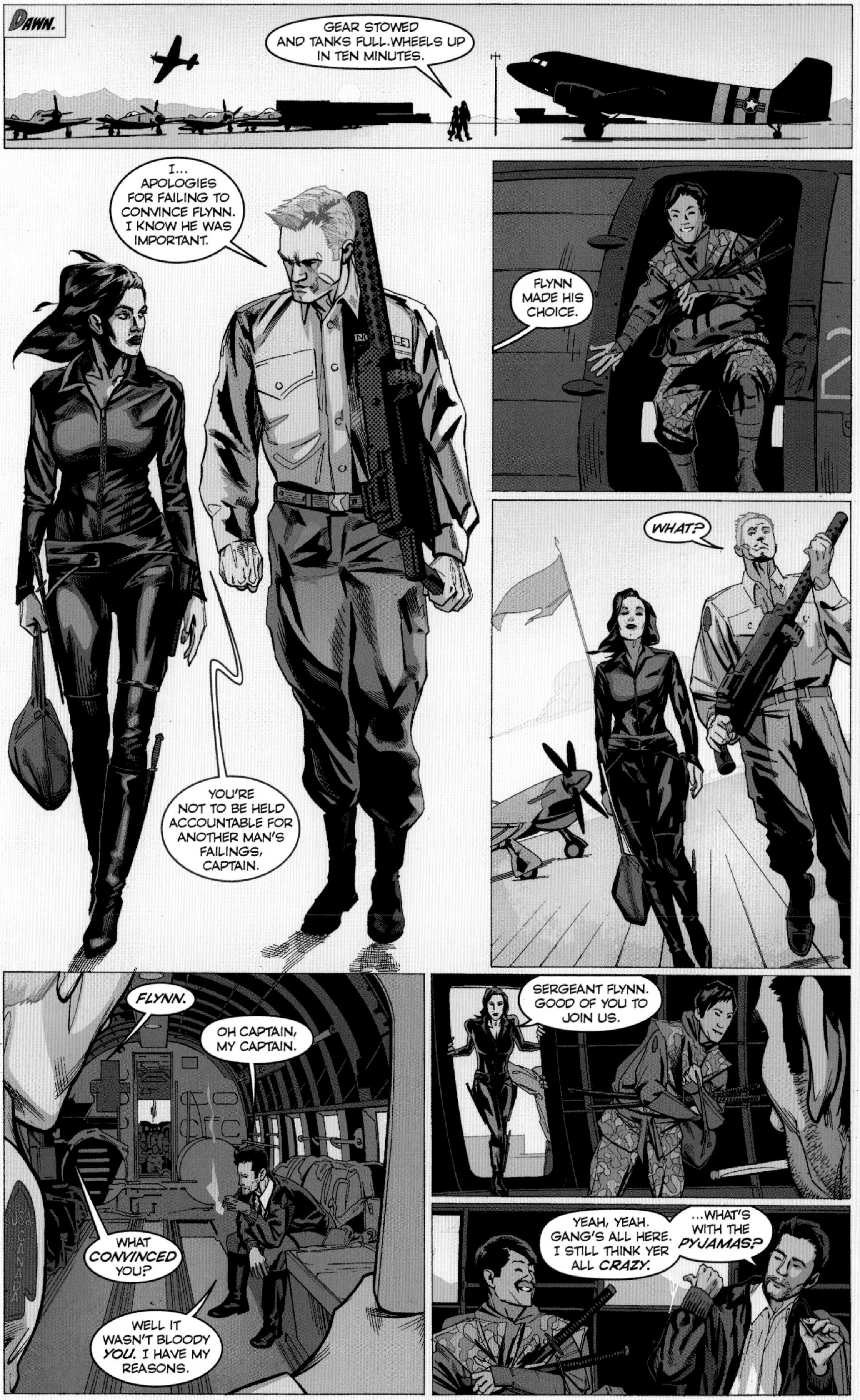
DAWN.
GEAR STOWED AND TANKS FULL.WHEELS UP IN TEN MINUTES.
I... APOLOGIES FOR FAILING TO CONVINCE FLYNN. I KNOW HE WAS IMPORTANT.
YOU'RE NOT TO BE HELD ACCOUNTABLE FOR ANOTHER MAN'S FAILINGS, CAPTAIN.
FLYNN MADE HIS CHOICE.
WHAT?
FLYNN.
OH CAPTAIN, MY CAPTAIN.
WHAT CONVINCED YOU?
WELL IT WASN'T BLOODY YOU. I HAVE MY REASONS.
SERGEANT FLYNN. GOOD OF YOU TO JOIN US.
YEAH, YEAH. GANG'S ALL HERE. I STILL THINK YER ALL CRAZY.
...WHAT'S WITH THE PYJAMAS?

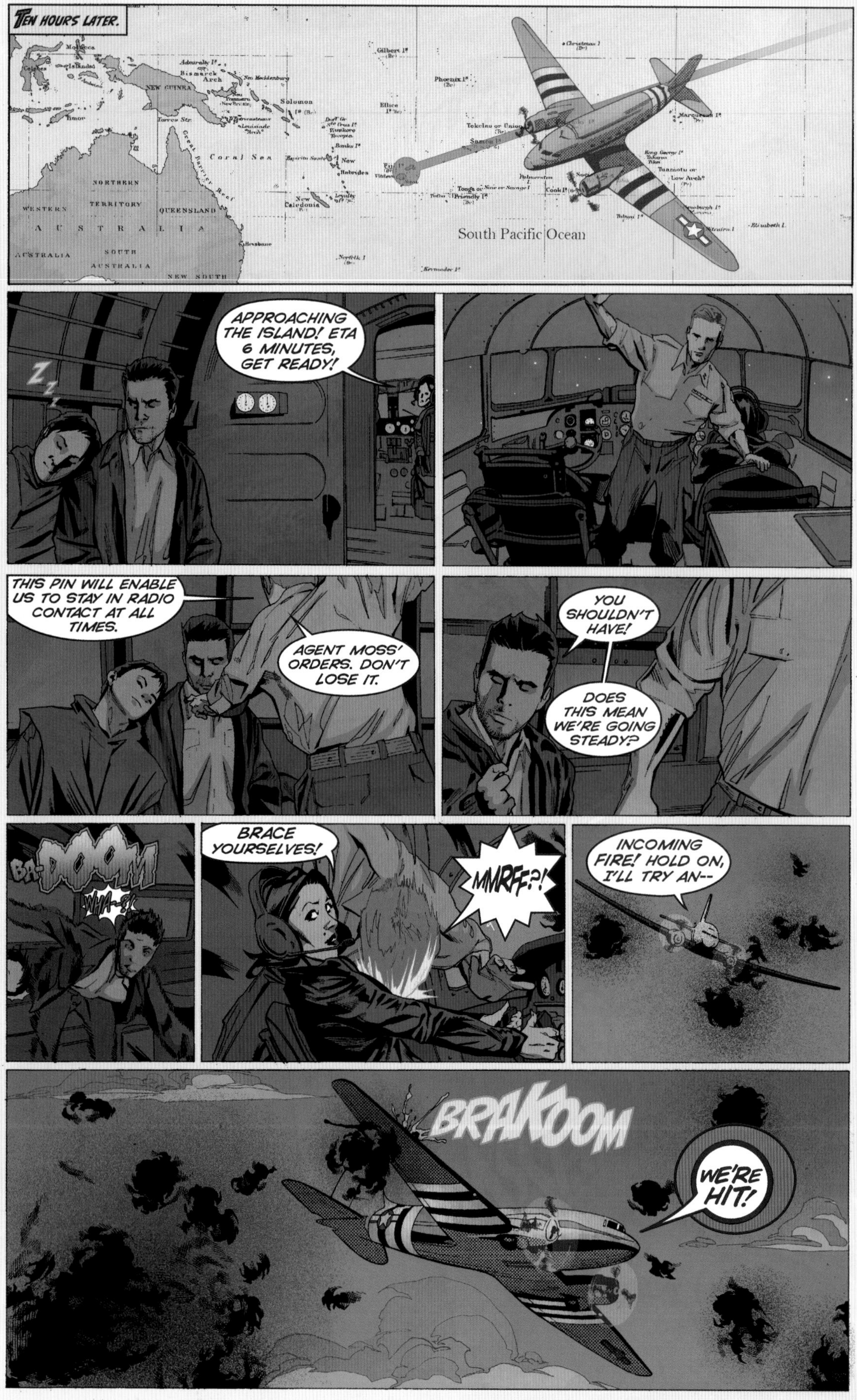
TEN HOURS LATER.
South Pacific Ocean
Coral Sea
NORTHERN TERRITORY
QUEENSLAND
WESTERN AUSTRALIA
SOUTH AUSTRALIA
A U S T R A L I A
APPROACHING THE ISLAND! ETA 6 MINUTES, GET READY!
Z Z Z
THIS PIN WILL ENABLE US TO STAY IN RADIO CONTACT AT ALL TIMES.
AGENT MOSS' ORDERS. DON'T LOSE IT.
YOU SHOULDN'T HAVE!
DOES THIS MEAN WE'RE GOING STEADY?
BA-DOOM
WHA--?!
BRACE YOURSELVES!
MMRFF?!
INCOMING FIRE! HOLD ON, I'LL TRY AN--
BRAKOOM
WE'RE HIT!

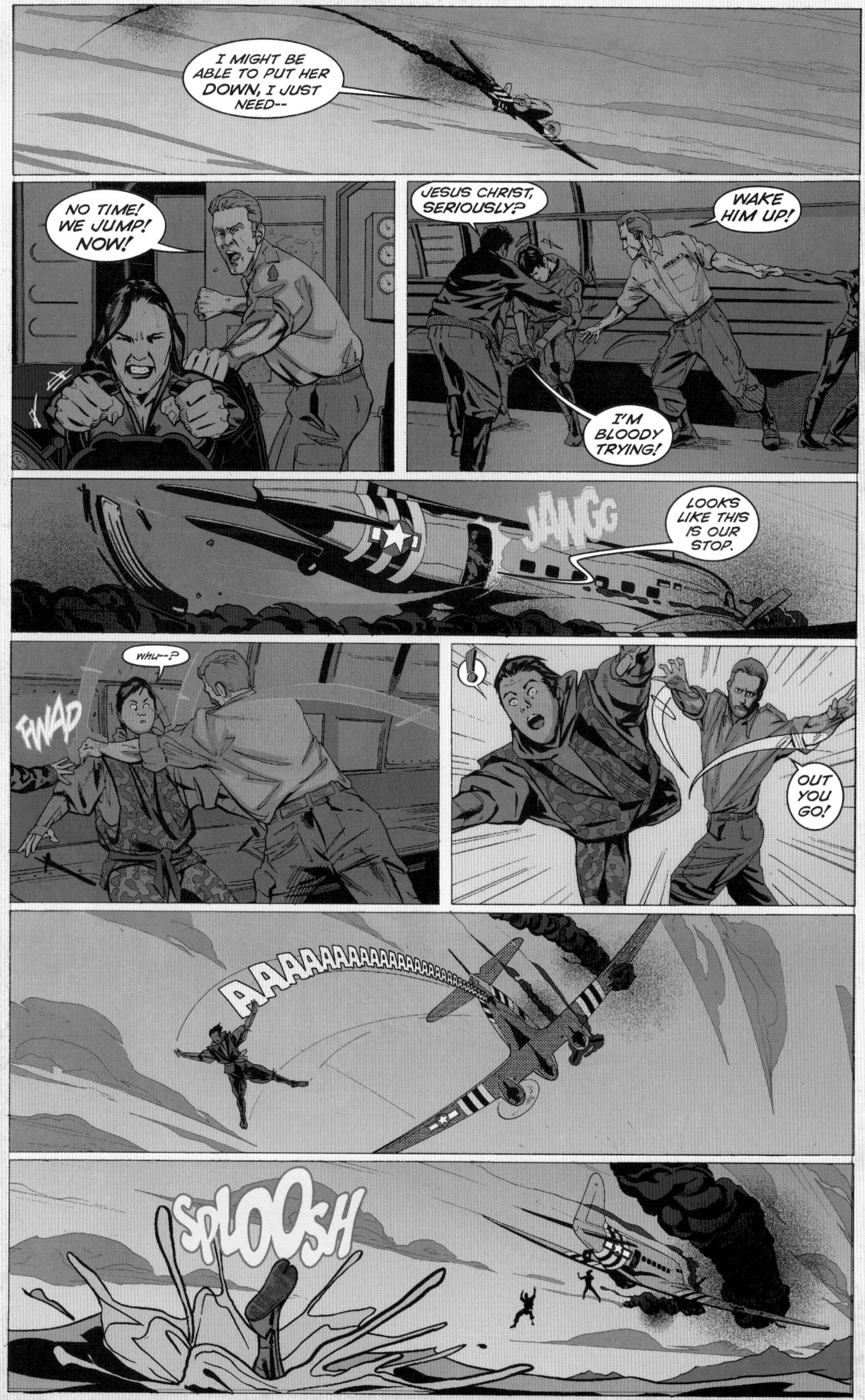

I MIGHT BE ABLE TO PUT HER DOWN, I JUST NEED--
NO TIME! WE JUMP! NOW!
JESUS CHRIST, SERIOUSLY?
WAKE HIM UP!
I'M BLOODY TRYING!
JANGG
LOOKS LIKE THIS IS OUR STOP.
WHU--?
FWAP
!
OUT YOU GO!
AAAAAAAAAAAAAAAAAAAAAAAAAAA
SPLOOSH

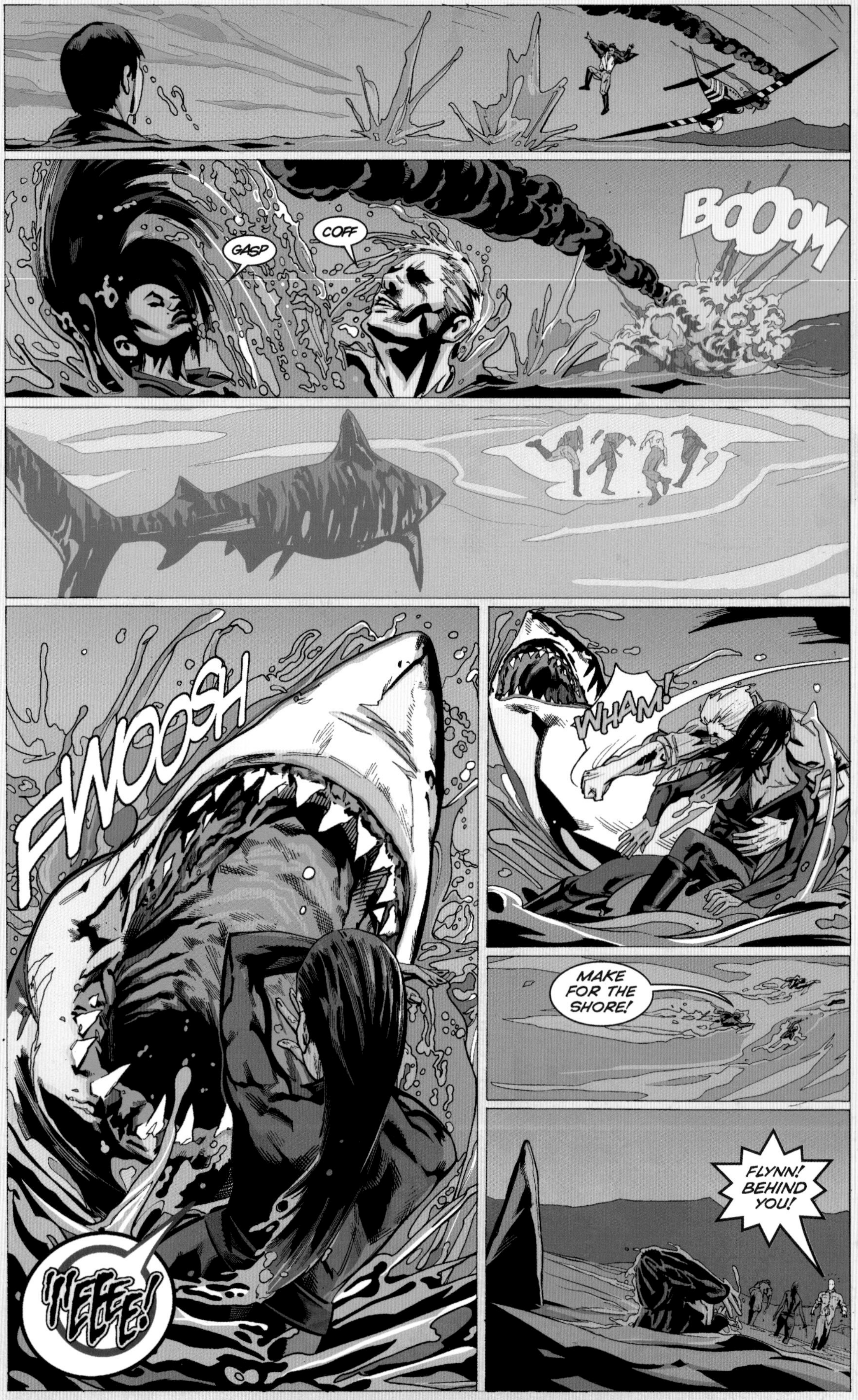
GASP
COFF
BOOOM
FWOOSH
YEEEE!
WHAM!
MAKE FOR THE SHORE!
FLYNN! BEHIND YOU!

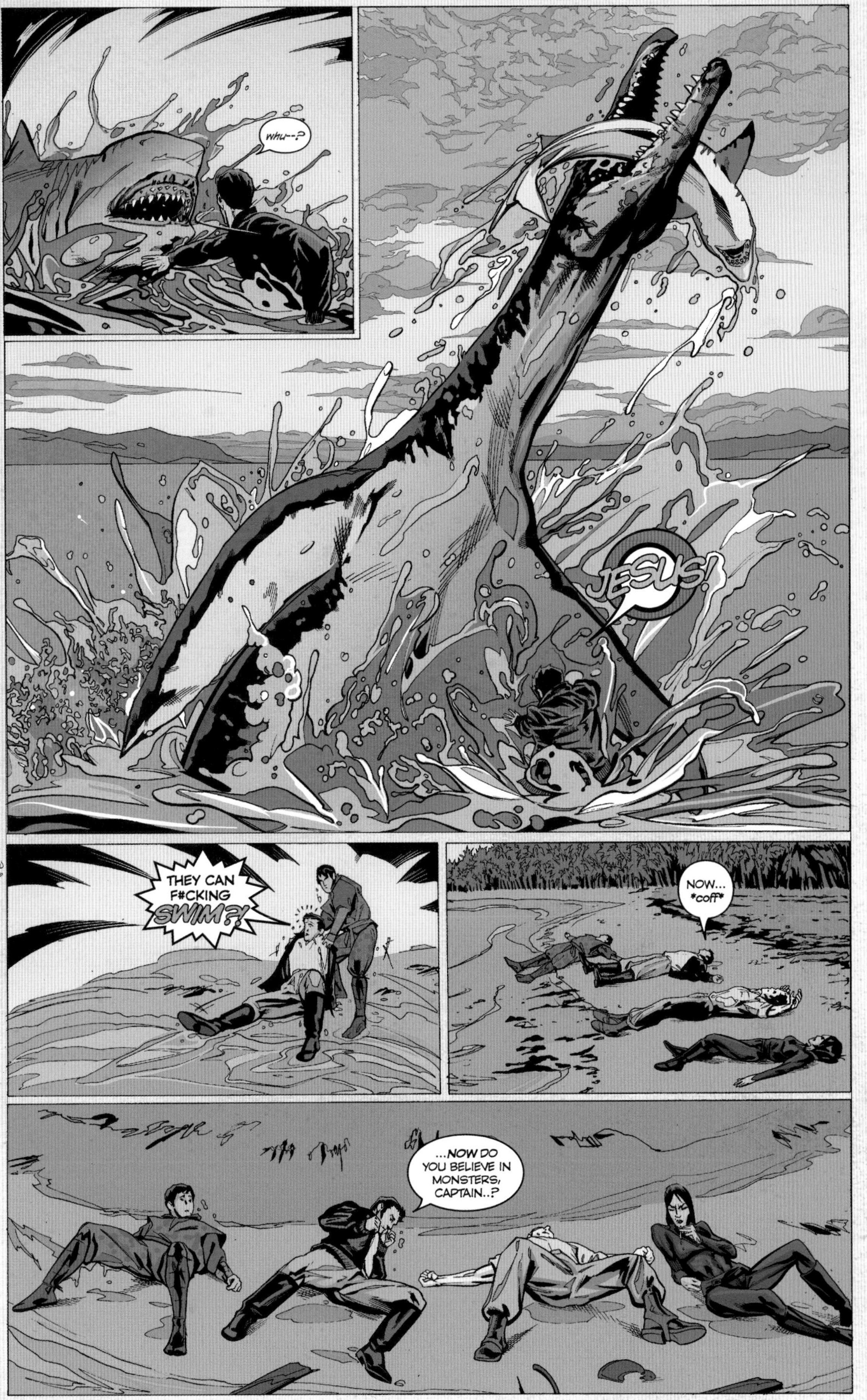
whu--?
JESUS!
THEY CAN F#CKING SWIM?!
NOW... *coff*
...NOW DO YOU BELIEVE IN MONSTERS, CAPTAIN..?

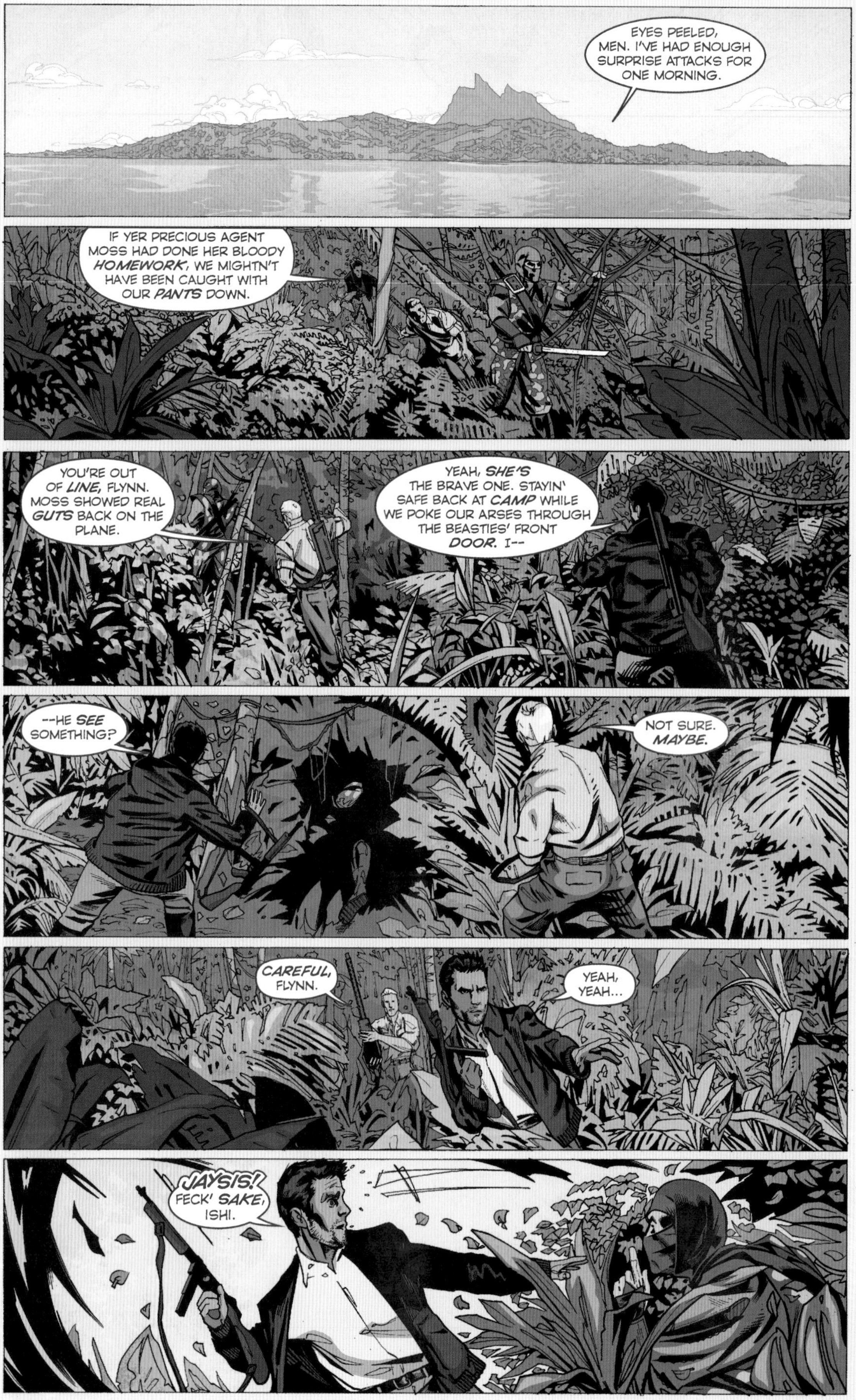
EYES PEELED, MEN. I'VE HAD ENOUGH SURPRISE ATTACKS FOR ONE MORNING.
IF YER PRECIOUS AGENT MOSS HAD DONE HER BLOODY *HOMEWORK*, WE MIGHTN'T HAVE BEEN CAUGHT WITH OUR *PANTS* DOWN.
YOU'RE OUT OF *LINE*, FLYNN. MOSS SHOWED REAL *GUTS* BACK ON THE PLANE.
YEAH, *SHE'S* THE BRAVE ONE. STAYIN' SAFE BACK AT *CAMP* WHILE WE POKE OUR ARSES THROUGH THE BEASTIES' FRONT *DOOR*. I--
--HE *SEE* SOMETHING?
NOT SURE. *MAYBE*.
CAREFUL, FLYNN.
YEAH, YEAH...
JAYSIS! FECK' *SAKE*, ISHI.

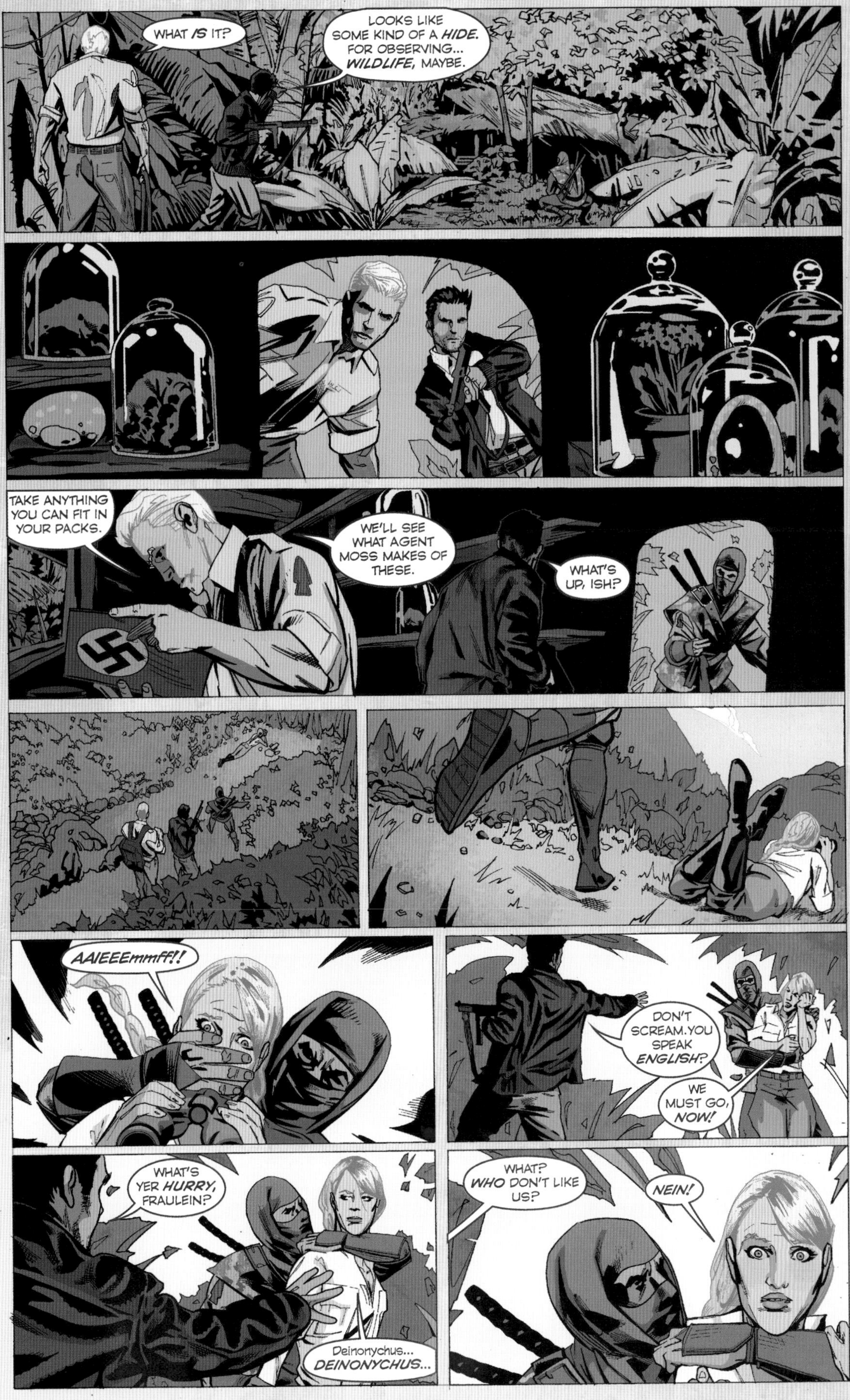
WHAT IS IT?
LOOKS LIKE SOME KIND OF A HIDE. FOR OBSERVING... WILDLIFE, MAYBE.
TAKE ANYTHING YOU CAN FIT IN YOUR PACKS.
WE'LL SEE WHAT AGENT MOSS MAKES OF THESE.
WHAT'S UP, ISH?
AAIEEEmmff!!
DON'T SCREAM. YOU SPEAK ENGLISH?
WE MUST GO, NOW!
WHAT'S YER HURRY, FRAULEIN?
Deinonychus... DEINONYCHUS...
WHAT? WHO DON'T LIKE US?
NEIN!

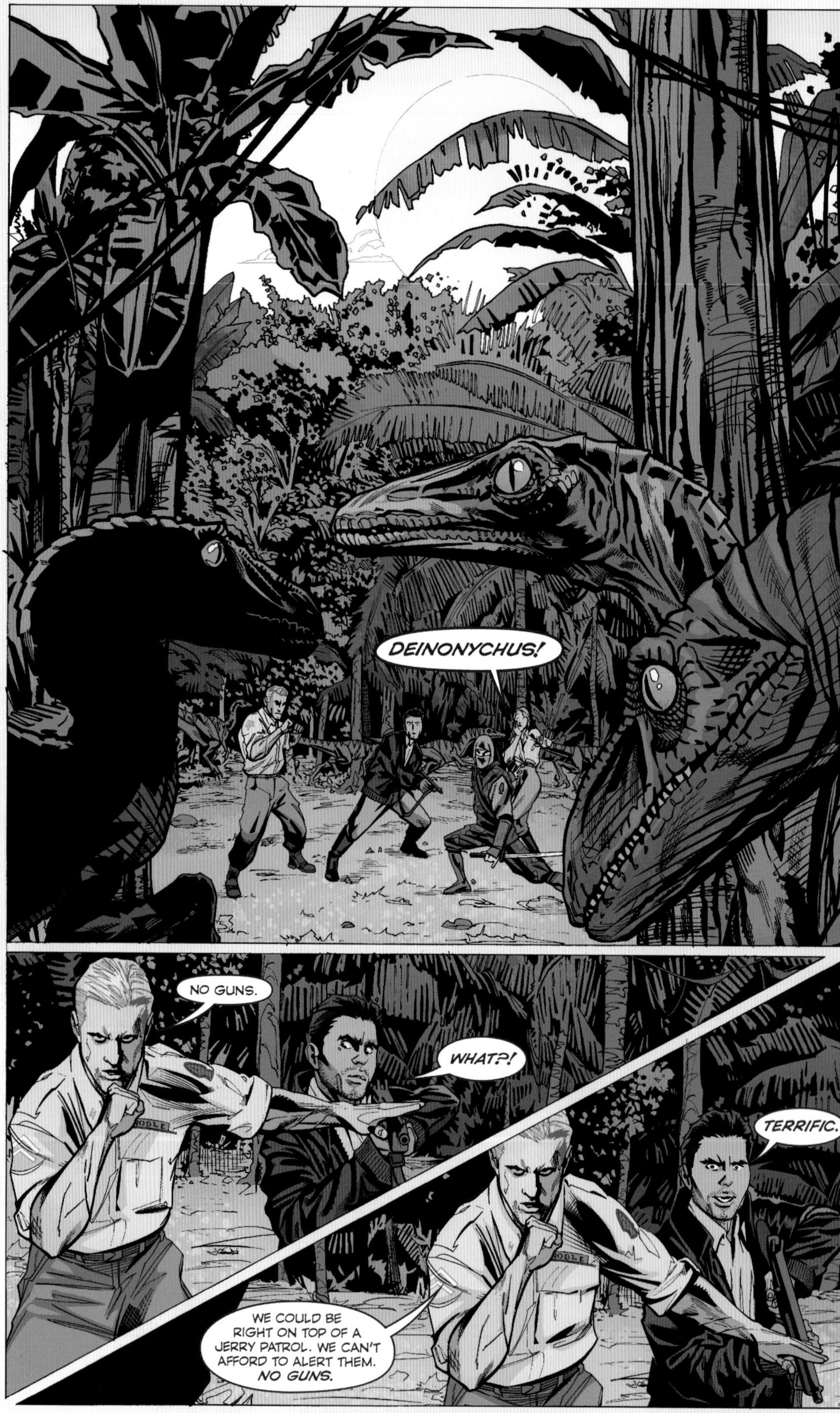
DEINONYCHUS!
NO GUNS.
WHAT?!
TERRIFIC.
WE COULD BE RIGHT ON TOP OF A JERRY PATROL. WE CAN'T AFFORD TO ALERT THEM. NO GUNS.

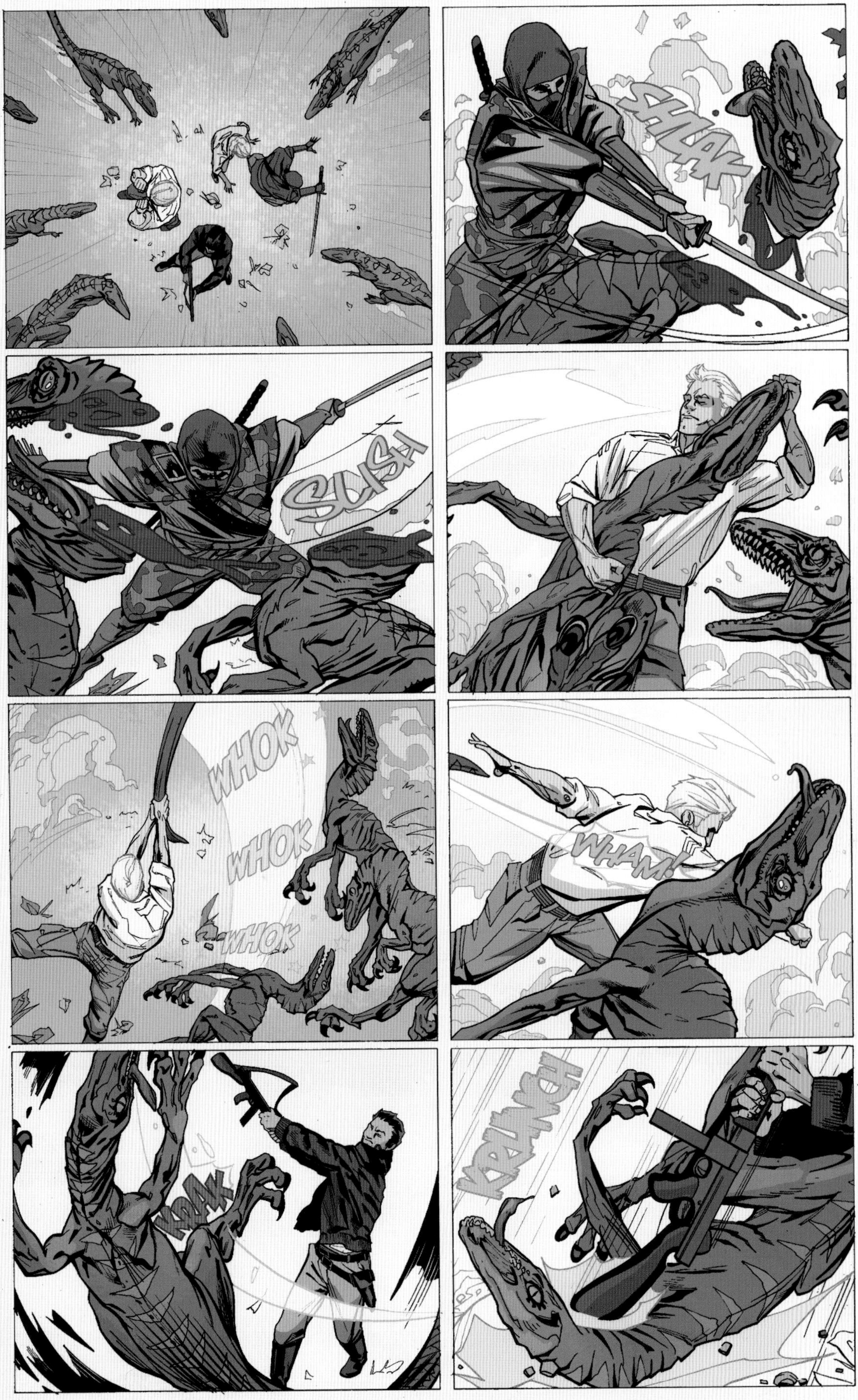
SHLAK
SLISH
WHOK
WHOK
WHOK
WHAM!
KRAK
KRUNCH

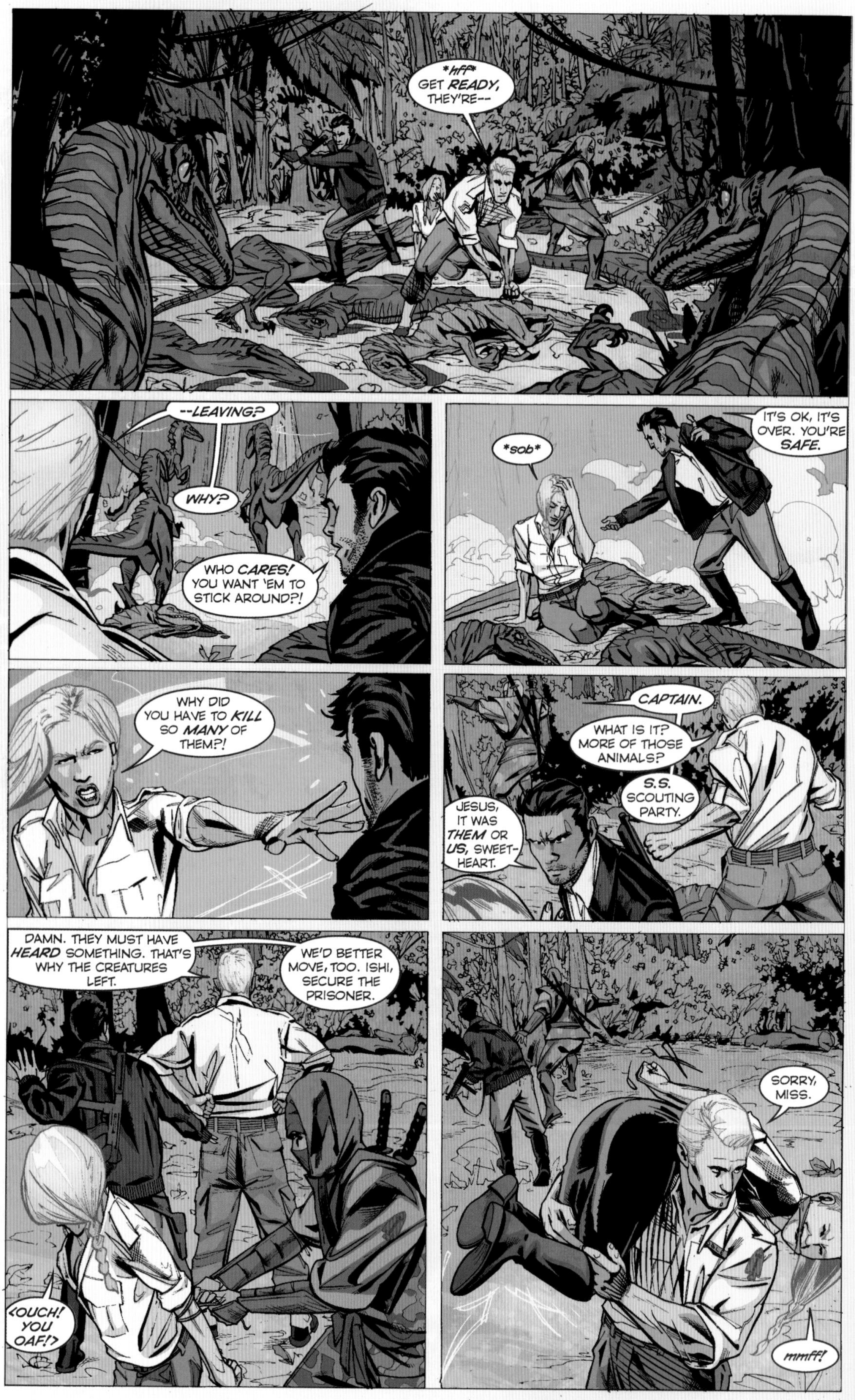
hff GET READY, THEY'RE--
--LEAVING?
WHY?
WHO CARES! YOU WANT 'EM TO STICK AROUND?!
sob
IT'S OK, IT'S OVER. YOU'RE SAFE.
WHY DID YOU HAVE TO KILL SO MANY OF THEM?!
CAPTAIN.
WHAT IS IT? MORE OF THOSE ANIMALS?
S.S. SCOUTING PARTY.
JESUS, IT WAS THEM OR US, SWEET-HEART.
DAMN. THEY MUST HAVE HEARD SOMETHING. THAT'S WHY THE CREATURES LEFT.
WE'D BETTER MOVE, TOO. ISHI, SECURE THE PRISONER.
<OUCH! YOU OAF!>
SORRY, MISS.
mmff!

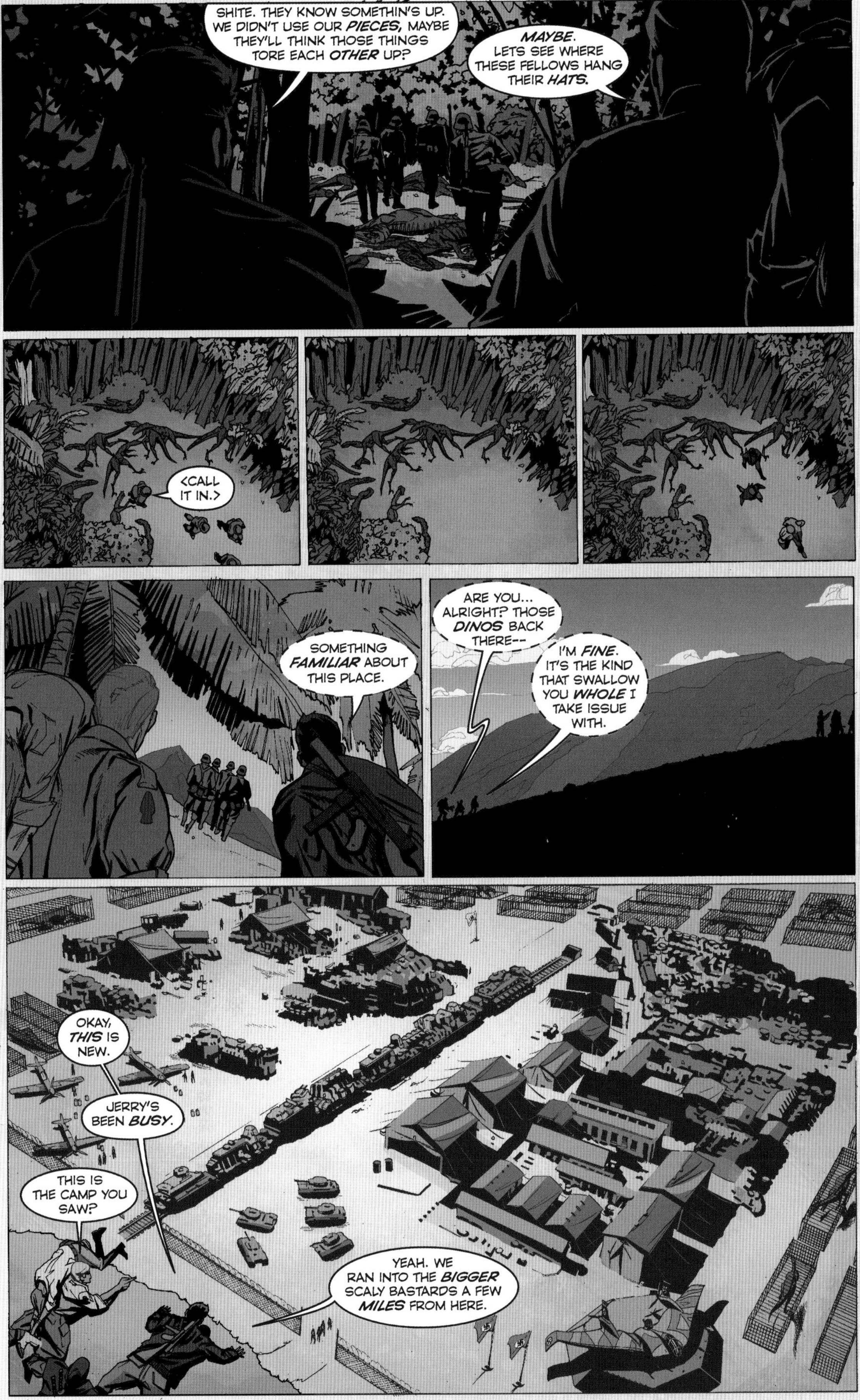
SHITE. THEY KNOW SOMETHIN'S UP. WE DIDN'T USE OUR PIECES, MAYBE THEY'LL THINK THOSE THINGS TORE EACH OTHER UP?
MAYBE. LETS SEE WHERE THESE FELLOWS HANG THEIR HATS.
<CALL IT IN.>
SOMETHING FAMILIAR ABOUT THIS PLACE.
ARE YOU... ALRIGHT? THOSE DINOS BACK THERE--
I'M FINE. IT'S THE KIND THAT SWALLOW YOU WHOLE I TAKE ISSUE WITH.
OKAY, THIS IS NEW.
JERRY'S BEEN BUSY.
THIS IS THE CAMP YOU SAW?
YEAH. WE RAN INTO THE BIGGER SCALY BASTARDS A FEW MILES FROM HERE.

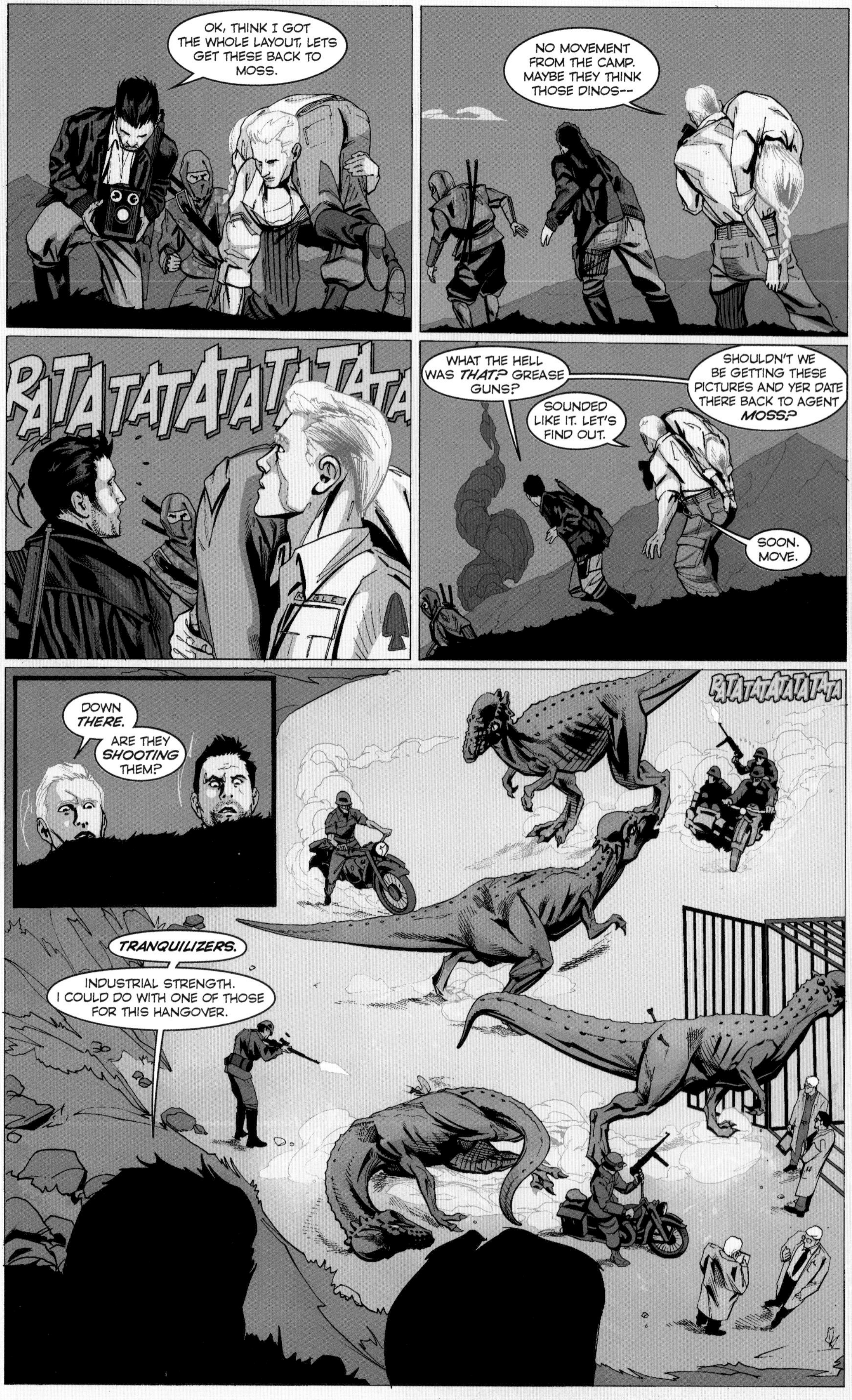
OK, THINK I GOT THE WHOLE LAYOUT, LETS GET THESE BACK TO MOSS.
NO MOVEMENT FROM THE CAMP. MAYBE THEY THINK THOSE DINOS--
RATATATATATATATA
WHAT THE HELL WAS THAT? GREASE GUNS?
SOUNDED LIKE IT. LET'S FIND OUT.
SHOULDN'T WE BE GETTING THESE PICTURES AND YER DATE THERE BACK TO AGENT MOSS?
SOON. MOVE.
DOWN THERE.
ARE THEY SHOOTING THEM?
RATATATATATATATA
TRANQUILIZERS.
INDUSTRIAL STRENGTH. I COULD DO WITH ONE OF THOSE FOR THIS HANGOVER.

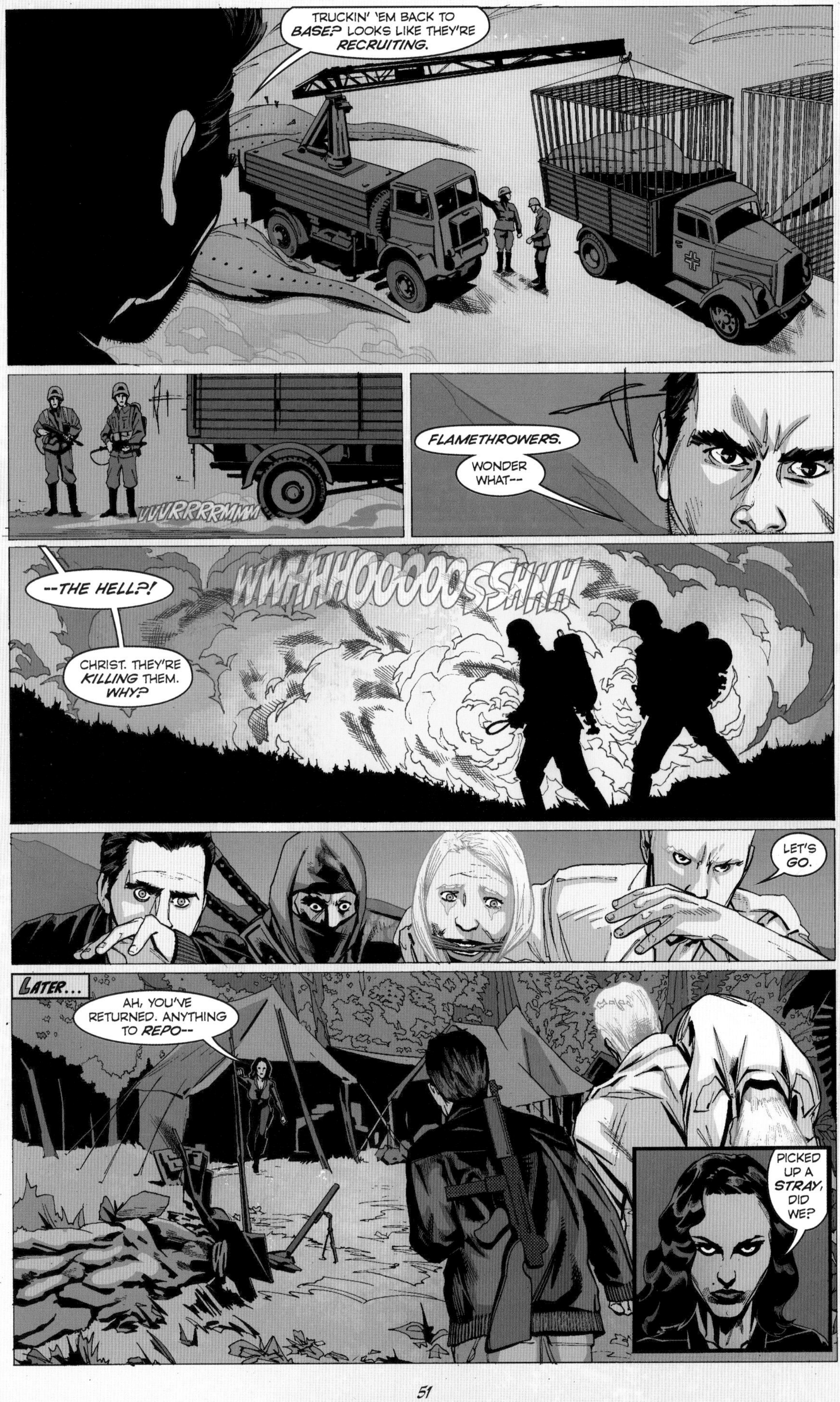
TRUCKIN' 'EM BACK TO BASE? LOOKS LIKE THEY'RE RECRUITING.
VVVRRRRMMM
FLAMETHROWERS.
WONDER WHAT--
--THE HELL?!
WWHHHOOOOOOSSHHH
CHRIST. THEY'RE KILLING THEM. WHY?
LET'S GO.
LATER...
AH, YOU'VE RETURNED. ANYTHING TO REPO--
PICKED UP A STRAY, DID WE?

GERMAN. *SCIENTIST*, WE THINK. SHE WAS STUDYING SOME OF THE CREATURES IN THE JUNGLE.

THOUGHT YOU MIGHT LIKE TO MEET HER, MAYBE COPY HER *HOMEWORK*.

IT WAS A *RISK* BRINGING HER HERE. THE SS WILL BE BENT ON HER *RETRIEVAL*.

STILL, LETS FIND OUT WHAT SHE *KNOWS*.

WHAT, YOU MEAN *INTERROGATE* HER? ARE YOU *TRAINED* FOR THAT?

OF COURSE. YOUR ARM, CAPTAIN. ARE YOU *INJURED?*

IT'S *NOTHING.* I MET MY FIRST DINOSAUR. AND HIS EXTENDED *FAMILY.*

WELL BE SURE AND INCLUDE IT IN YOUR *REPORT.*

LOOKS LIKE WE KNOW WHO TEACHER'S *PET* IS.

MAN, THEY WEREN'T KIDDIN' WHEN THEY SAID YOU WERE *GOOD*, ISH.

NO KRAUT WILL BE GETTING IN HERE WITHOUT RAISING AN ALMIGHTY BLOODY *RACKET.*

CAPTAIN, STAFF SERGEANT. IF YOU WOULD. *ISHIKAWA,* PLEASE CONTINUE SECURING THE PERIMETER, THANK YOU.

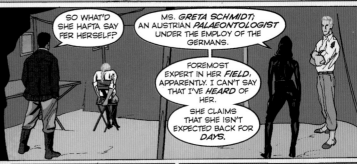

SO WHAT'D SHE HAFTA SAY FER HERSELF?

MS. *GRETA SCHMIDT;* AN AUSTRIAN *PALAEONTOLOGIST* UNDER THE EMPLOY OF THE GERMANS.

FOREMOST EXPERT IN HER *FIELD,* APPARENTLY. I CAN'T SAY THAT I'VE *HEARD* OF HER.

SHE CLAIMS THAT SHE ISN'T EXPECTED BACK FOR *DAYS.*

SHE OFFERED THAT ALL UP WILLINGLY?

SHE'S A *RATIONAL* WOMAN.

CAPTAIN, IF YOU'D JOIN ME IN REVIEWING MS. SCHMIDT'S FILES?

YOU CRIED WHEN THEY TORCHED THOSE CRITTERS. PERSONALLY I COULDN'T CARE LESS IF THEY BURNED 'EM ALL TO A *CINDER.* SO *TELL* ME.

WHY ARE YOU IN BED WITH THE SS?

I HAVE NO INTEREST WHATSOEVER IN MEN AND THEIR *WARS.*

THEY NAME THESE BEAUTIFUL CREATURES *'MONSTERS'.*

IT IS YOU IDIOT *MEN* WHO ARE THE MONSTERS.

AH HERE NOW, HANG *ON* A SEC.

WE'RE THE *GOOD* GUYS.

I AM *SURE.* HERE OUT OF THE GOODNESS OF YOUR *HEARTS.* NAZI, U.S.– YOU SIMPLY BEAR DIFFERENT EMBLEMS ON YOUR *SLEEVES.* THE CREATURES WOULD MEET THE SAME *FATE* REGARDLESS. INSTRUMENTS IN THE AGENDAS OF *MADMEN.*

YEAH? AND YER A BLOODY *ANGEL,* RIGHT? WOULDN'T HURT A FLY? YOU PEOPLE ARE MASSACRING MILLIONS OF INNOCENT FOLKS AND *WE'RE* THE MONSTERS? GIMME A BLOODY *BREAK,* LADY.

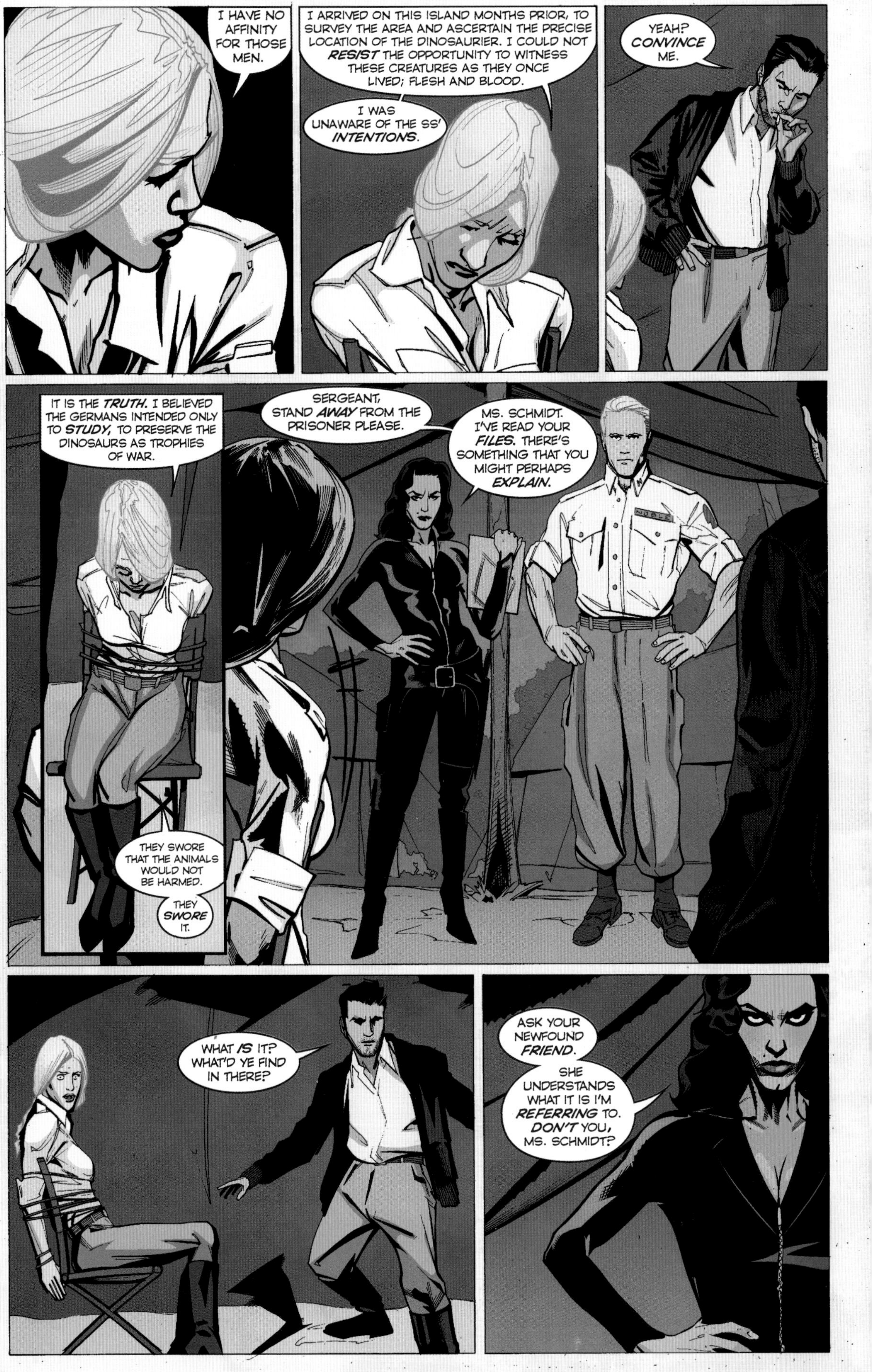
I HAVE NO AFFINITY FOR THOSE MEN.
I ARRIVED ON THIS ISLAND MONTHS PRIOR, TO SURVEY THE AREA AND ASCERTAIN THE PRECISE LOCATION OF THE DINOSAURIER. I COULD NOT RESIST THE OPPORTUNITY TO WITNESS THESE CREATURES AS THEY ONCE LIVED; FLESH AND BLOOD.
I WAS UNAWARE OF THE SS' INTENTIONS.
YEAH? CONVINCE ME.
IT IS THE TRUTH. I BELIEVED THE GERMANS INTENDED ONLY TO STUDY, TO PRESERVE THE DINOSAURS AS TROPHIES OF WAR.
THEY SWORE THAT THE ANIMALS WOULD NOT BE HARMED.
THEY SWORE IT.
SERGEANT, STAND AWAY FROM THE PRISONER PLEASE.
MS. SCHMIDT. I'VE READ YOUR FILES. THERE'S SOMETHING THAT YOU MIGHT PERHAPS EXPLAIN.
WHAT IS IT? WHAT'D YE FIND IN THERE?
ASK YOUR NEWFOUND FRIEND.
SHE UNDERSTANDS WHAT IT IS I'M REFERRING TO. DON'T YOU, MS. SCHMIDT?

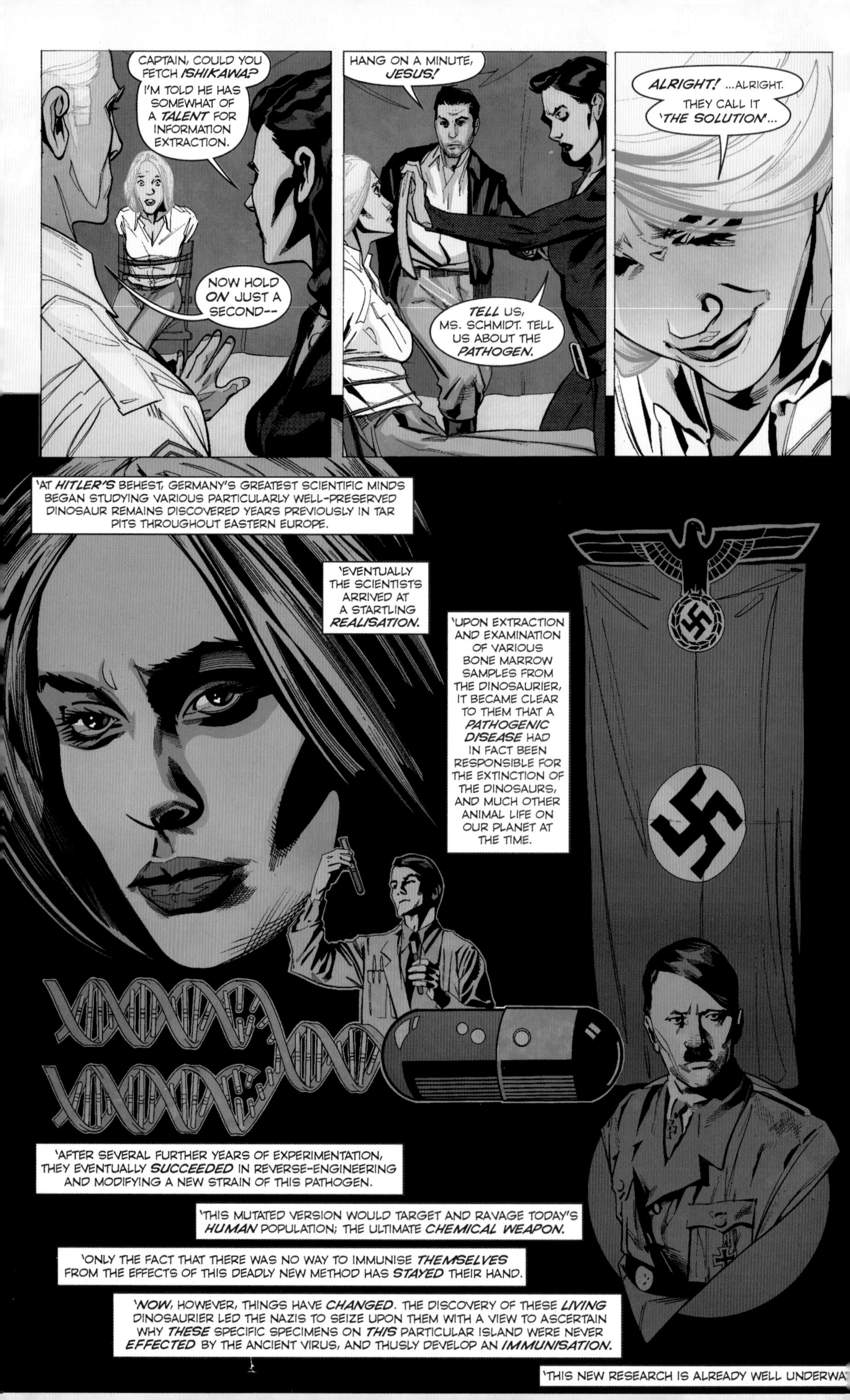
CAPTAIN, COULD YOU FETCH ISHIKAWA?
I'M TOLD HE HAS SOMEWHAT OF A TALENT FOR INFORMATION EXTRACTION.
NOW HOLD ON JUST A SECOND--
HANG ON A MINUTE, JESUS!
TELL US, MS. SCHMIDT. TELL US ABOUT THE PATHOGEN.
ALRIGHT! ...ALRIGHT.
THEY CALL IT 'THE SOLUTION'...
'AT HITLER'S BEHEST, GERMANY'S GREATEST SCIENTIFIC MINDS BEGAN STUDYING VARIOUS PARTICULARLY WELL-PRESERVED DINOSAUR REMAINS DISCOVERED YEARS PREVIOUSLY IN TAR PITS THROUGHOUT EASTERN EUROPE.
'EVENTUALLY THE SCIENTISTS ARRIVED AT A STARTLING REALISATION.
'UPON EXTRACTION AND EXAMINATION OF VARIOUS BONE MARROW SAMPLES FROM THE DINOSAURIER, IT BECAME CLEAR TO THEM THAT A PATHOGENIC DISEASE HAD IN FACT BEEN RESPONSIBLE FOR THE EXTINCTION OF THE DINOSAURS, AND MUCH OTHER ANIMAL LIFE ON OUR PLANET AT THE TIME.
'AFTER SEVERAL FURTHER YEARS OF EXPERIMENTATION, THEY EVENTUALLY SUCCEEDED IN REVERSE-ENGINEERING AND MODIFYING A NEW STRAIN OF THIS PATHOGEN.
'THIS MUTATED VERSION WOULD TARGET AND RAVAGE TODAY'S HUMAN POPULATION; THE ULTIMATE CHEMICAL WEAPON.
'ONLY THE FACT THAT THERE WAS NO WAY TO IMMUNISE THEMSELVES FROM THE EFFECTS OF THIS DEADLY NEW METHOD HAS STAYED THEIR HAND.
'NOW, HOWEVER, THINGS HAVE CHANGED. THE DISCOVERY OF THESE LIVING DINOSAURIER LED THE NAZIS TO SEIZE UPON THEM WITH A VIEW TO ASCERTAIN WHY THESE SPECIFIC SPECIMENS ON THIS PARTICULAR ISLAND WERE NEVER EFFECTED BY THE ANCIENT VIRUS, AND THUSLY DEVELOP AN IMMUNISATION.
'THIS NEW RESEARCH IS ALREADY WELL UNDERWA

SO THAT'S IT. THE *ENDGAME*.

IF THESE ANIMALS ARE SO *IMPORTANT* TO HITLER, WHY HAS HE ONLY COMMITTED THIS SMALL FORCE TO THE ISLAND? IF WHAT YOU'RE SAYING IS *TRUE*, THEN THIS COULD BE THE DEFINING FACTOR THAT SWINGS THE WHOLE *WAR* IN THE NAZIS' *FAVOUR*.

SECRECY WAS OF THE UPPERMOST CONCERN. A LARGE FORCE WOULD DRAW UNDUE *ATTENTION*.

I'M INCLINED TO AGREE WITH CAPTAIN NOBLE. A FEW PLATOONS TO RECOVER WHAT IS POTENTIALLY THE MOST POTENT BIOLOGICAL WEAPON HUMANKIND HAS EVER *POSSESSED*?

THERE MUST BE SOMETHING *MORE*.

THEY *NEED* NOTHING MORE. THESE WAFFEN-SS ARE LED BY *COMMANDANT TÖHT*.

THERE IS NO MAN THAT HITLER TRUSTS MORE. HE IS RUTHLESS. BEYOND CAPABLE. *UNDERESTIMATE* HIM AT YOUR *PERIL*.

BESIDES. HE IS NOT *ALONE*. THEY HAVE A MIGHTY *WARSHIP*. *SUBMARINES*. *ARTILLERY*.

YOU ARE ONLY *FOUR*. YOU PRESUME TO THINK *HE* IS UNDERPOWERED? *HA!*

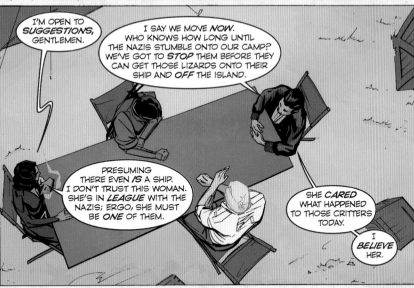

I'M OPEN TO *SUGGESTIONS*, GENTLEMEN.

I SAY WE MOVE *NOW*. WHO KNOWS HOW LONG UNTIL THE NAZIS STUMBLE ONTO OUR CAMP? WE'VE GOT TO *STOP* THEM BEFORE THEY CAN GET THOSE LIZARDS ONTO THEIR SHIP AND *OFF* THE ISLAND.

PRESUMING THERE EVEN *IS* A SHIP. I DON'T TRUST THIS WOMAN. SHE'S IN *LEAGUE* WITH THE NAZIS; ERGO, SHE MUST BE *ONE* OF THEM.

SHE *CARED* WHAT HAPPENED TO THOSE CRITTERS TODAY. I *BELIEVE* HER.

IT MAKES NO *DIFFERENCE* ANYWAY. REGARDLESS OF YER WOMAN, WE NEED TO *STOP* THEM, AND IT HAS TO BE *SOON*. WHAT ARE WE *WAITING* FOR?!

WHAT WE *NEED* IS TO ASSESS THE SITUATION CAREFULLY. WHAT WE ARE *WAITING* FOR IS TO REPORT OUR FINDINGS TO OUR SUPERIORS AND IN TURN RECEIVE ORDERS ON HOW TO *PROCEED*.

I SHALL NOT RISK MY ENTIRE TEAM'S LIVES BASED ON WHAT YOU *BELIEVE*, SERGEANT.

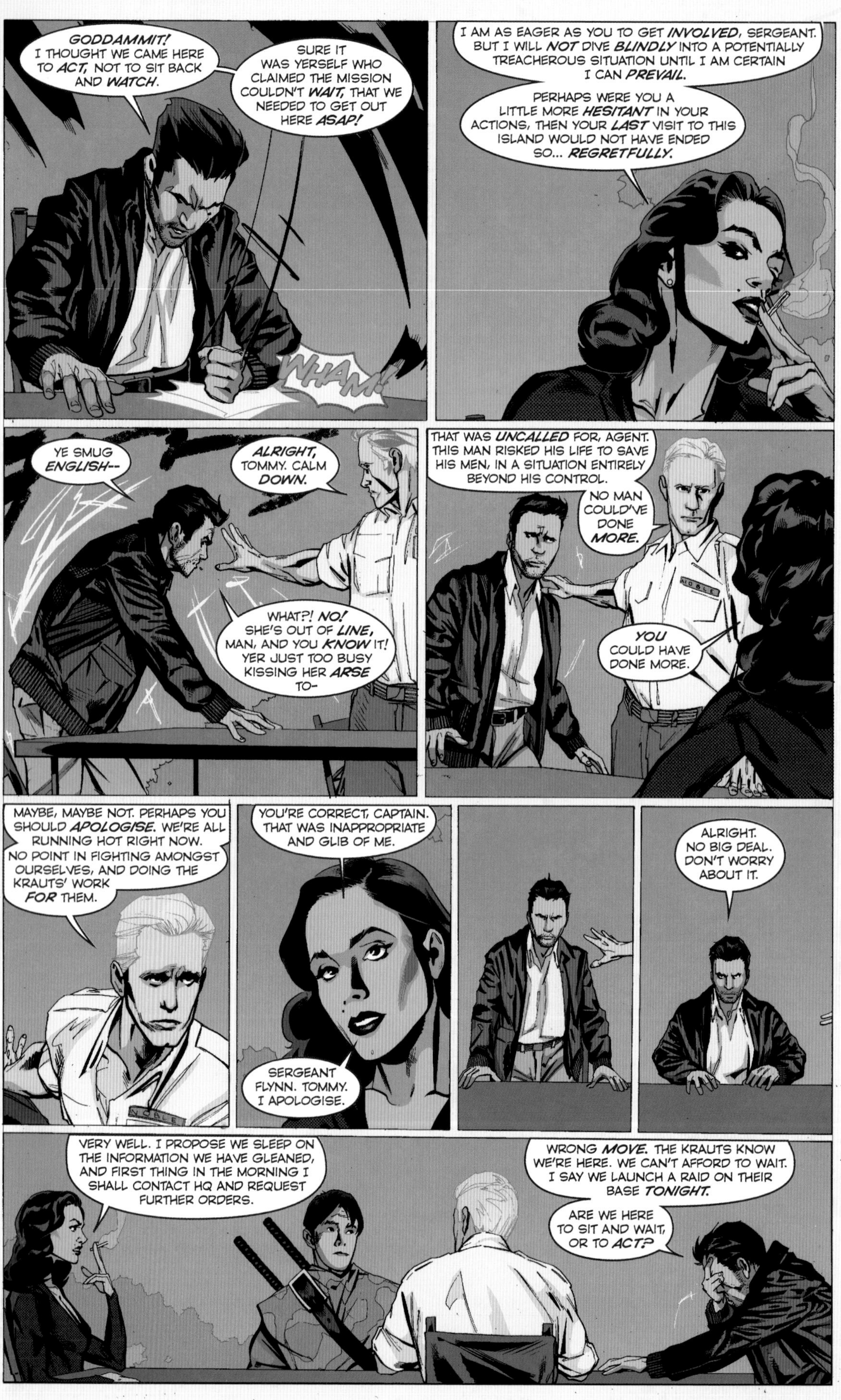
GODDAMMIT! I THOUGHT WE CAME HERE TO ACT, NOT TO SIT BACK AND WATCH.
SURE IT WAS YERSELF WHO CLAIMED THE MISSION COULDN'T WAIT, THAT WE NEEDED TO GET OUT HERE ASAP!
WHAM!
I AM AS EAGER AS YOU TO GET INVOLVED, SERGEANT. BUT I WILL NOT DIVE BLINDLY INTO A POTENTIALLY TREACHEROUS SITUATION UNTIL I AM CERTAIN I CAN PREVAIL.
PERHAPS WERE YOU A LITTLE MORE HESITANT IN YOUR ACTIONS, THEN YOUR LAST VISIT TO THIS ISLAND WOULD NOT HAVE ENDED SO... REGRETFULLY.
YE SMUG ENGLISH--
ALRIGHT, TOMMY. CALM DOWN.
WHAT?! NO! SHE'S OUT OF LINE, MAN, AND YOU KNOW IT! YER JUST TOO BUSY KISSING HER ARSE TO-
THAT WAS UNCALLED FOR, AGENT. THIS MAN RISKED HIS LIFE TO SAVE HIS MEN, IN A SITUATION ENTIRELY BEYOND HIS CONTROL.
NO MAN COULD'VE DONE MORE.
YOU COULD HAVE DONE MORE.
MAYBE, MAYBE NOT. PERHAPS YOU SHOULD APOLOGISE. WE'RE ALL RUNNING HOT RIGHT NOW. NO POINT IN FIGHTING AMONGST OURSELVES, AND DOING THE KRAUTS' WORK FOR THEM.
YOU'RE CORRECT, CAPTAIN. THAT WAS INAPPROPRIATE AND GLIB OF ME.
SERGEANT FLYNN. TOMMY. I APOLOGISE.
ALRIGHT. NO BIG DEAL. DON'T WORRY ABOUT IT.
VERY WELL. I PROPOSE WE SLEEP ON THE INFORMATION WE HAVE GLEANED, AND FIRST THING IN THE MORNING I SHALL CONTACT HQ AND REQUEST FURTHER ORDERS.
WRONG MOVE. THE KRAUTS KNOW WE'RE HERE. WE CAN'T AFFORD TO WAIT. I SAY WE LAUNCH A RAID ON THEIR BASE TONIGHT.
ARE WE HERE TO SIT AND WAIT, OR TO ACT?

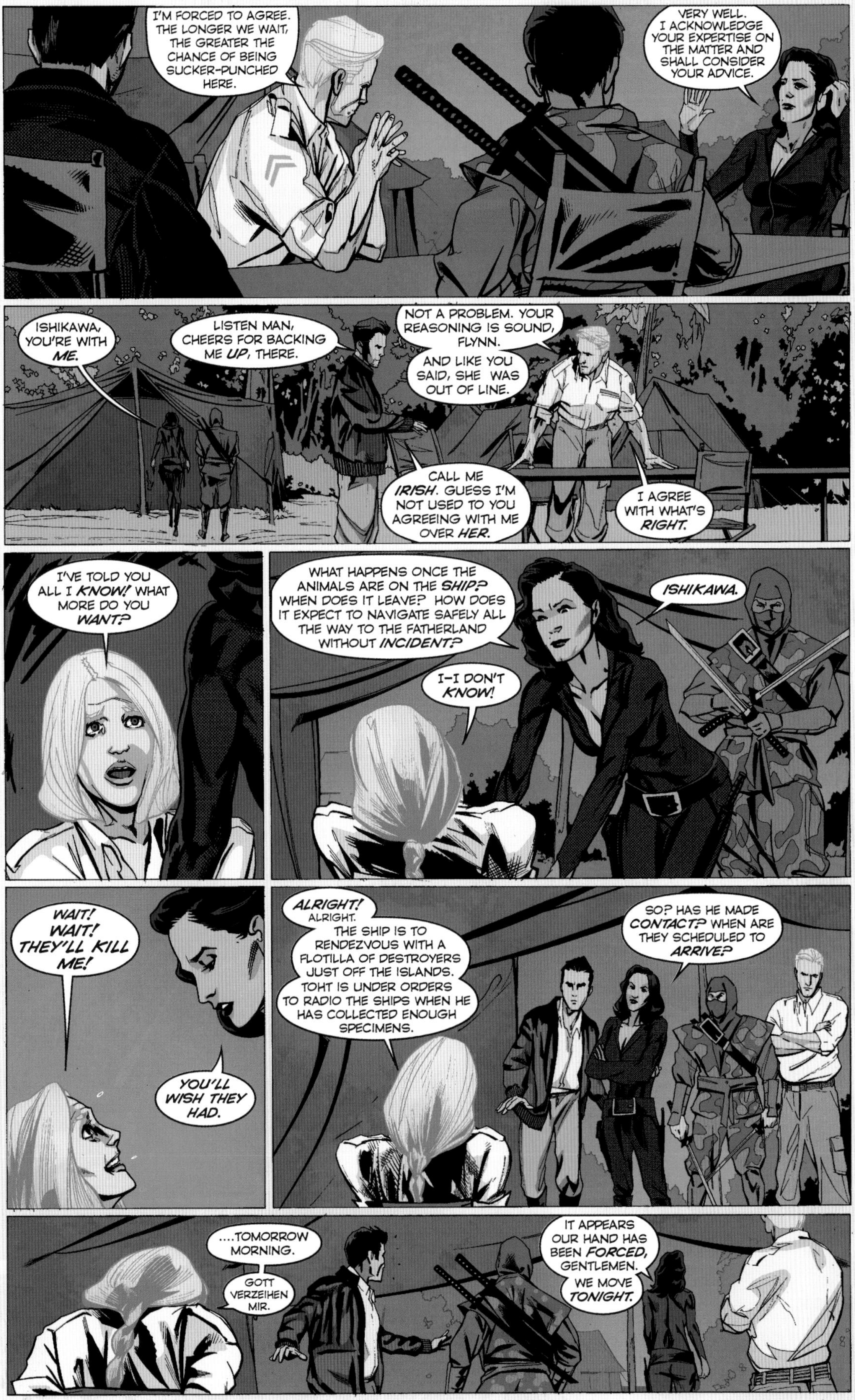
I'M FORCED TO AGREE. THE LONGER WE WAIT, THE GREATER THE CHANCE OF BEING SUCKER-PUNCHED HERE.
VERY WELL. I ACKNOWLEDGE YOUR EXPERTISE ON THE MATTER AND SHALL CONSIDER YOUR ADVICE.
ISHIKAWA, YOU'RE WITH ME.
LISTEN MAN, CHEERS FOR BACKING ME UP, THERE.
NOT A PROBLEM. YOUR REASONING IS SOUND, FLYNN.
AND LIKE YOU SAID, SHE WAS OUT OF LINE.
CALL ME IRISH. GUESS I'M NOT USED TO YOU AGREEING WITH ME OVER HER.
I AGREE WITH WHAT'S RIGHT.
I'VE TOLD YOU ALL I KNOW! WHAT MORE DO YOU WANT?
WHAT HAPPENS ONCE THE ANIMALS ARE ON THE SHIP? WHEN DOES IT LEAVE? HOW DOES IT EXPECT TO NAVIGATE SAFELY ALL THE WAY TO THE FATHERLAND WITHOUT INCIDENT?
ISHIKAWA.
I-I DON'T KNOW!
WAIT! WAIT! THEY'LL KILL ME!
YOU'LL WISH THEY HAD.
ALRIGHT! ALRIGHT. THE SHIP IS TO RENDEZVOUS WITH A FLOTILLA OF DESTROYERS JUST OFF THE ISLANDS. TOHT IS UNDER ORDERS TO RADIO THE SHIPS WHEN HE HAS COLLECTED ENOUGH SPECIMENS.
SO? HAS HE MADE CONTACT? WHEN ARE THEY SCHEDULED TO ARRIVE?
....TOMORROW MORNING.
GOTT VERZEIHEN MIR.
IT APPEARS OUR HAND HAS BEEN FORCED, GENTLEMEN.
WE MOVE TONIGHT.

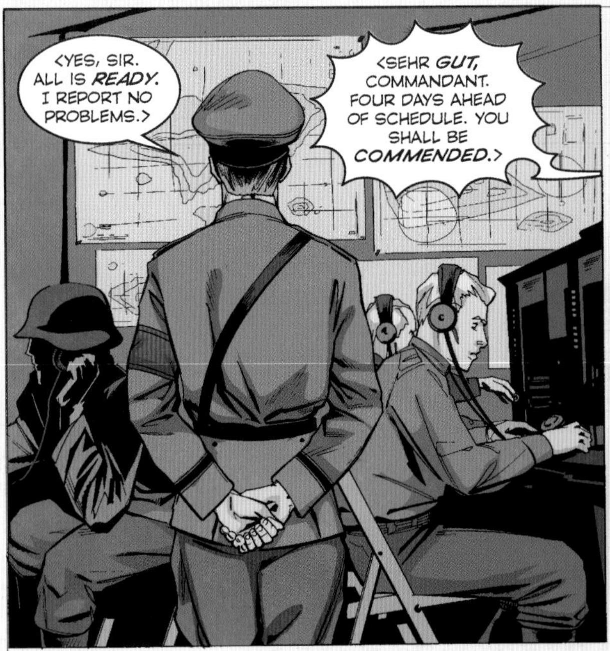
<YES, SIR. ALL IS *READY.* I REPORT NO PROBLEMS.>
<SEHR *GUT,* COMMANDANT. FOUR DAYS AHEAD OF SCHEDULE. YOU SHALL BE *COMMENDED.*>

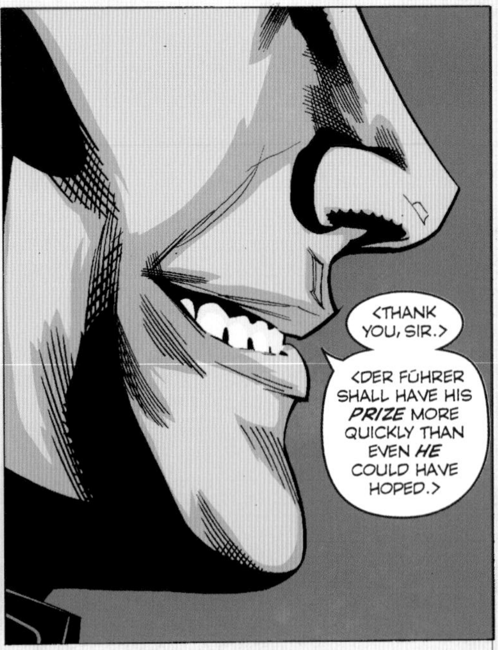
<THANK YOU, SIR.>
<DER FÜHRER SHALL HAVE HIS *PRIZE* MORE QUICKLY THAN EVEN *HE* COULD HAVE HOPED.>

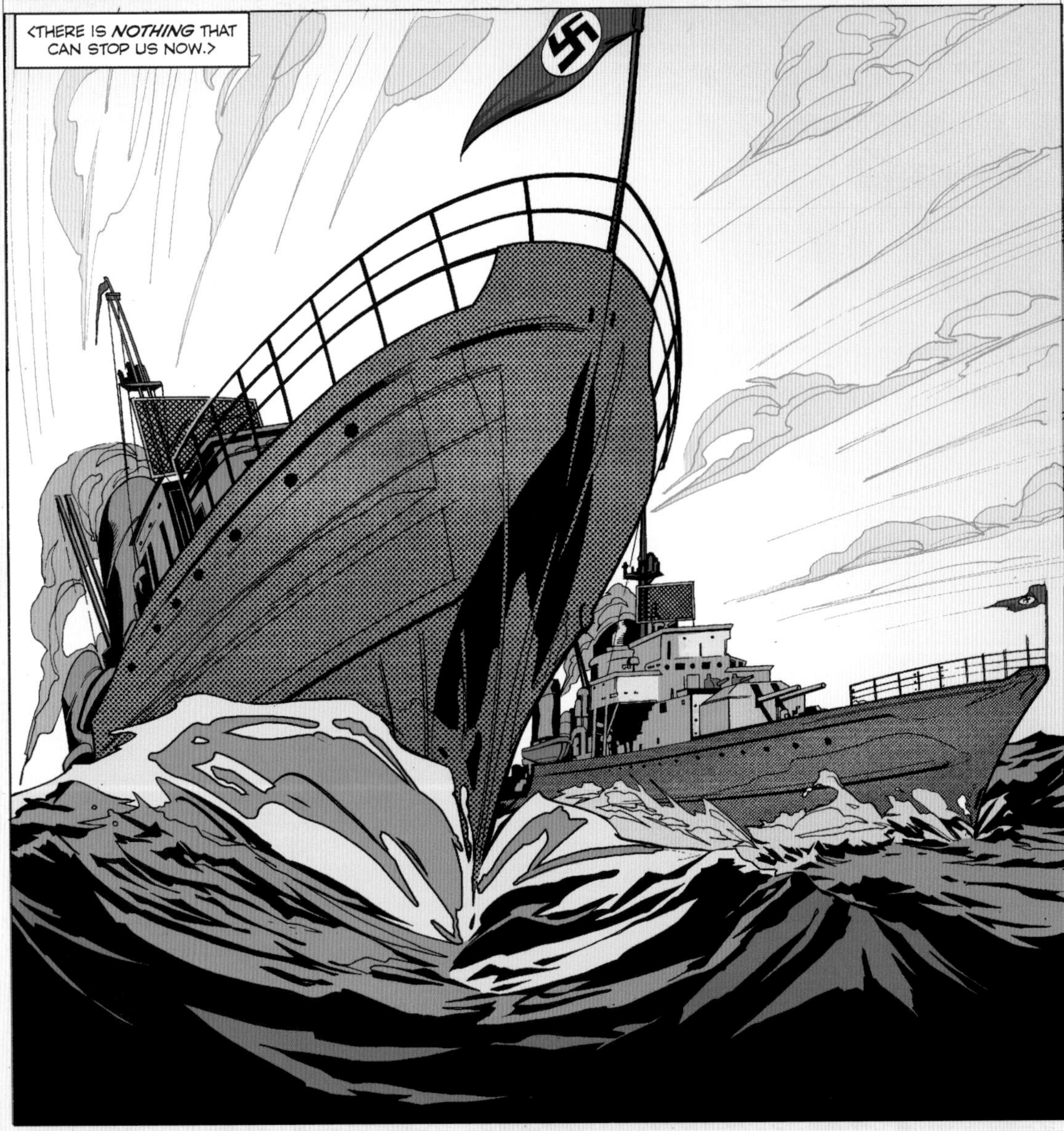
<THERE IS *NOTHING* THAT CAN STOP US NOW.>

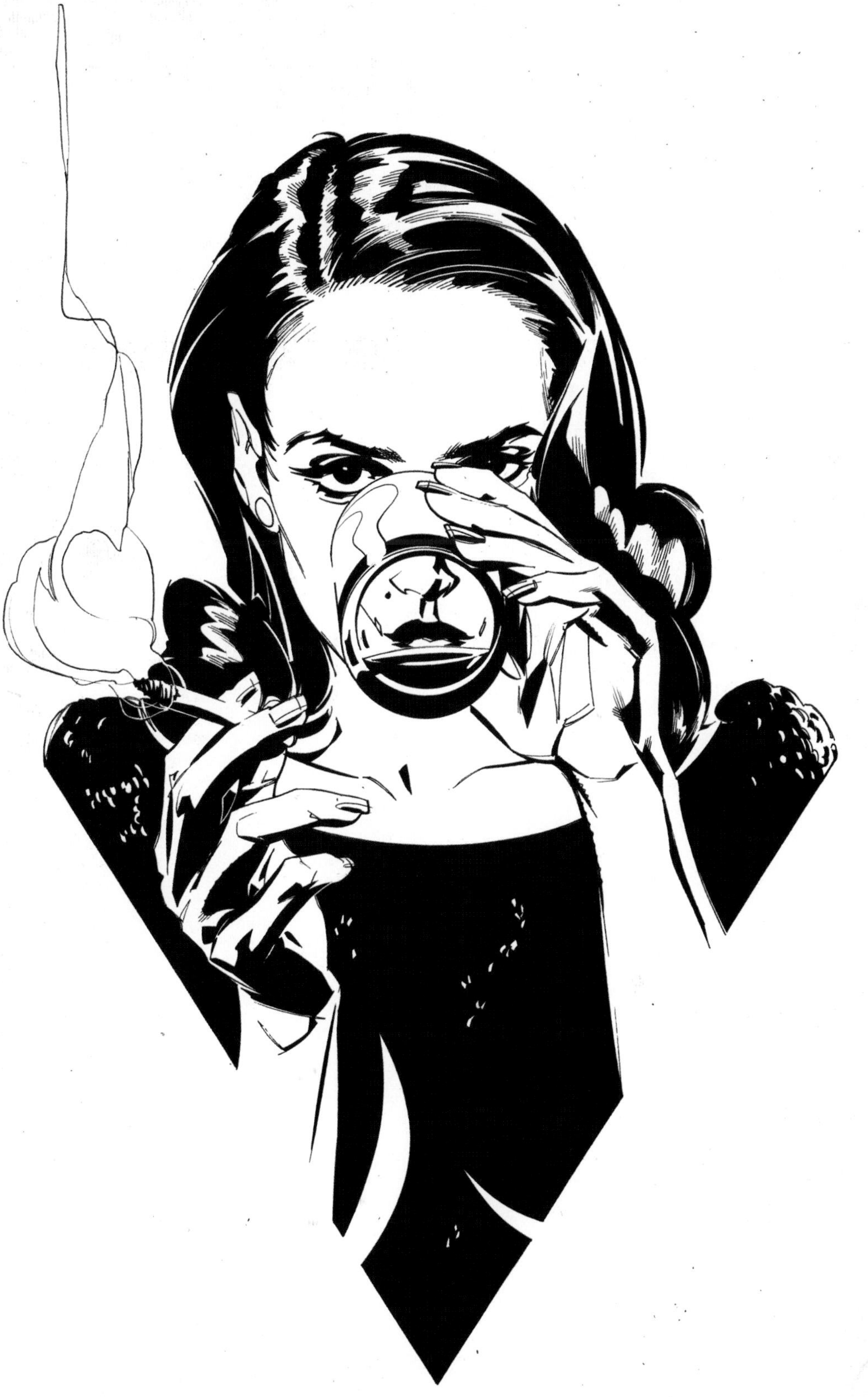

Chapter Three

SOMETHING WICKED THIS WAY COMES

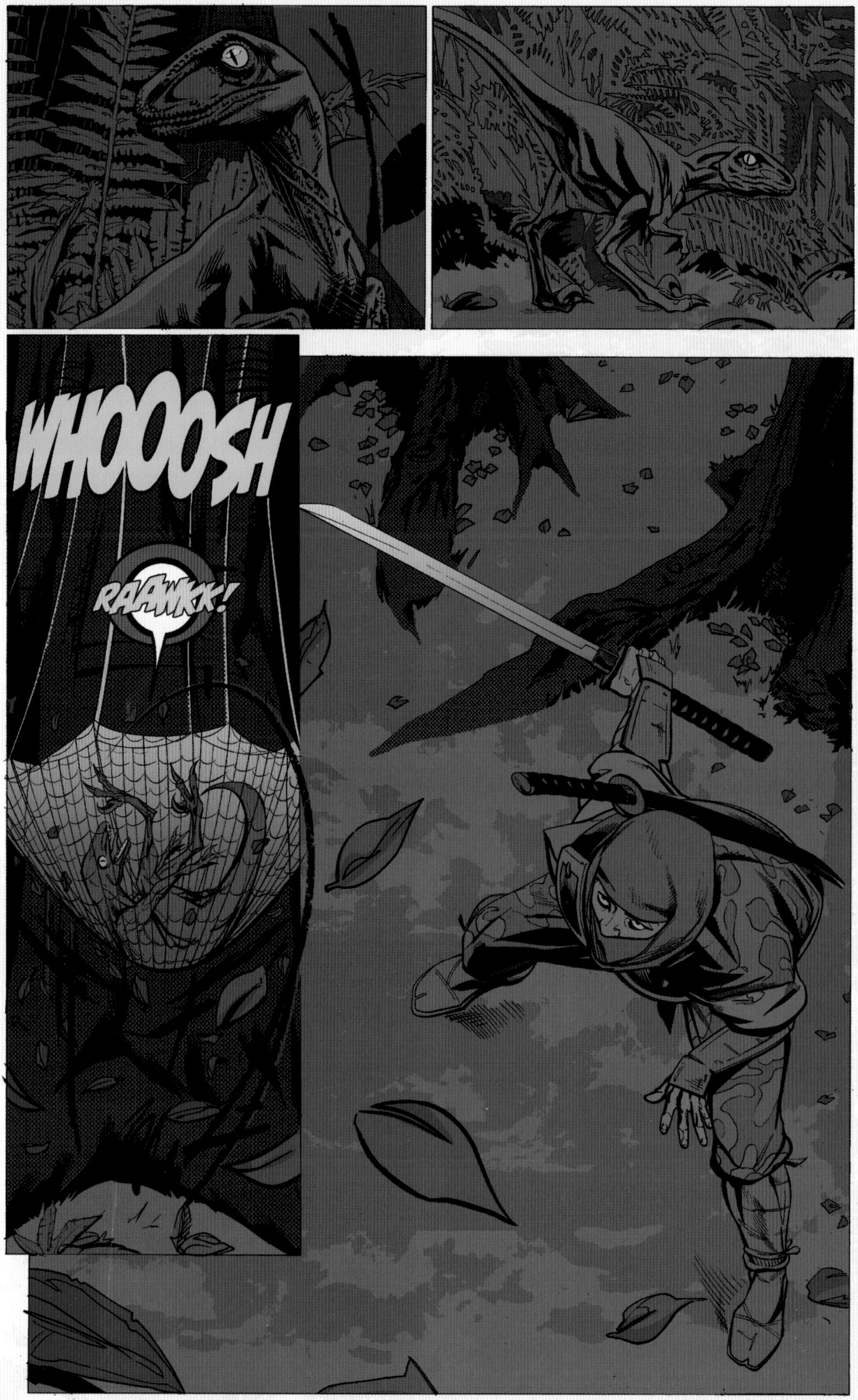
WHOOOSH
RAAWKK!

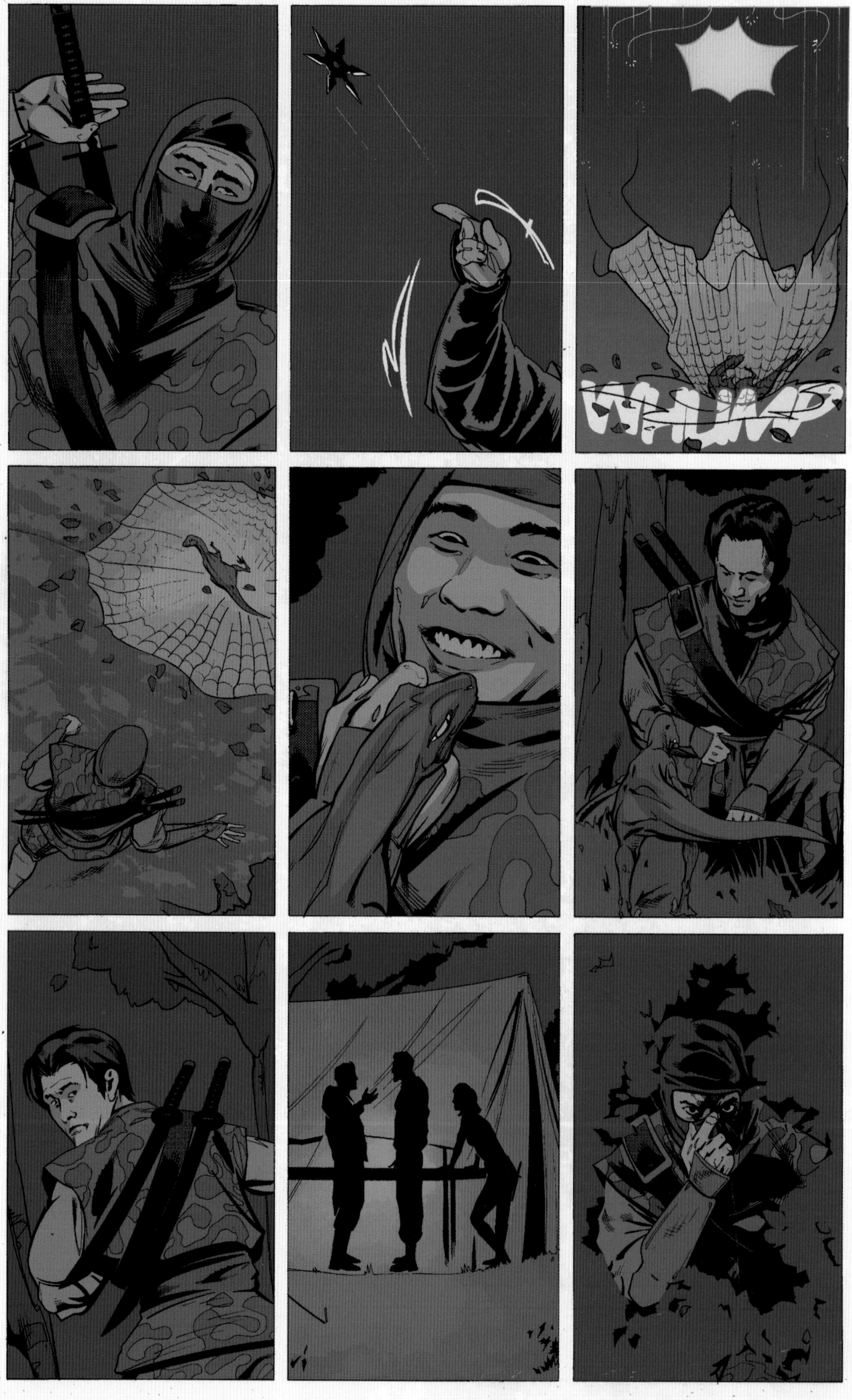
WHUMP

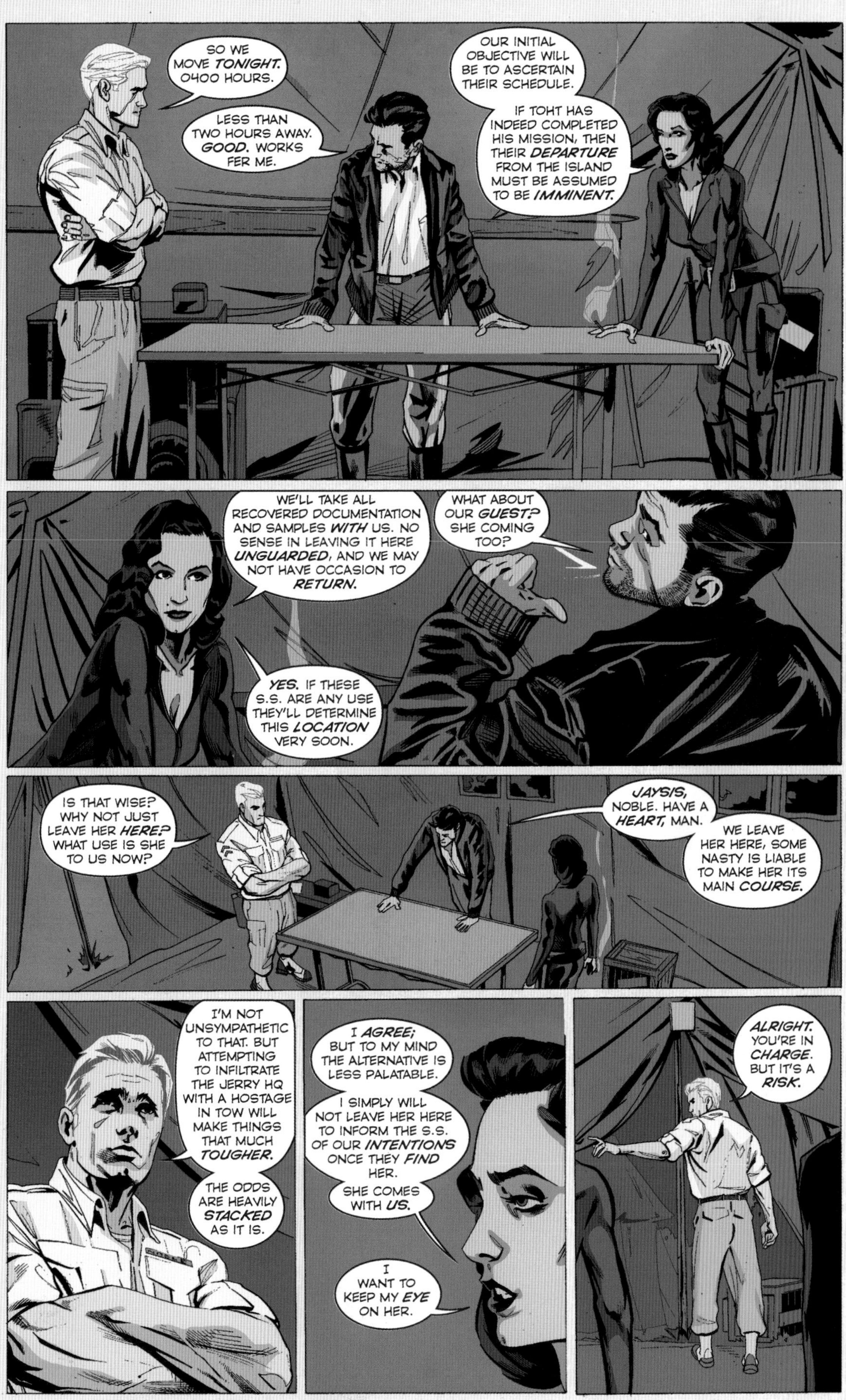
SO WE MOVE TONIGHT. 0400 HOURS.
LESS THAN TWO HOURS AWAY. GOOD. WORKS FER ME.
OUR INITIAL OBJECTIVE WILL BE TO ASCERTAIN THEIR SCHEDULE.
IF TOHT HAS INDEED COMPLETED HIS MISSION, THEN THEIR DEPARTURE FROM THE ISLAND MUST BE ASSUMED TO BE IMMINENT.
WE'LL TAKE ALL RECOVERED DOCUMENTATION AND SAMPLES WITH US. NO SENSE IN LEAVING IT HERE UNGUARDED, AND WE MAY NOT HAVE OCCASION TO RETURN.
WHAT ABOUT OUR GUEST? SHE COMING TOO?
YES. IF THESE S.S. ARE ANY USE THEY'LL DETERMINE THIS LOCATION VERY SOON.
IS THAT WISE? WHY NOT JUST LEAVE HER HERE? WHAT USE IS SHE TO US NOW?
JAYSIS, NOBLE. HAVE A HEART, MAN.
WE LEAVE HER HERE, SOME NASTY IS LIABLE TO MAKE HER ITS MAIN COURSE.
I'M NOT UNSYMPATHETIC TO THAT. BUT ATTEMPTING TO INFILTRATE THE JERRY HQ WITH A HOSTAGE IN TOW WILL MAKE THINGS THAT MUCH TOUGHER.
THE ODDS ARE HEAVILY STACKED AS IT IS.
I AGREE; BUT TO MY MIND THE ALTERNATIVE IS LESS PALATABLE.
I SIMPLY WILL NOT LEAVE HER HERE TO INFORM THE S.S. OF OUR INTENTIONS ONCE THEY FIND HER.
SHE COMES WITH US.
I WANT TO KEEP MY EYE ON HER.
ALRIGHT. YOU'RE IN CHARGE. BUT IT'S A RISK.

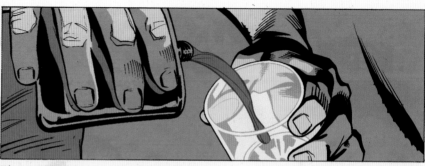

ROOM FOR ONE *MORE*, SERGEANT?

MAKE YERSELF AT *HOME*, CAPTAIN.

JOHN. CALL ME *JOHN*.

FAIR ENOUGH, *JOHN*. AN' HERE, FORGET THE *'SERGEANT'* CRAP. IT'S TOMMY. OR *IRISH*.

'IRISH'. THERE'S AN *ENIGMATIC* NICKNAME.

HEH, YEAH. THEY DON'T HIRE US GRUNTS FOR OUR *IMAGINATION*, Y'KNOW?

DIDN'T TAKE YOU FOR A *DRINKER*. AGAINST *REGULATIONS*.

YEAH, WELL. I'VE A FEELING THIS COULD BE A ONE-WAY *TRIP*.

CHRIST, DON'T BE SO BLOODY *MELODRAMATIC*. WAY I SEE IT, YER PRETTY MUCH *INDESTRUCTIBLE*.

HA, *MAYBE*. GUESS WE'LL FIND *OUT*.

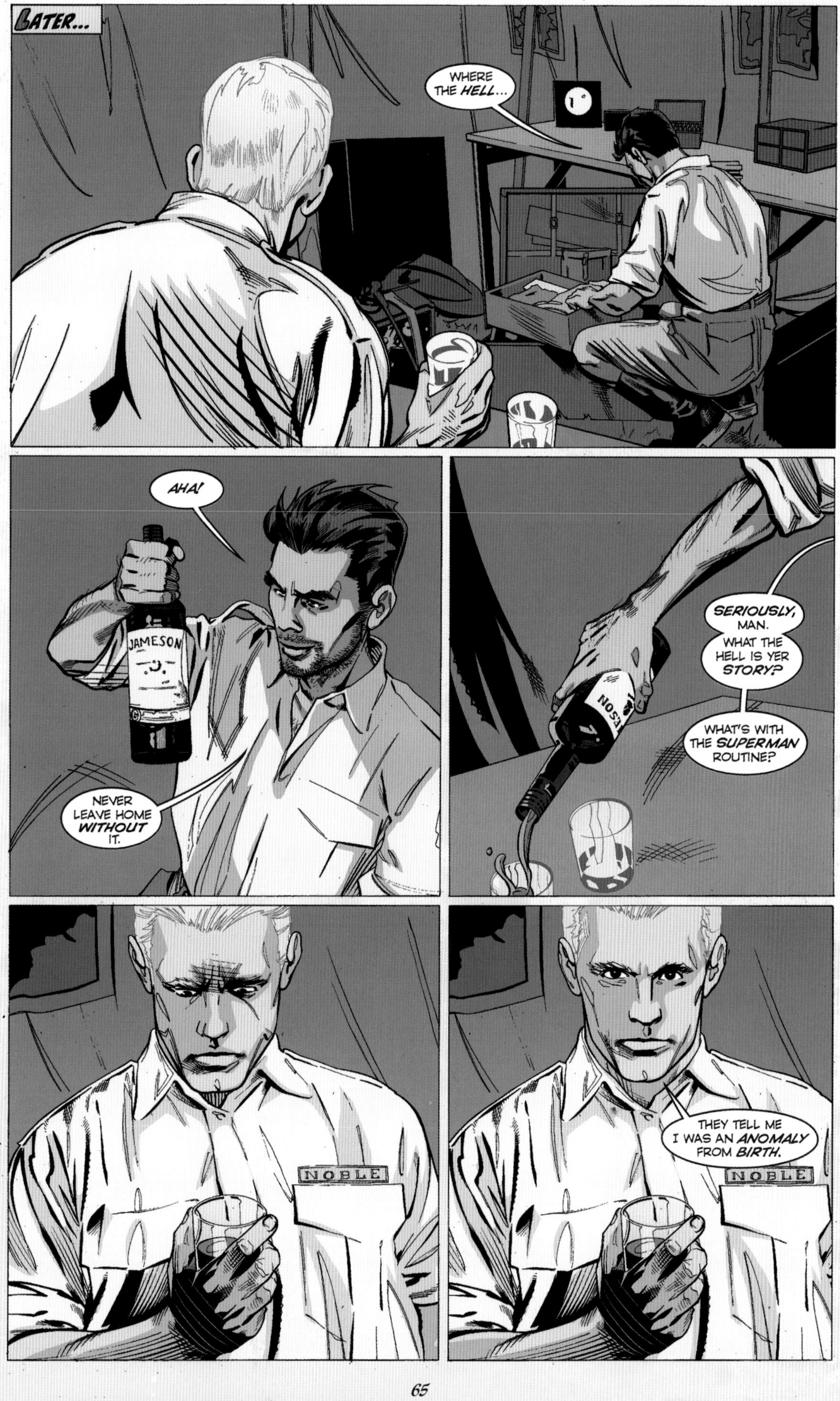
LATER...
WHERE THE HELL...
AHA!
NEVER LEAVE HOME WITHOUT IT.
JAMESON
SERIOUSLY, MAN. WHAT THE HELL IS YER STORY?
WHAT'S WITH THE SUPERMAN ROUTINE?
NOBLE
NOBLE
THEY TELL ME I WAS AN ANOMALY FROM BIRTH.

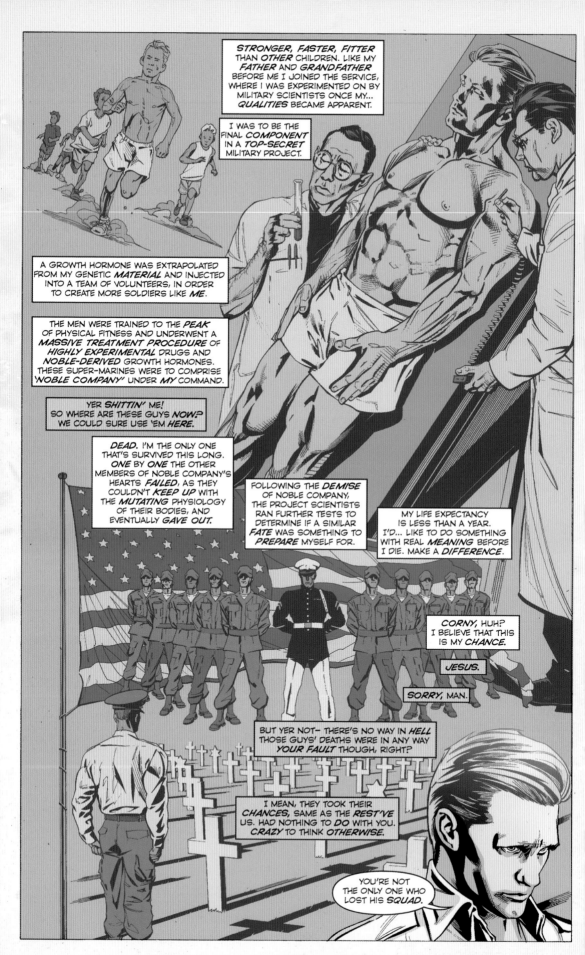

STRONGER, FASTER, FITTER THAN OTHER CHILDREN. LIKE MY FATHER AND GRANDFATHER BEFORE ME I JOINED THE SERVICE, WHERE I WAS EXPERIMENTED ON BY MILITARY SCIENTISTS ONCE MY... QUALITIES BECAME APPARENT.

I WAS TO BE THE FINAL COMPONENT IN A TOP-SECRET MILITARY PROJECT.

A GROWTH HORMONE WAS EXTRAPOLATED FROM MY GENETIC MATERIAL AND INJECTED INTO A TEAM OF VOLUNTEERS, IN ORDER TO CREATE MORE SOLDIERS LIKE ME.

THE MEN WERE TRAINED TO THE PEAK OF PHYSICAL FITNESS AND UNDERWENT A MASSIVE TREATMENT PROCEDURE OF HIGHLY EXPERIMENTAL DRUGS AND NOBLE-DERIVED GROWTH HORMONES. THESE SUPER-MARINES WERE TO COMPRISE 'NOBLE COMPANY' UNDER MY COMMAND.

YER SHITTIN' ME! SO WHERE ARE THESE GUYS NOW!? WE COULD SURE USE 'EM HERE.

DEAD. I'M THE ONLY ONE THAT'S SURVIVED THIS LONG. ONE BY ONE THE OTHER MEMBERS OF NOBLE COMPANY'S HEARTS FAILED, AS THEY COULDN'T KEEP UP WITH THE MUTATING PHYSIOLOGY OF THEIR BODIES, AND EVENTUALLY GAVE OUT.

FOLLOWING THE DEMISE OF NOBLE COMPANY, THE PROJECT SCIENTISTS RAN FURTHER TESTS TO DETERMINE IF A SIMILAR FATE WAS SOMETHING TO PREPARE MYSELF FOR.

MY LIFE EXPECTANCY IS LESS THAN A YEAR. I'D... LIKE TO DO SOMETHING WITH REAL MEANING BEFORE I DIE. MAKE A DIFFERENCE.

CORNY, HUH? I BELIEVE THAT THIS IS MY CHANCE.

JESUS.

SORRY, MAN.

BUT YER NOT– THERE'S NO WAY IN HELL THOSE GUYS' DEATHS WERE IN ANY WAY YOUR FAULT THOUGH, RIGHT?

I MEAN, THEY TOOK THEIR CHANCES, SAME AS THE REST'VE US. HAD NOTHING TO DO WITH YOU. CRAZY TO THINK OTHERWISE.

YOU'RE NOT THE ONLY ONE WHO LOST HIS SQUAD.

TO FALLEN COMRADES.

SLÁINTE.

coff

C'MON, WE'RE TOO GOOD-LOOKIN' TO BE FEELIN' SORRY FER OURSELVES.

AN' BESIDES, YOU'VE LASTED THIS LONG, WHY ALL OF A SUDDEN YOU ONLY HAVE A YEAR? I CALL BULLSHIT.

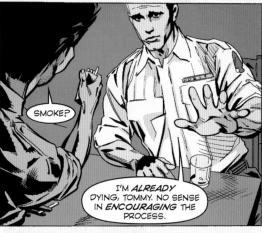

SMOKE?

I'M ALREADY DYING, TOMMY. NO SENSE IN ENCOURAGING THE PROCESS.

I'VE JUST BEEN ON THE RADIO WITH COMMAND.

THE NAVY ARE ON THEIR WAY. WHEN WE NEED THE CAVALRY, THEY'LL BE THERE.

JAMESON

JUST WHAT THE DOCTOR ORDERED.

HEY!

67

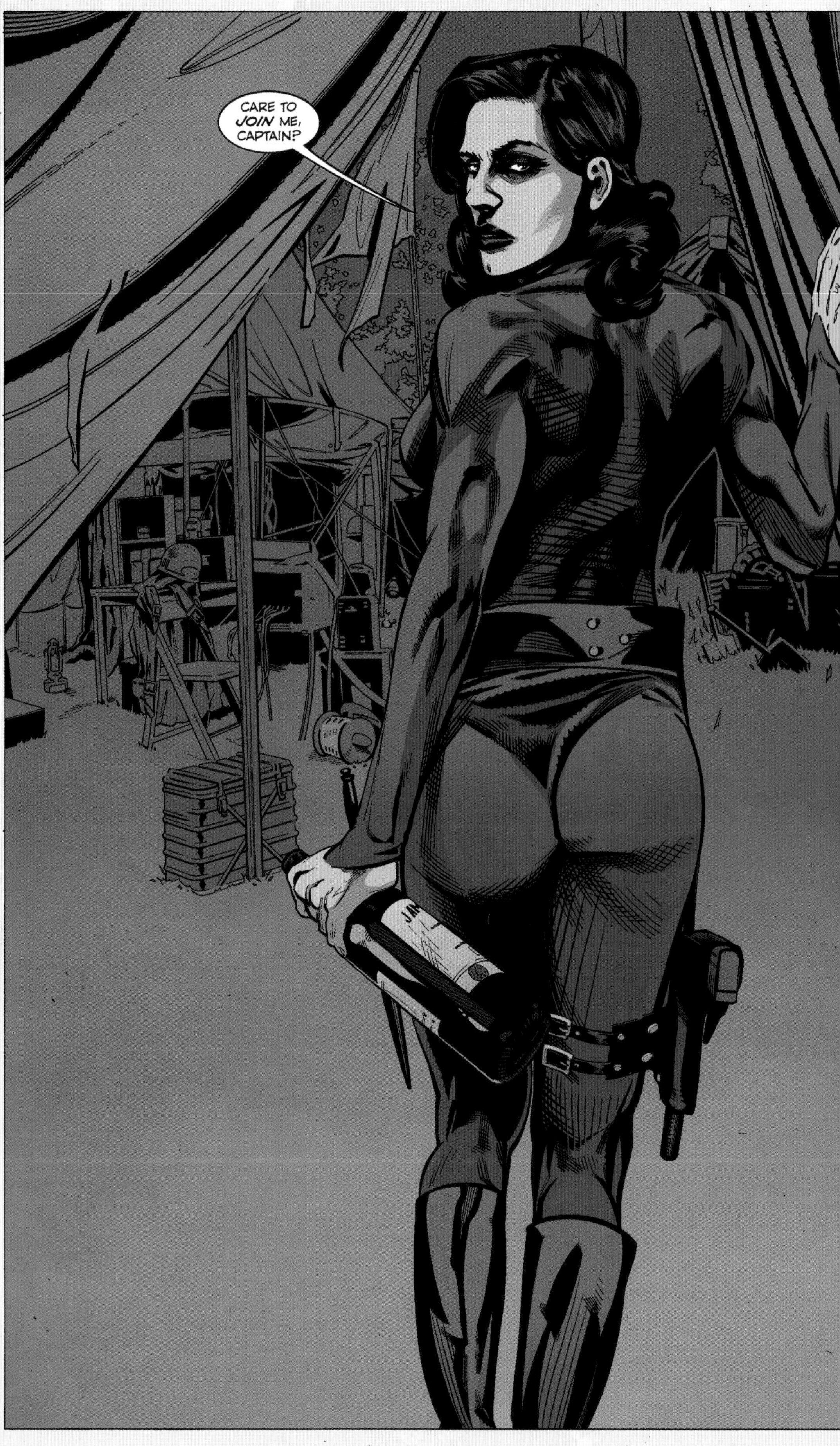
CARE TO *JOIN* ME, CAPTAIN?

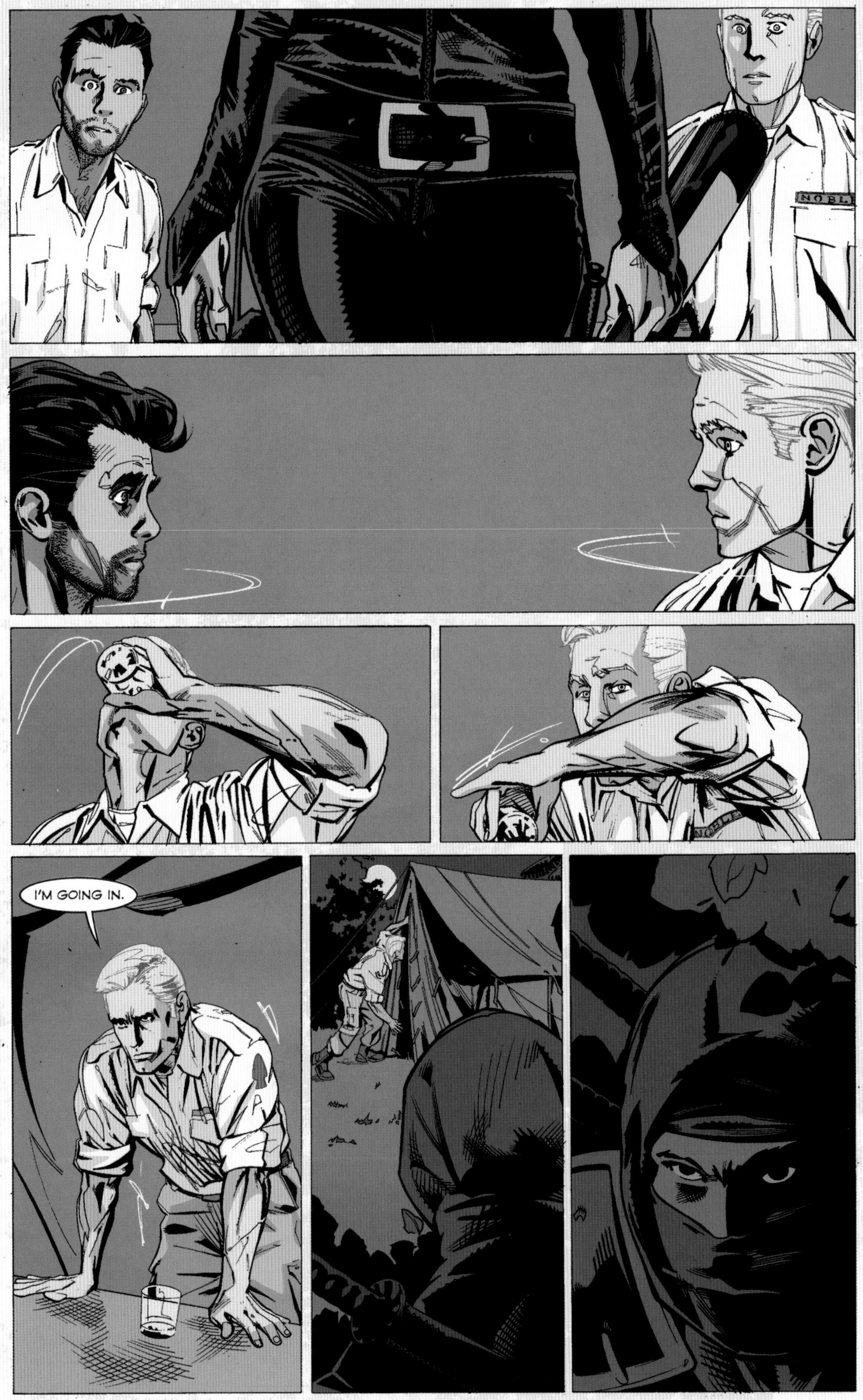
NOBLE
NOBLE
I'M GOING IN.

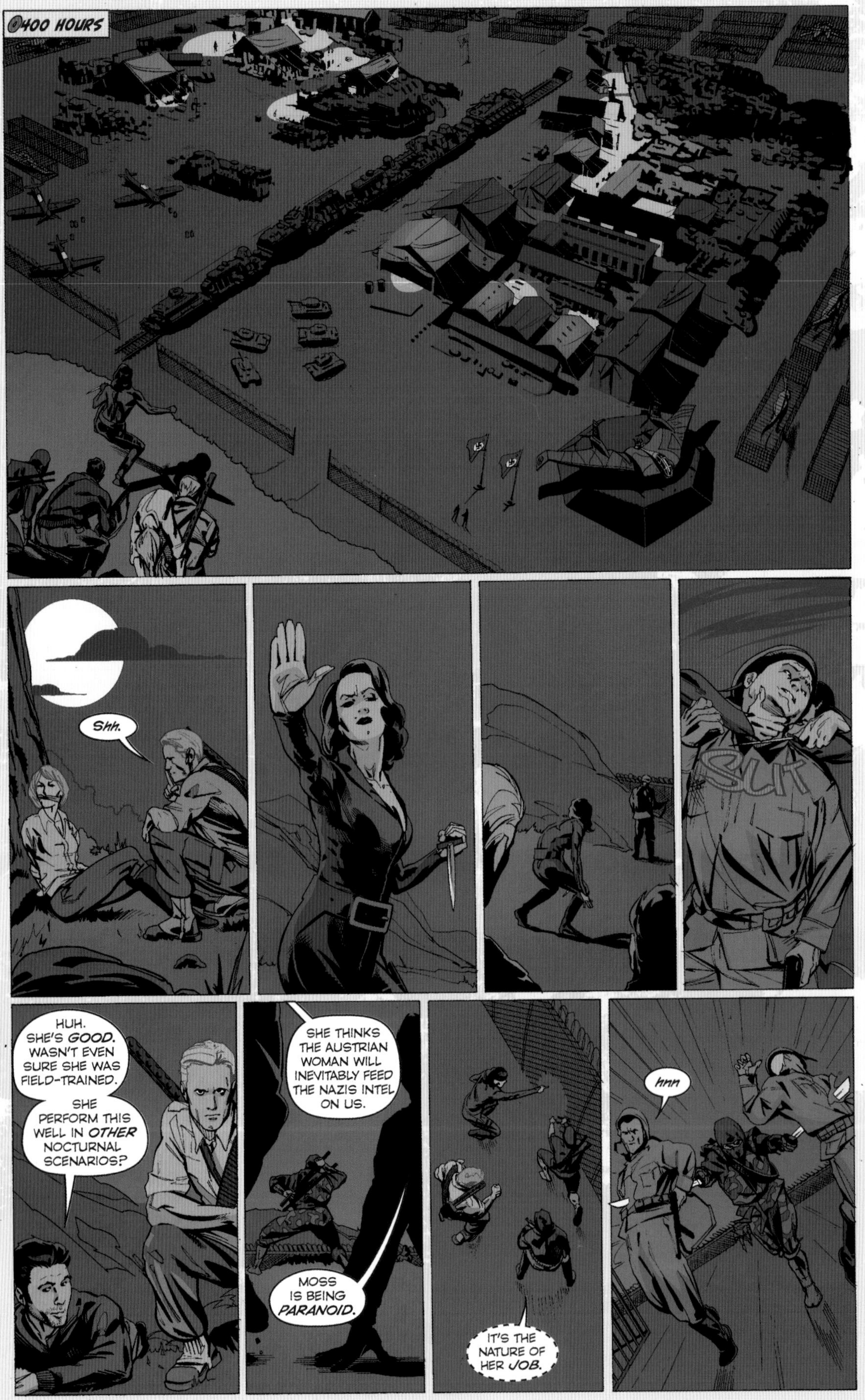
0400 HOURS
Shh.
SLIT
HUH. SHE'S GOOD. WASN'T EVEN SURE SHE WAS FIELD-TRAINED.
SHE PERFORM THIS WELL IN OTHER NOCTURNAL SCENARIOS?
SHE THINKS THE AUSTRIAN WOMAN WILL INEVITABLY FEED THE NAZIS INTEL ON US.
MOSS IS BEING PARANOID.
IT'S THE NATURE OF HER JOB.
hnn

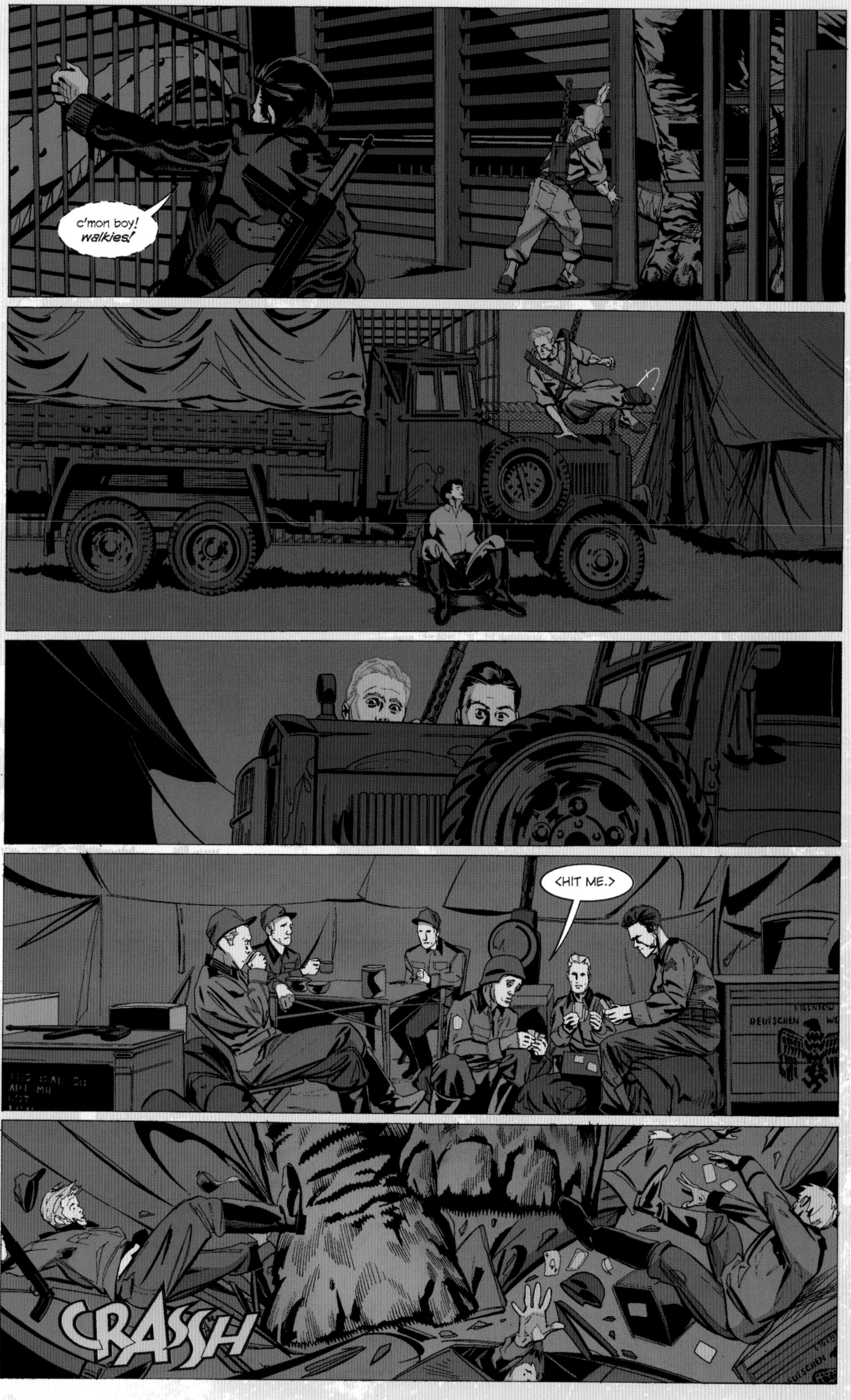
c'mon boy! walkies!
<HIT ME.>
DEUTSCHEN
CRASH

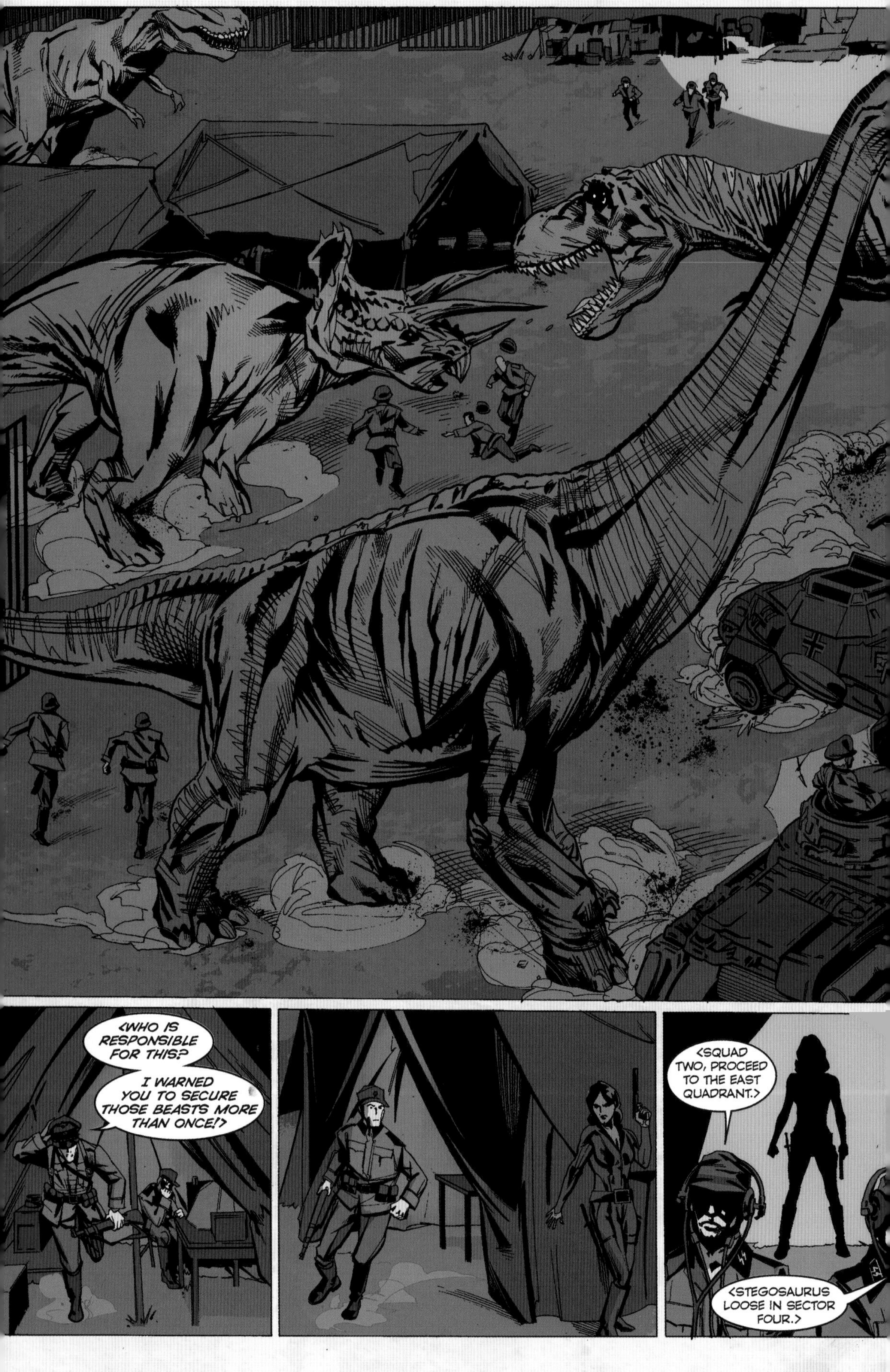
<WHO IS RESPONSIBLE FOR THIS?
I WARNED YOU TO SECURE THOSE BEASTS MORE THAN ONCE!>
<SQUAD TWO, PROCEED TO THE EAST QUADRANT.>
<STEGOSAURUS LOOSE IN SECTOR FOUR.>

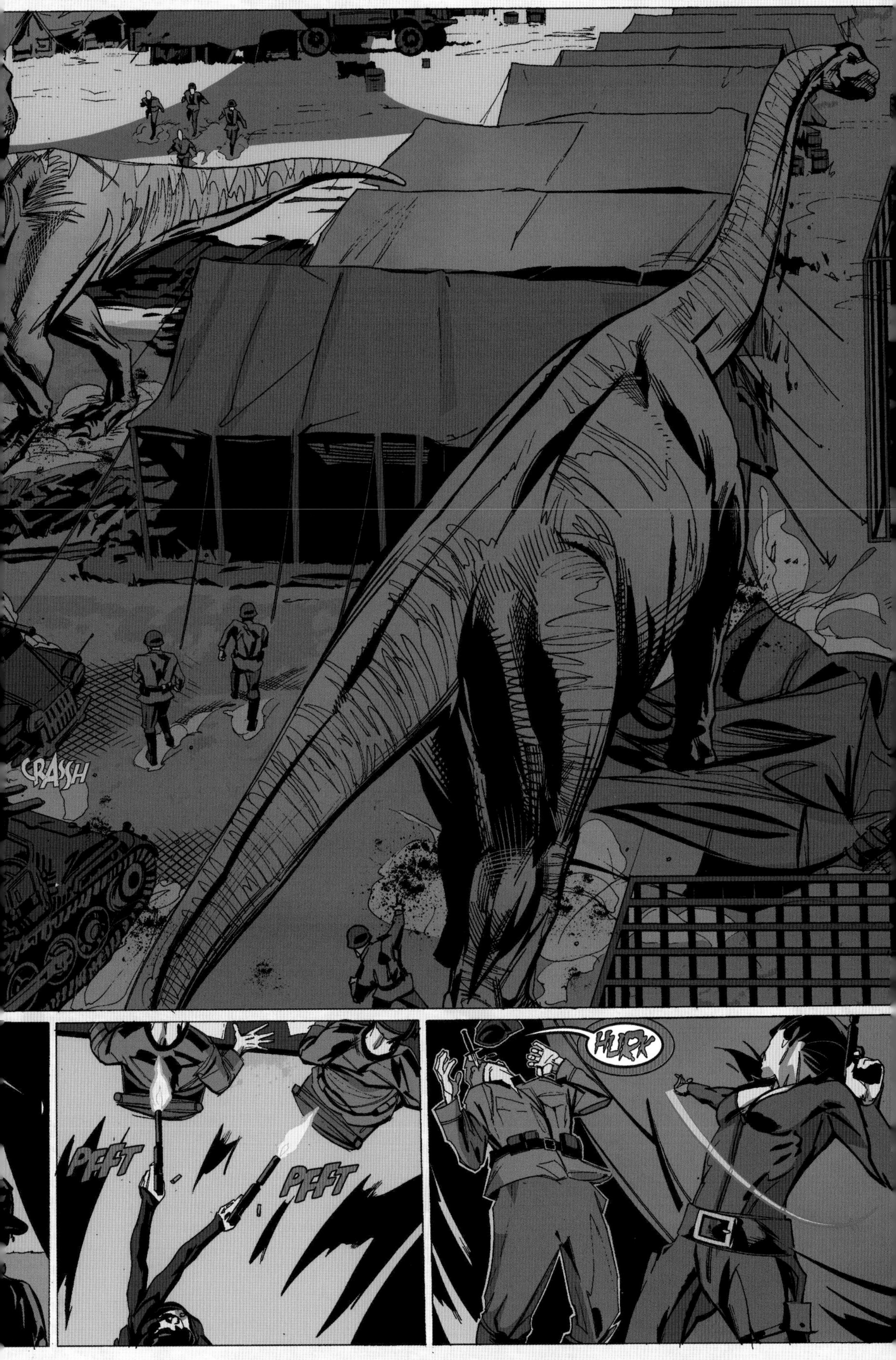
CRASSH
PFFT
PFFT
HURK

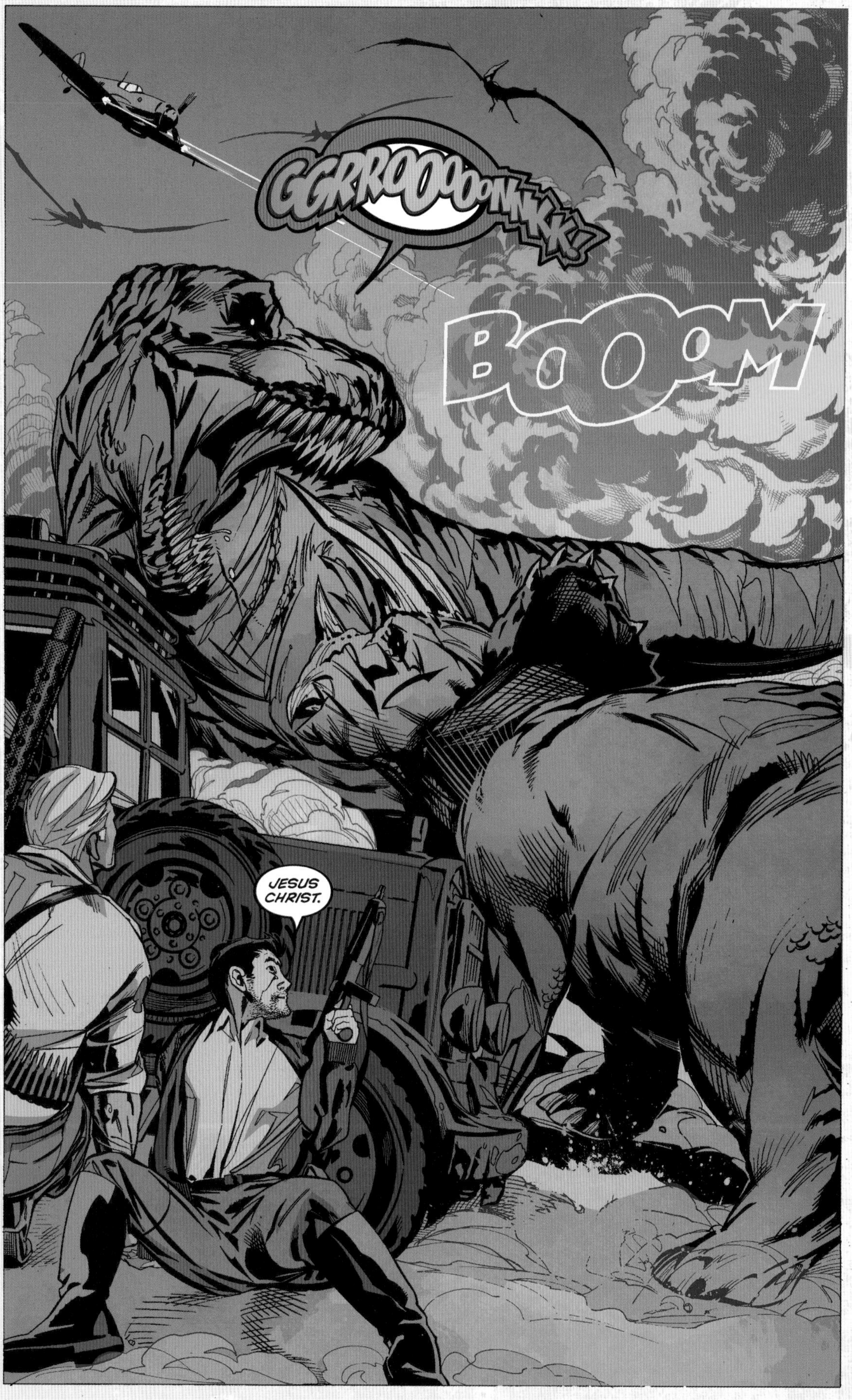
GGRROOOOOONNKKK!
BOOOM
JESUS CHRIST.

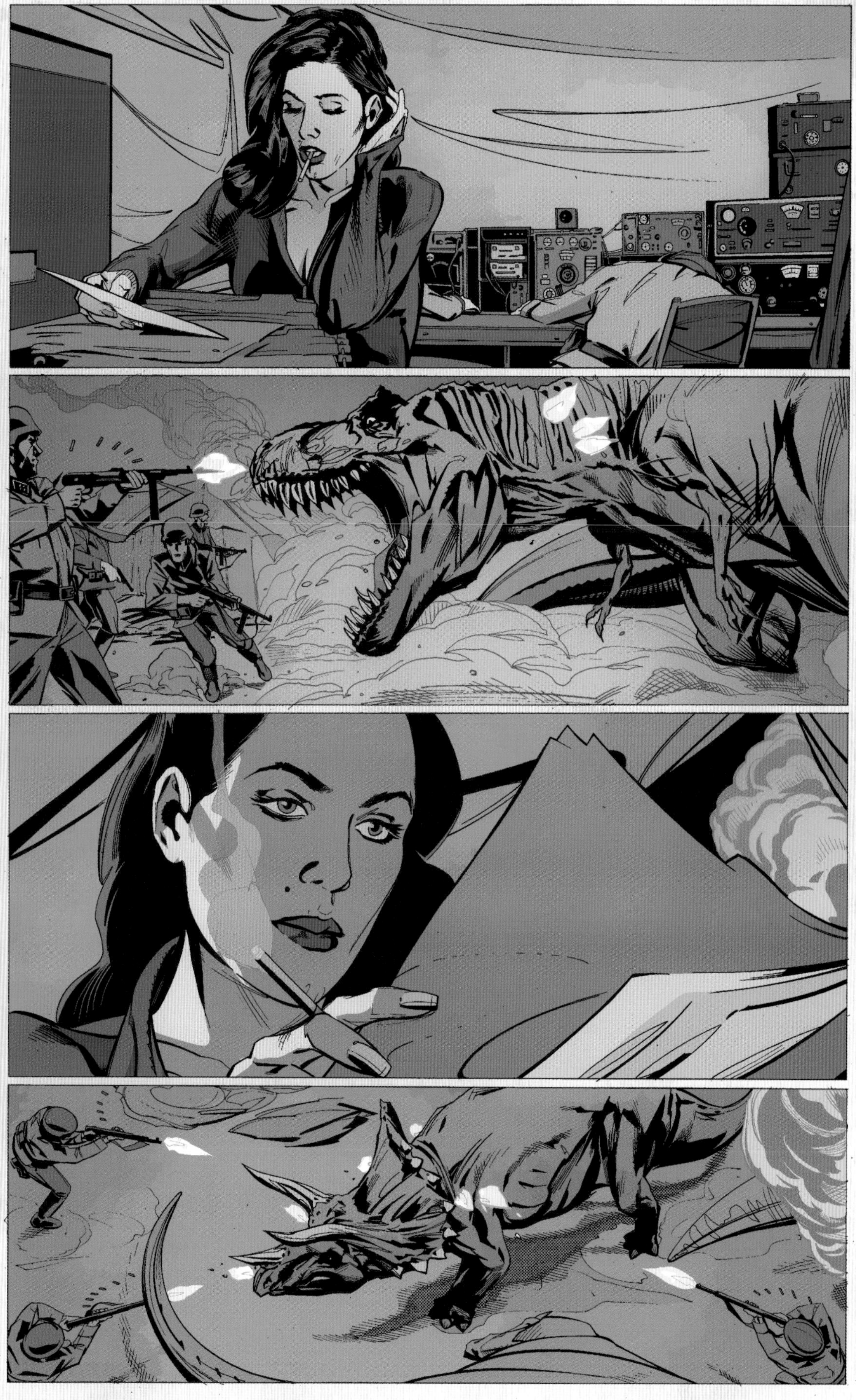

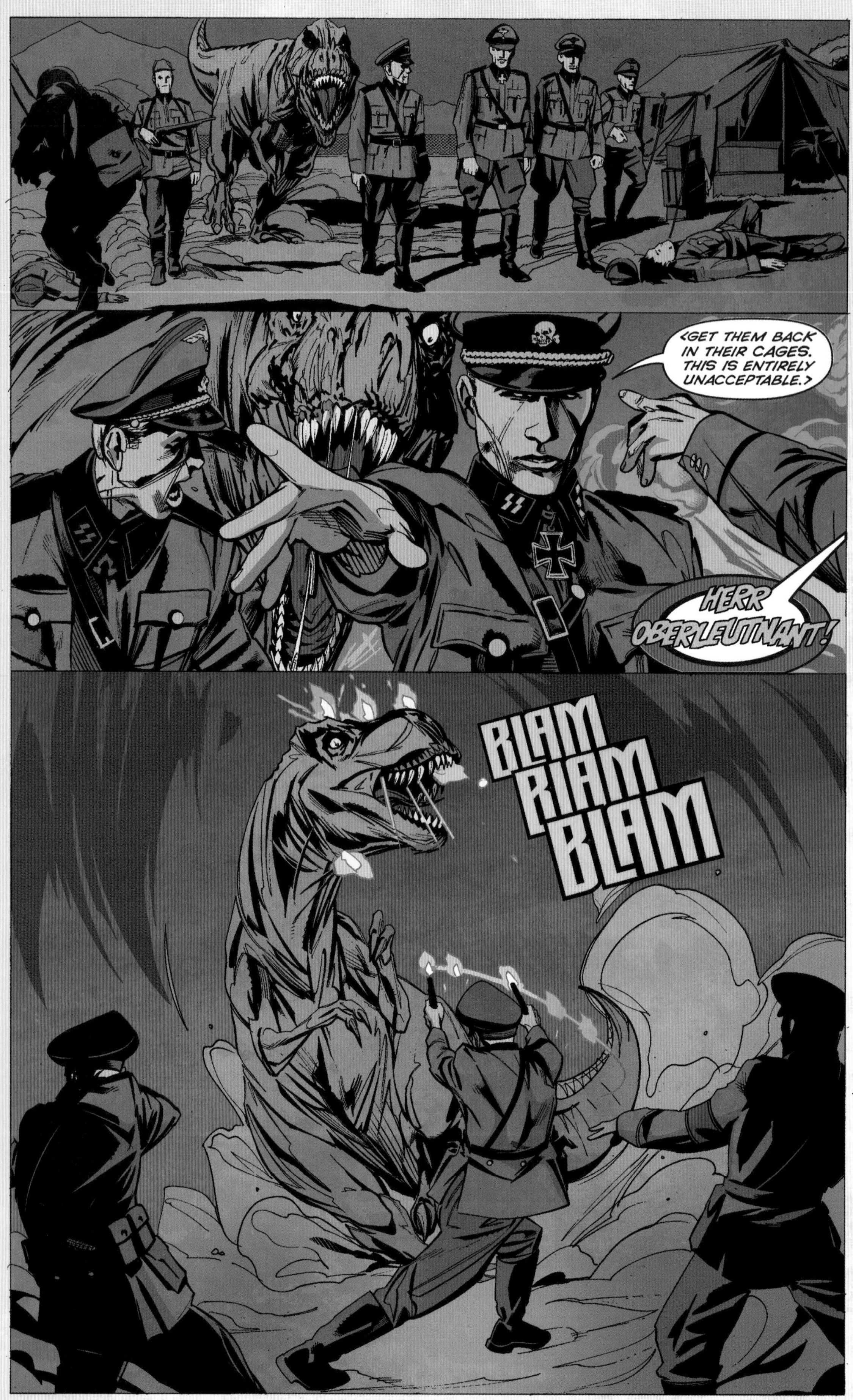
<GET THEM BACK IN THEIR CAGES. THIS IS ENTIRELY UNACCEPTABLE.>
HERR OBERLEUTNANT!
BLAM
BLAM
BLAM

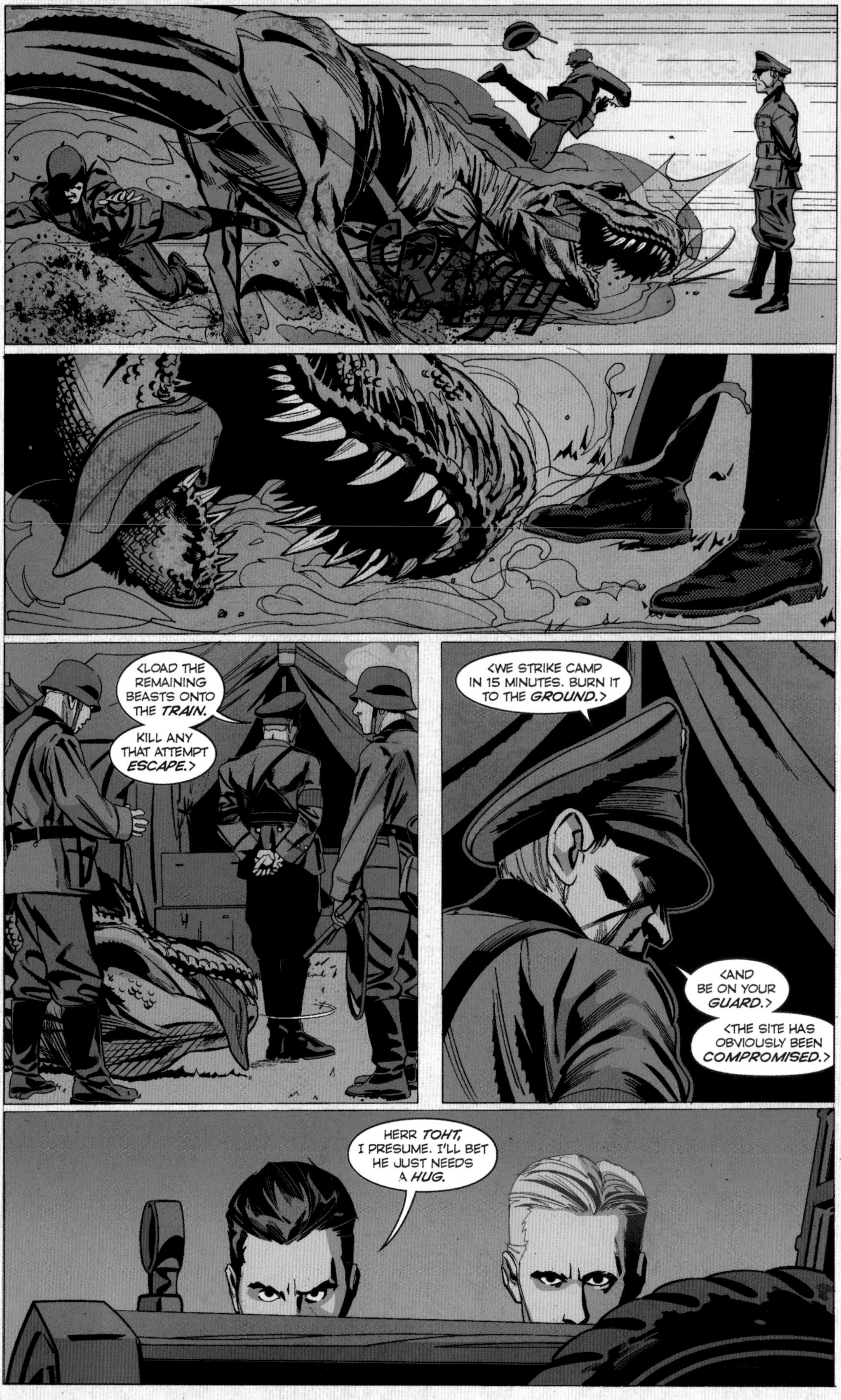
<LOAD THE REMAINING BEASTS ONTO THE *TRAIN*.
KILL ANY THAT ATTEMPT *ESCAPE*.>
<WE STRIKE CAMP IN 15 MINUTES. BURN IT TO THE *GROUND*.>
<AND BE ON YOUR *GUARD*.>
<THE SITE HAS OBVIOUSLY BEEN *COMPROMISED*.>
HERR *TOHT*, I PRESUME. I'LL BET HE JUST NEEDS A *HUG*.

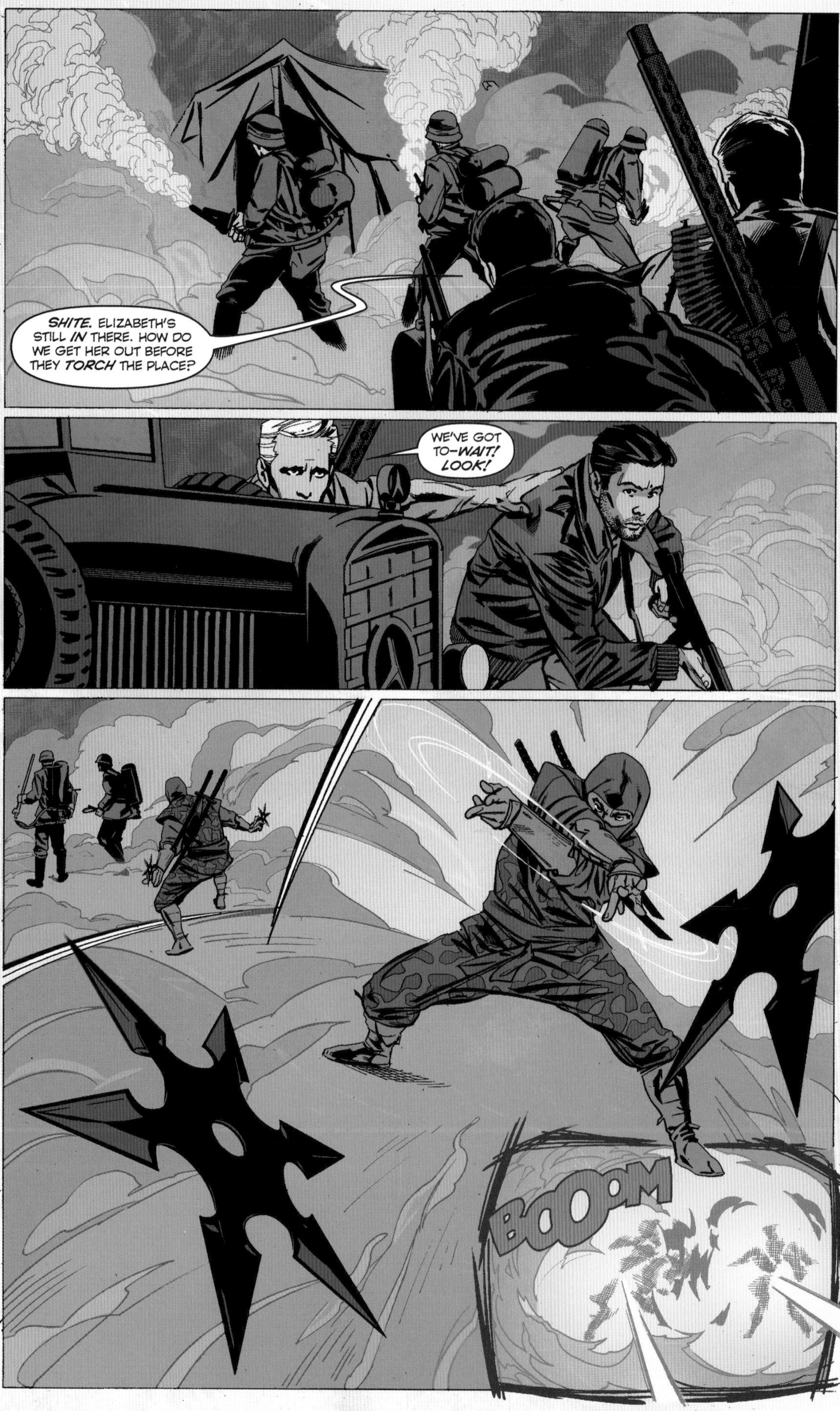
SHITE. ELIZABETH'S STILL IN THERE. HOW DO WE GET HER OUT BEFORE THEY TORCH THE PLACE?
WE'VE GOT TO—WAIT! LOOK!
BOOOM

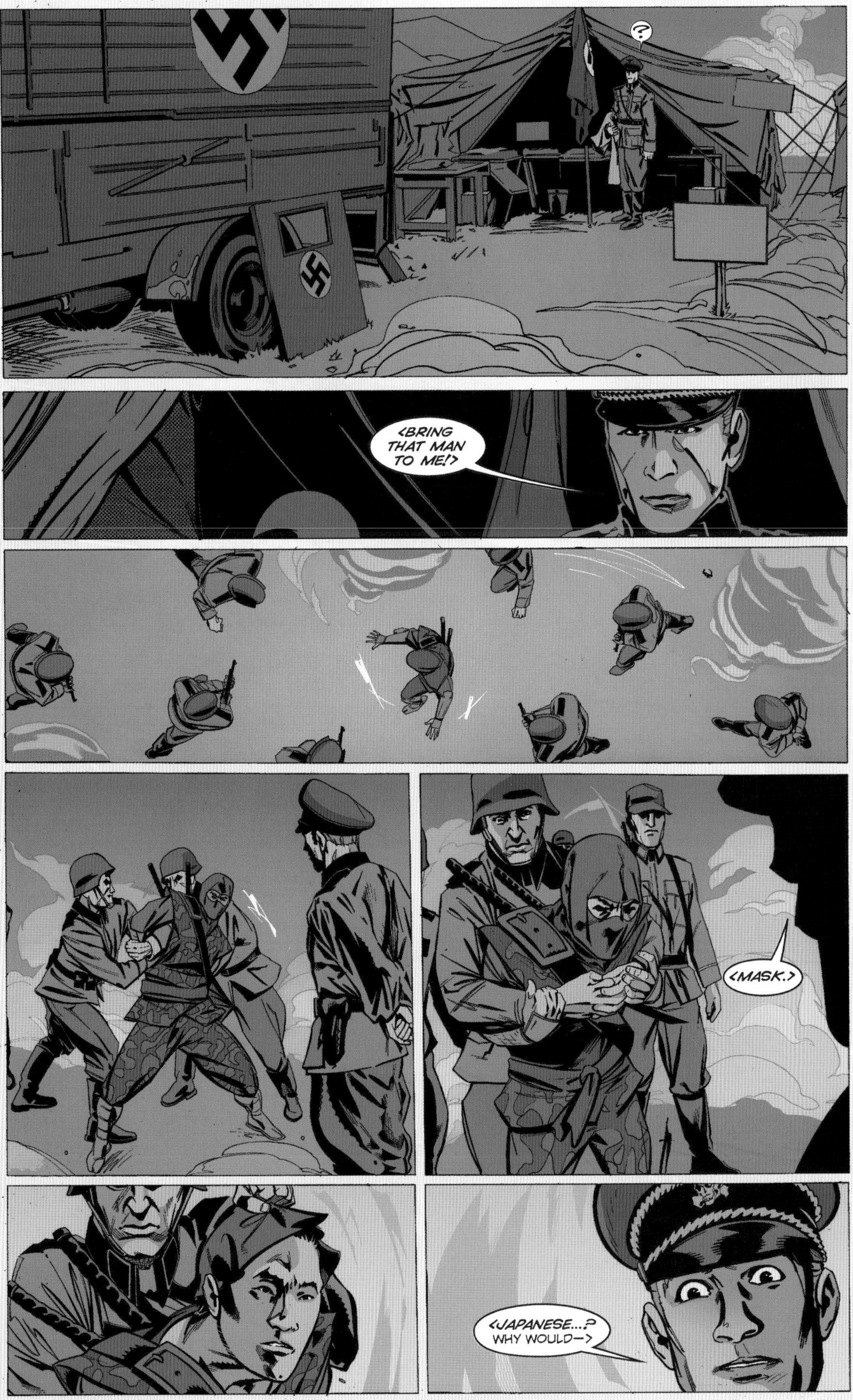
?
<BRING THAT MAN TO ME!>
<MASK.>
<JAPANESE...? WHY WOULD—>

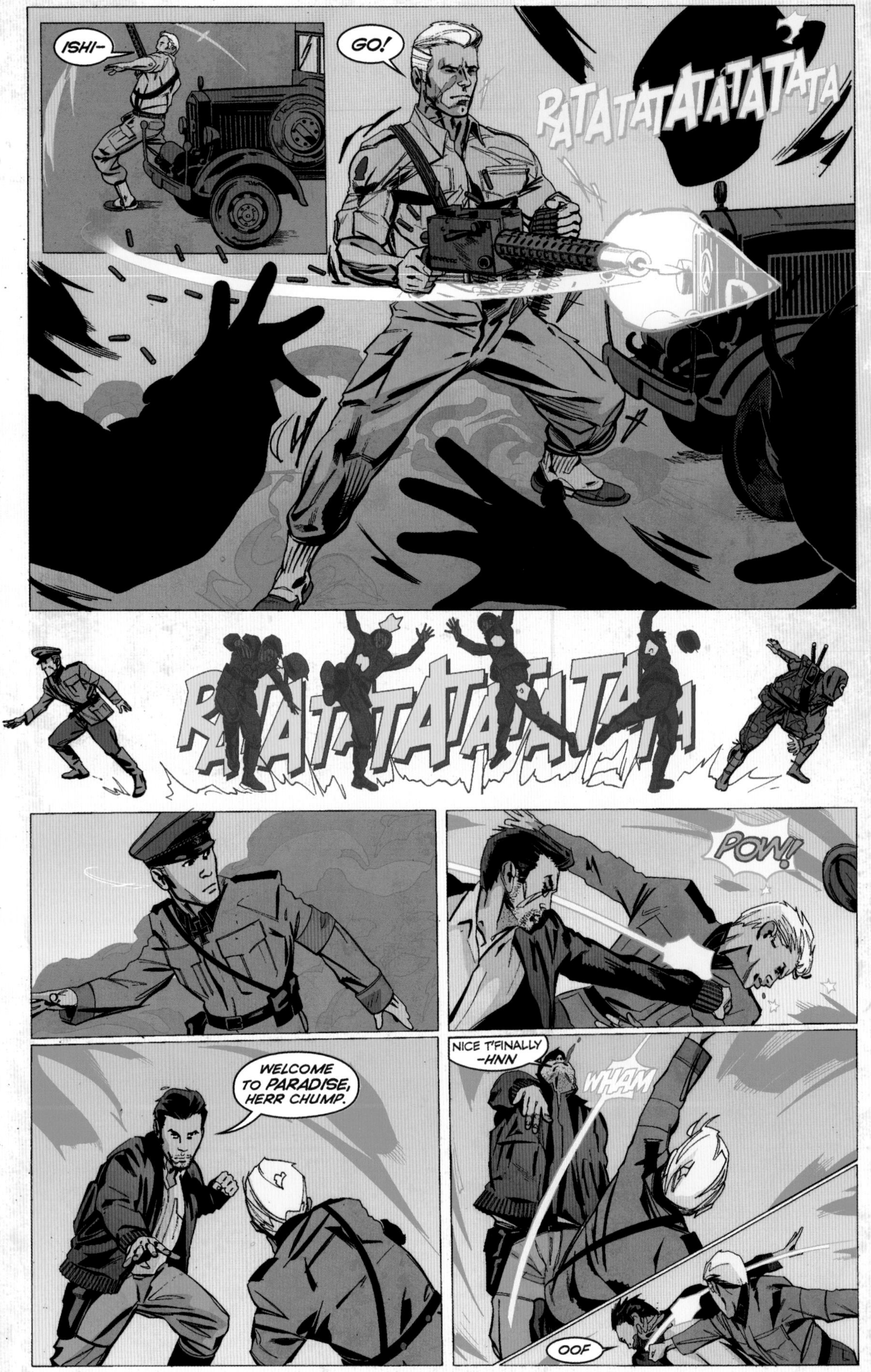
ISHI-
GO!
RATATATATATATATATA
RATATATATATATATA
POW!
WELCOME TO PARADISE, HERR CHUMP.
NICE T'FINALLY -HNN
WHAM
OOF

IRISHMAN. WHAT ARE—

KRAK

UNGH!

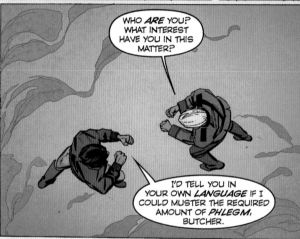

WHO *ARE* YOU? WHAT INTEREST HAVE YOU IN THIS MATTER?

I'D TELL YOU IN YOUR OWN *LANGUAGE* IF I COULD MUSTER THE REQUIRED AMOUNT OF *PHLEGM,* BUTCHER.

NOW—

—ORDER YOUR MEN TO HAND OVER THE *ANIMALS!*

AMUSING. I THINK *NOT.* IN ANY CASE, IT APPEARS YOU HAVE MORE *PRESSING* CONCERNS IN MY *COMMAND* TENT.

HOW *STUPID* DO YOU—

AIEeEEE!

?

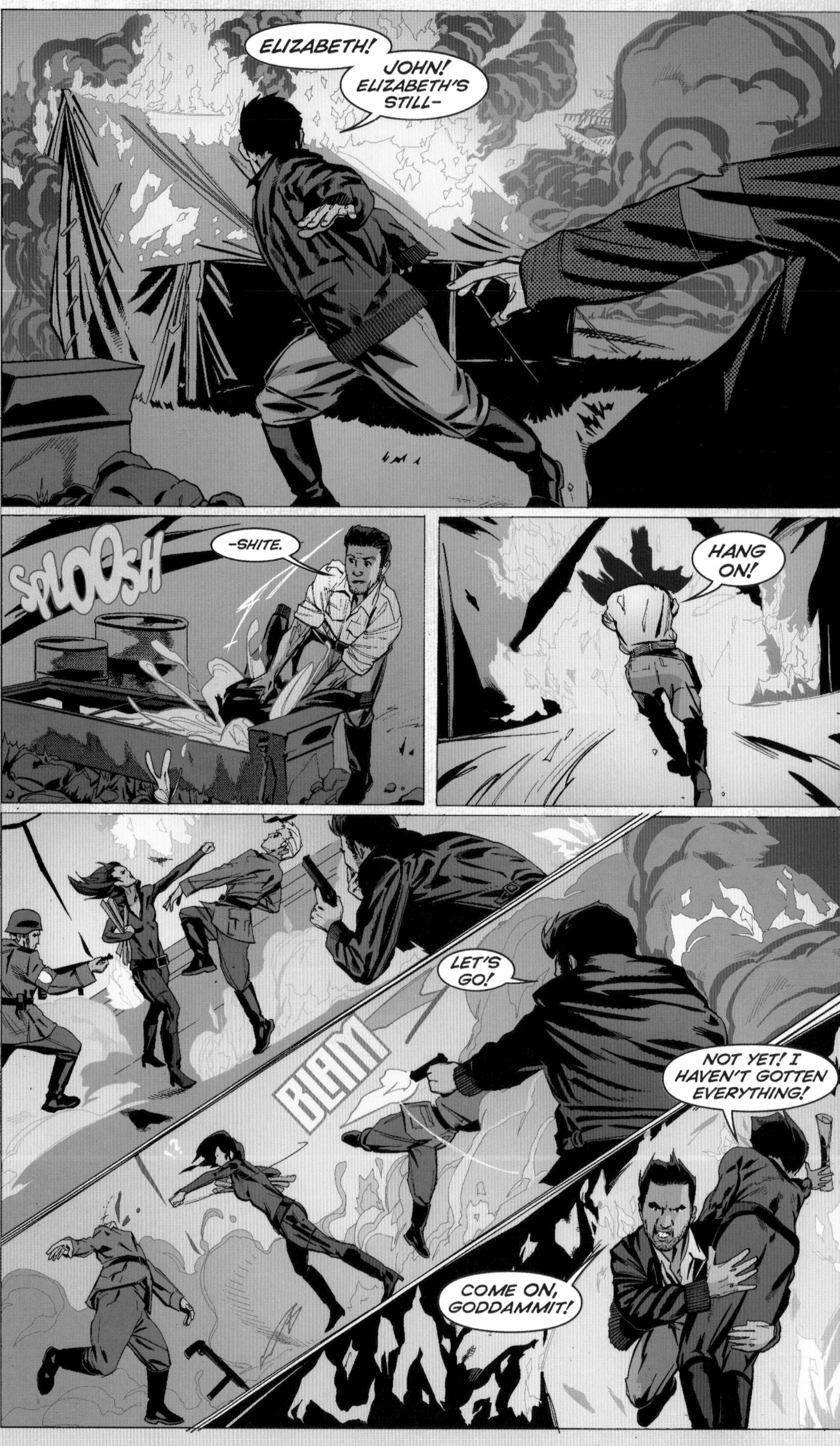
ELIZABETH!
JOHN! ELIZABETH'S STILL-
SPLOOSH
-SHITE.
HANG ON!
LET'S GO!
BLAM
NOT YET! I HAVEN'T GOTTEN EVERYTHING!
COME ON, GODDAMMIT!

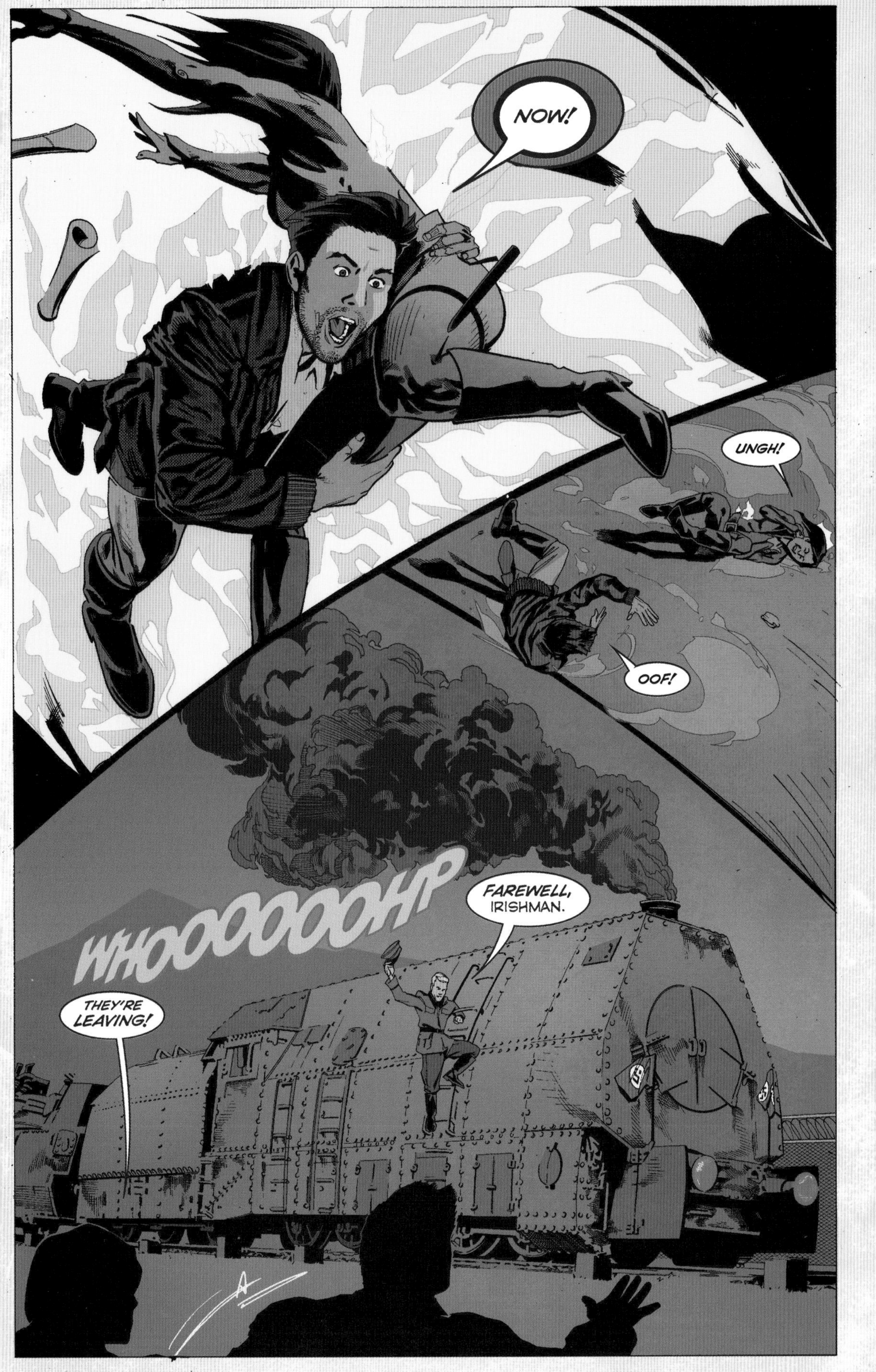
NOW!
UNGH!
OOF!
WHOOOOOOOHP
FAREWELL, IRISHMAN.
THEY'RE LEAVING!

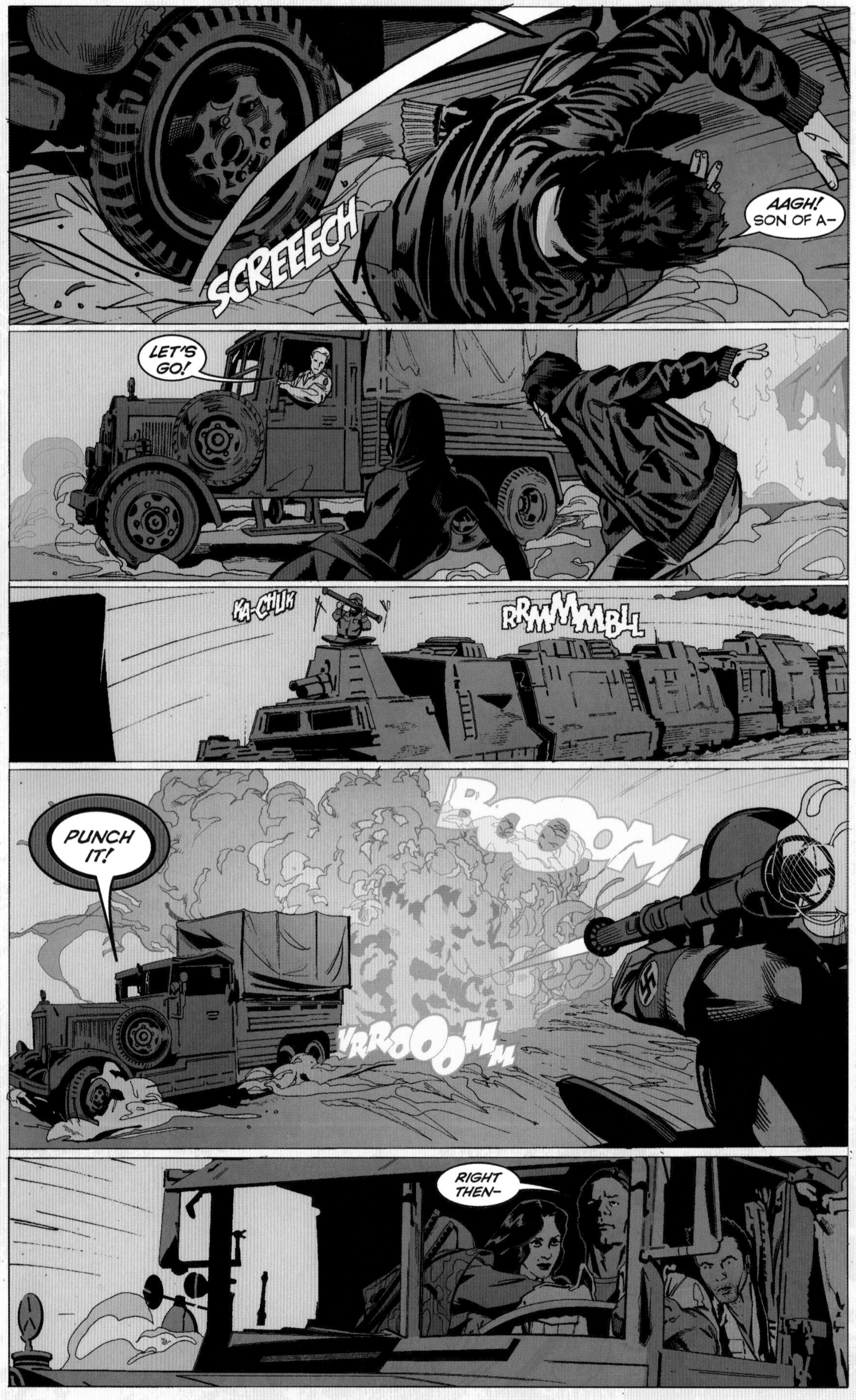
SCREEECH
AAGH! SON OF A–
LET'S GO!
KA-CHUK
RRMMMMBLL
PUNCH IT!
BOOOM
VRROOOMM
RIGHT THEN–

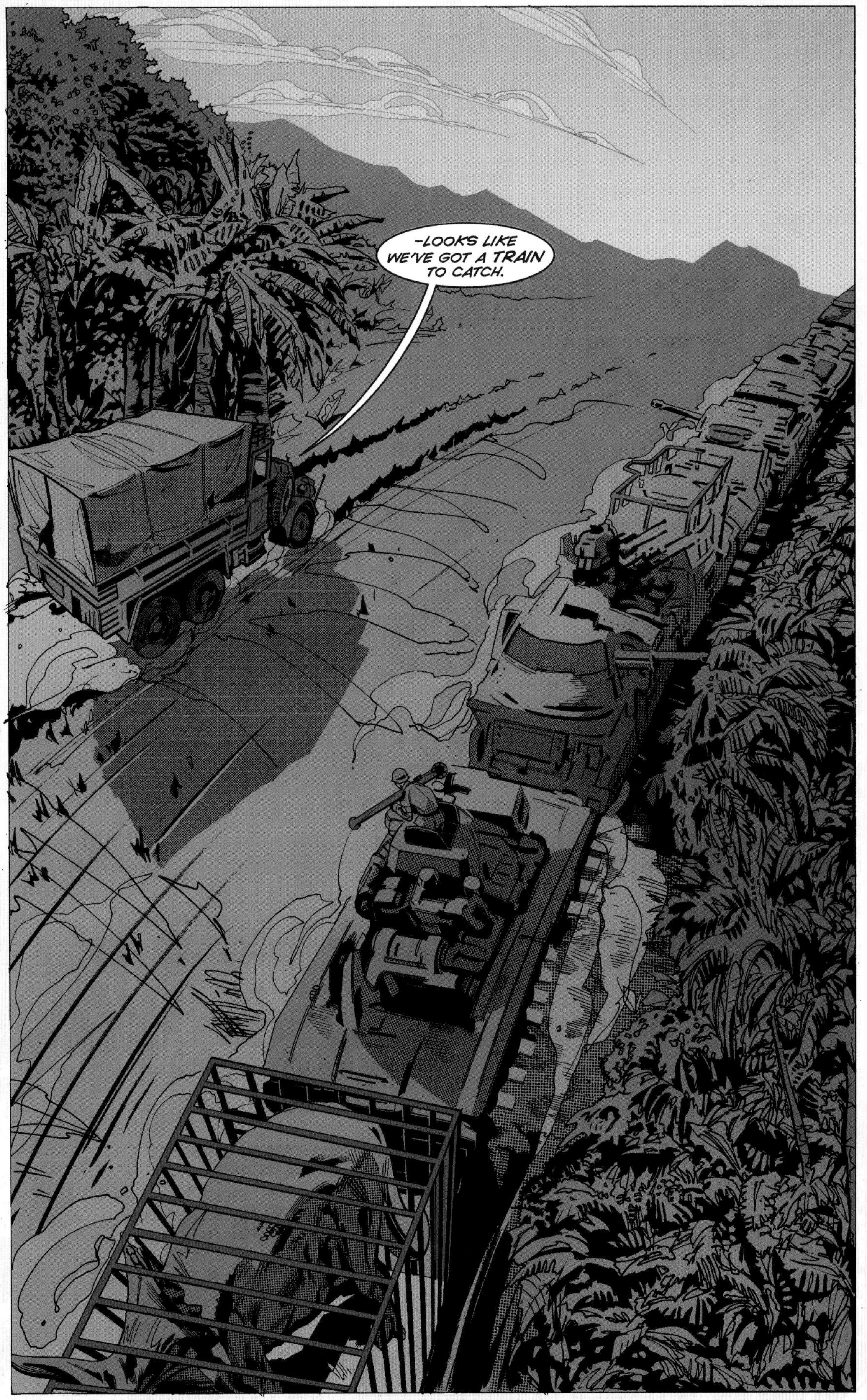
-LOOKS LIKE WE'VE GOT A TRAIN TO CATCH.

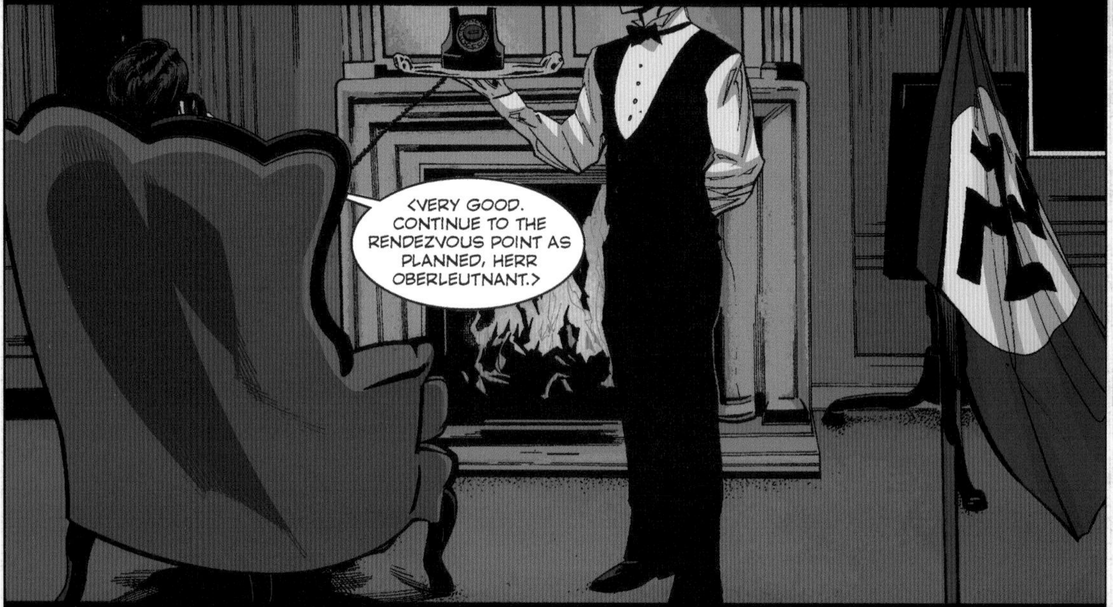
<VERY GOOD. CONTINUE TO THE RENDEZVOUS POINT AS PLANNED, HERR OBERLEUTNANT.>

Chapter Four

CURIOUSER AND CURIOUSER!

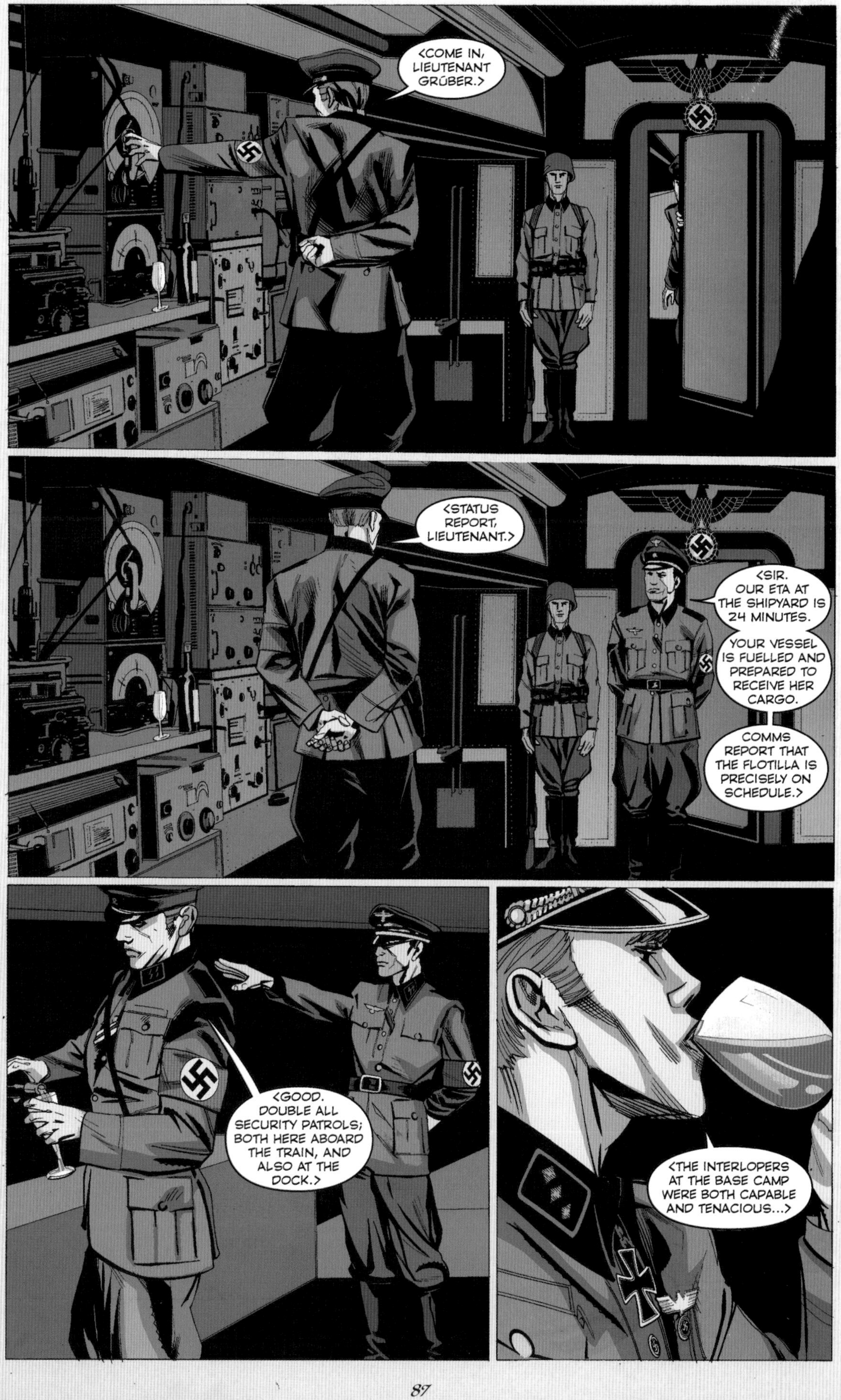
<COME IN, LIEUTENANT GRÜBER.>
<STATUS REPORT, LIEUTENANT.>
<SIR. OUR ETA AT THE SHIPYARD IS 24 MINUTES.
YOUR VESSEL IS FUELLED AND PREPARED TO RECEIVE HER CARGO.
COMMS REPORT THAT THE FLOTILLA IS PRECISELY ON SCHEDULE.>
<GOOD. DOUBLE ALL SECURITY PATROLS; BOTH HERE ABOARD THE TRAIN, AND ALSO AT THE DOCK.>
<THE INTERLOPERS AT THE BASE CAMP WERE BOTH CAPABLE AND TENACIOUS...>

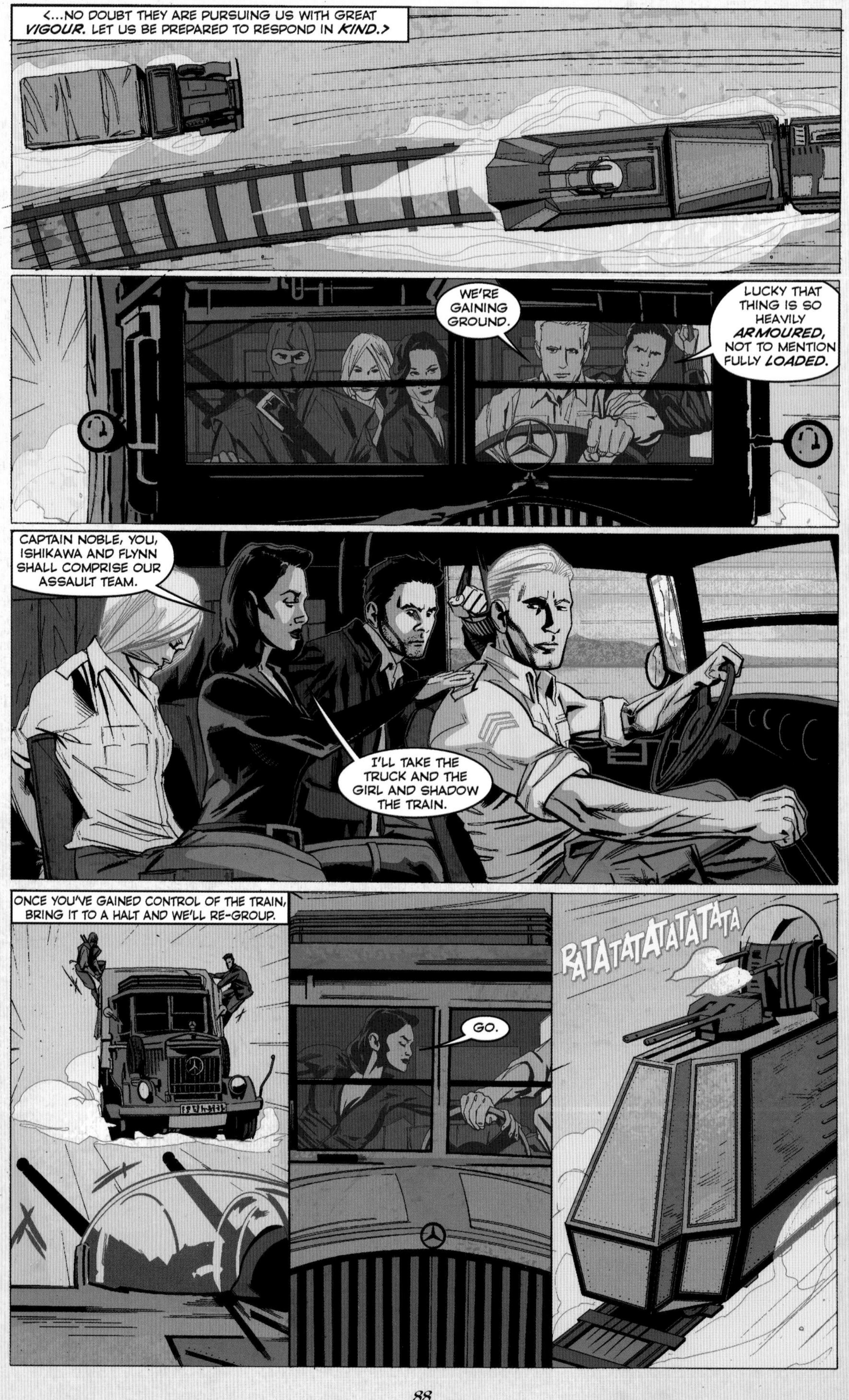

<...NO DOUBT THEY ARE PURSUING US WITH GREAT VIGOUR. LET US BE PREPARED TO RESPOND IN KIND.>
WE'RE GAINING GROUND.
LUCKY THAT THING IS SO HEAVILY ARMOURED, NOT TO MENTION FULLY LOADED.
CAPTAIN NOBLE, YOU, ISHIKAWA AND FLYNN SHALL COMPRISE OUR ASSAULT TEAM.
I'LL TAKE THE TRUCK AND THE GIRL AND SHADOW THE TRAIN.
ONCE YOU'VE GAINED CONTROL OF THE TRAIN, BRING IT TO A HALT AND WE'LL RE-GROUP.
GO.
RATATATATATATATA

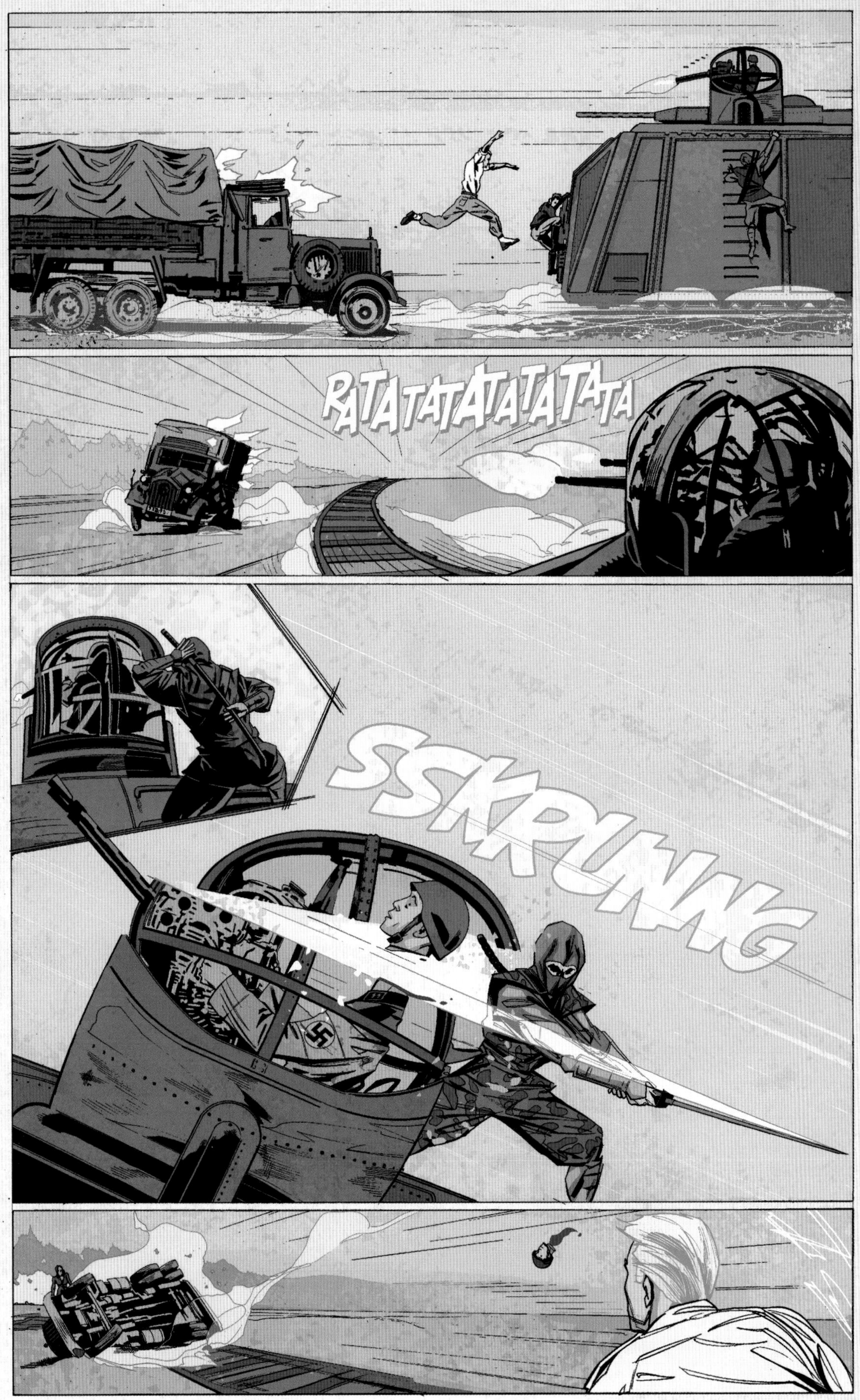
RATATATATATATATA
SSKRUNNG

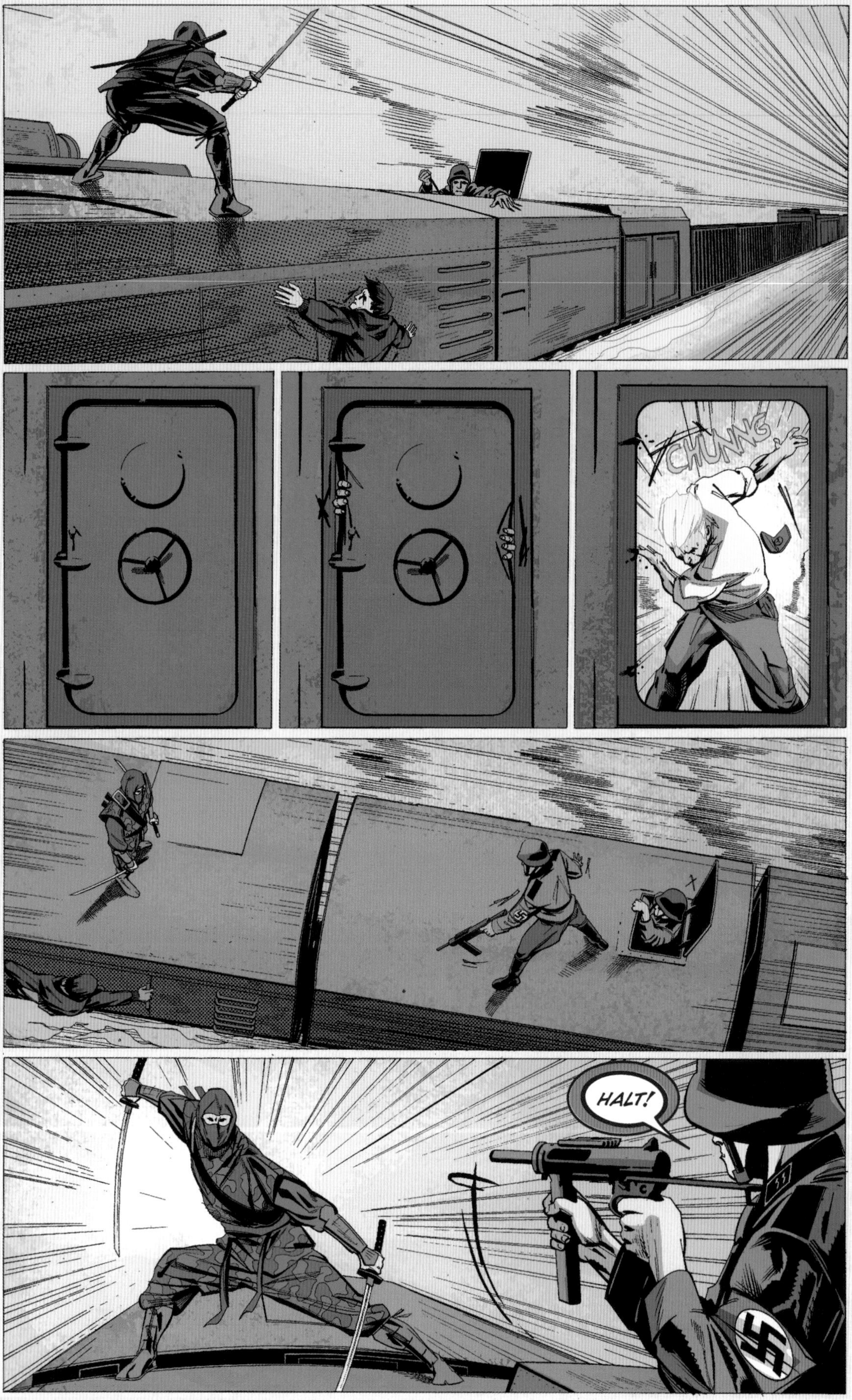
CHUNNG
HALT!

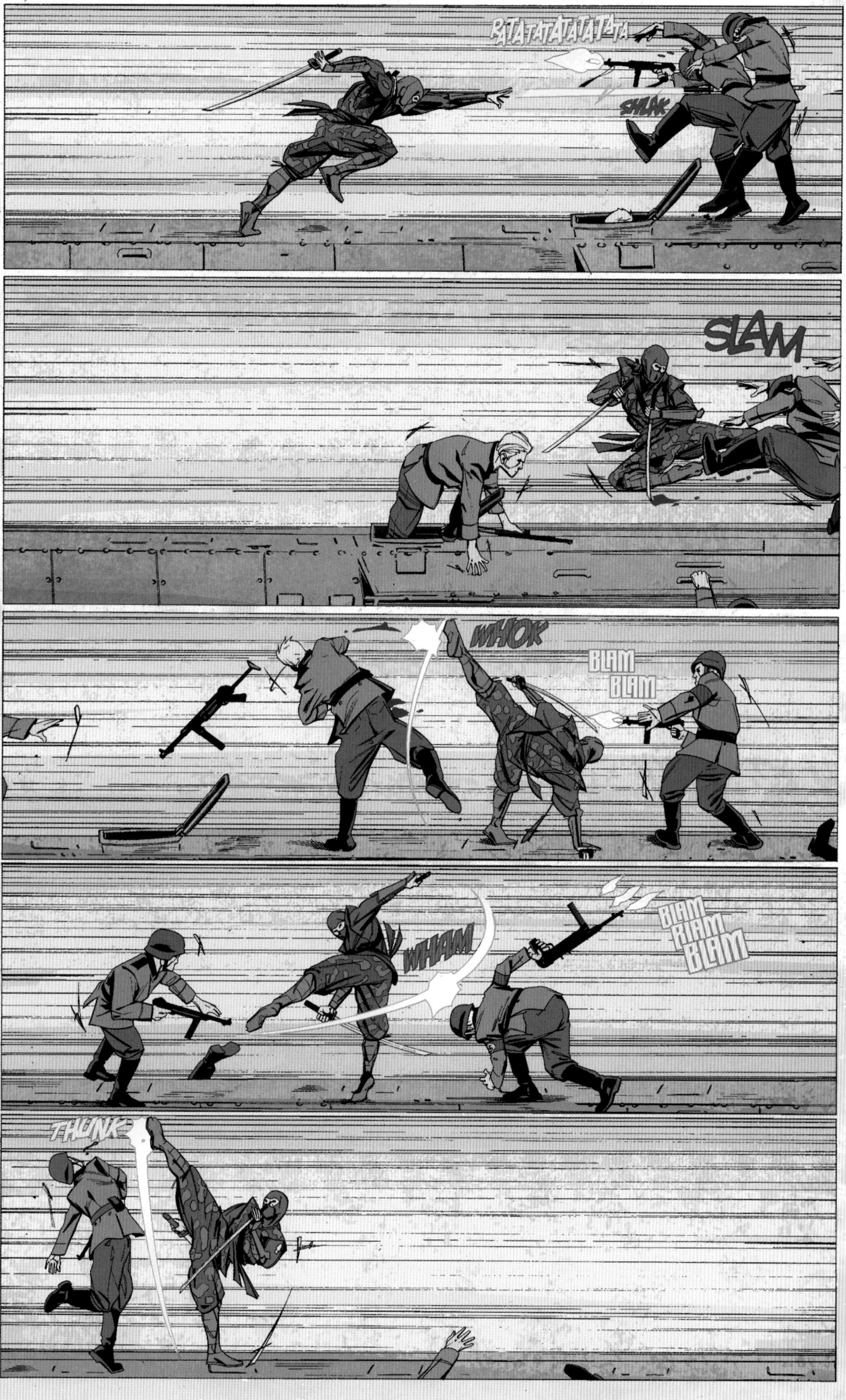
RATATATATATATATA
SHLAK
SLAM
WHOK
BLAM
BLAM
BLAM
BLAM
BLAM
WHAM
THUNK

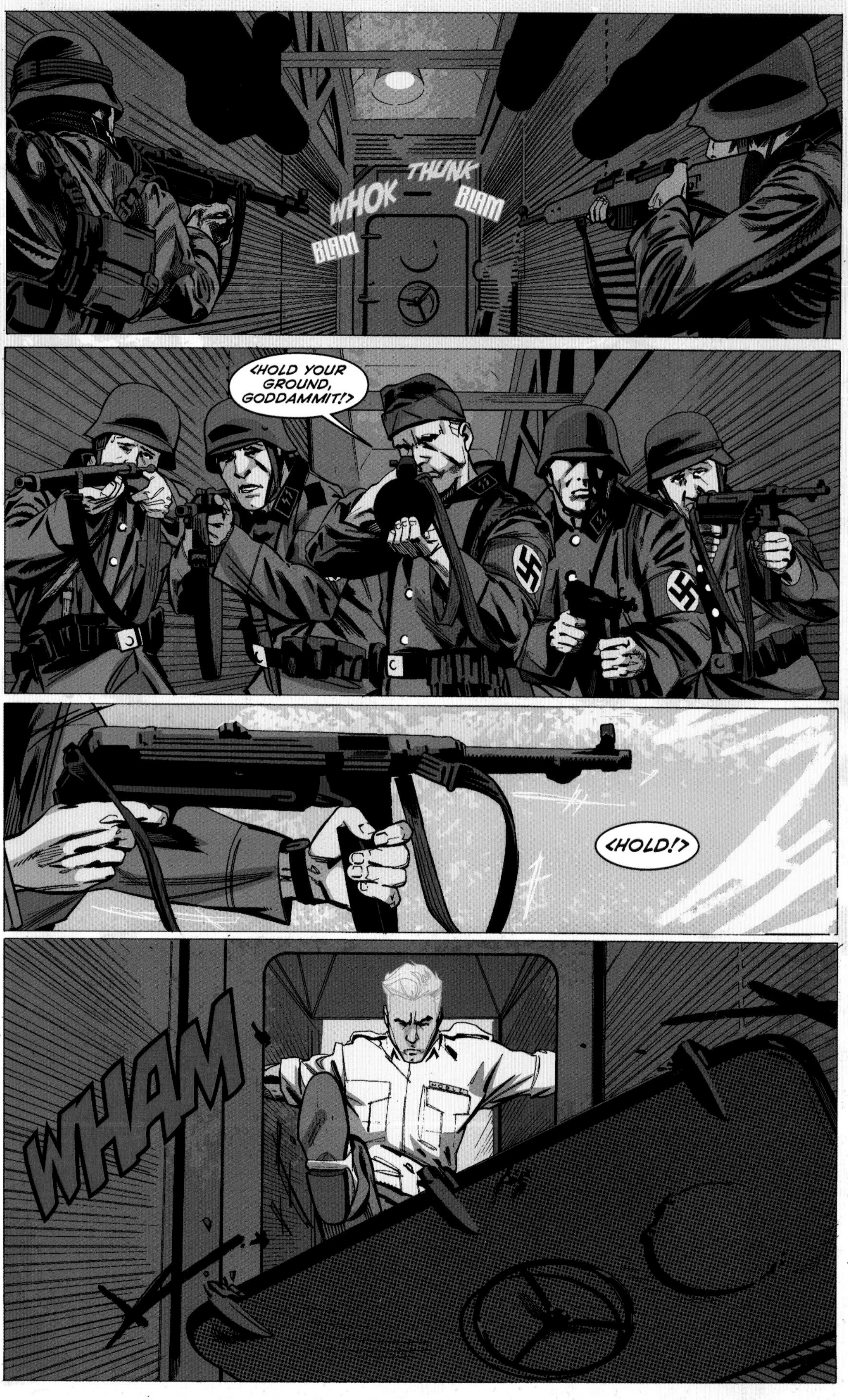
WHOK
THUNK
BLAM
BLAM
<HOLD YOUR GROUND, GODDAMMIT!>
<HOLD!>
WHAM

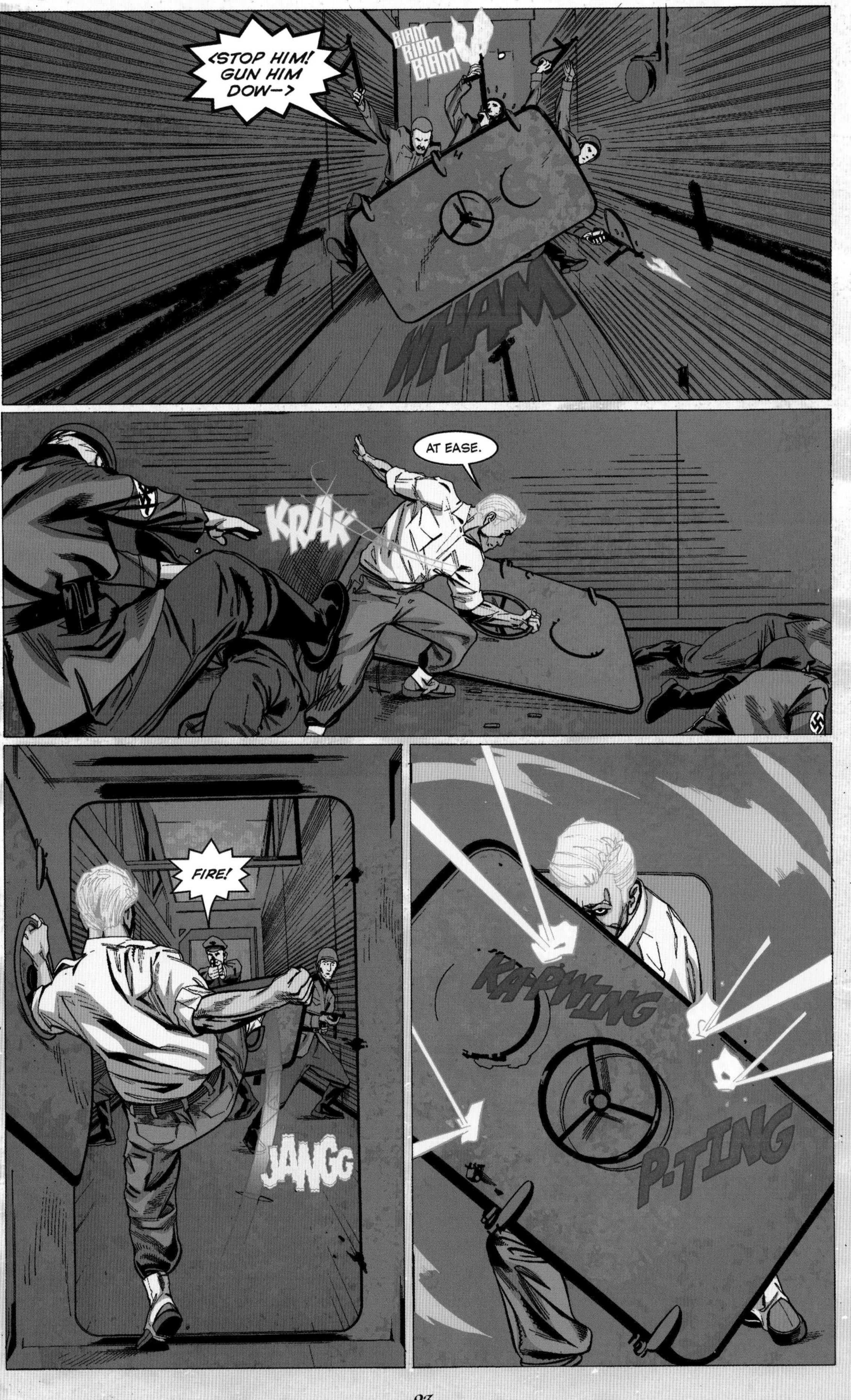
<STOP HIM! GUN HIM DOW—>
BLAM BLAM BLAM
WHAM
AT EASE.
KRAK
FIRE!
JANGG
KA-PWING
P-TING

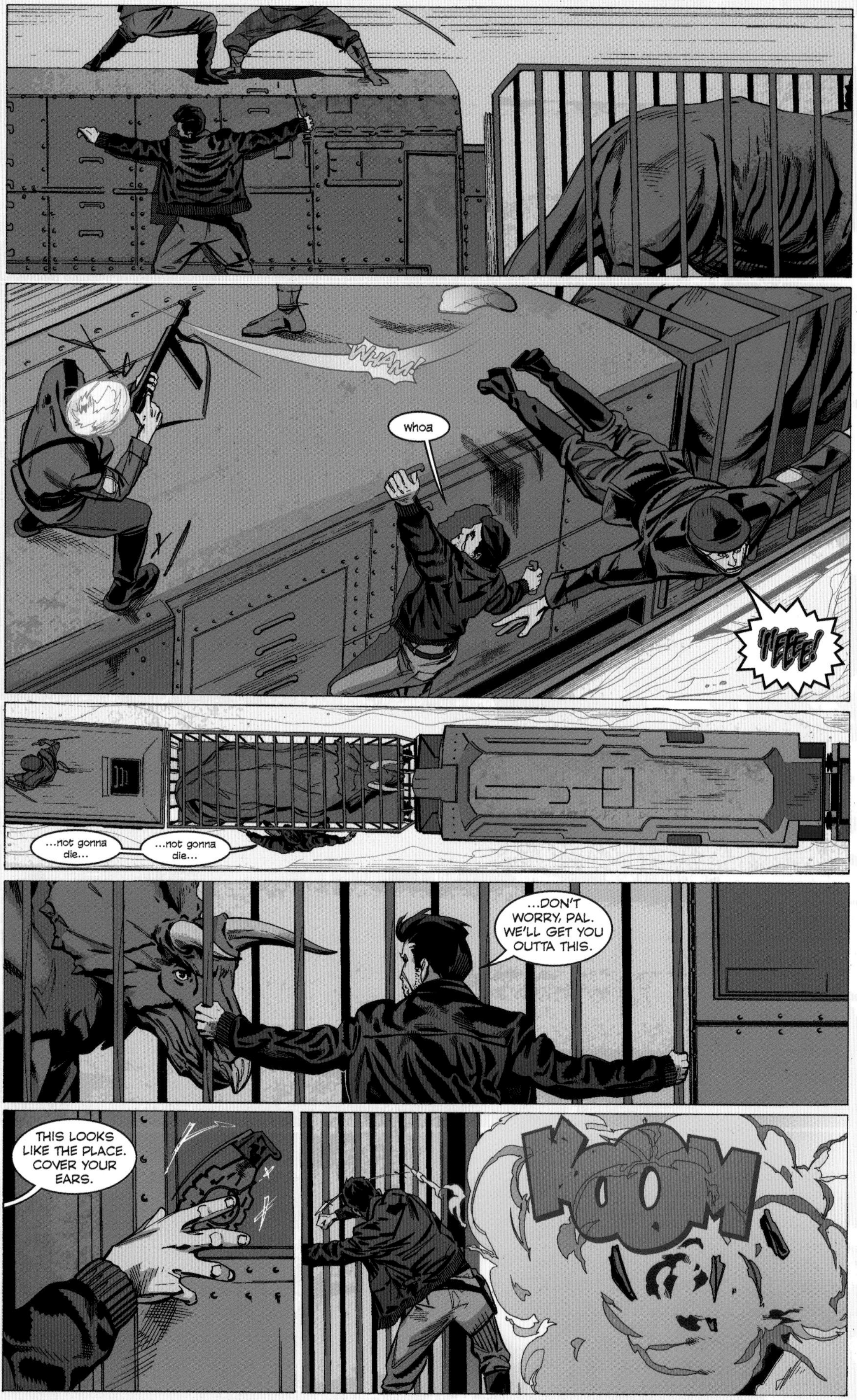
WHAM!
whoa
YEEEE!
...not gonna die...
...not gonna die...
...DON'T WORRY, PAL. WE'LL GET YOU OUTTA THIS.
THIS LOOKS LIKE THE PLACE. COVER YOUR EARS.
BOOM

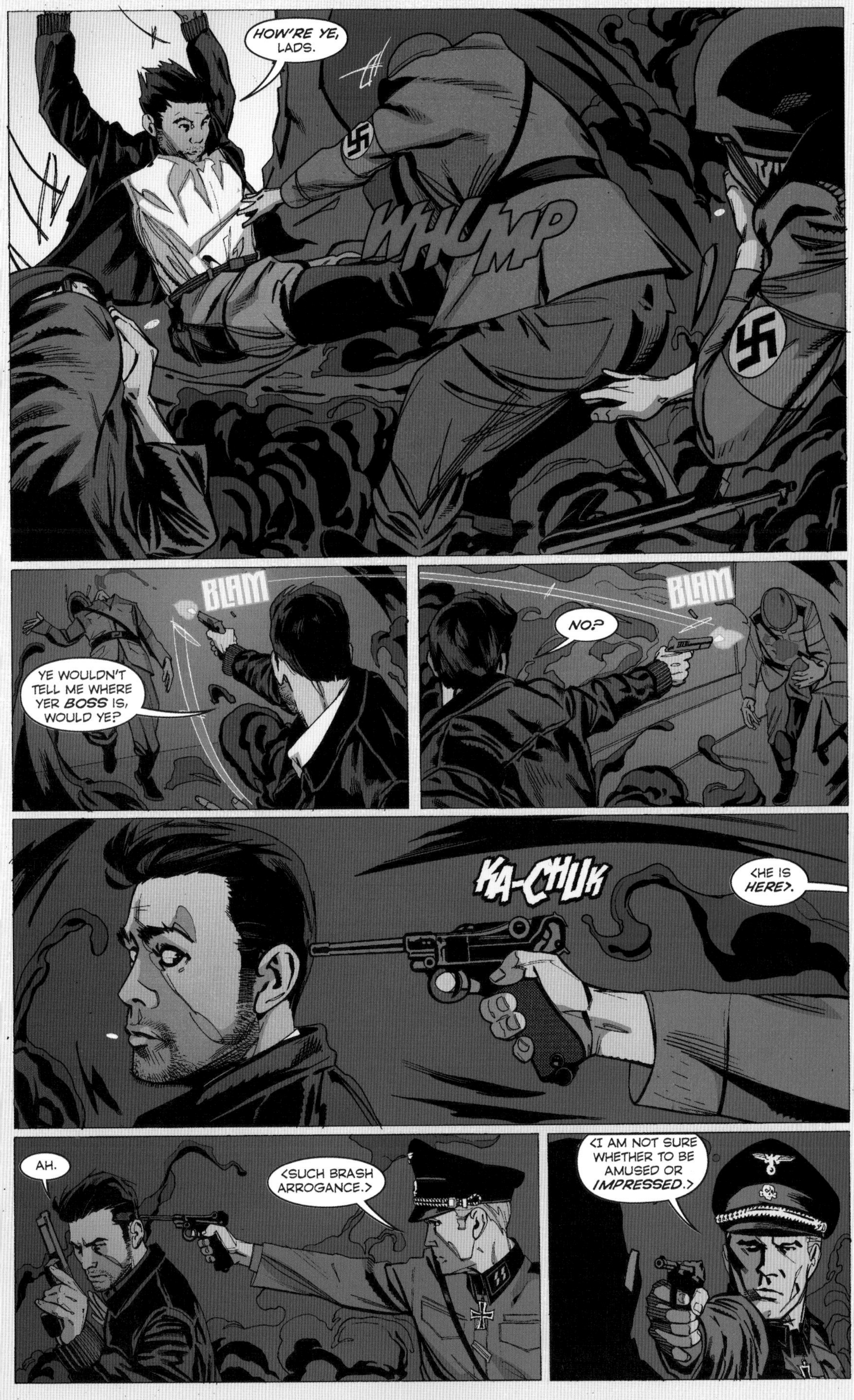
HOW'RE YE, LADS.
WHUMP
BLAM
YE WOULDN'T TELL ME WHERE YER BOSS IS, WOULD YE?
BLAM
NO?
KA-CHUK
<HE IS HERE>.
AH.
<SUCH BRASH ARROGANCE.>
<I AM NOT SURE WHETHER TO BE AMUSED OR IMPRESSED.>

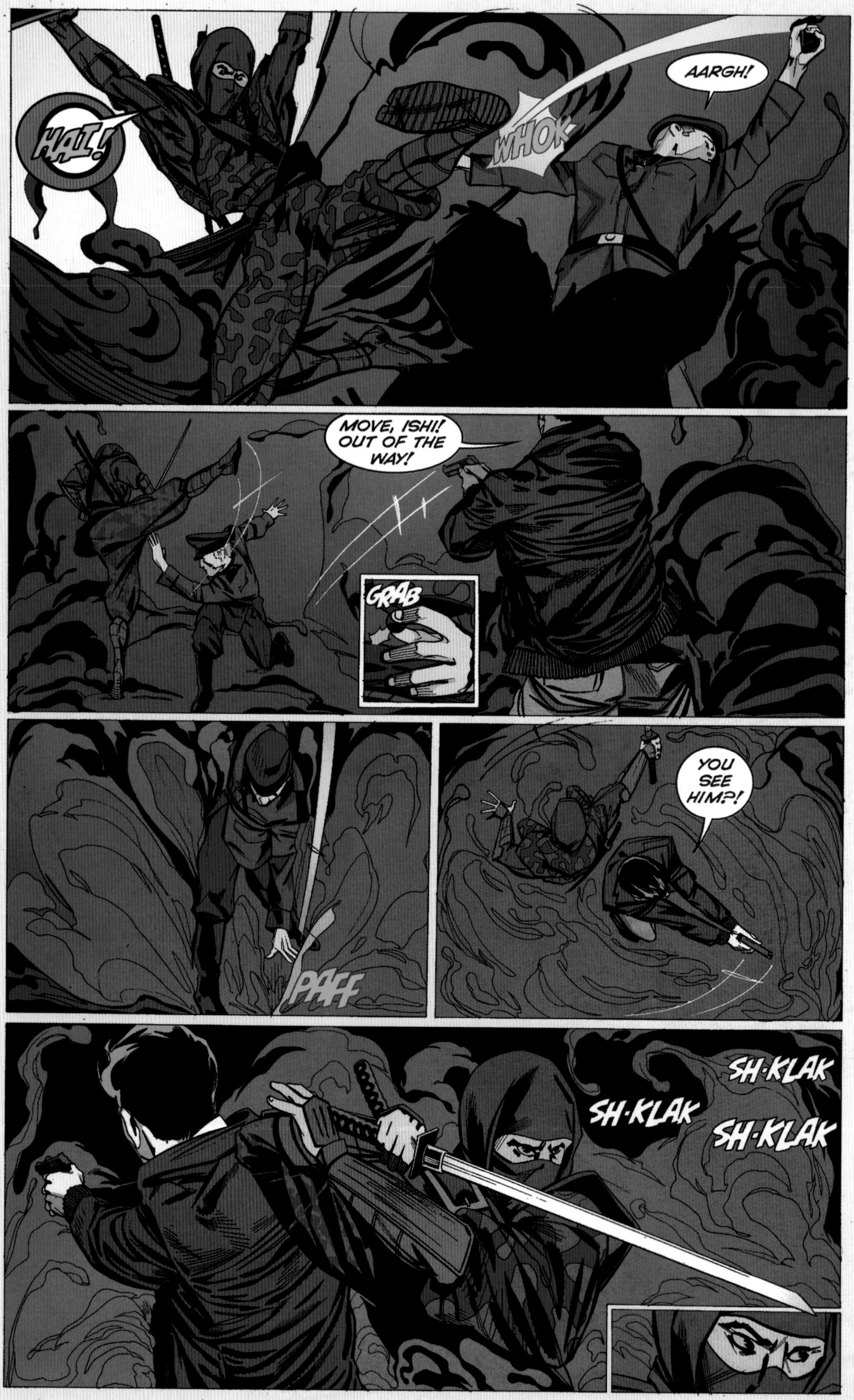
HAI!
WHOK
AARGH!
MOVE, ISHI! OUT OF THE WAY!
GRAB
PAFF
YOU SEE HIM?!
SH-KLAK
SH-KLAK
SH-KLAK

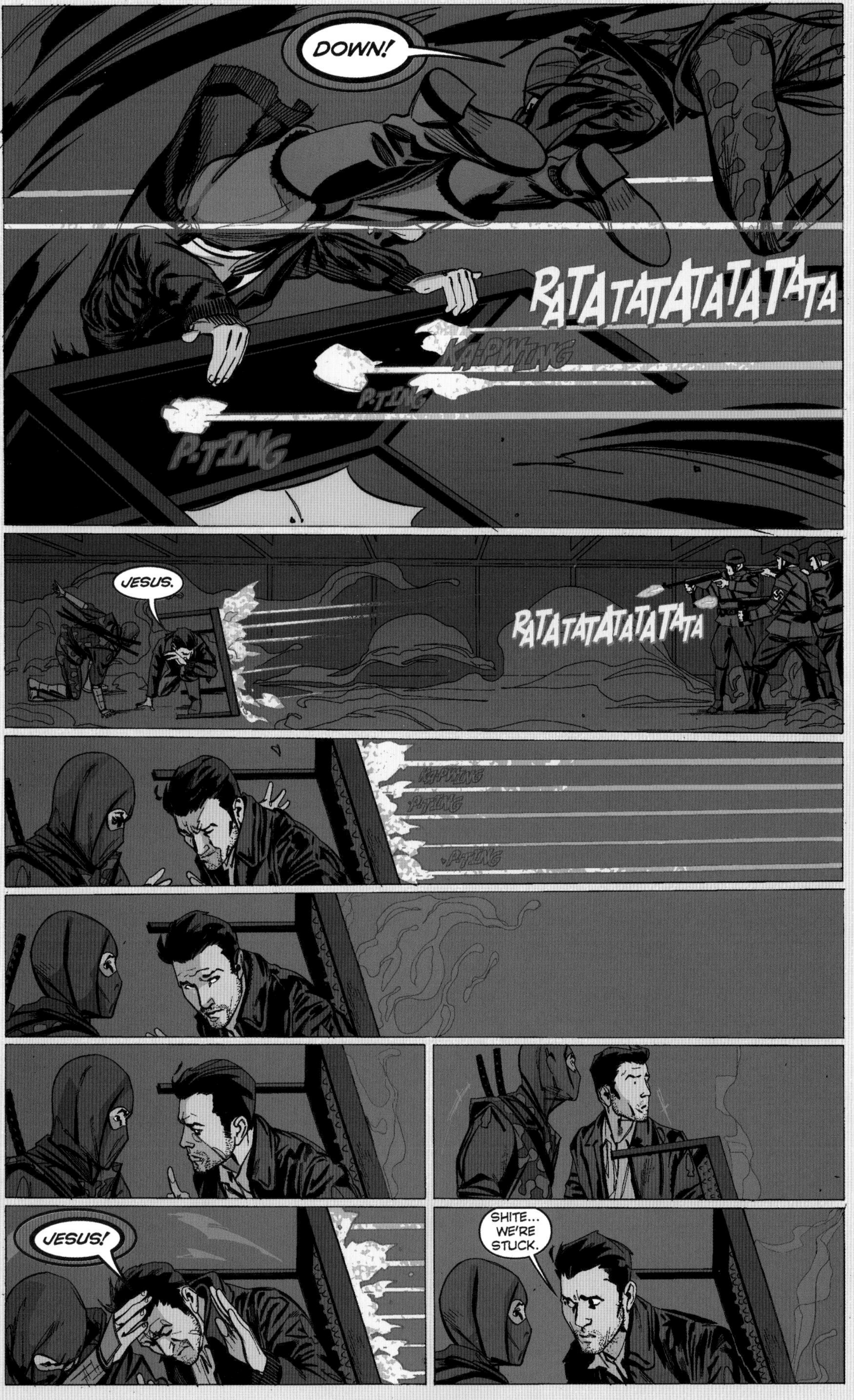
DOWN!
RATATATATATATATATA
KA-PWING
P-TING
P-TING
JESUS.
RATATATATATATATATA
KA-PWING
P-TING
P-TING
JESUS!
SHITE... WE'RE STUCK.

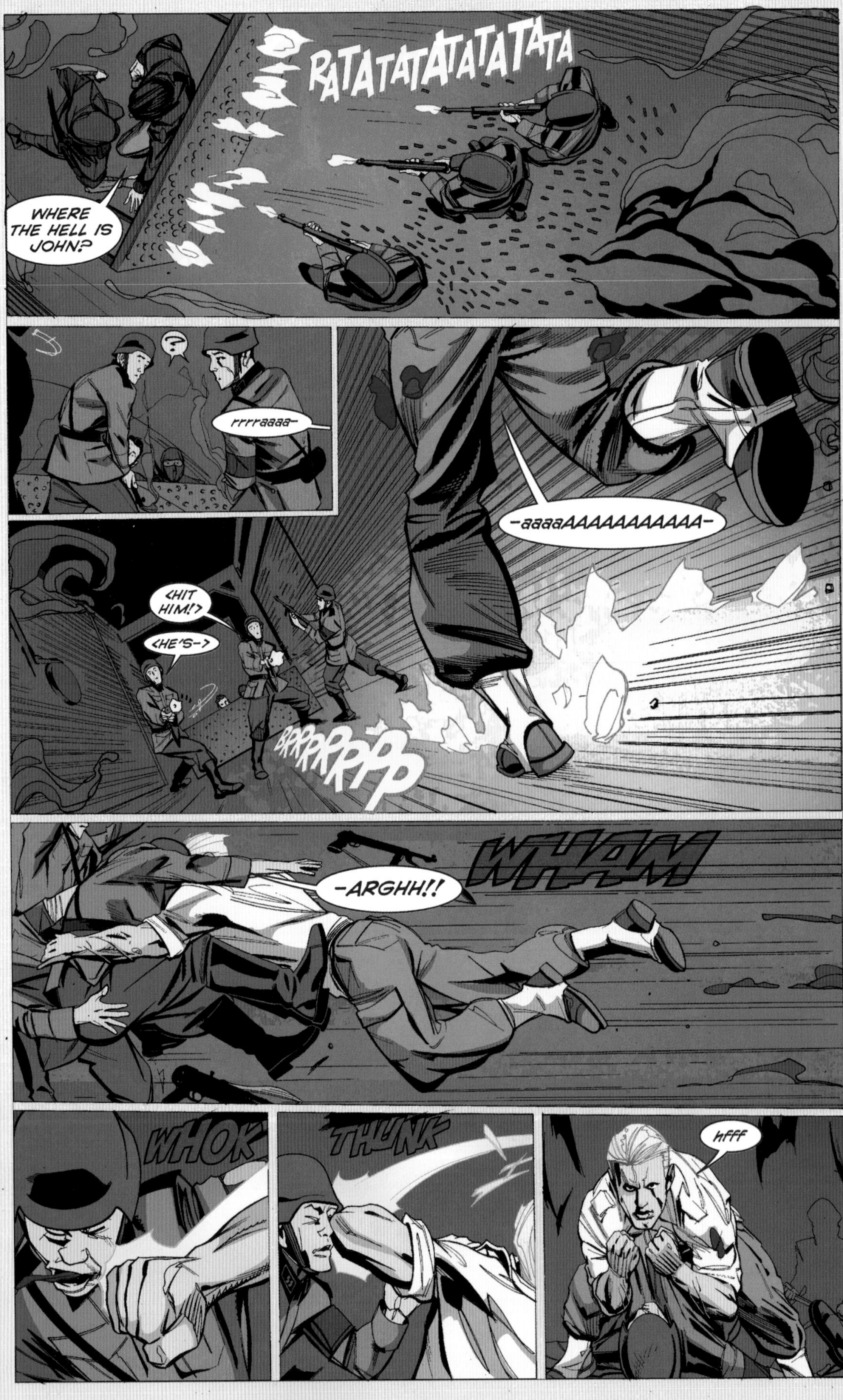
RATATATATATATATA
WHERE THE HELL IS JOHN?
?
rrrraaaa-
-aaaaAAAAAAAAAAA-
<HIT HIM!>
<HE'S->
BRRRRRPP
WHAM
-ARGHH!!
WHOK
THUNK
hfff

STAB

hnn

JOHN!

<HOW *FITTING* THAT YOUR COUNTRY WILL SHARE YOUR *FATE*, AMERICAN; PUNCTURED BY OUR FLAG AS SHE *BLEEDS* LIKE THE PROVERBIAL *STUCK PIG*.>

HEIL HITLER.

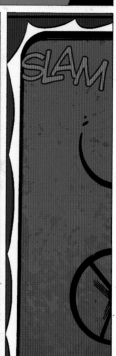

SLAM

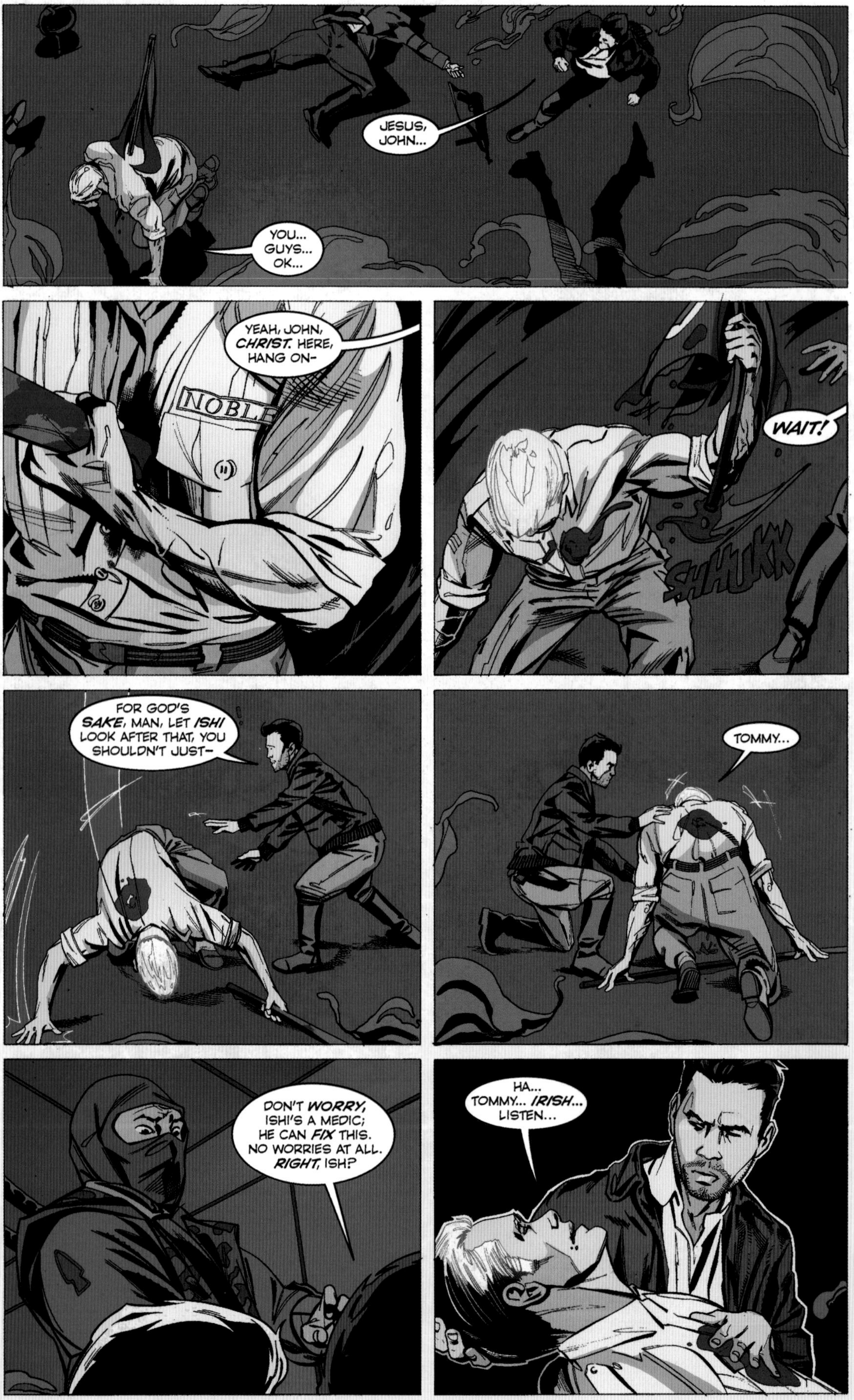
JESUS, JOHN...
YOU... GUYS... OK...
YEAH, JOHN, CHRIST. HERE, HANG ON-
NOBLE
WAIT!
SHHUKK
FOR GOD'S SAKE, MAN, LET ISHI LOOK AFTER THAT, YOU SHOULDN'T JUST-
TOMMY...
DON'T WORRY, ISHI'S A MEDIC; HE CAN FIX THIS. NO WORRIES AT ALL. RIGHT, ISH?
HA... TOMMY... IRISH... LISTEN...

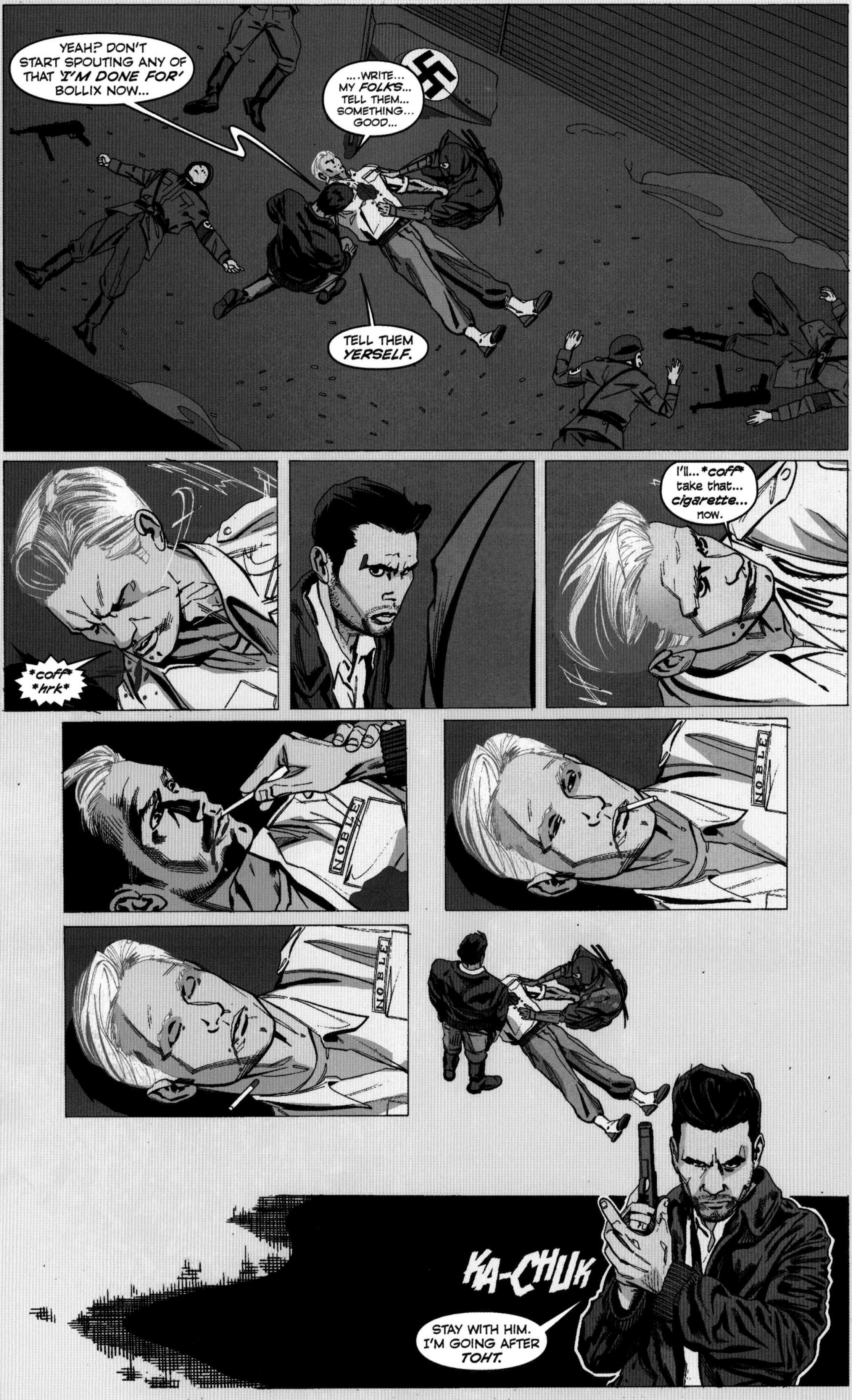
YEAH? DON'T START SPOUTING ANY OF THAT 'I'M DONE FOR' BOLLIX NOW...
....WRITE... MY FOLKS... TELL THEM... SOMETHING... GOOD...
TELL THEM YERSELF.
coff *hrk*
I'll... *coff* take that... cigarette... now.
NOBLE
NOBLE
NOBLE
KA-CHUK
STAY WITH HIM. I'M GOING AFTER TOHT.

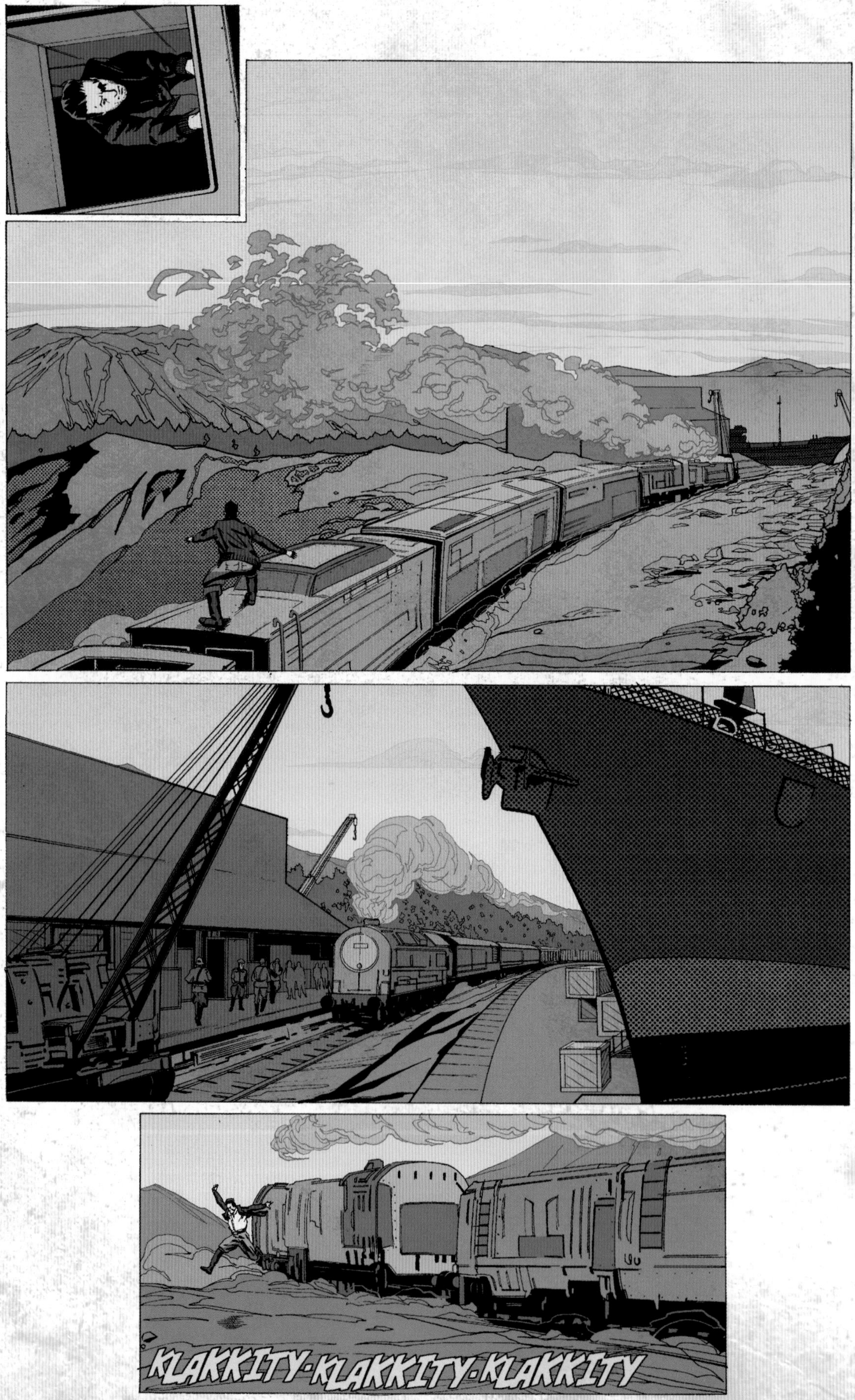
KLAKKITY-KLAKKITY-KLAKKITY

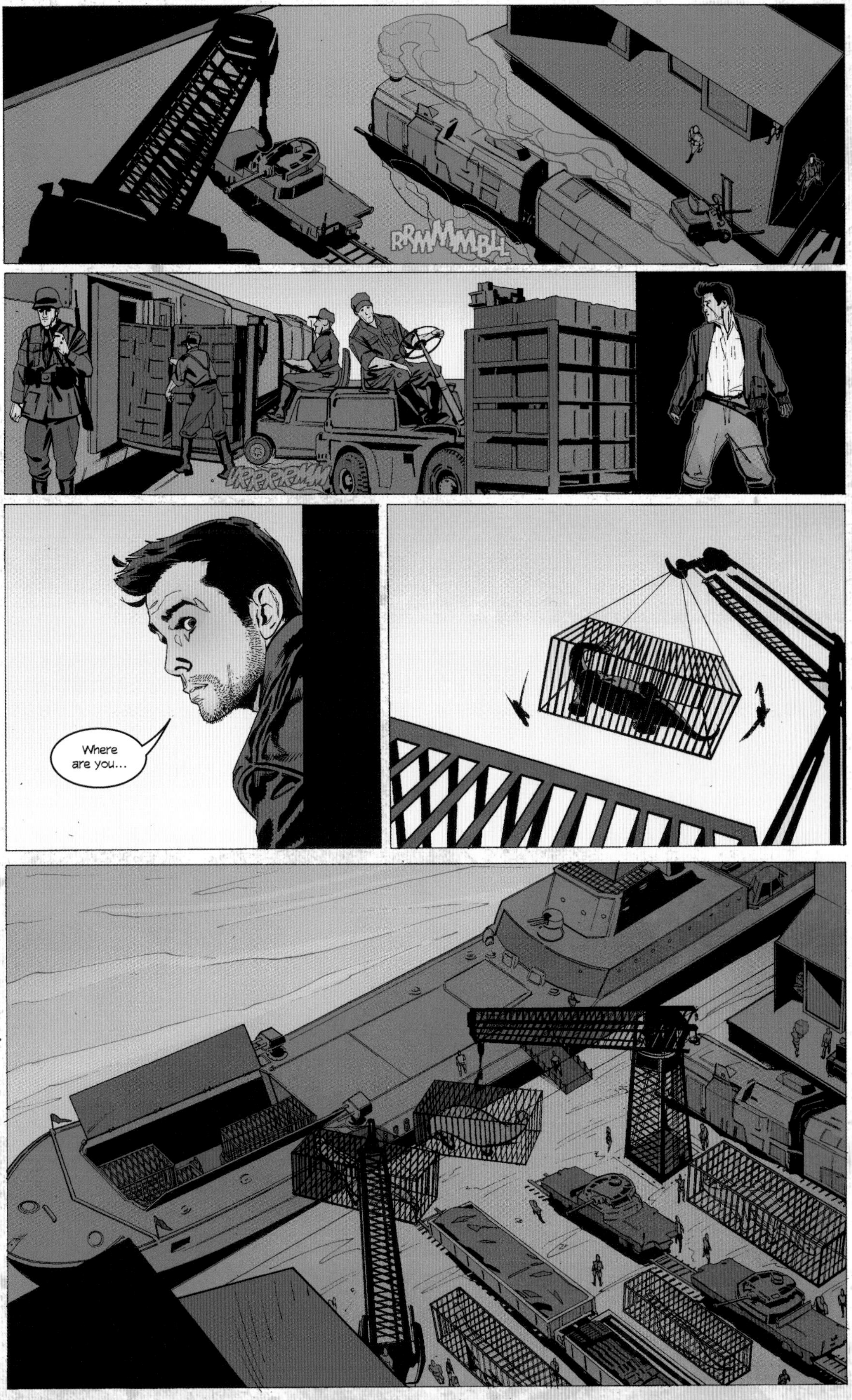
RRMMMMBLL
URRRRRMM
Where are you...

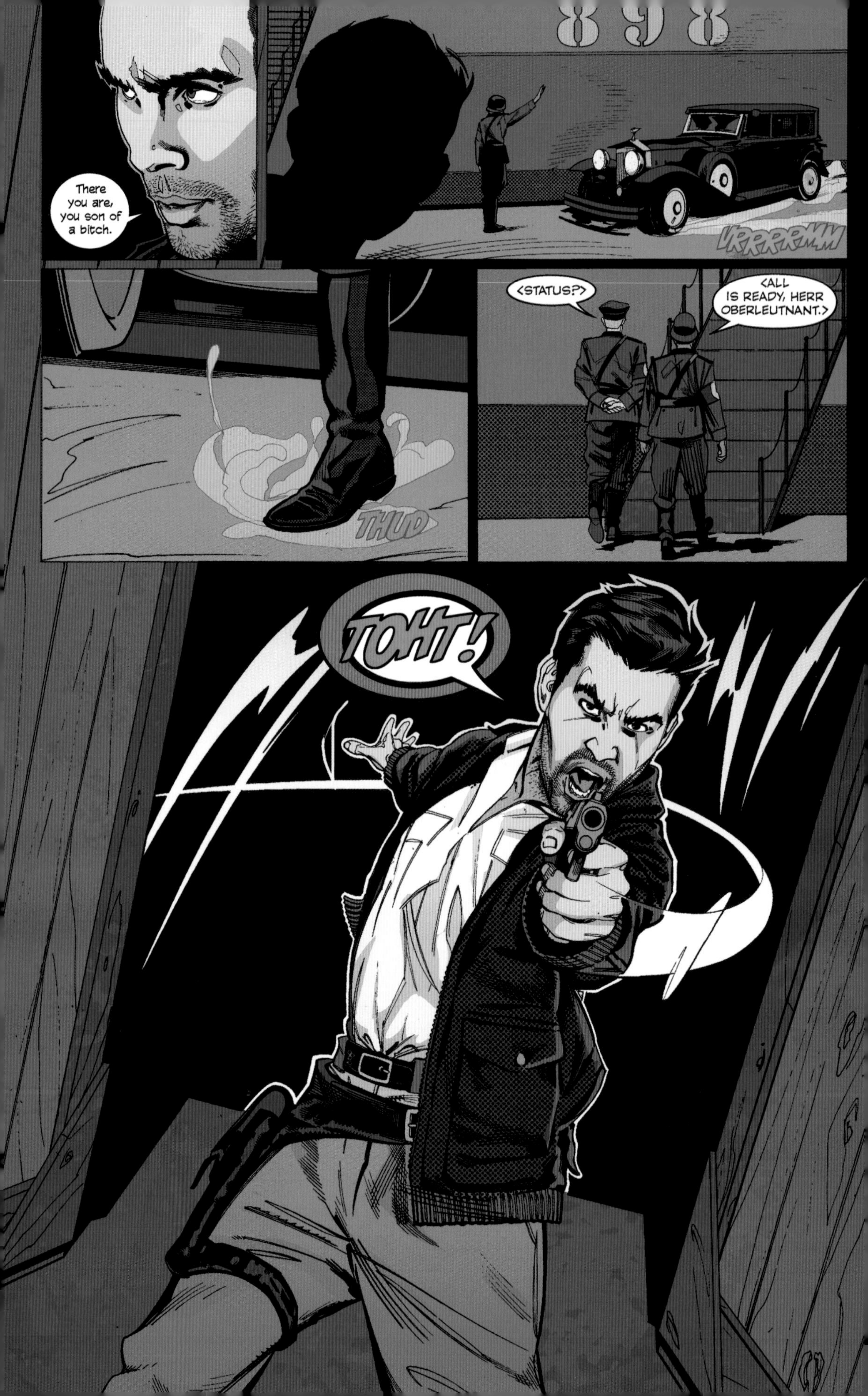

There you are, you son of a bitch.
898
VRRRRMM
THUD
<STATUS?>
<ALL IS READY, HERR OBERLEUTNANT.>
TOHT!

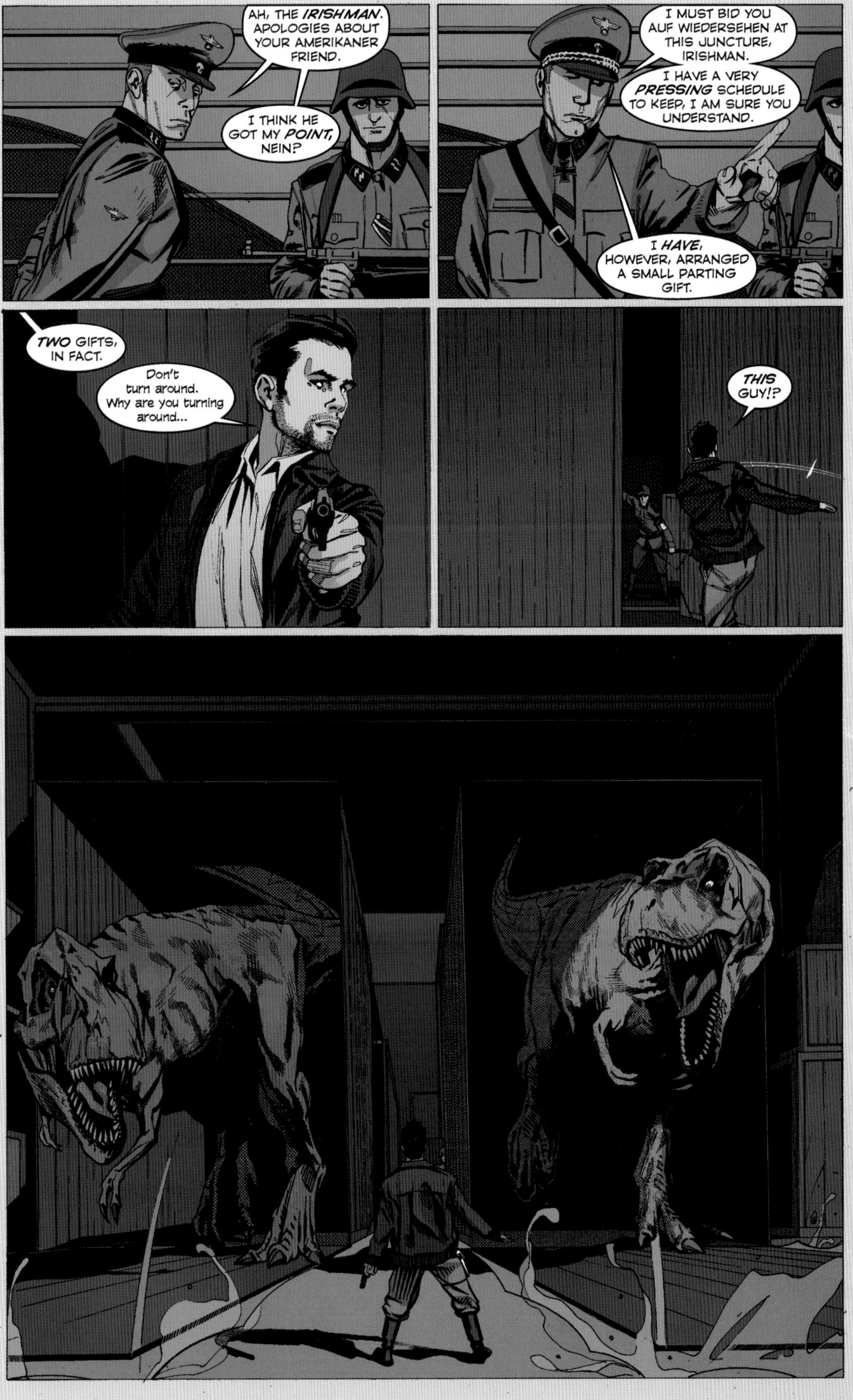
AH, THE IRISHMAN. APOLOGIES ABOUT YOUR AMERIKANER FRIEND.
I THINK HE GOT MY POINT, NEIN?
I MUST BID YOU AUF WIEDERSEHEN AT THIS JUNCTURE, IRISHMAN.
I HAVE A VERY PRESSING SCHEDULE TO KEEP, I AM SURE YOU UNDERSTAND.
I HAVE, HOWEVER, ARRANGED A SMALL PARTING GIFT.
TWO GIFTS, IN FACT.
Don't turn around. Why are you turning around...
THIS GUY!?

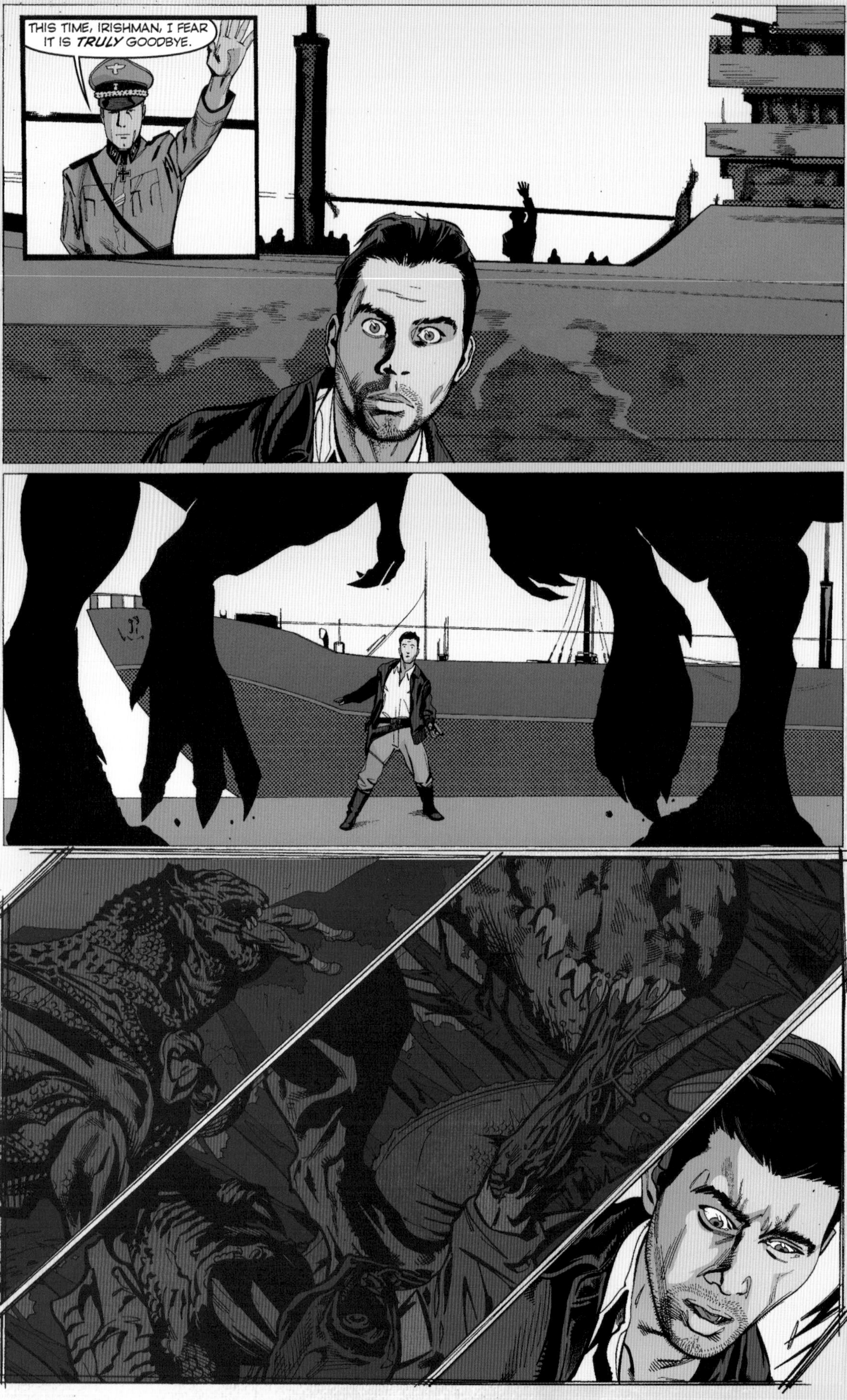
THIS TIME, IRISHMAN, I FEAR IT IS TRULY GOODBYE.

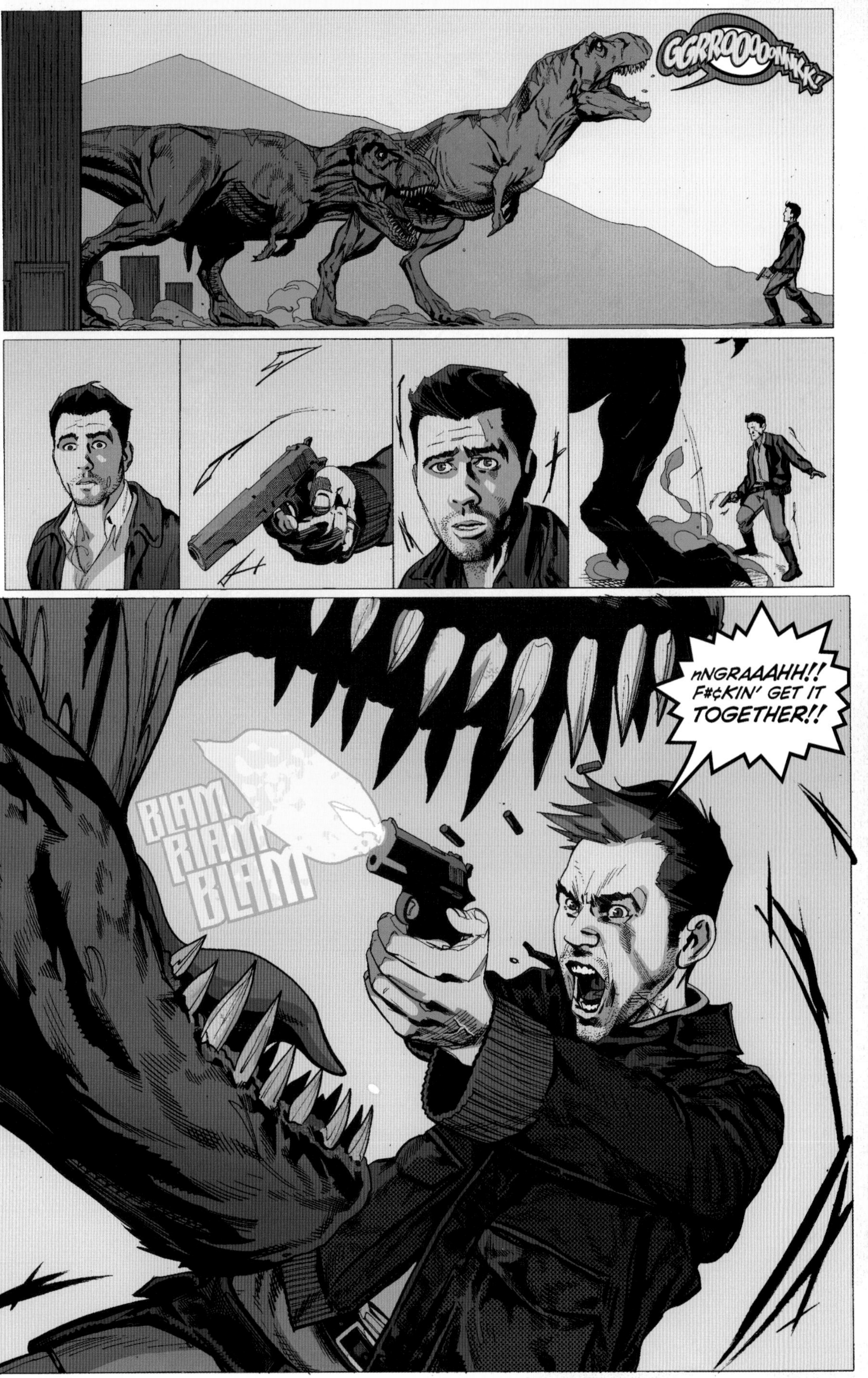
GGRROOOOOONNKK!
nNGRAAAHH!! F#¢KIN' GET IT TOGETHER!!
BLAM BLAM BLAM

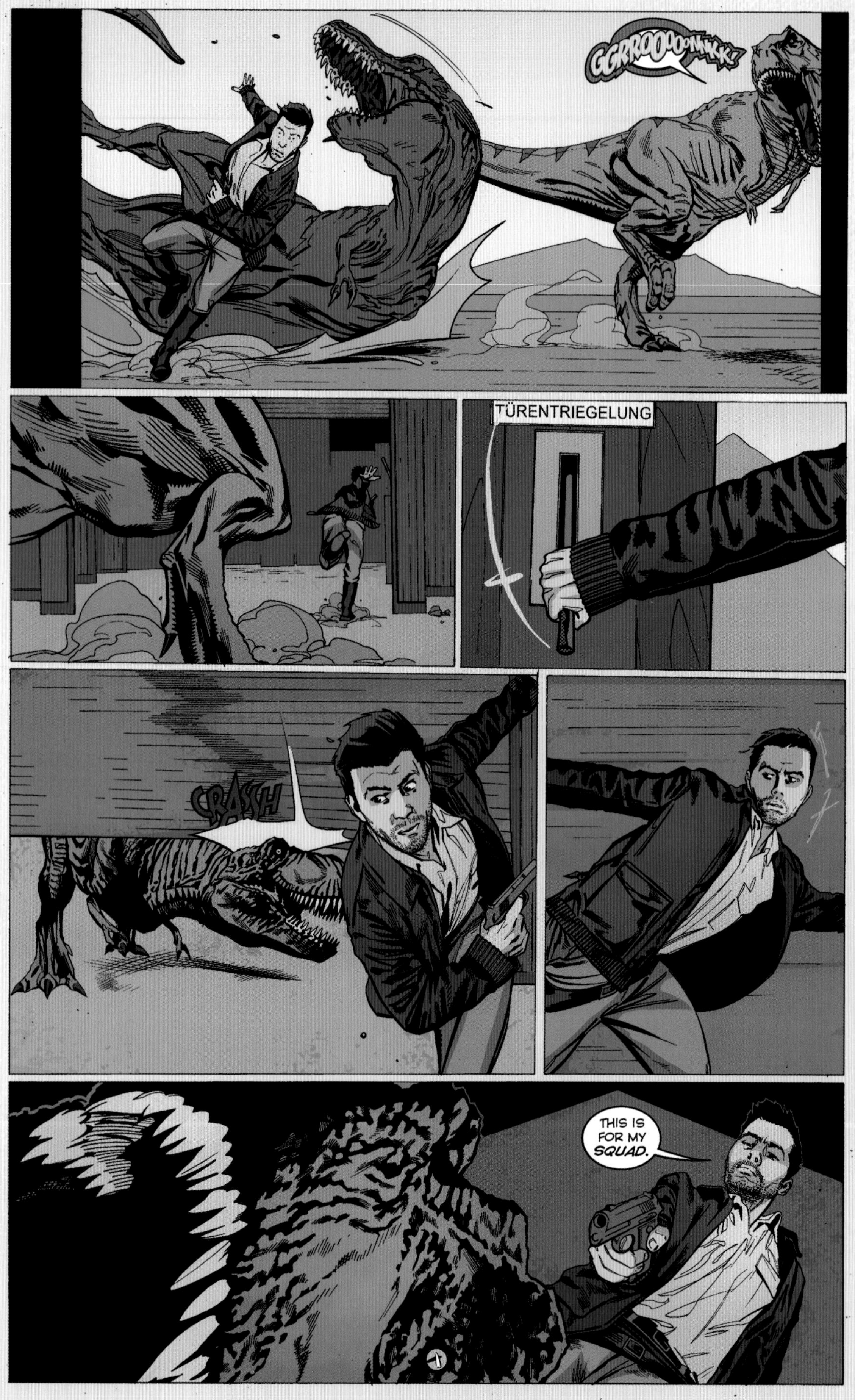
GGRROOOOONNKK!
TÜRENTRIEGELUNG
CRASH
THIS IS FOR MY SQUAD.

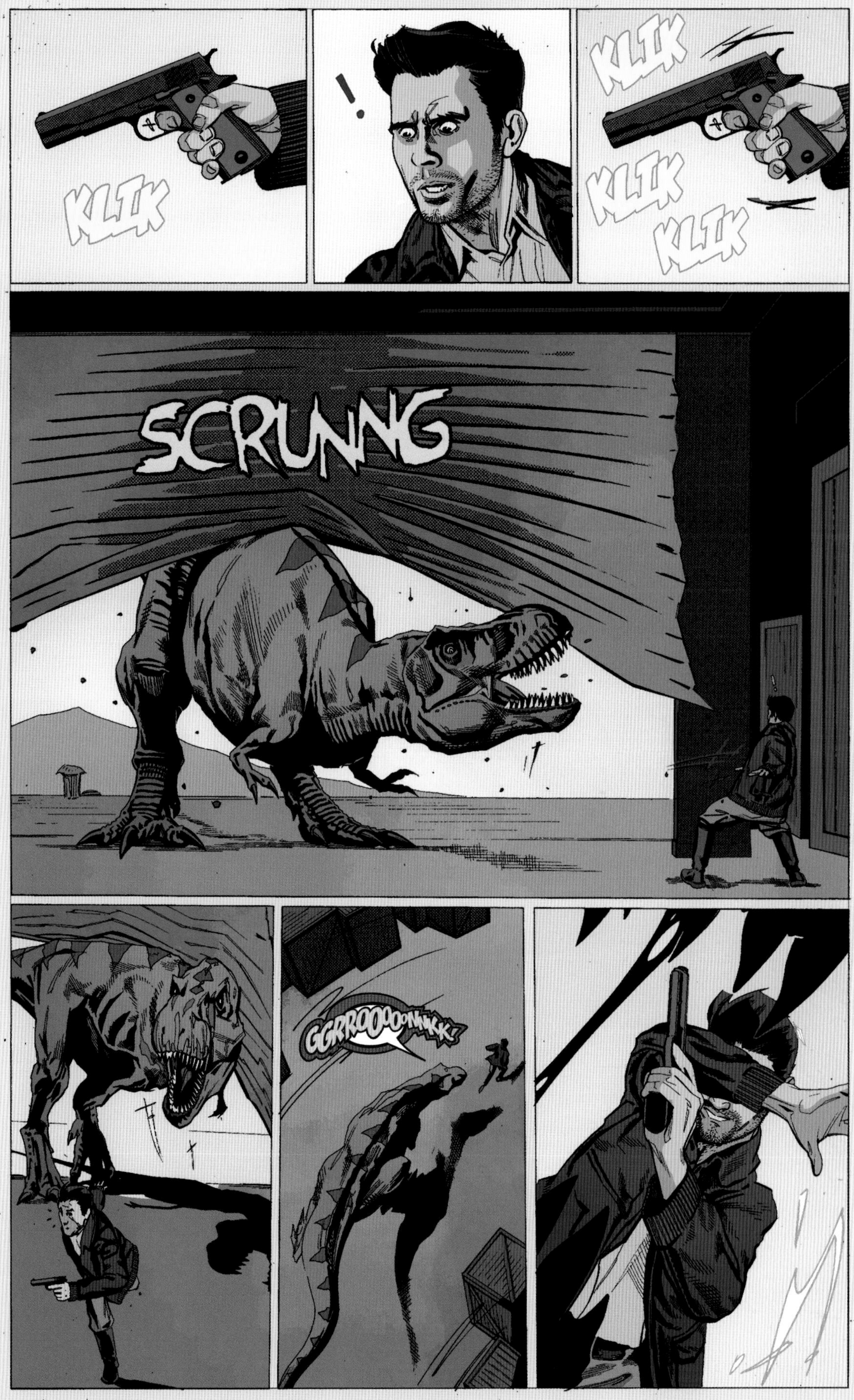

KLIK
!
KLIK
KLIK
KLIK
SCRUNNG
GGRROOOOONNKK!

GGRROOOOOMKK!

BLAM BLAM BLAM

?!

GRETA!?

BLOODY HELL, AM I GLAD TO SEE *YOU!* I THOUGHT THAT WAS *IT.*

YOU *SAVED* ME!

AND YOU MANAGED TO TAKE THAT THING DOWN WITHOUT *KILLING* IT.

WAIT—

—WHAT THE HELL ARE YOU EVEN *DOING* HERE? WHERE'S *ELIZABETH?*

I—

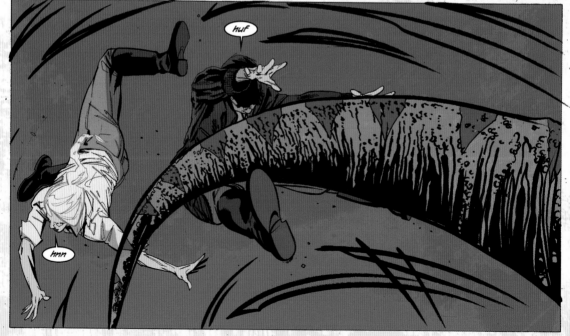

huf

hnn

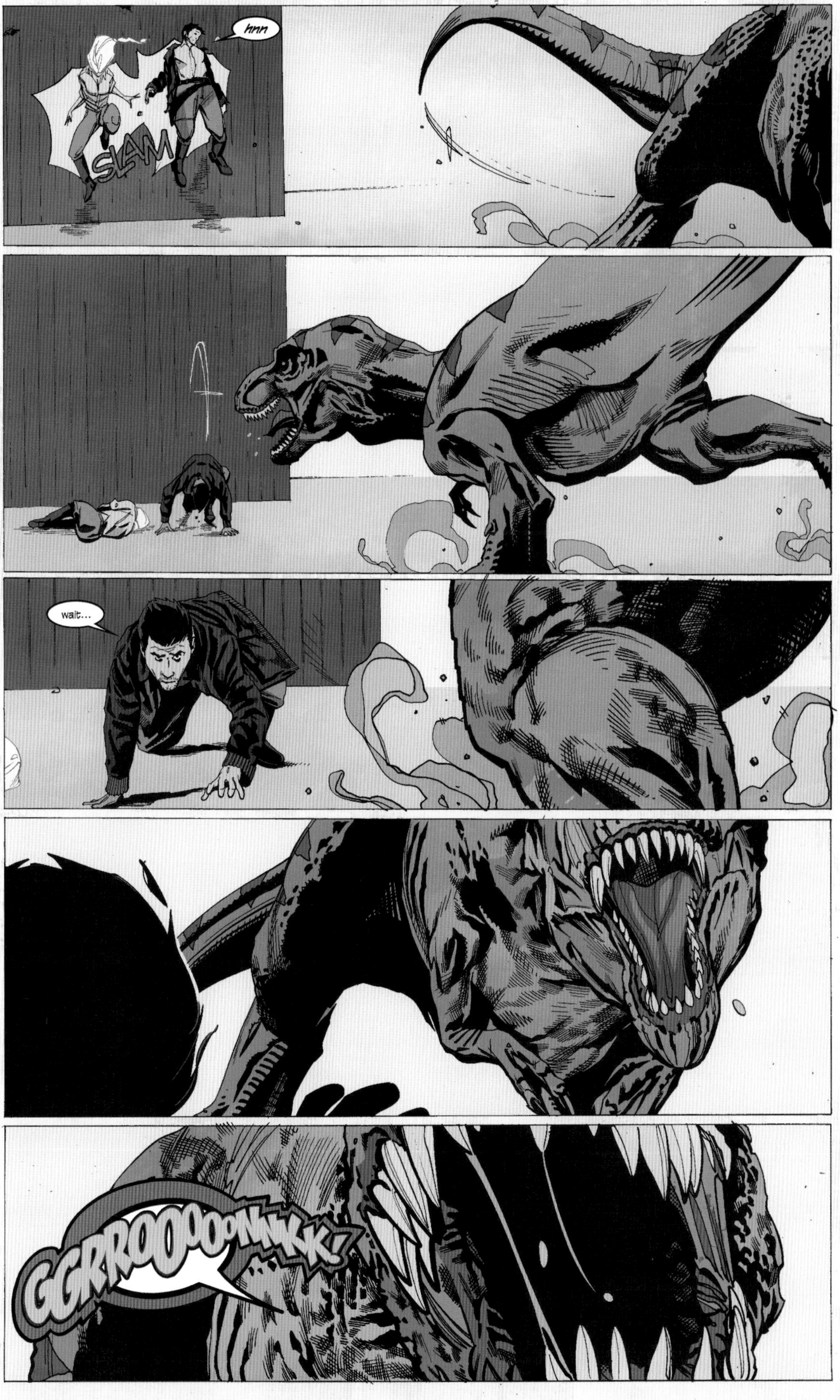
hnn
SLAM
wait...
GGRROOOOONNKK!

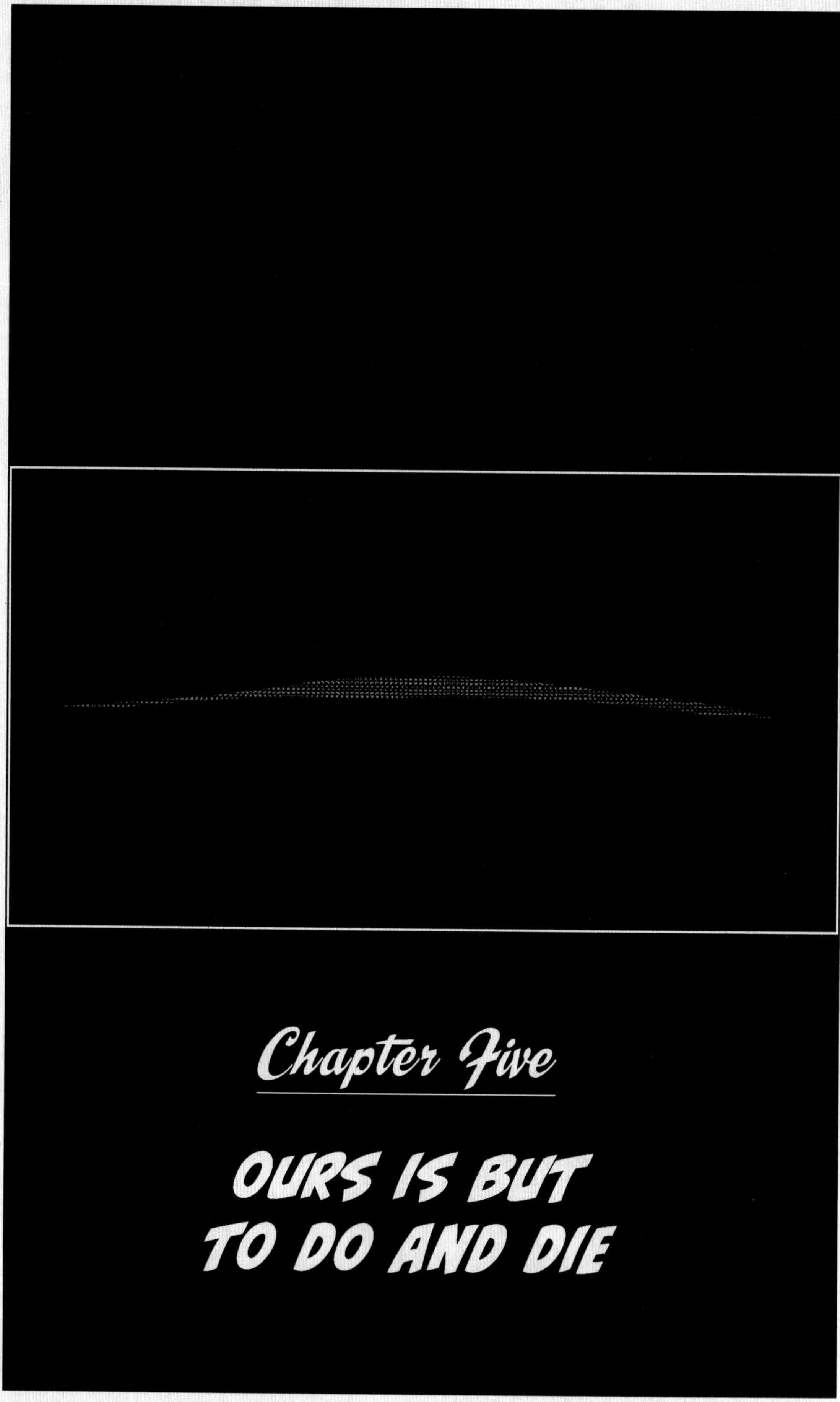
Chapter Five
OURS IS BUT
TO DO AND DIE

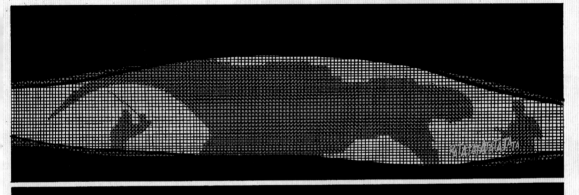

SUSH RATATATATATATATA

STAB

THOOM

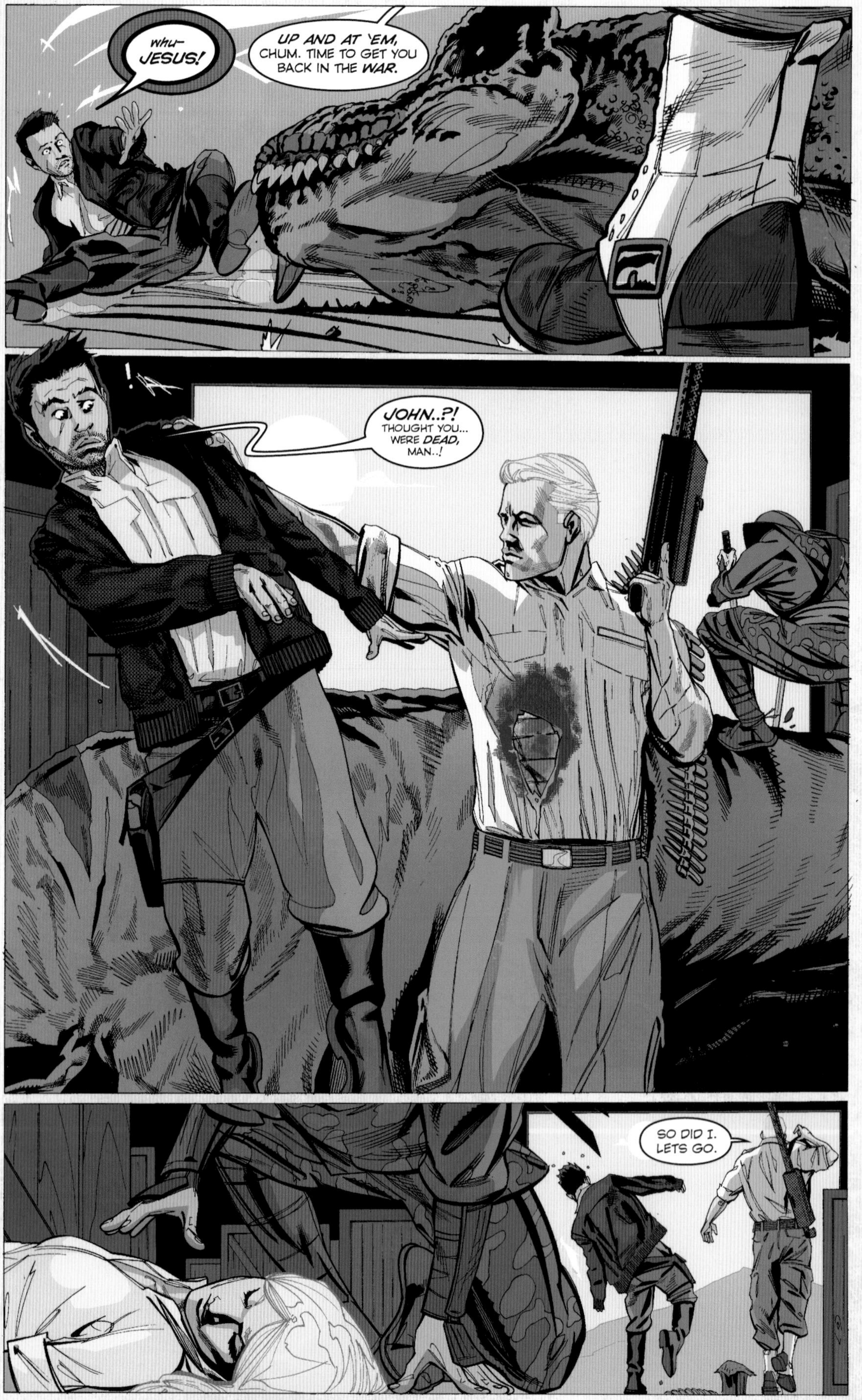
whu-
JESUS!
UP AND AT 'EM, CHUM. TIME TO GET YOU BACK IN THE WAR.
JOHN..?! THOUGHT YOU... WERE DEAD, MAN..!
SO DID I. LETS GO.

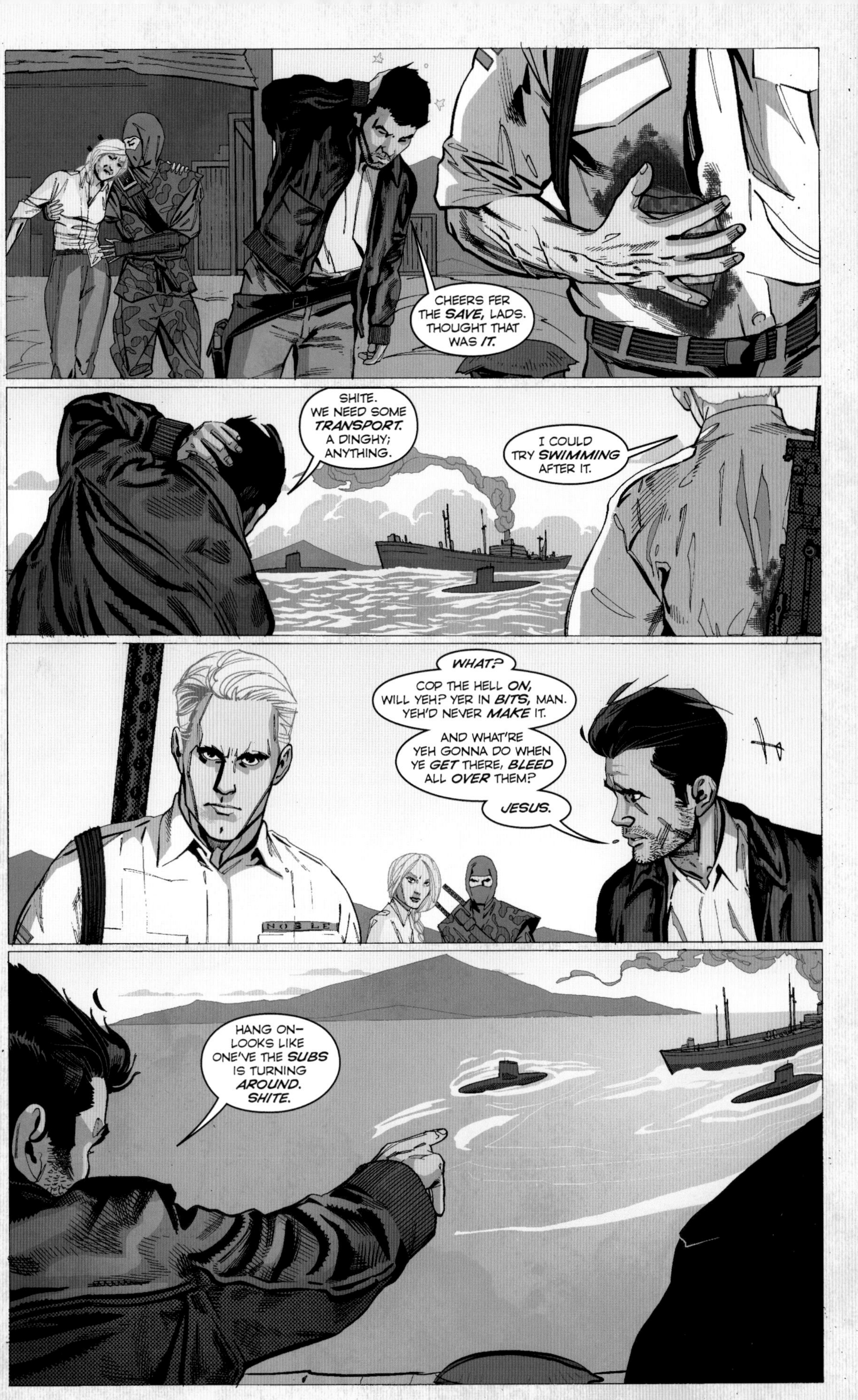
CHEERS FER THE SAVE, LADS. THOUGHT THAT WAS IT.
SHITE. WE NEED SOME TRANSPORT. A DINGHY; ANYTHING.
I COULD TRY SWIMMING AFTER IT.
WHAT?
COP THE HELL ON, WILL YEH? YER IN BITS, MAN. YEH'D NEVER MAKE IT.
AND WHAT'RE YEH GONNA DO WHEN YE GET THERE, BLEED ALL OVER THEM?
JESUS.
NOBLE
HANG ON– LOOKS LIKE ONE'VE THE SUBS IS TURNING AROUND. SHITE.

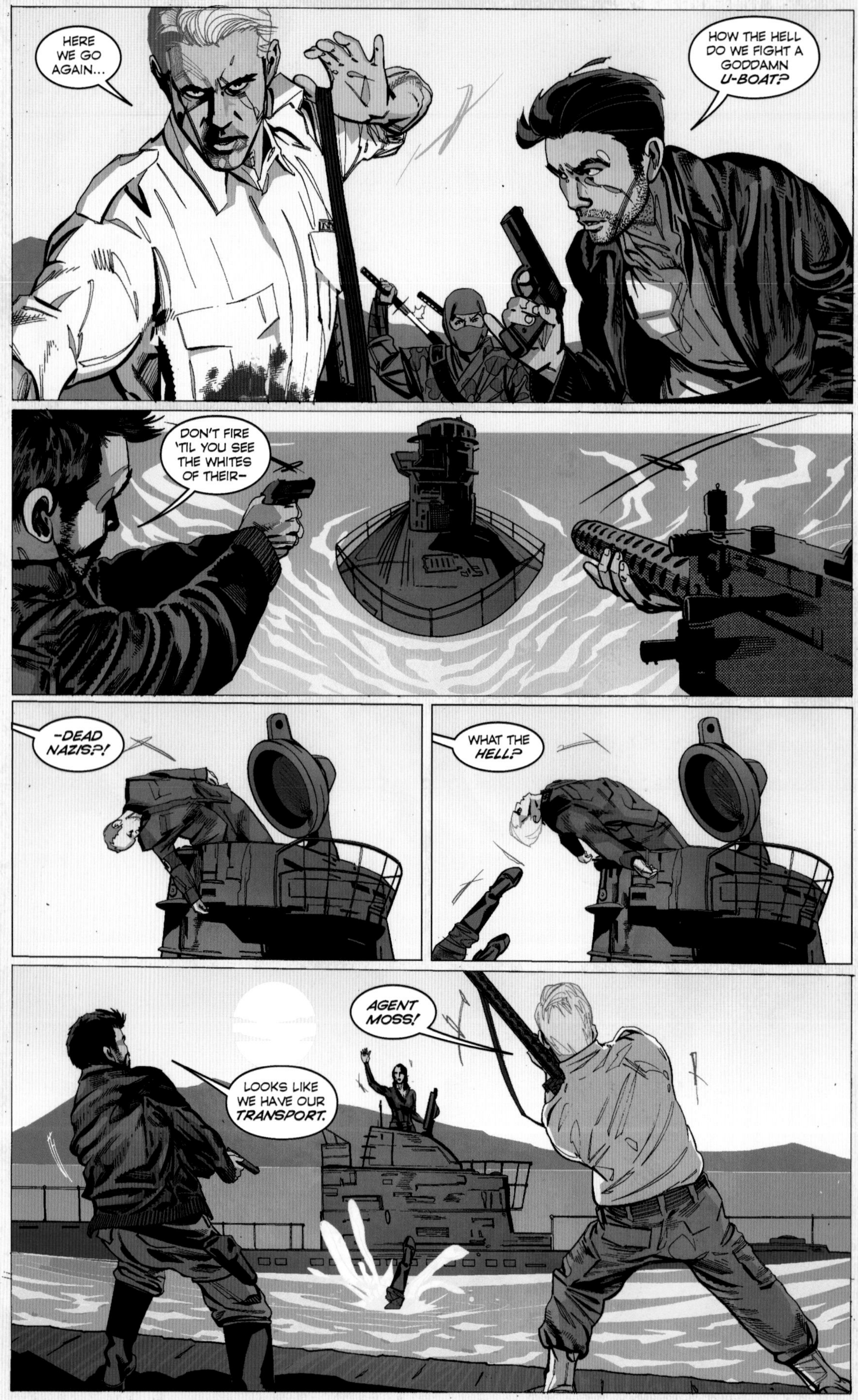
HERE WE GO AGAIN...
HOW THE HELL DO WE FIGHT A GODDAMN U-BOAT?
DON'T FIRE 'TIL YOU SEE THE WHITES OF THEIR-
-DEAD NAZIS?!
WHAT THE HELL?
AGENT MOSS!
LOOKS LIKE WE HAVE OUR TRANSPORT.

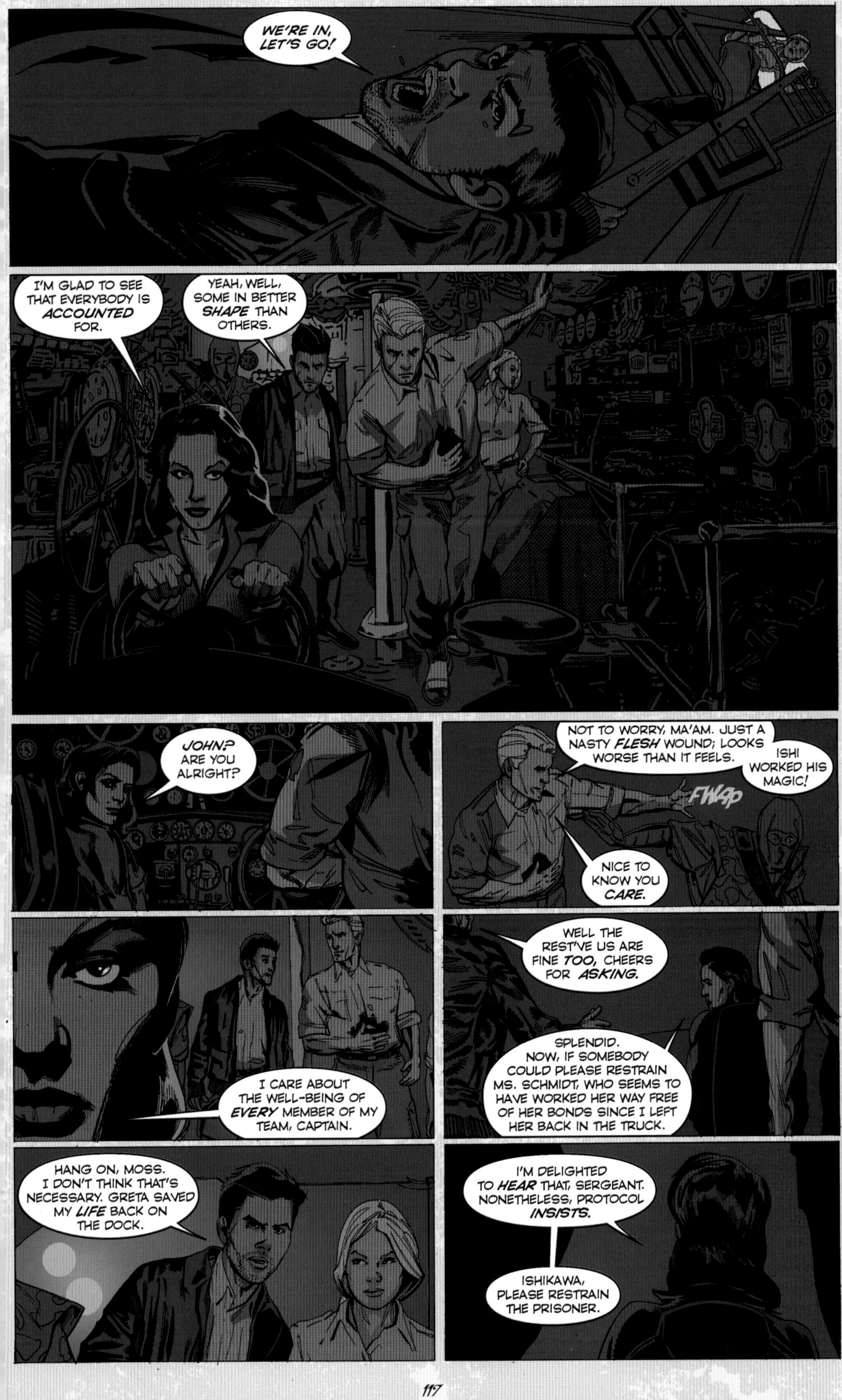
WE'RE IN, LET'S GO!
I'M GLAD TO SEE THAT EVERYBODY IS ACCOUNTED FOR.
YEAH, WELL, SOME IN BETTER SHAPE THAN OTHERS.
JOHN? ARE YOU ALRIGHT?
NOT TO WORRY, MA'AM. JUST A NASTY FLESH WOUND; LOOKS WORSE THAN IT FEELS.
ISHI WORKED HIS MAGIC!
FWAP
NICE TO KNOW YOU CARE.
I CARE ABOUT THE WELL-BEING OF EVERY MEMBER OF MY TEAM, CAPTAIN.
WELL THE REST'VE US ARE FINE TOO, CHEERS FOR ASKING.
SPLENDID. NOW, IF SOMEBODY COULD PLEASE RESTRAIN MS. SCHMIDT, WHO SEEMS TO HAVE WORKED HER WAY FREE OF HER BONDS SINCE I LEFT HER BACK IN THE TRUCK.
HANG ON, MOSS. I DON'T THINK THAT'S NECESSARY. GRETA SAVED MY LIFE BACK ON THE DOCK.
I'M DELIGHTED TO HEAR THAT, SERGEANT. NONETHELESS, PROTOCOL INSISTS.
ISHIKAWA, PLEASE RESTRAIN THE PRISONER.

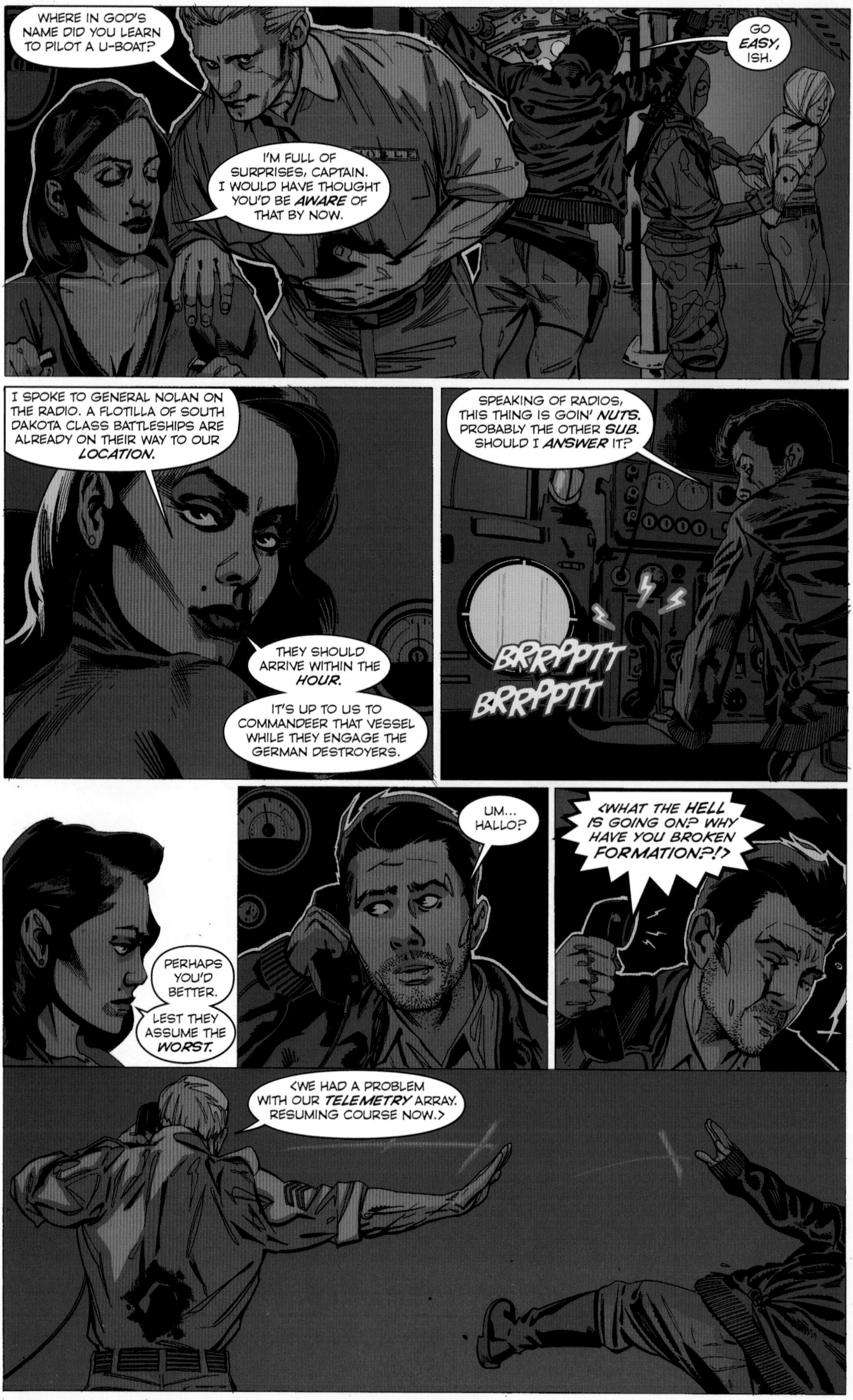

WHERE IN GOD'S NAME DID YOU LEARN TO PILOT A U-BOAT?
GO EASY, ISH.
I'M FULL OF SURPRISES, CAPTAIN. I WOULD HAVE THOUGHT YOU'D BE AWARE OF THAT BY NOW.
I SPOKE TO GENERAL NOLAN ON THE RADIO. A FLOTILLA OF SOUTH DAKOTA CLASS BATTLESHIPS ARE ALREADY ON THEIR WAY TO OUR LOCATION.
THEY SHOULD ARRIVE WITHIN THE HOUR.
IT'S UP TO US TO COMMANDEER THAT VESSEL WHILE THEY ENGAGE THE GERMAN DESTROYERS.
SPEAKING OF RADIOS, THIS THING IS GOIN' NUTS. PROBABLY THE OTHER SUB. SHOULD I ANSWER IT?
BRRPPTT
BRRPPTT
PERHAPS YOU'D BETTER.
LEST THEY ASSUME THE WORST.
UM... HALLO?
<WHAT THE HELL IS GOING ON? WHY HAVE YOU BROKEN FORMATION?!>
<WE HAD A PROBLEM WITH OUR TELEMETRY ARRAY. RESUMING COURSE NOW.>

<HELLO?>

...YOU THINK THEY *BOUGHT* IT?

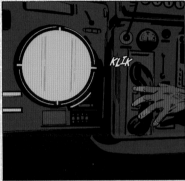

KLIK

CAPTAIN KÖLLER, THIS IS OBERLEUTNANT TOHT. SINK THAT VESSEL, PLEASE.

BLIP BLIP

GUESS THAT ANSWERS OUR QUESTION. THE OTHER SUB IS COMING *ABOUT.*

THEY'RE HEADING STRAIGHT FOR US.

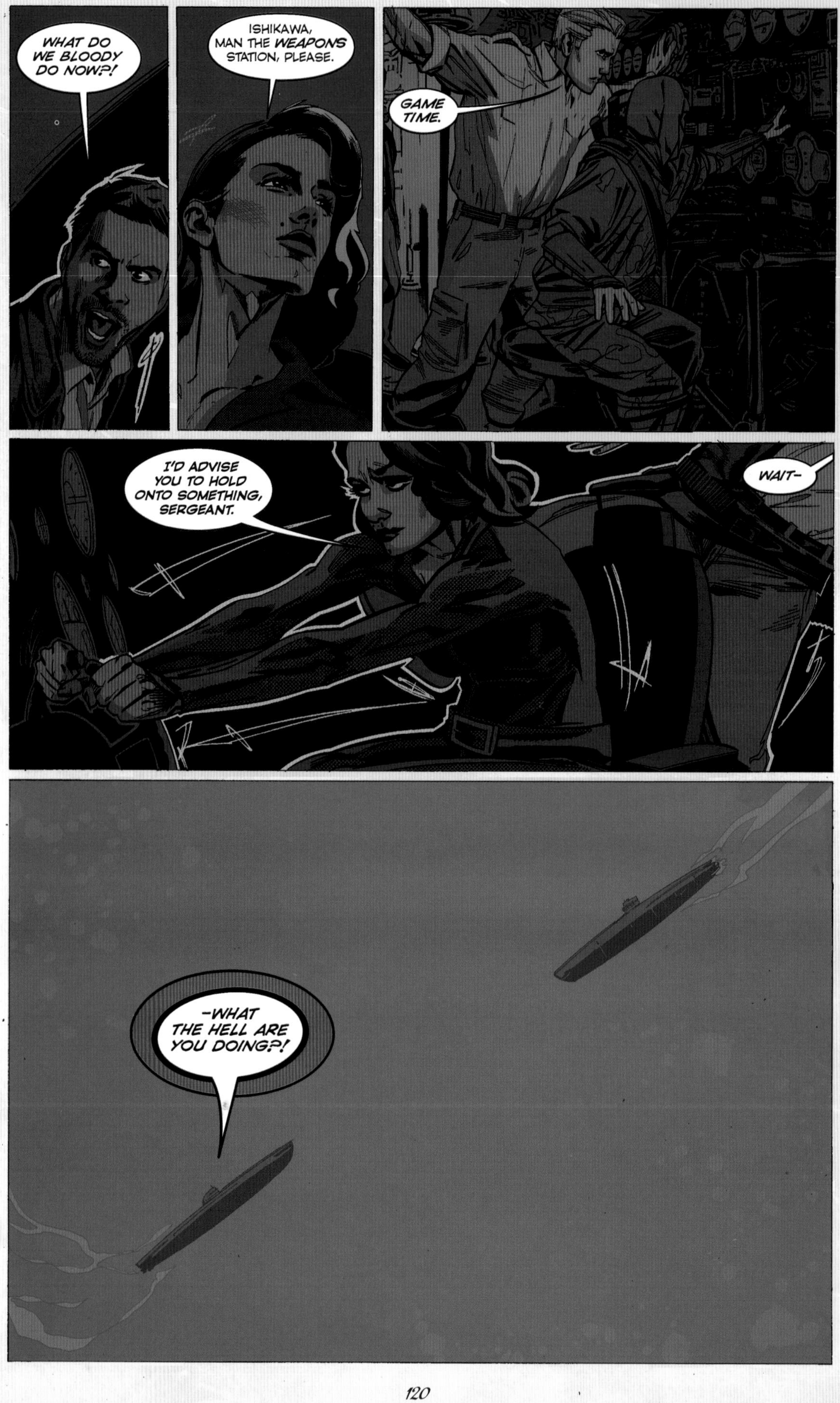
WHAT DO WE BLOODY DO NOW?!
ISHIKAWA, MAN THE WEAPONS STATION, PLEASE.
GAME TIME.
I'D ADVISE YOU TO HOLD ONTO SOMETHING, SERGEANT.
WAIT-
-WHAT THE HELL ARE YOU DOING?!

THESE ARE THE NEW TYPE *XXIII* BOATS, DEVELOPED TO REPLACE THE TYPE *II'S*. ONLY TWO TORPEDOES EACH, PRE-LOADED *EXTERNALLY*.

TWO SHOTS *APIECE.*

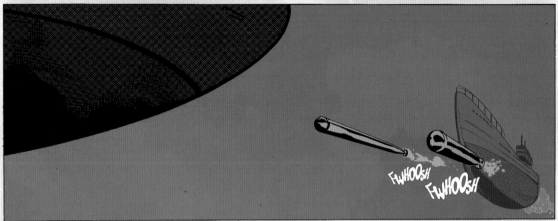

FWHOOSH FWHOOSH

TWO ENEMY TORPEDOES BEARING DOWN ON US, 150 YARDS OUT!

Sweet Jesus.

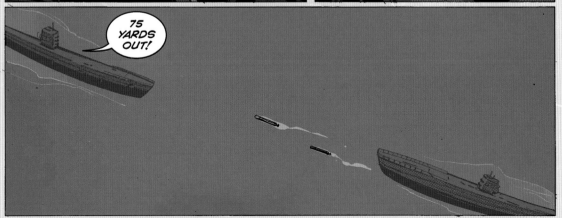

75 YARDS OUT!

NOW, ISHI!
FIRE!
SLAM
FWHOOSH
FWHOOSH
BRACE YOURSELVES!
BOOOM

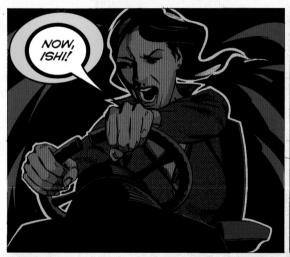

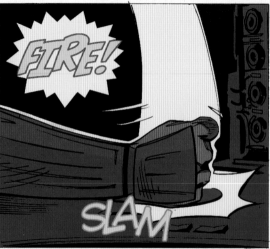

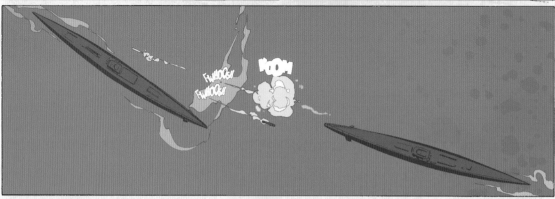

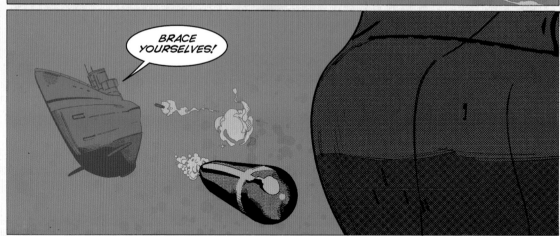

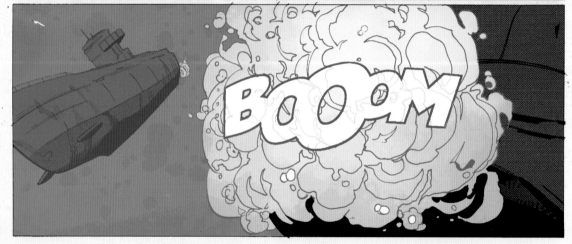

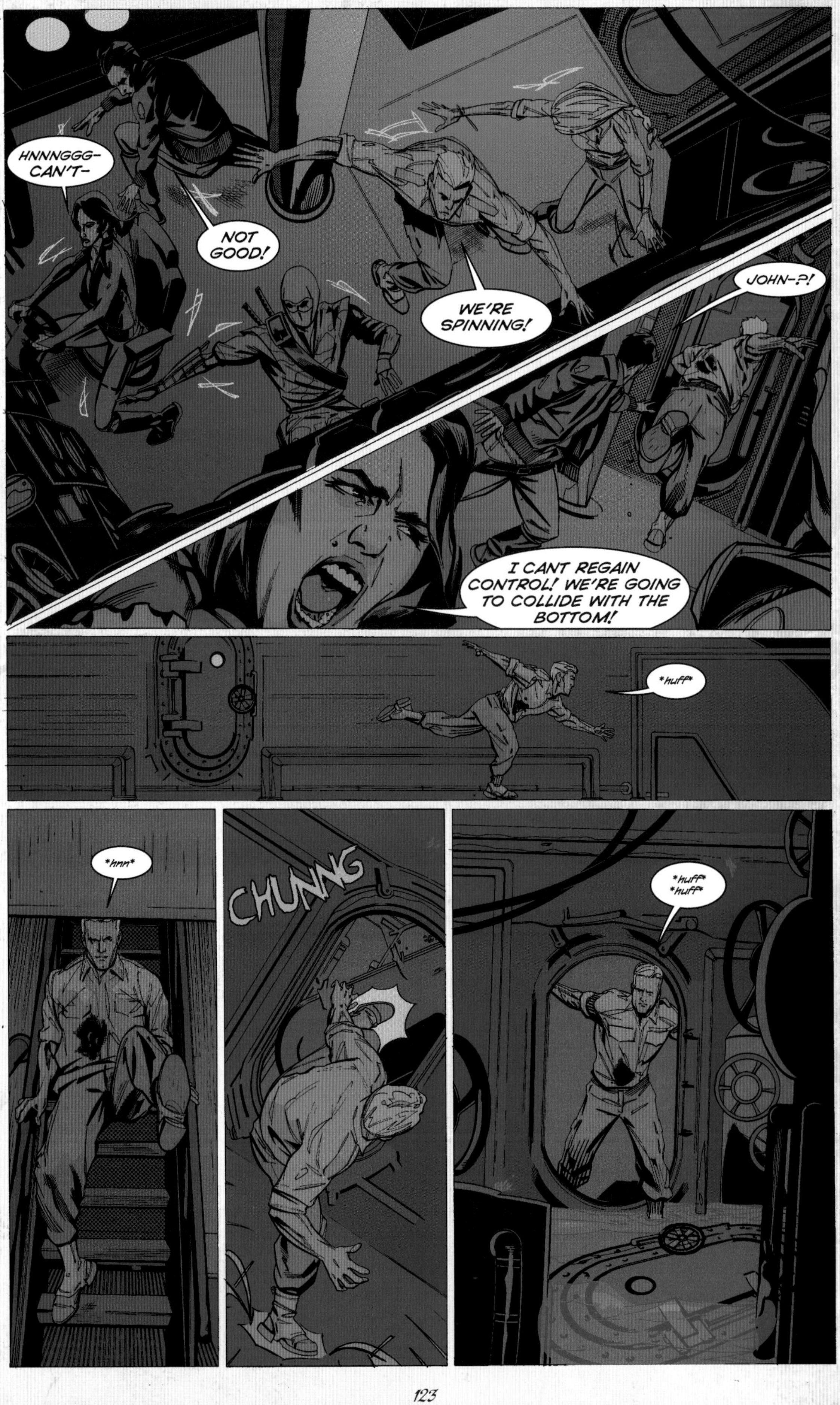
HNNNGGG-
CAN'T-
NOT GOOD!
WE'RE SPINNING!
JOHN-?!
I CANT REGAIN CONTROL! WE'RE GOING TO COLLIDE WITH THE BOTTOM!
huff
hnn
CHUNNG
huff
huff

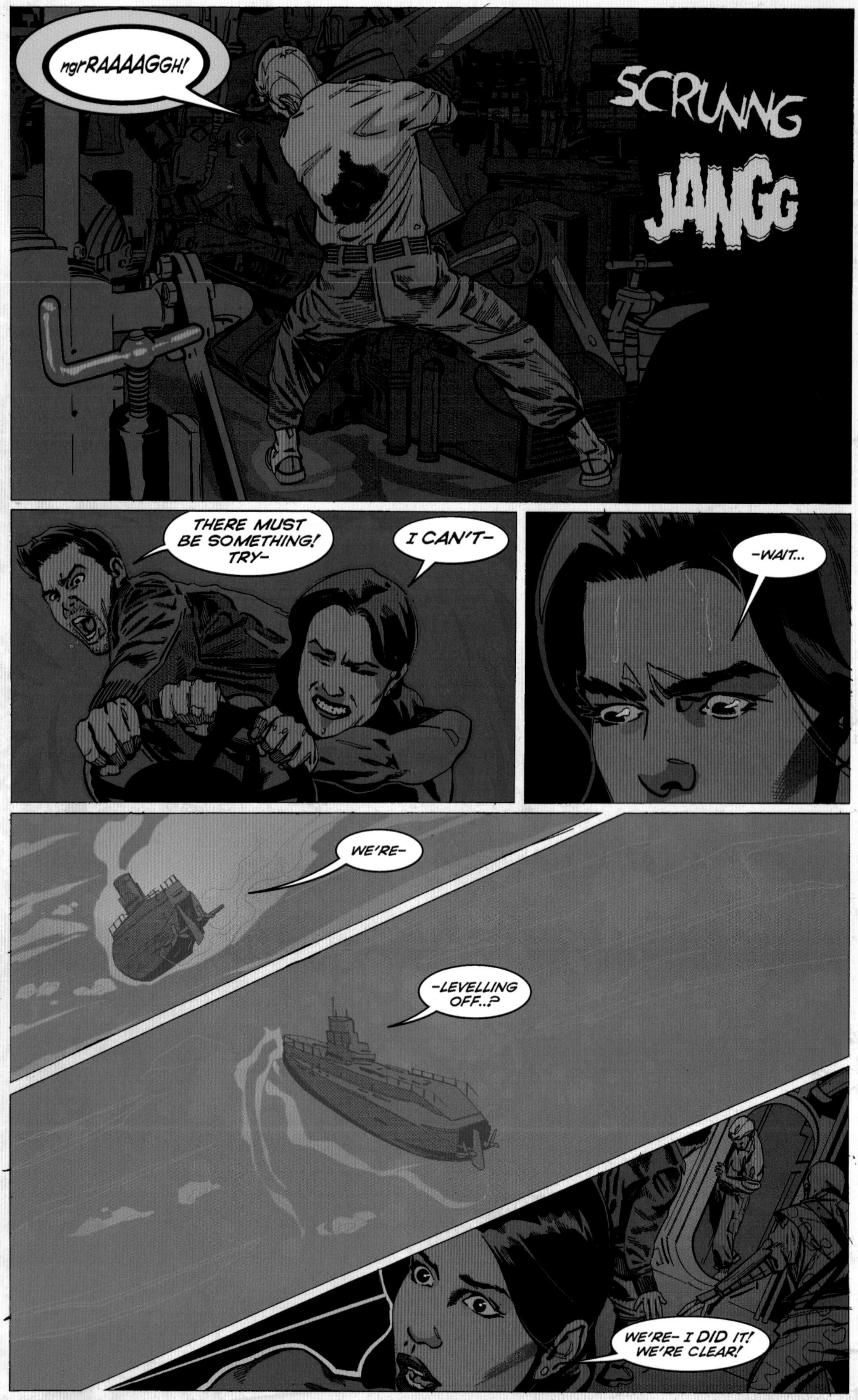
ngrRAAAAGGH!
SCRUNNG
JANGG
THERE MUST BE SOMETHING! TRY-
I CAN'T-
-WAIT...
WE'RE-
-LEVELLING OFF..?
WE'RE- I DID IT! WE'RE CLEAR!

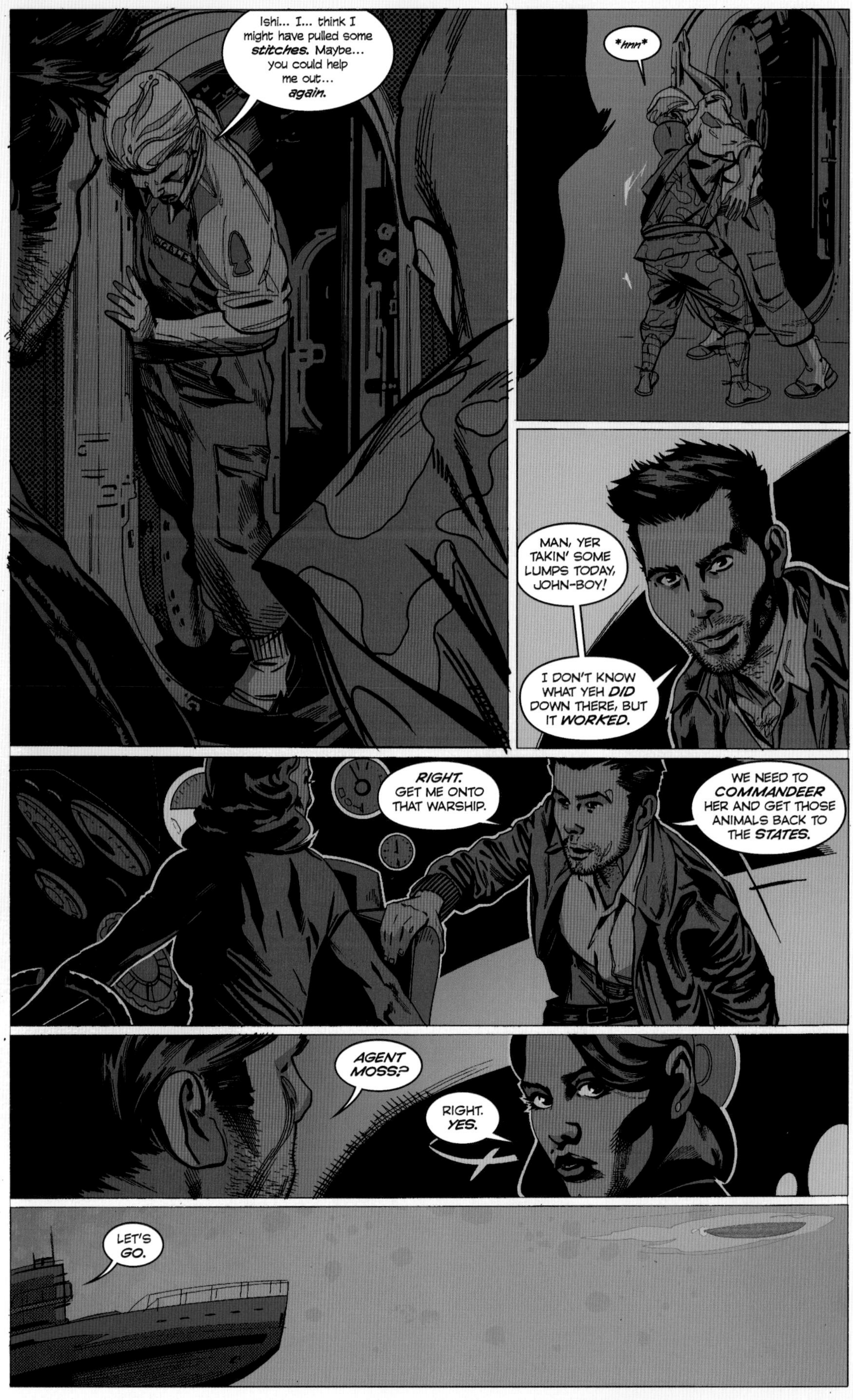
Ishi... I... think I might have pulled some stitches. Maybe... you could help me out... again.
hnn
MAN, YER TAKIN' SOME LUMPS TODAY, JOHN-BOY!
I DON'T KNOW WHAT YEH DID DOWN THERE, BUT IT WORKED.
RIGHT. GET ME ONTO THAT WARSHIP.
WE NEED TO COMMANDEER HER AND GET THOSE ANIMALS BACK TO THE STATES.
AGENT MOSS?
RIGHT. YES.
LET'S GO.

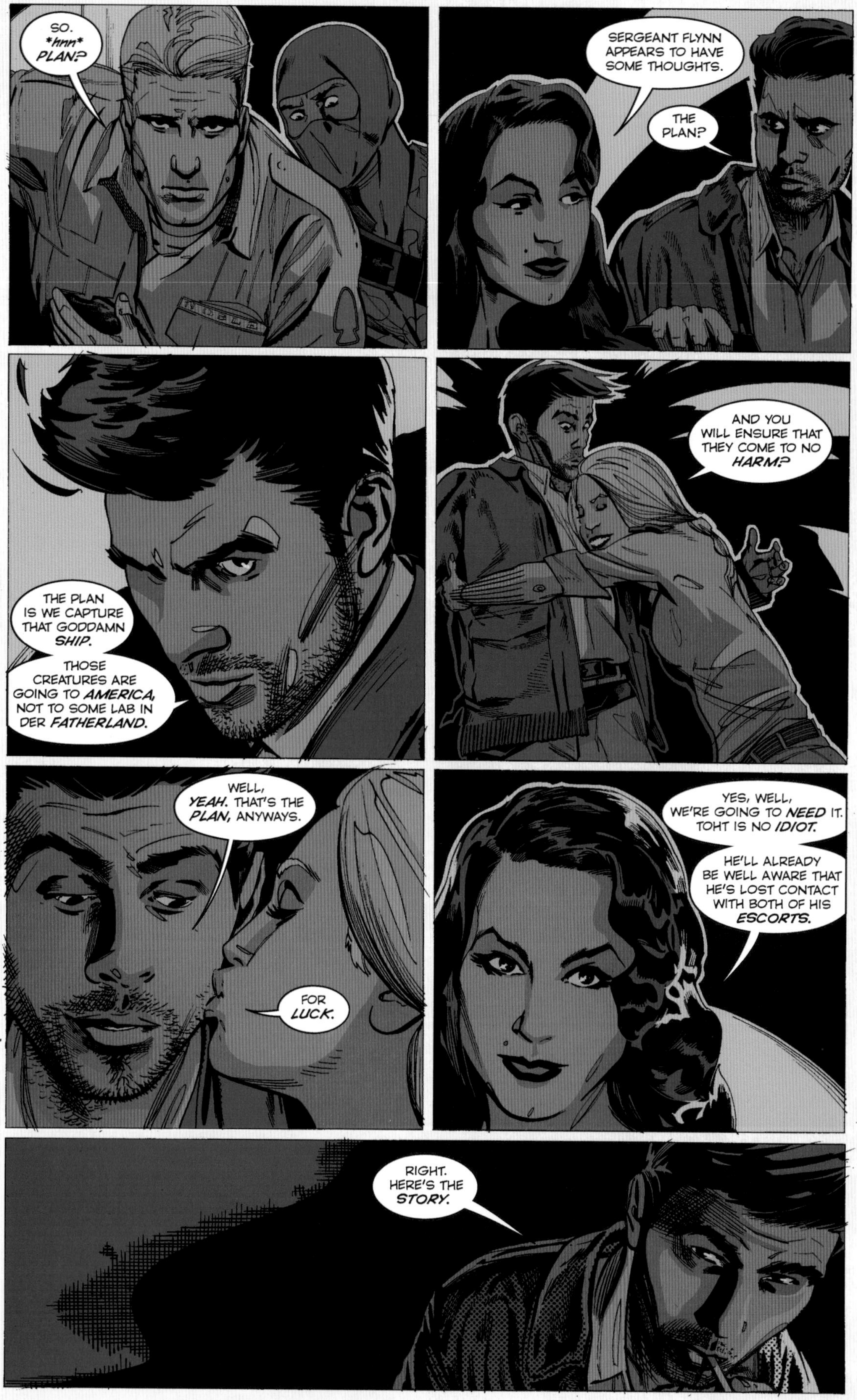
SO. *hnn* PLAN?
SERGEANT FLYNN APPEARS TO HAVE SOME THOUGHTS.
THE PLAN?
THE PLAN IS WE CAPTURE THAT GODDAMN SHIP.
THOSE CREATURES ARE GOING TO AMERICA, NOT TO SOME LAB IN DER FATHERLAND.
AND YOU WILL ENSURE THAT THEY COME TO NO HARM?
WELL, YEAH. THAT'S THE PLAN, ANYWAYS.
FOR LUCK.
YES, WELL, WE'RE GOING TO NEED IT. TOHT IS NO IDIOT.
HE'LL ALREADY BE WELL AWARE THAT HE'S LOST CONTACT WITH BOTH OF HIS ESCORTS.
RIGHT. HERE'S THE STORY.

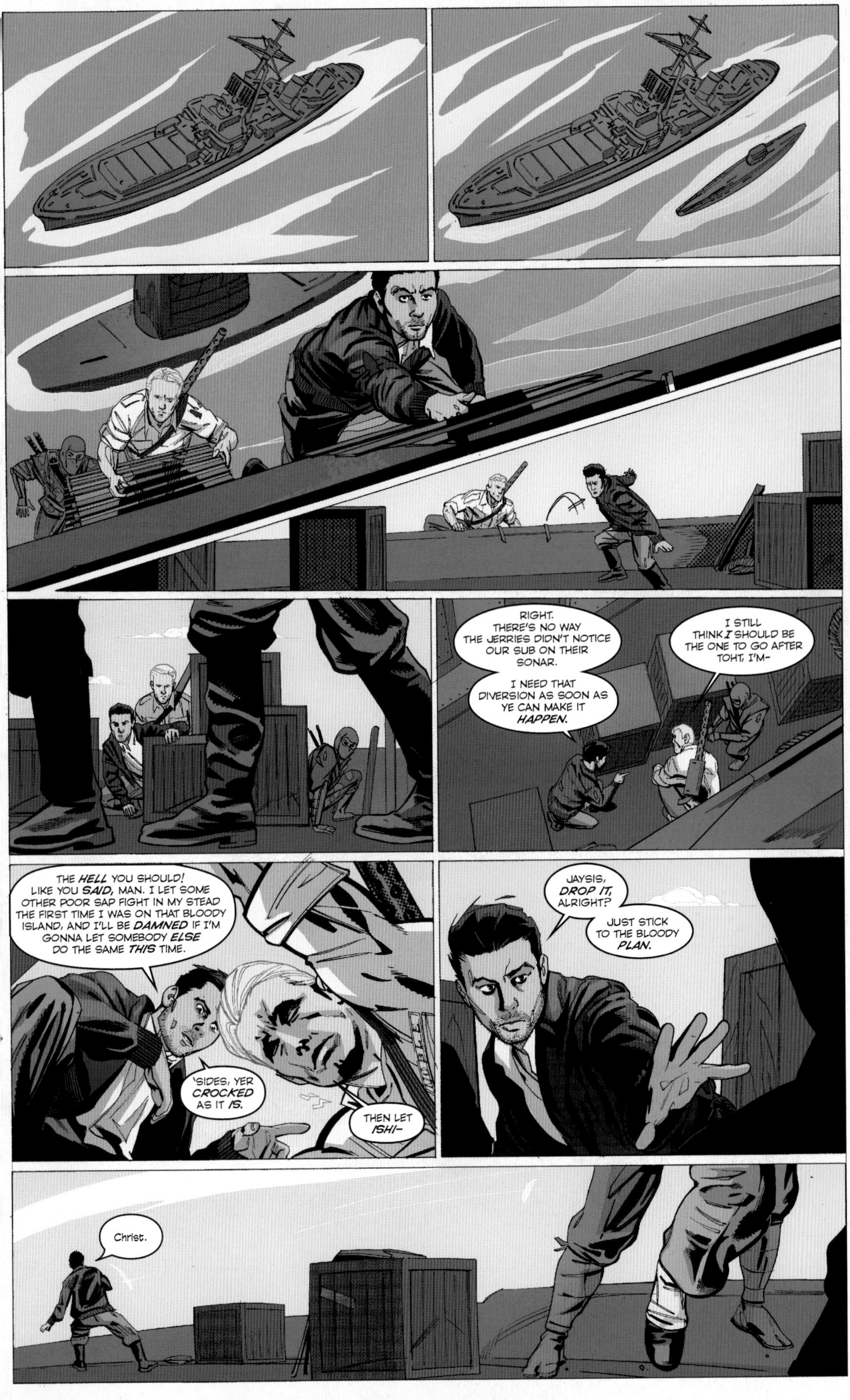
RIGHT. THERE'S NO WAY THE JERRIES DIDN'T NOTICE OUR SUB ON THEIR SONAR.
I NEED THAT DIVERSION AS SOON AS YE CAN MAKE IT HAPPEN.
I STILL THINK I SHOULD BE THE ONE TO GO AFTER TOHT, I'M-
THE HELL YOU SHOULD! LIKE YOU SAID, MAN. I LET SOME OTHER POOR SAP FIGHT IN MY STEAD THE FIRST TIME I WAS ON THAT BLOODY ISLAND, AND I'LL BE DAMNED IF I'M GONNA LET SOMEBODY ELSE DO THE SAME THIS TIME.
'SIDES, YER CROCKED AS IT IS.
THEN LET ISHI-
JAYSIS, DROP IT, ALRIGHT?
JUST STICK TO THE BLOODY PLAN.
Christ.

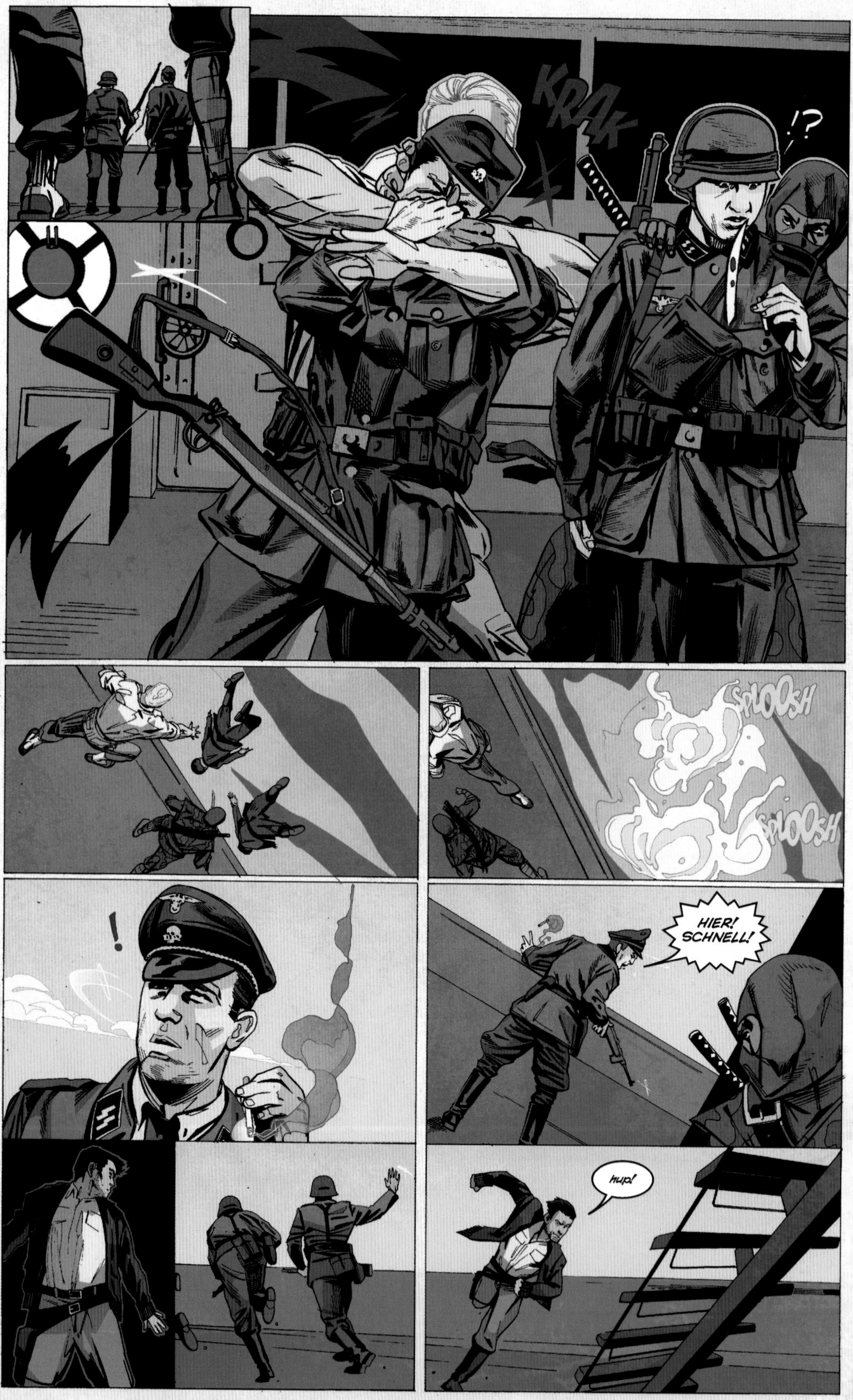
KRAK
!?
SPLOOSH
SPLOOSH
!
HIER! SCHNELL!
hup!

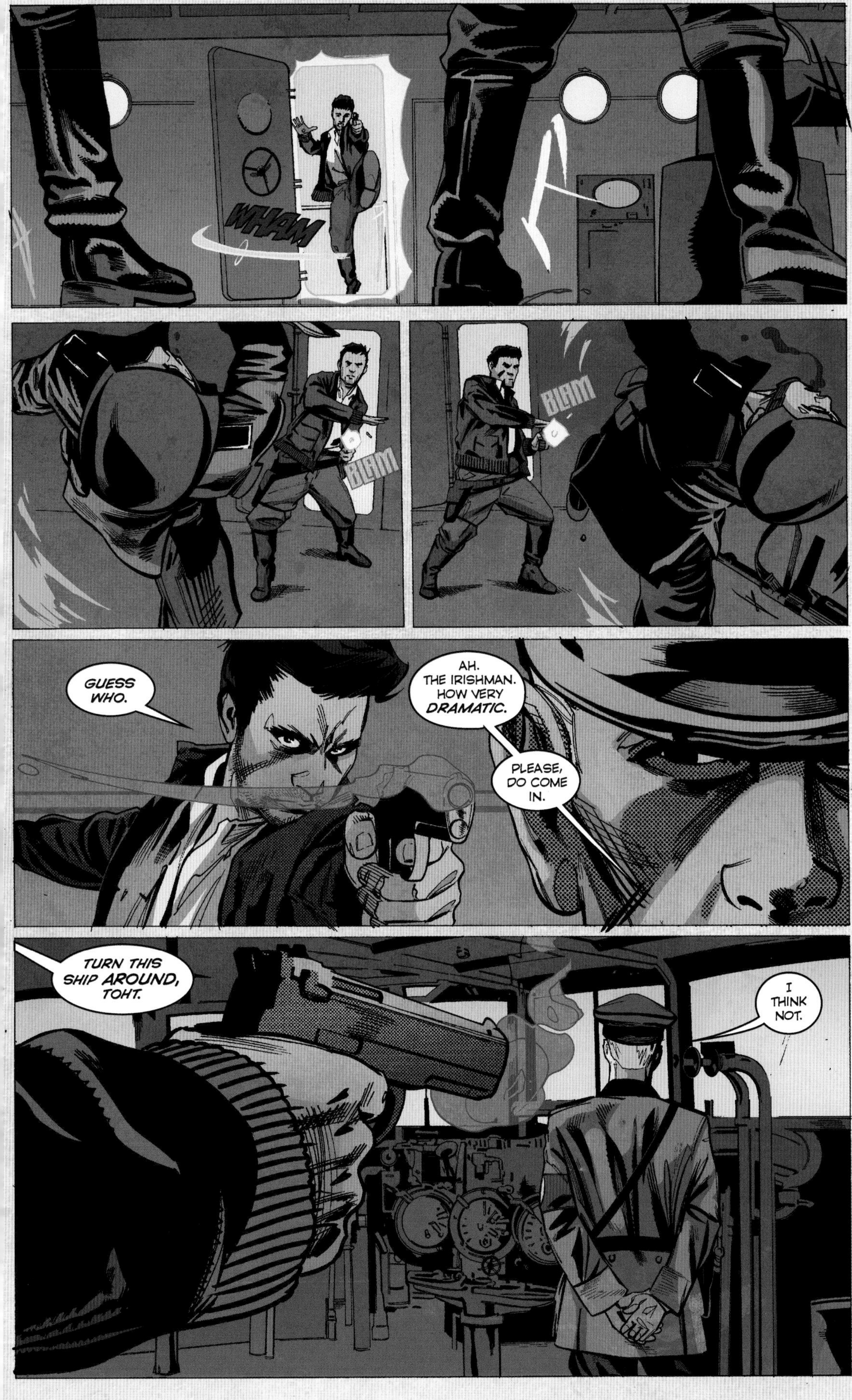
WHAM
BLAM
BLAM
GUESS WHO.
AH. THE IRISHMAN. HOW VERY *DRAMATIC*.
PLEASE, DO COME IN.
*TURN THIS SHIP **AROUND**, TOHT.*
I THINK NOT.

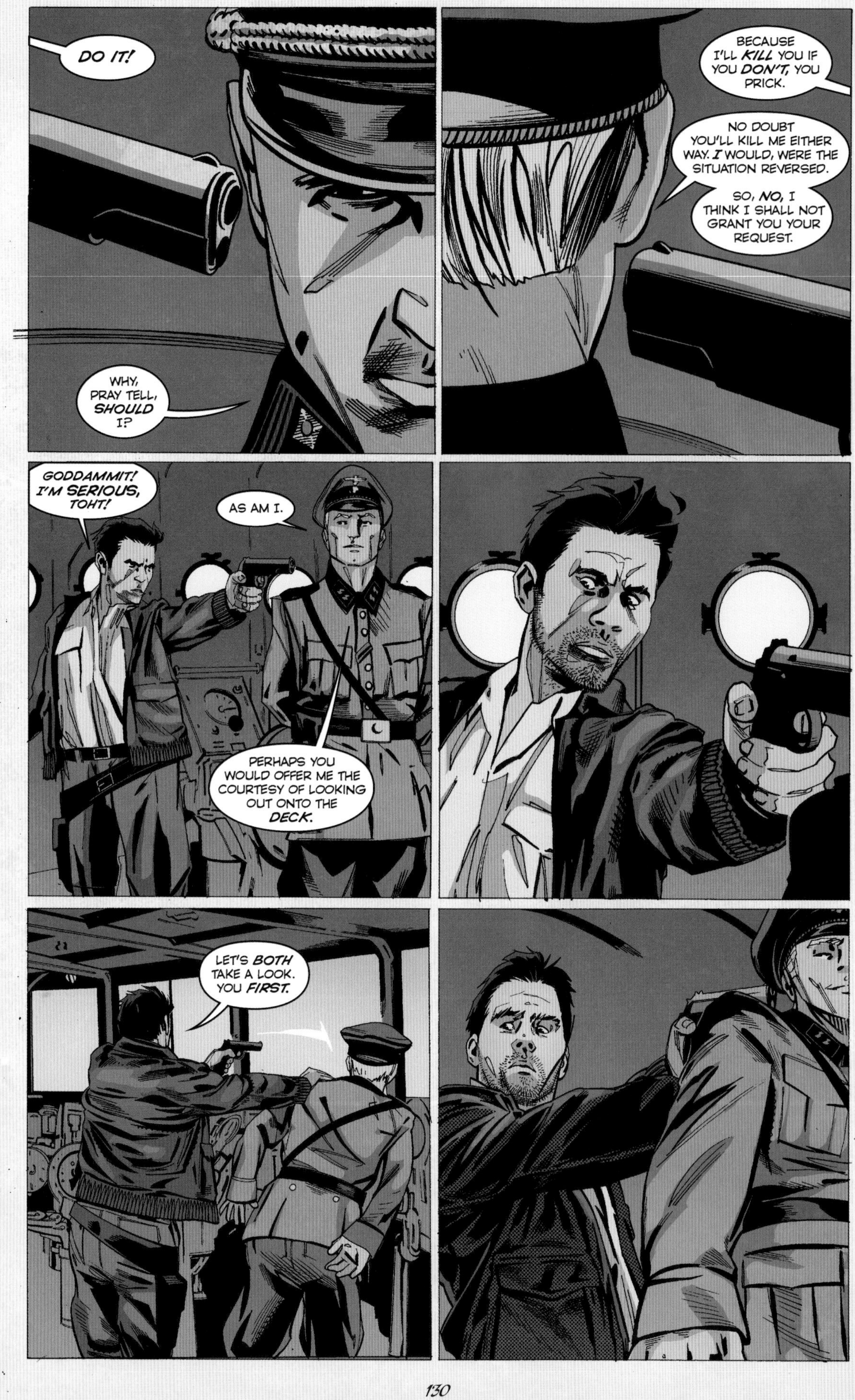
DO IT!
WHY, PRAY TELL, SHOULD I?
BECAUSE I'LL KILL YOU IF YOU DON'T, YOU PRICK.
NO DOUBT YOU'LL KILL ME EITHER WAY. I WOULD, WERE THE SITUATION REVERSED.
SO, NO, I THINK I SHALL NOT GRANT YOU YOUR REQUEST.
GODDAMMIT! I'M SERIOUS, TOHT!
AS AM I.
PERHAPS YOU WOULD OFFER ME THE COURTESY OF LOOKING OUT ONTO THE DECK.
LET'S BOTH TAKE A LOOK. YOU FIRST.

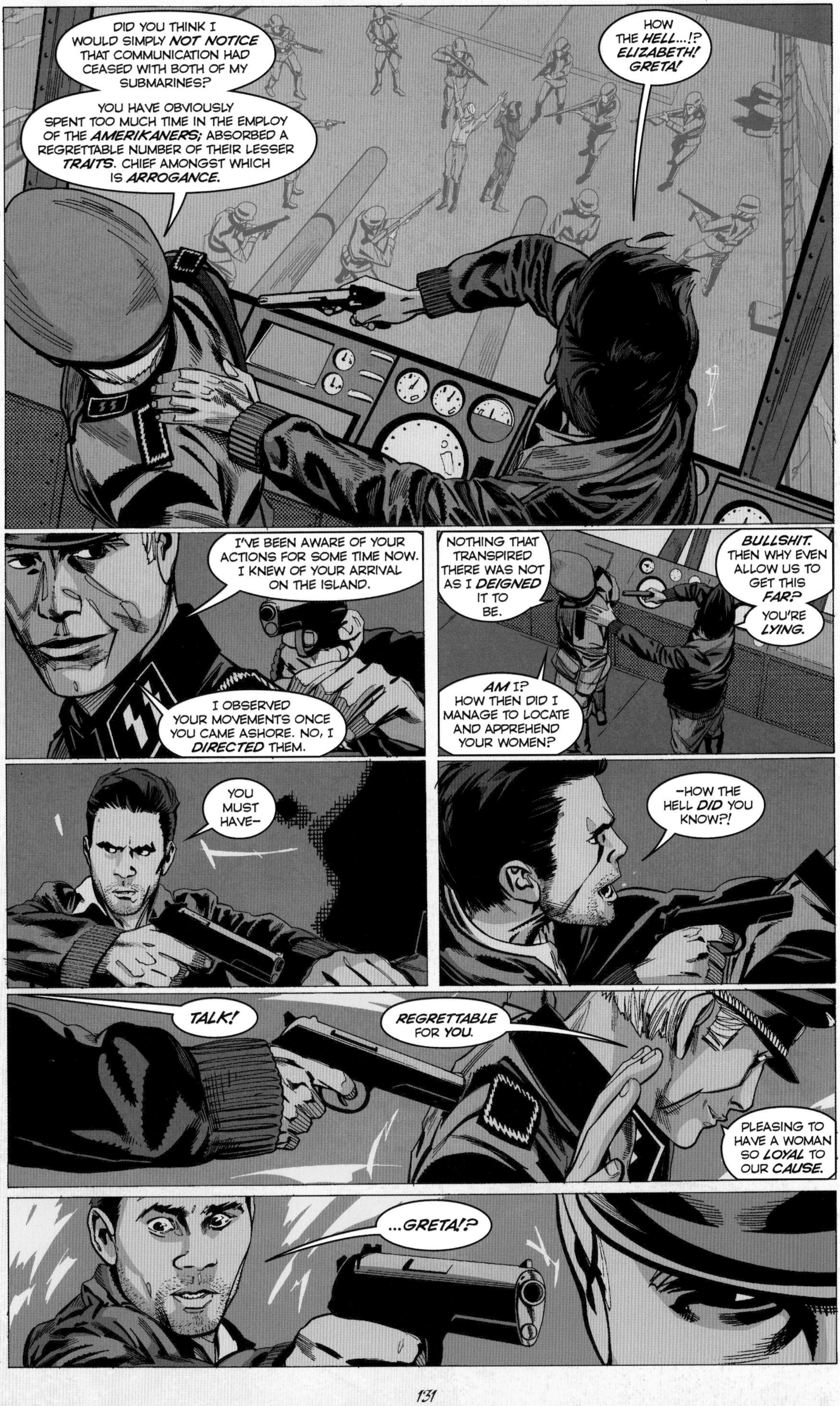
DID YOU THINK I WOULD SIMPLY NOT NOTICE THAT COMMUNICATION HAD CEASED WITH BOTH OF MY SUBMARINES?
YOU HAVE OBVIOUSLY SPENT TOO MUCH TIME IN THE EMPLOY OF THE AMERIKANERS; ABSORBED A REGRETTABLE NUMBER OF THEIR LESSER TRAITS. CHIEF AMONGST WHICH IS ARROGANCE.
HOW THE HELL...!? ELIZABETH! GRETA!
I'VE BEEN AWARE OF YOUR ACTIONS FOR SOME TIME NOW. I KNEW OF YOUR ARRIVAL ON THE ISLAND.
I OBSERVED YOUR MOVEMENTS ONCE YOU CAME ASHORE. NO, I DIRECTED THEM.
NOTHING THAT TRANSPIRED THERE WAS NOT AS I DEIGNED IT TO BE.
BULLSHIT. THEN WHY EVEN ALLOW US TO GET THIS FAR?
YOU'RE LYING.
AM I? HOW THEN DID I MANAGE TO LOCATE AND APPREHEND YOUR WOMEN?
YOU MUST HAVE-
-HOW THE HELL DID YOU KNOW?!
TALK!
REGRETTABLE FOR YOU.
PLEASING TO HAVE A WOMAN SO LOYAL TO OUR CAUSE.
...GRETA!?

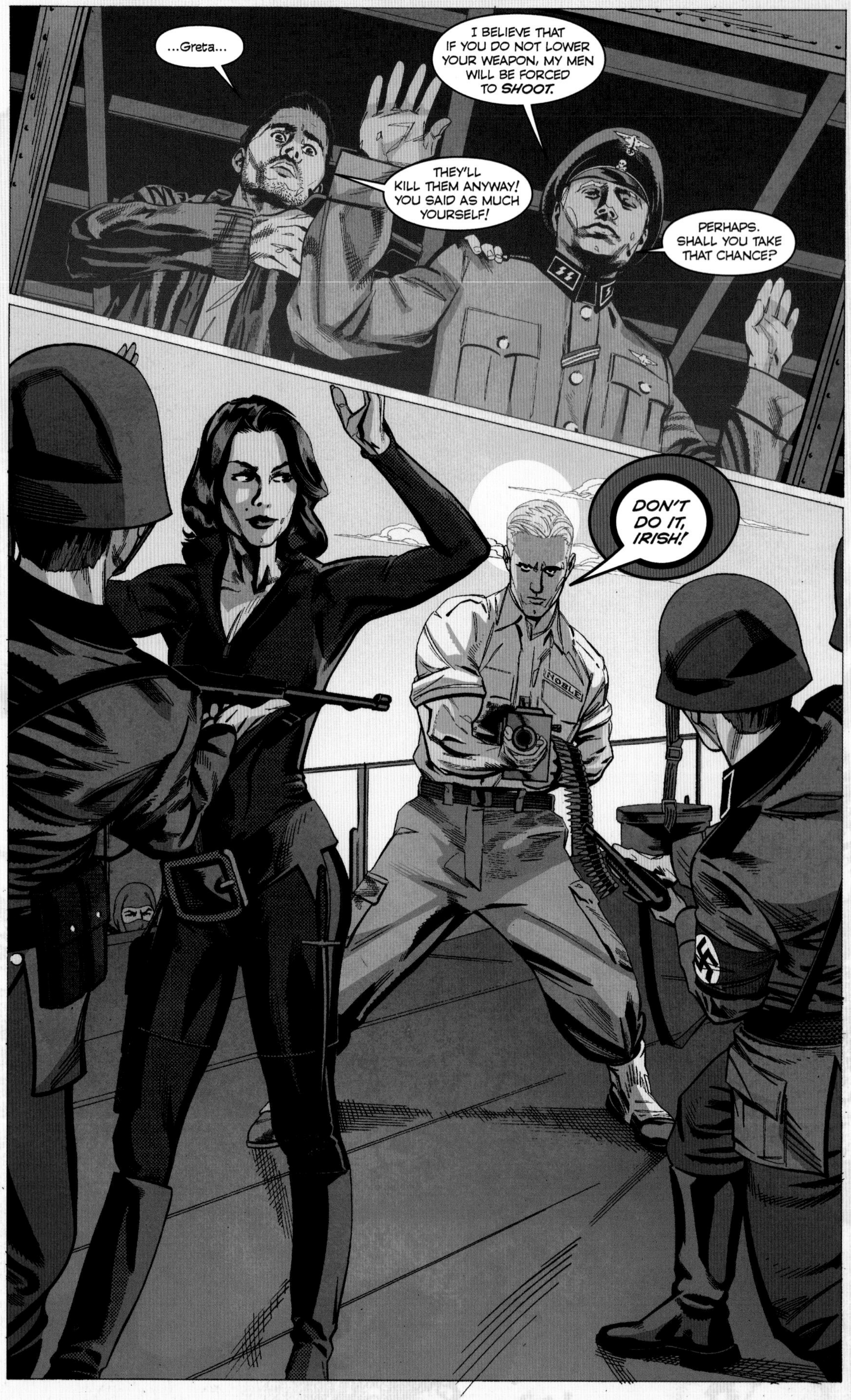
...Greta...
I BELIEVE THAT IF YOU DO NOT LOWER YOUR WEAPON, MY MEN WILL BE FORCED TO *SHOOT*.
THEY'LL KILL THEM ANYWAY! YOU SAID AS MUCH YOURSELF!
PERHAPS. SHALL YOU TAKE THAT CHANCE?
NOBLE
DON'T DO IT, IRISH!

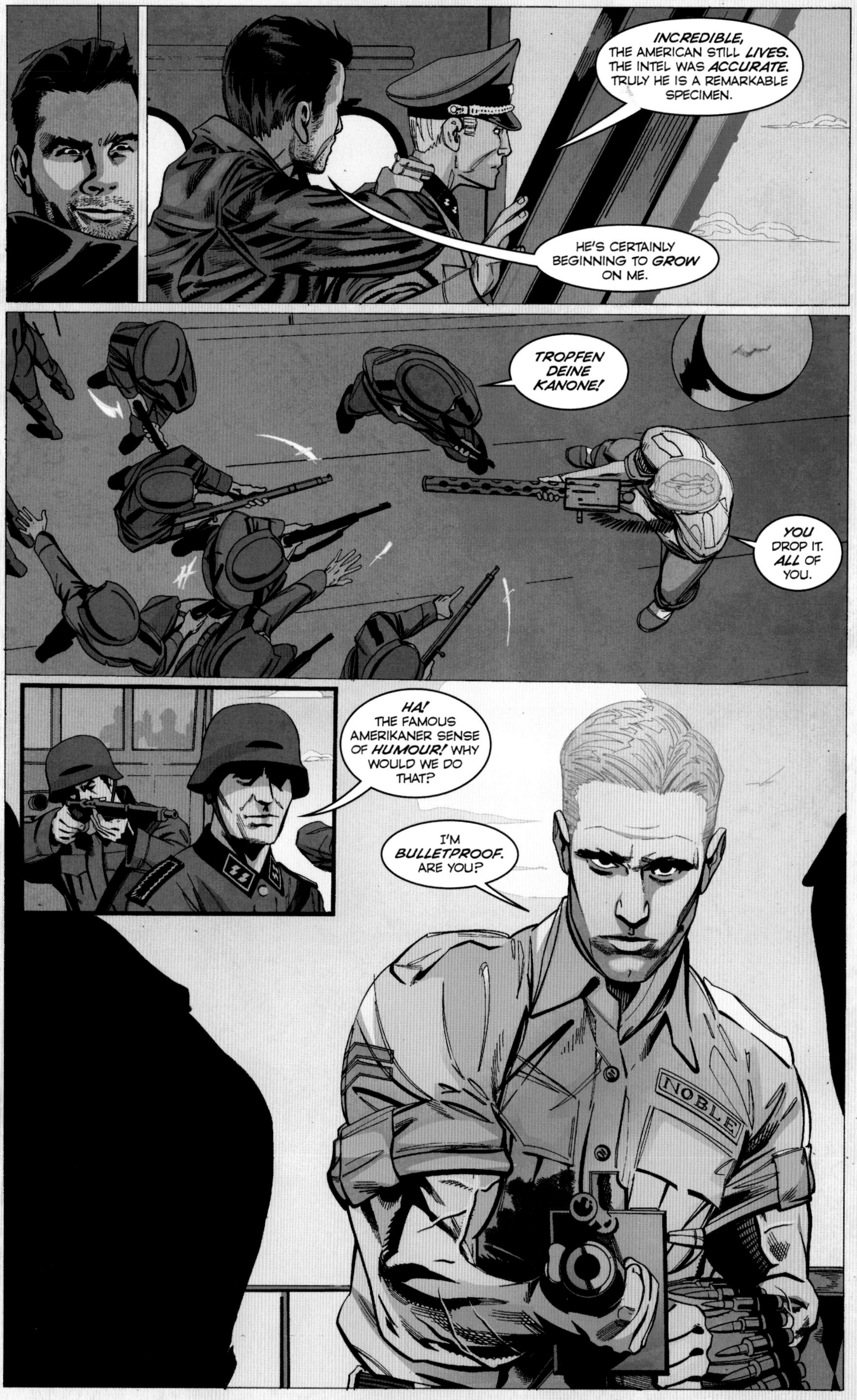

INCREDIBLE, THE AMERICAN STILL LIVES. THE INTEL WAS ACCURATE. TRULY HE IS A REMARKABLE SPECIMEN.
HE'S CERTAINLY BEGINNING TO GROW ON ME.
TROPFEN DEINE KANONE!
YOU DROP IT. ALL OF YOU.
HA! THE FAMOUS AMERIKANER SENSE OF HUMOUR! WHY WOULD WE DO THAT?
I'M BULLETPROOF. ARE YOU?
NOBLE

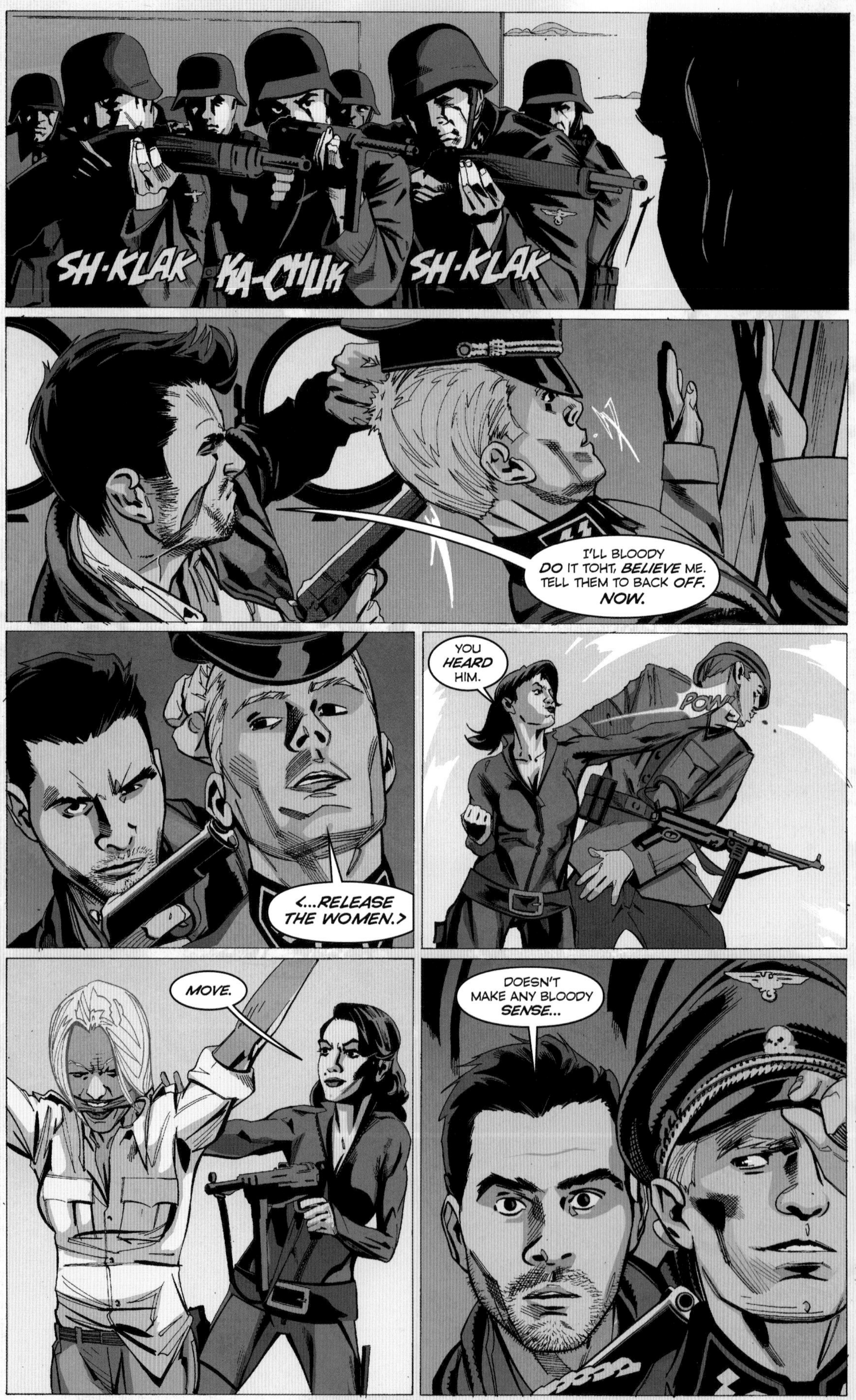
SH-KLAK KA-CHUK SH-KLAK
I'LL BLOODY DO IT TOHT, BELIEVE ME. TELL THEM TO BACK OFF. NOW.
<...RELEASE THE WOMEN.>
YOU HEARD HIM.
POW
MOVE.
DOESN'T MAKE ANY BLOODY SENSE...

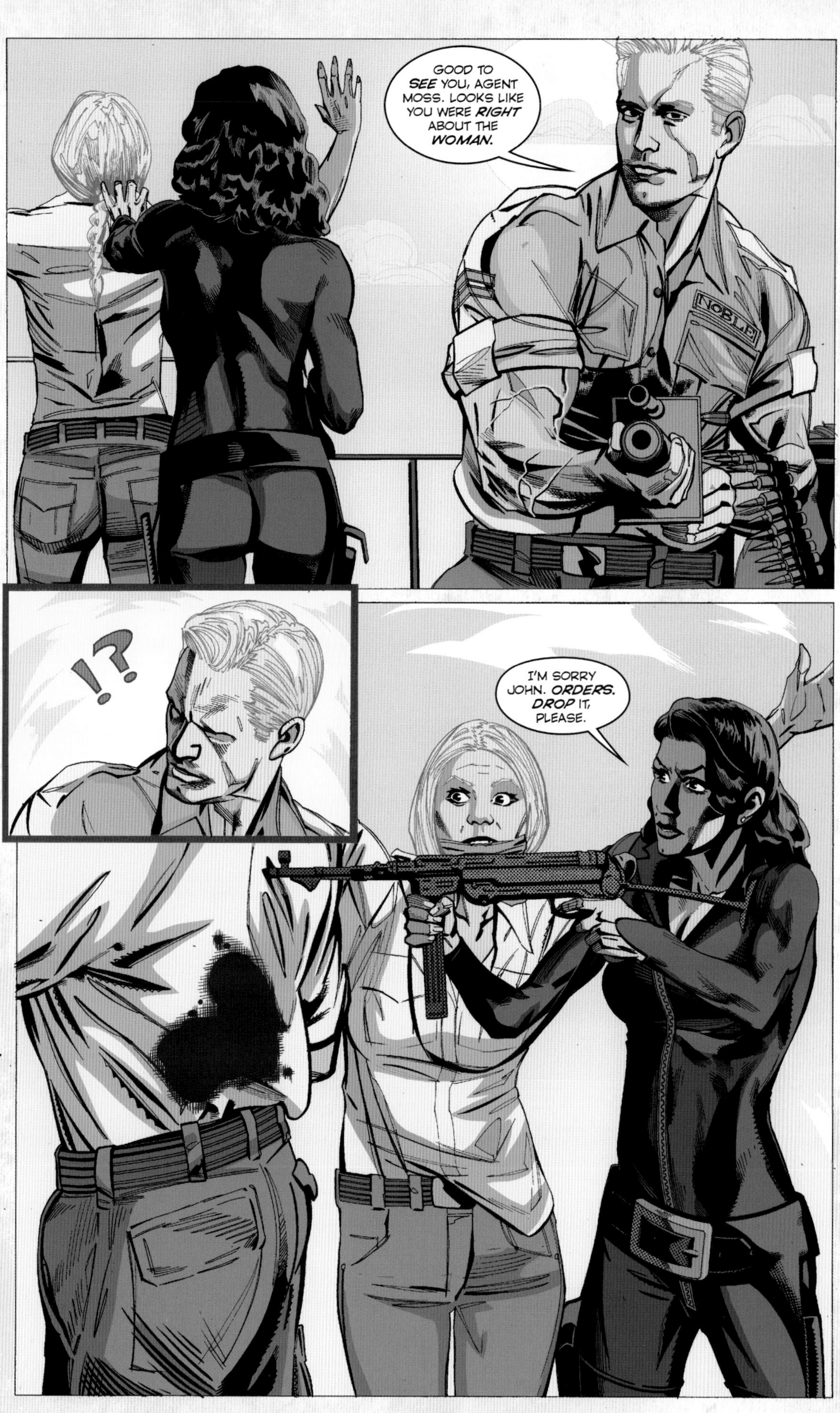
GOOD TO SEE YOU, AGENT MOSS. LOOKS LIKE YOU WERE RIGHT ABOUT THE WOMAN.
NOBLE
!?
I'M SORRY JOHN. ORDERS. DROP IT, PLEASE.

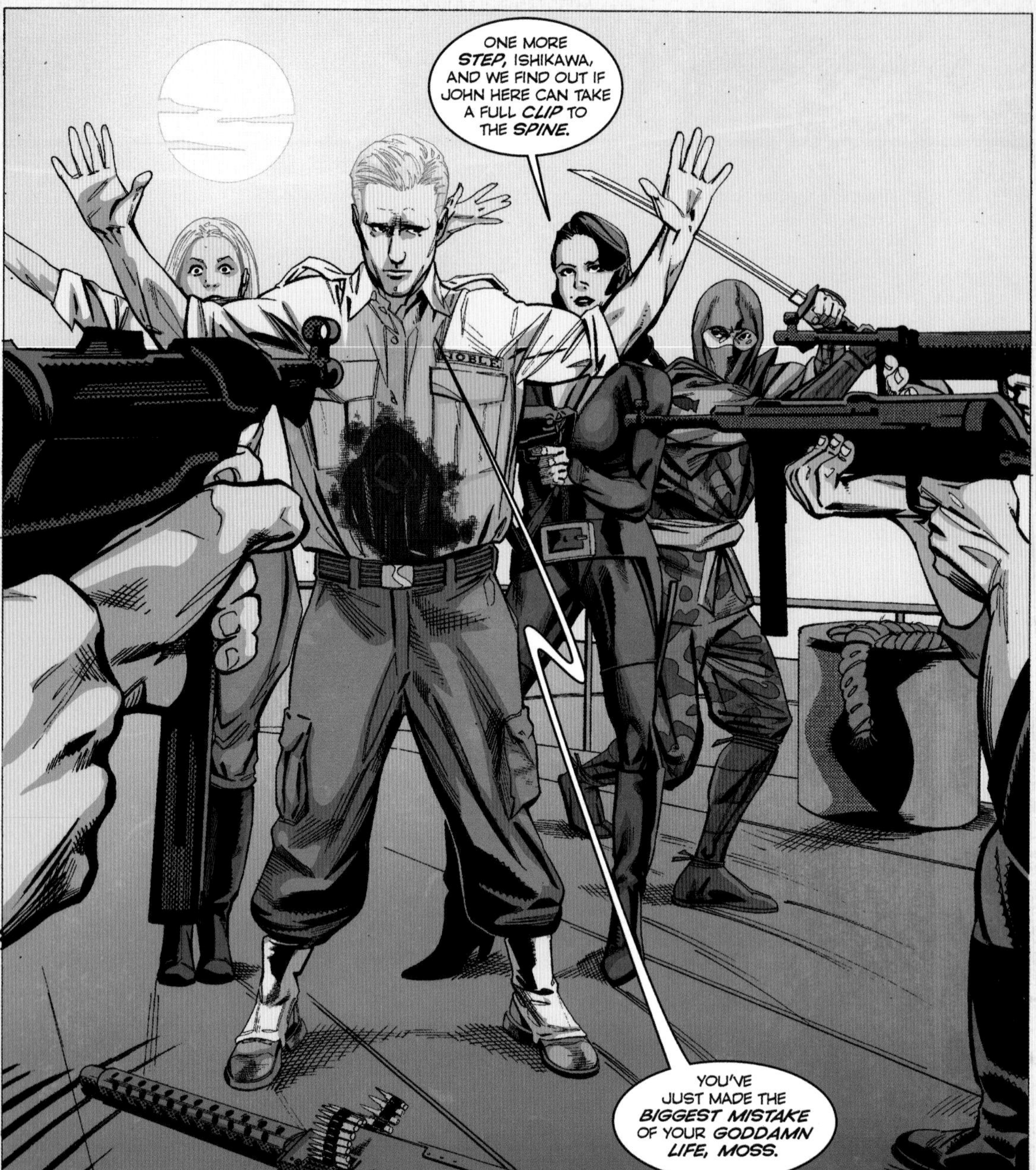
ONE MORE STEP, ISHIKAWA, AND WE FIND OUT IF JOHN HERE CAN TAKE A FULL CLIP TO THE SPINE.
YOU'VE JUST MADE THE BIGGEST MISTAKE OF YOUR GODDAMN LIFE, MOSS.

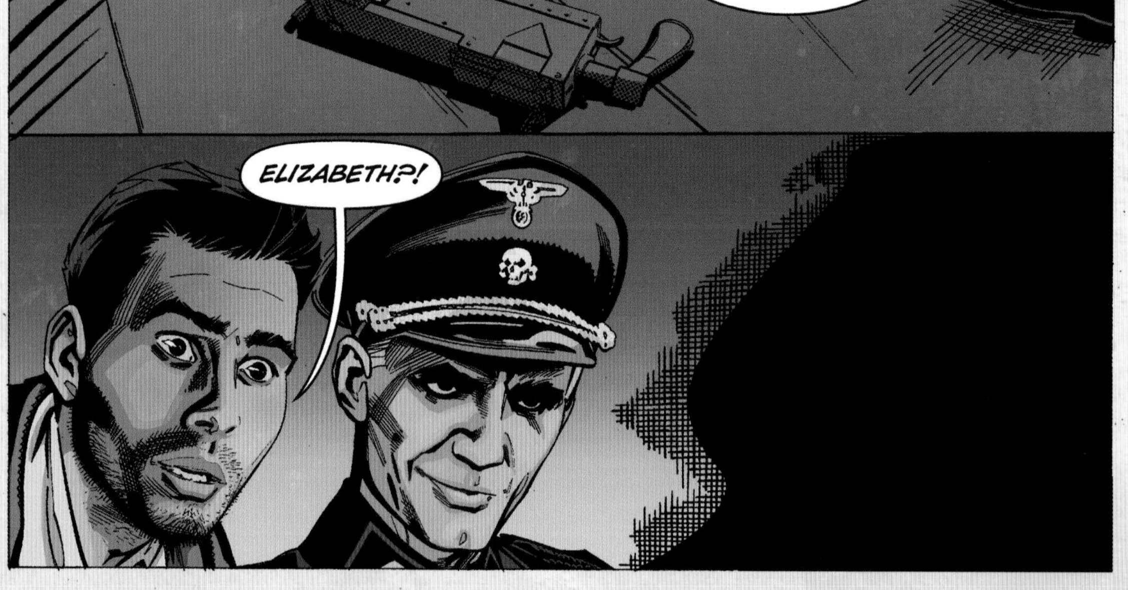
ELIZABETH?!

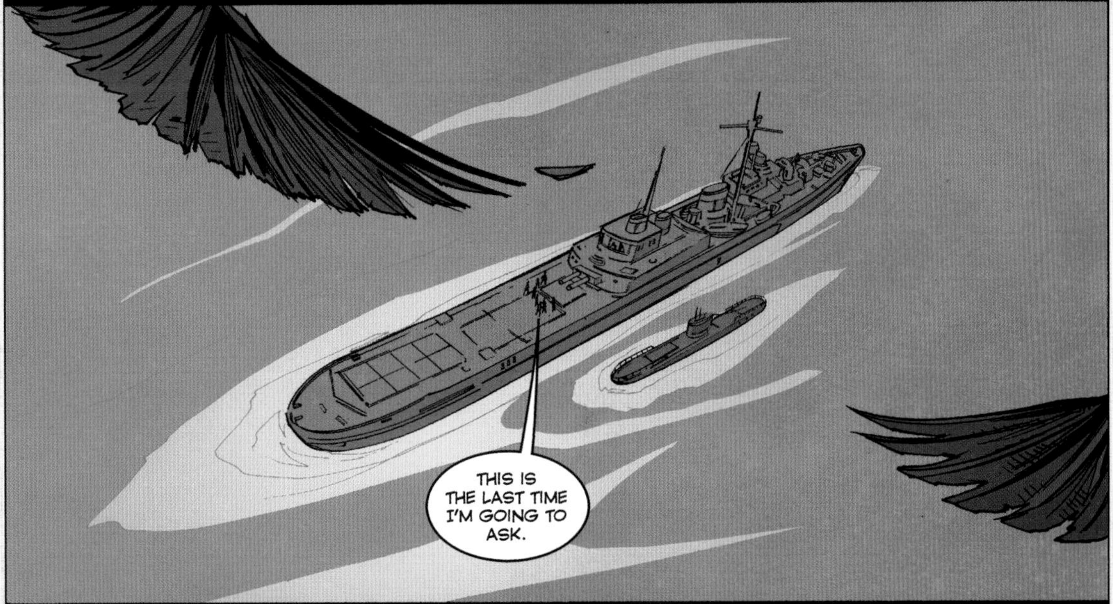
THIS IS THE LAST TIME I'M GOING TO ASK.

Chapter Six

KILLING WITH KINDNESS

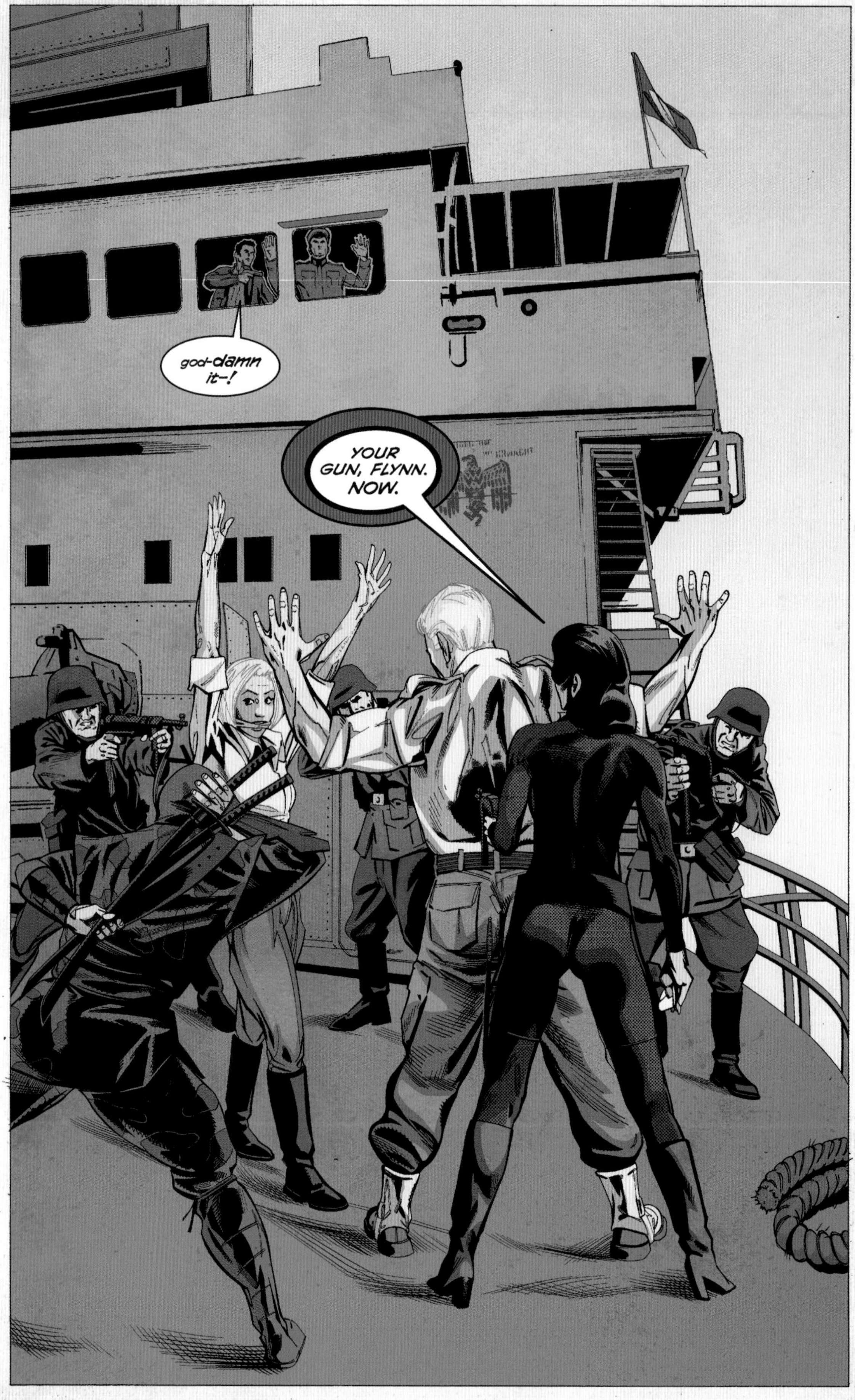
god-damn it-!
YOUR GUN, FLYNN. NOW.

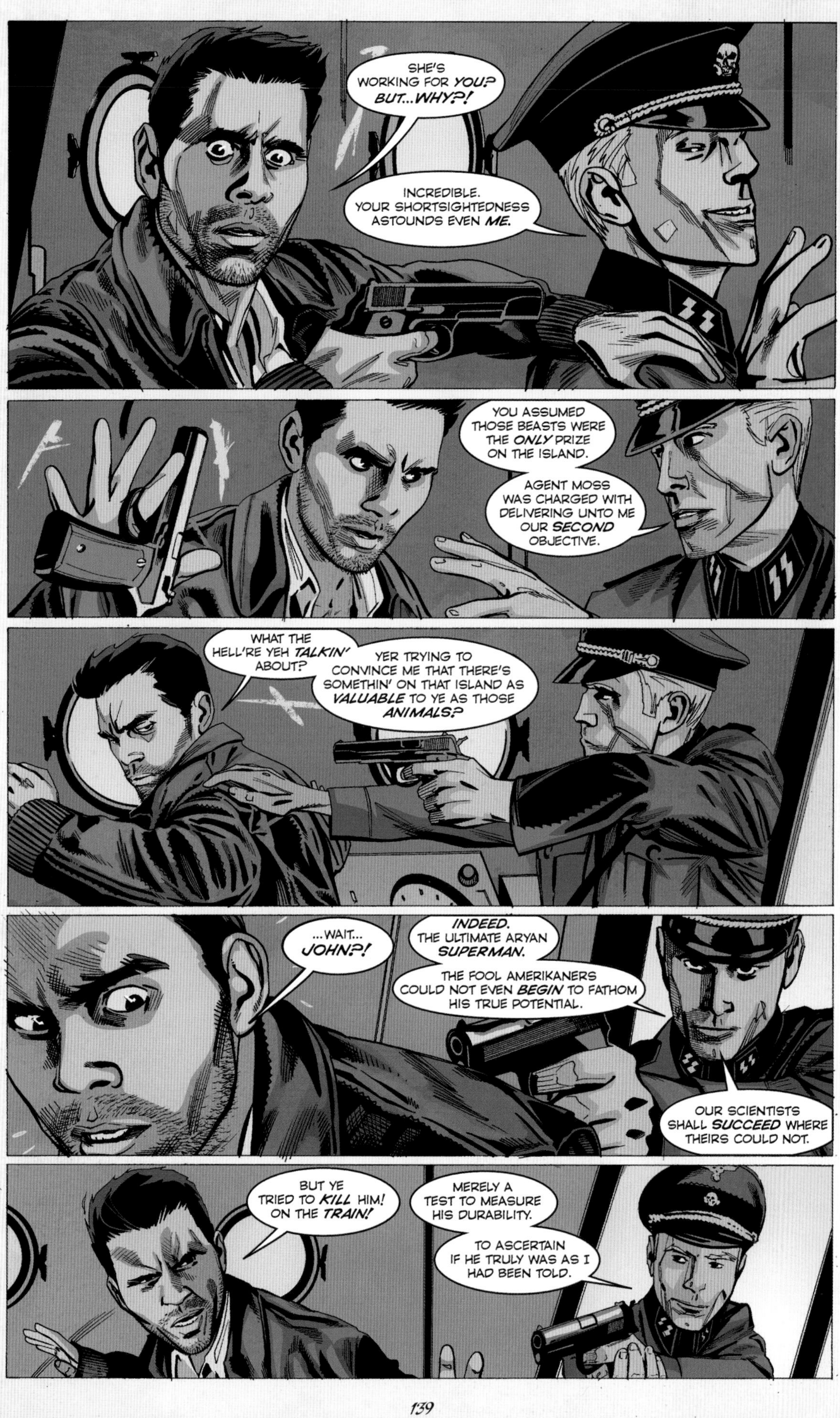
SHE'S WORKING FOR YOU? BUT...WHY?!
INCREDIBLE. YOUR SHORTSIGHTEDNESS ASTOUNDS EVEN ME.
YOU ASSUMED THOSE BEASTS WERE THE ONLY PRIZE ON THE ISLAND.
AGENT MOSS WAS CHARGED WITH DELIVERING UNTO ME OUR SECOND OBJECTIVE.
WHAT THE HELL'RE YEH TALKIN' ABOUT?
YER TRYING TO CONVINCE ME THAT THERE'S SOMETHIN' ON THAT ISLAND AS VALUABLE TO YE AS THOSE ANIMALS?
...WAIT... JOHN?!
INDEED. THE ULTIMATE ARYAN SUPERMAN.
THE FOOL AMERIKANERS COULD NOT EVEN BEGIN TO FATHOM HIS TRUE POTENTIAL.
OUR SCIENTISTS SHALL SUCCEED WHERE THEIRS COULD NOT.
BUT YE TRIED TO KILL HIM! ON THE TRAIN!
MERELY A TEST TO MEASURE HIS DURABILITY.
TO ASCERTAIN IF HE TRULY WAS AS I HAD BEEN TOLD.

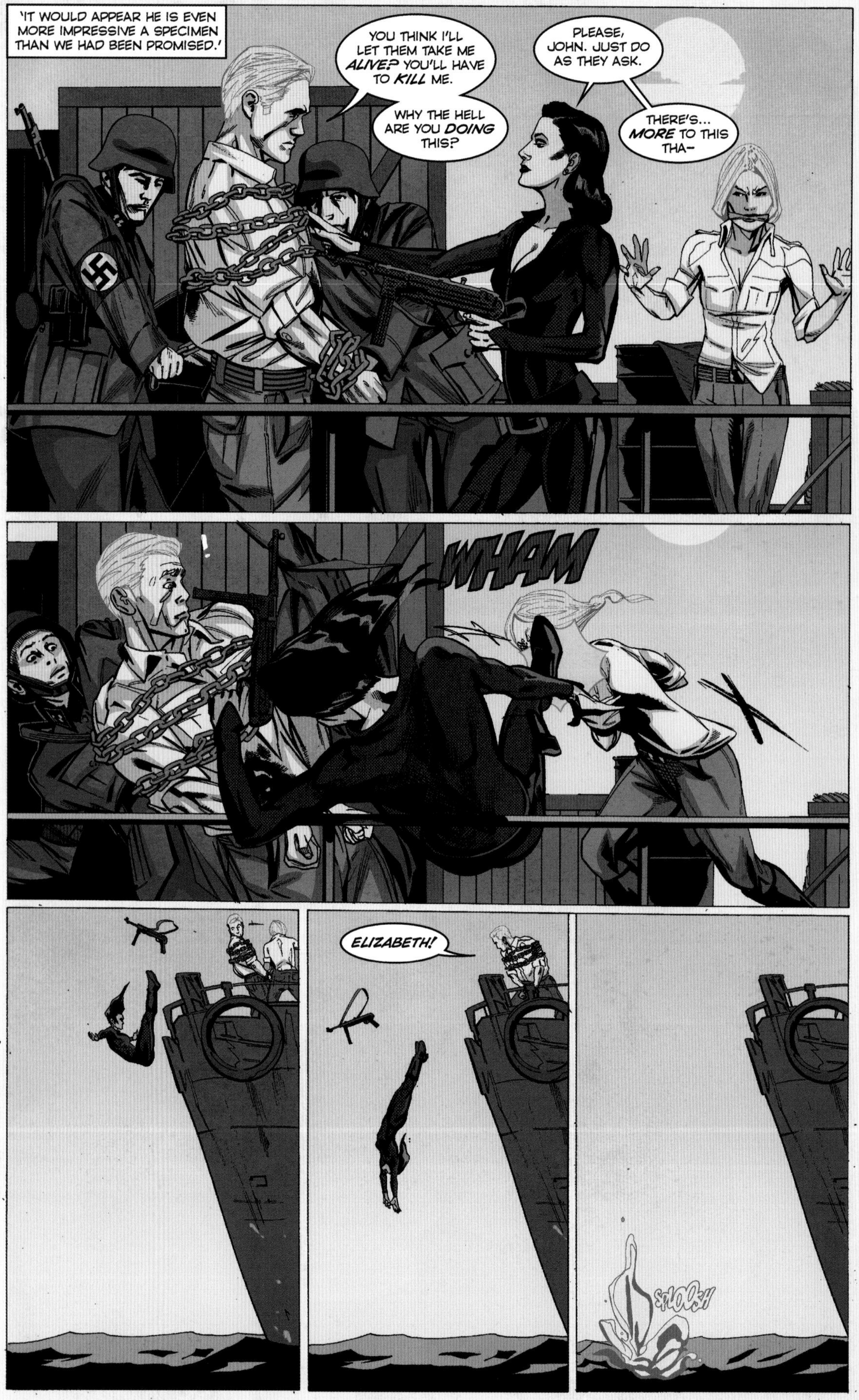
'IT WOULD APPEAR HE IS EVEN MORE IMPRESSIVE A SPECIMEN THAN WE HAD BEEN PROMISED.'
YOU THINK I'LL LET THEM TAKE ME ALIVE? YOU'LL HAVE TO KILL ME.
WHY THE HELL ARE YOU DOING THIS?
PLEASE, JOHN. JUST DO AS THEY ASK.
THERE'S... MORE TO THIS THA-
!
WHAM
ELIZABETH!
SPLOOSH

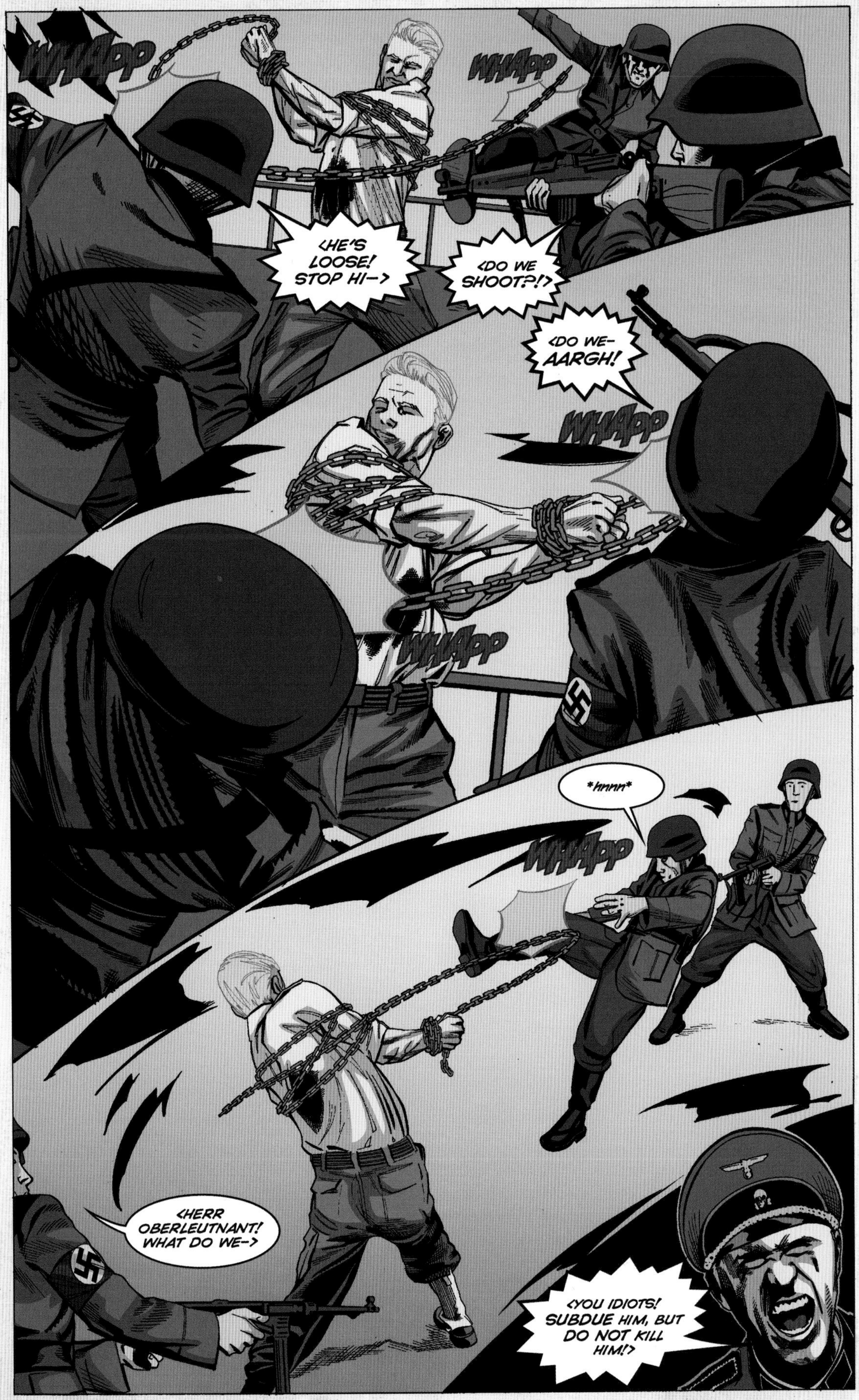
WHAPP
WHAPP
<HE'S LOOSE! STOP HI–>
<DO WE SHOOT?!>
<DO WE– AARGH!
WHAPP
WHAPP
hnnn
WHAPP
<HERR OBERLEUTNANT! WHAT DO WE–>
<YOU IDIOTS! SUBDUE HIM, BUT DO NOT KILL HIM!>

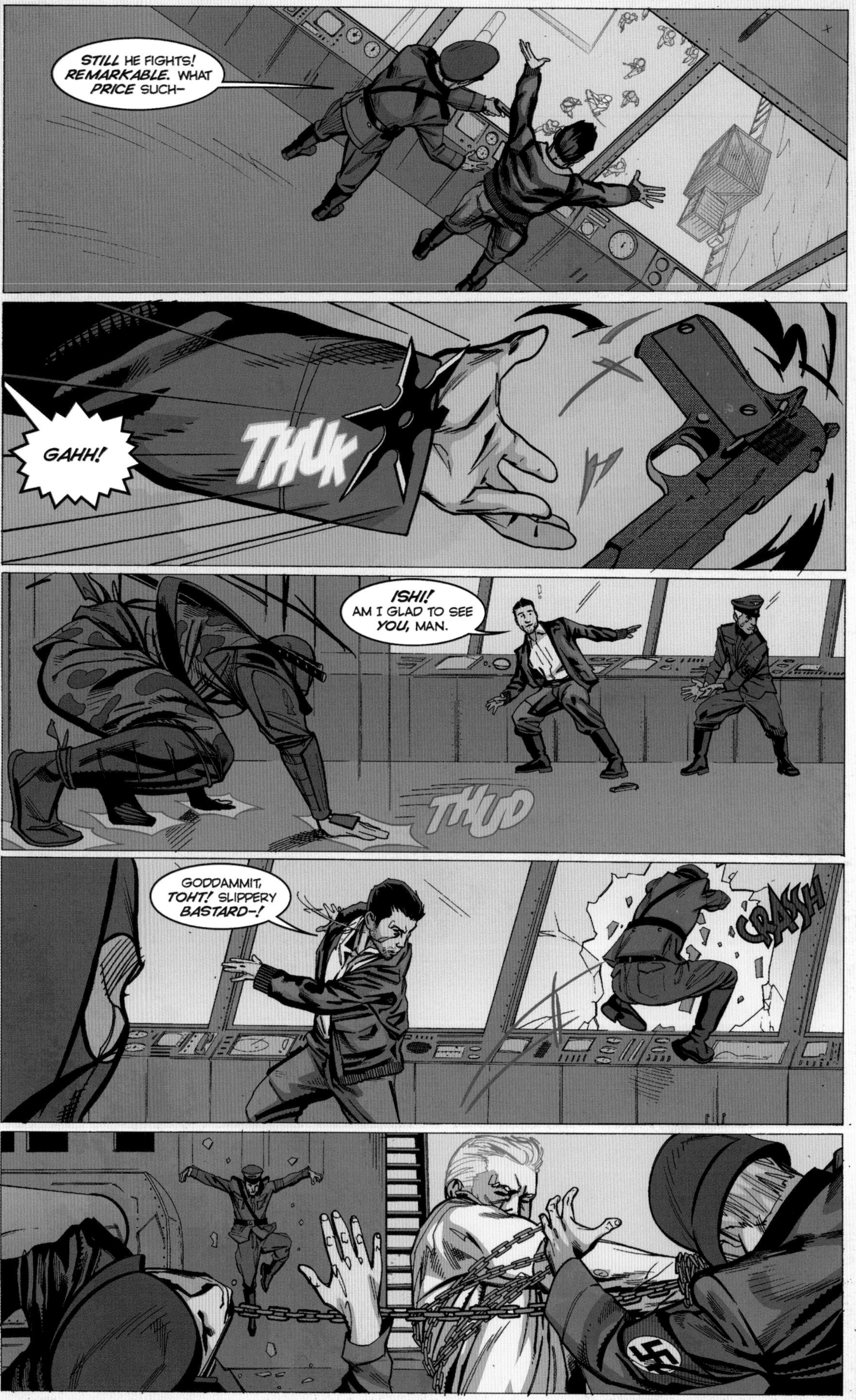
STILL HE FIGHTS! REMARKABLE. WHAT PRICE SUCH-
GAHH!
THUK
ISHI! AM I GLAD TO SEE YOU, MAN.
THUD
GODDAMMIT, TOHT! SLIPPERY BASTARD-!
CRASH

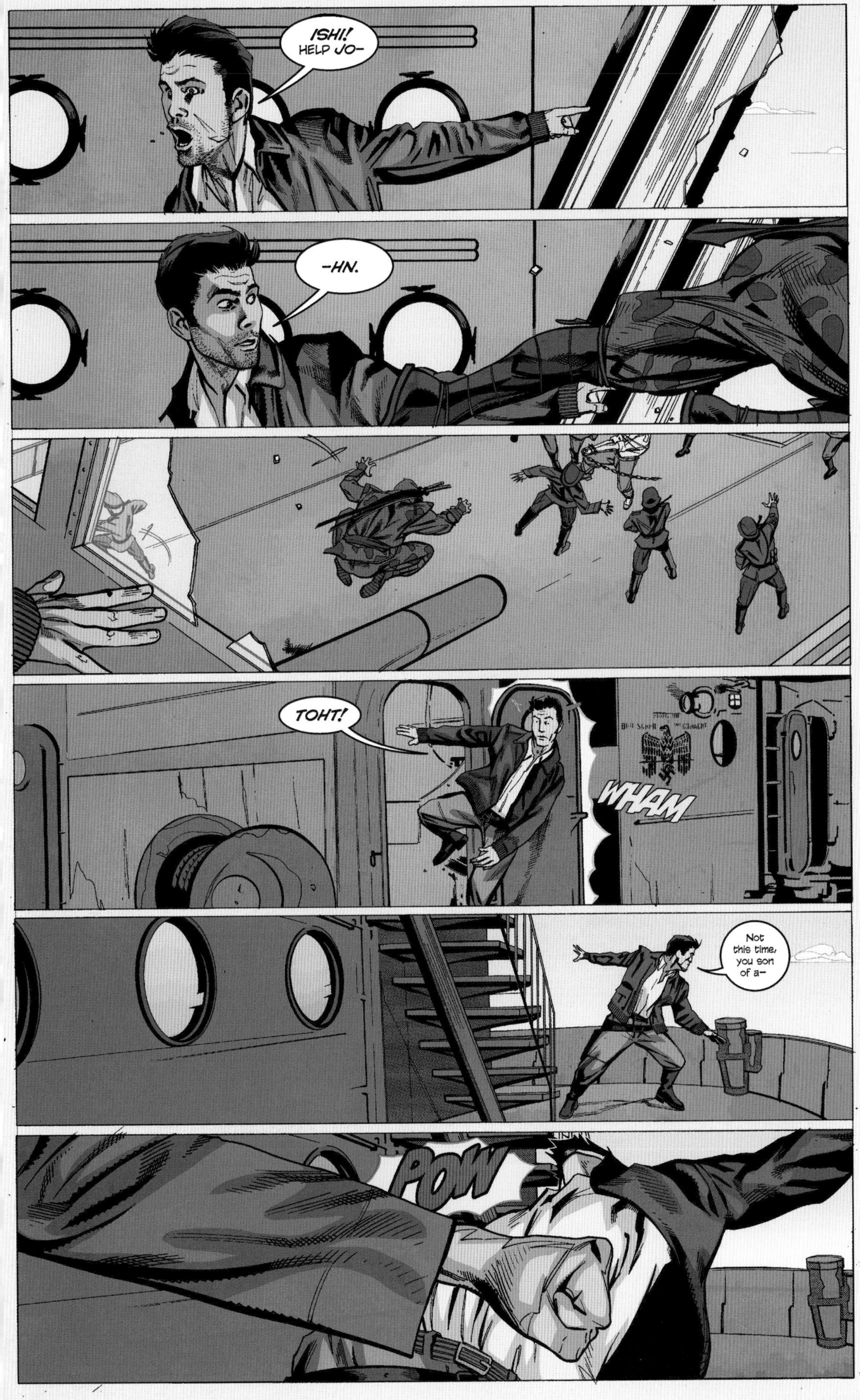
ISHI! HELP JO-
-HN.
TOHT!
WHAM
Not this time, you son of a-
POW

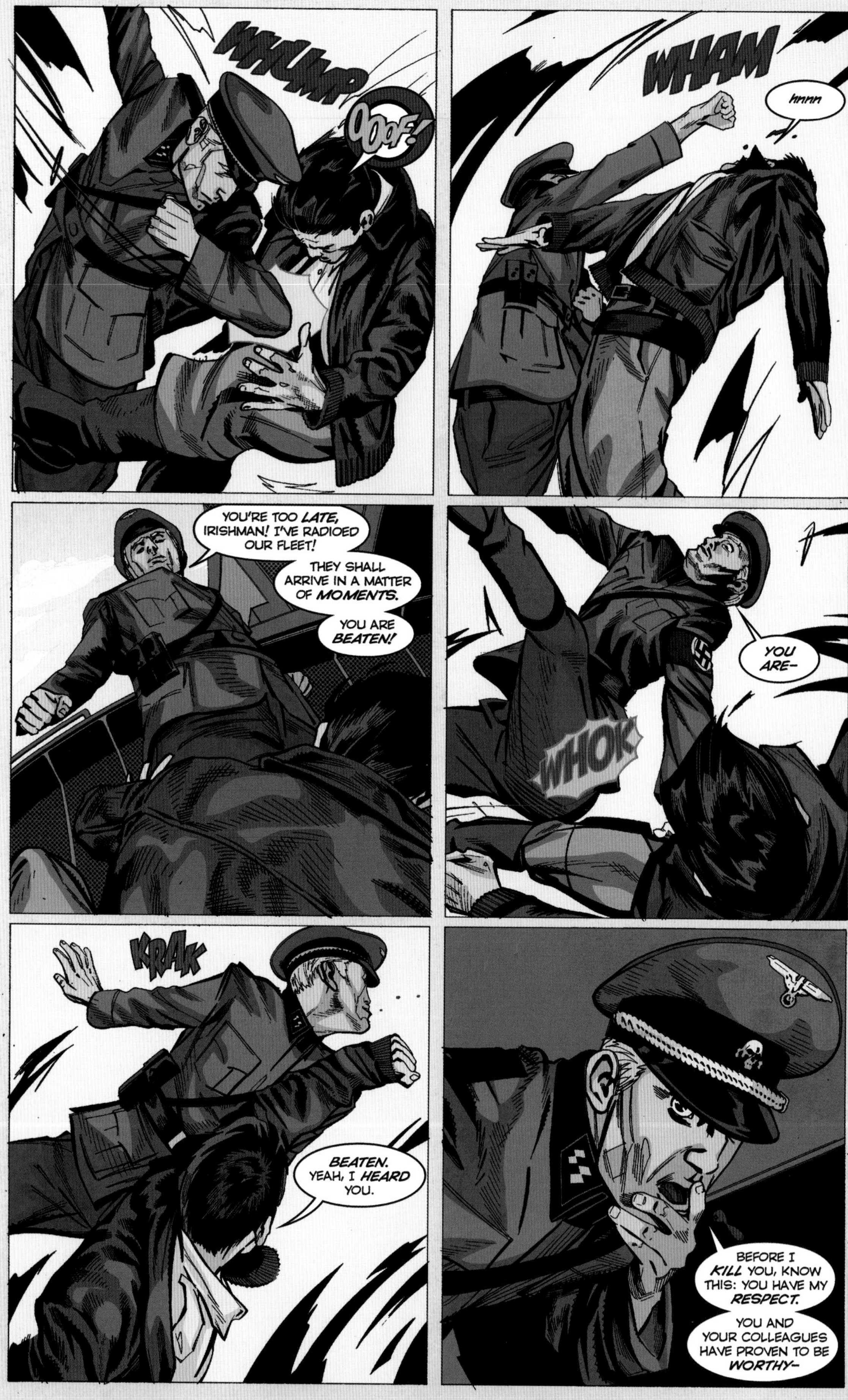
WHUMP
OOOF!
WHAM
hnnn
YOU'RE TOO LATE, IRISHMAN! I'VE RADIOED OUR FLEET!
THEY SHALL ARRIVE IN A MATTER OF MOMENTS.
YOU ARE BEATEN!
YOU ARE–
WHOK
KRAK
BEATEN. YEAH, I HEARD YOU.
BEFORE I KILL YOU, KNOW THIS: YOU HAVE MY RESPECT.
YOU AND YOUR COLLEAGUES HAVE PROVEN TO BE WORTHY–

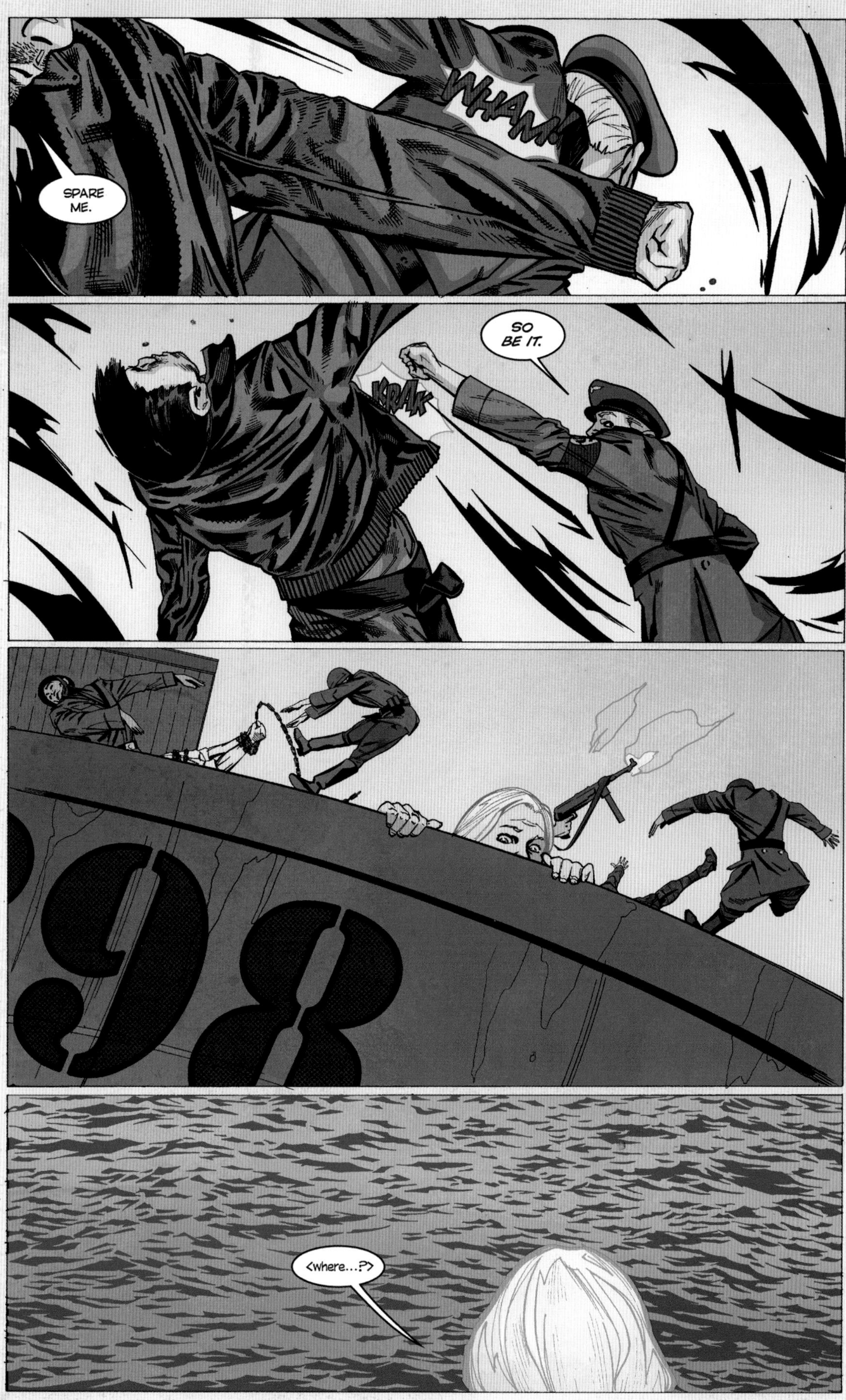
WHAM!
SPARE ME.
SO BE IT.
KRAK
<where...?>

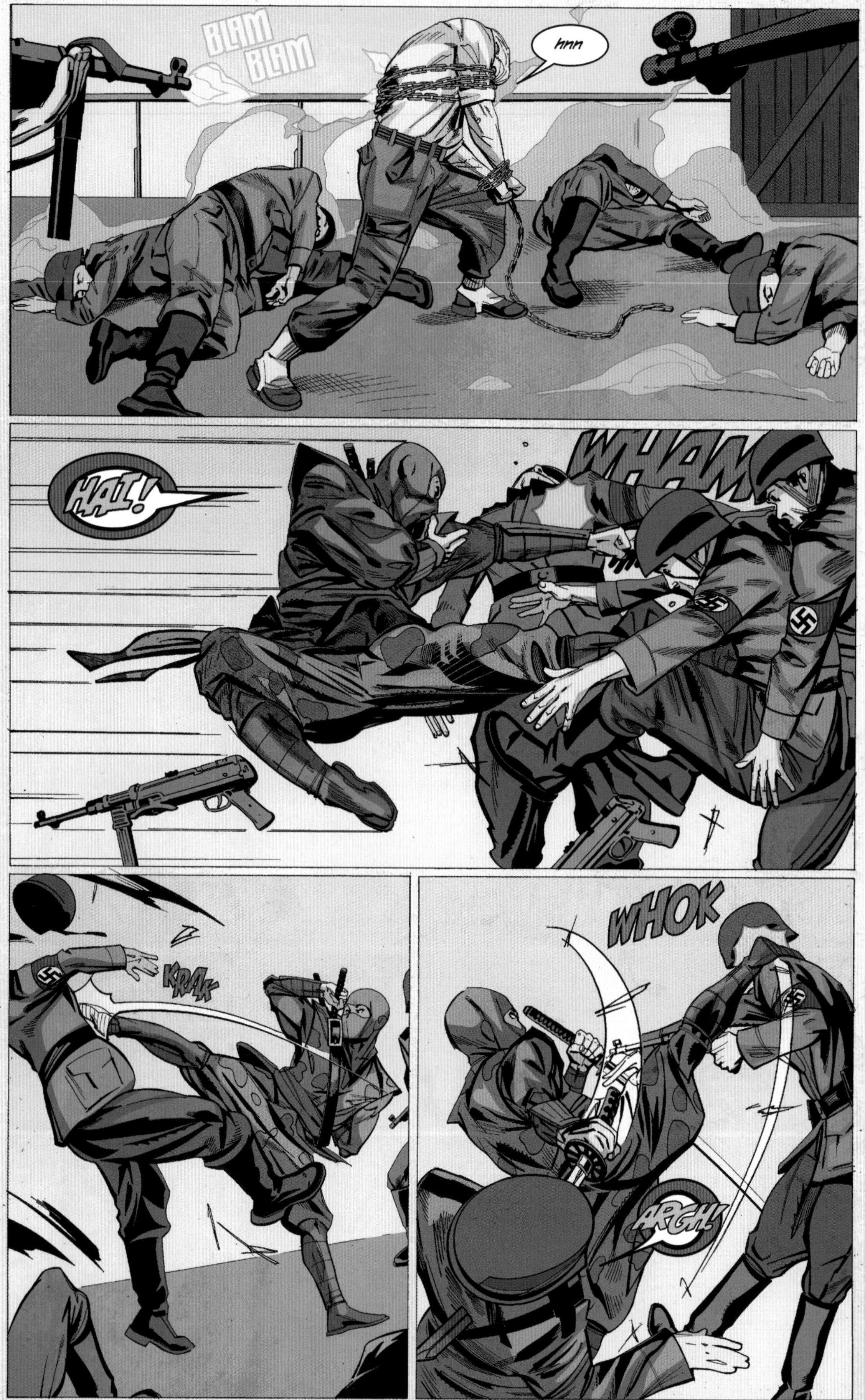
BLAM
BLAM
hnn
HAI!
WHAM
KRAK
WHOK
ARGH!

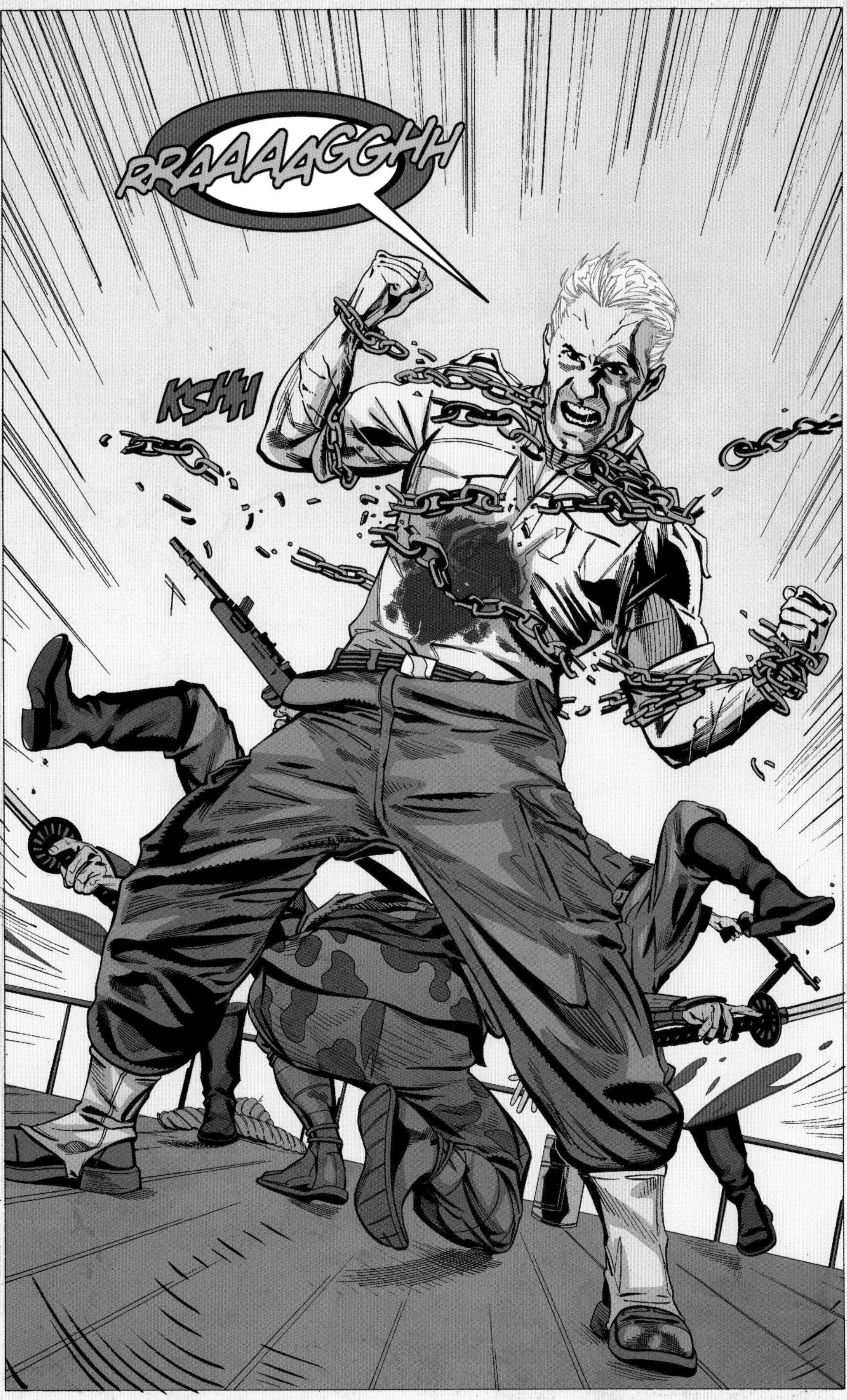
RRAAAAGGHH
KSHH

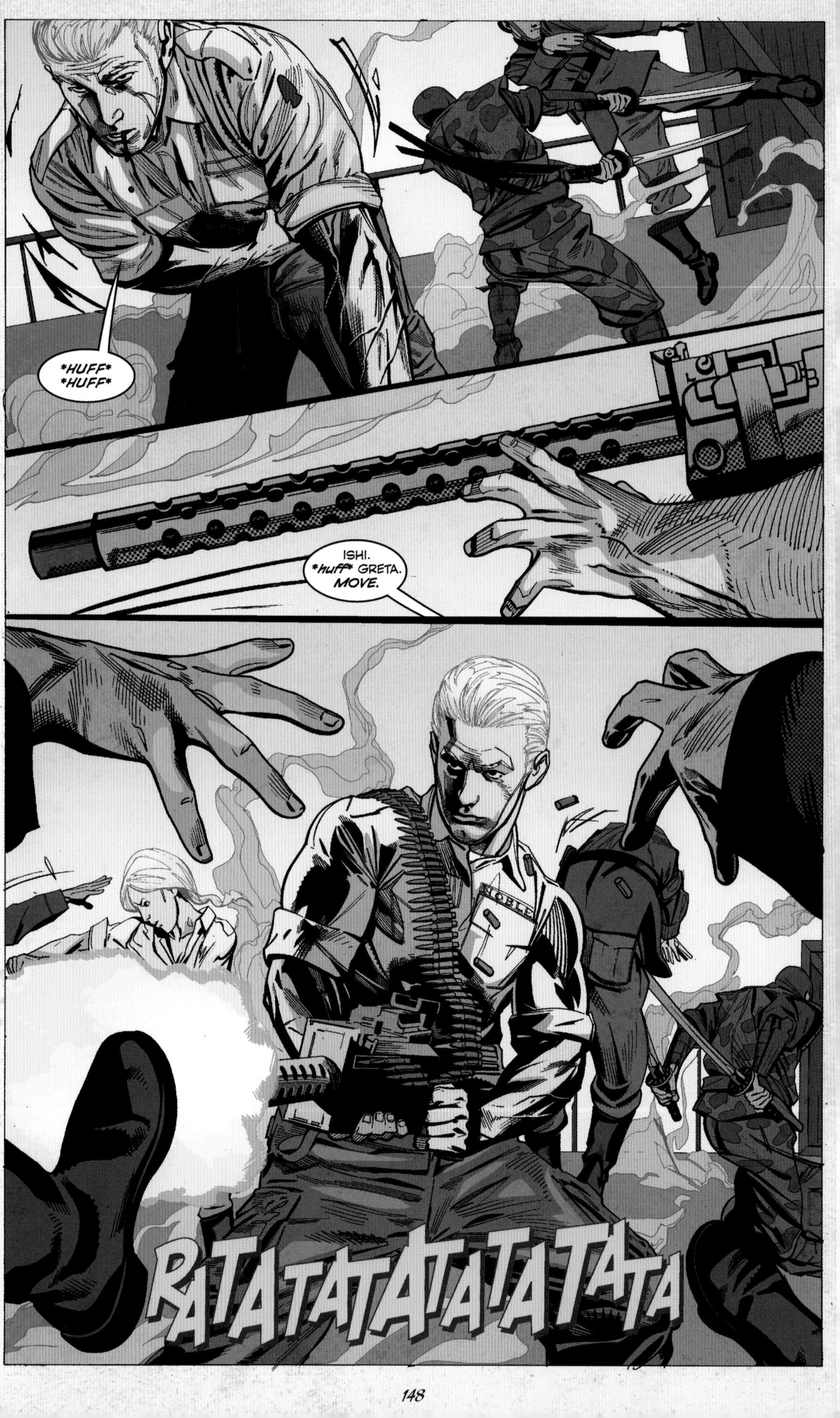
HUFF
HUFF
ISHI. *huff* GRETA. MOVE.
RATATATATATATATA

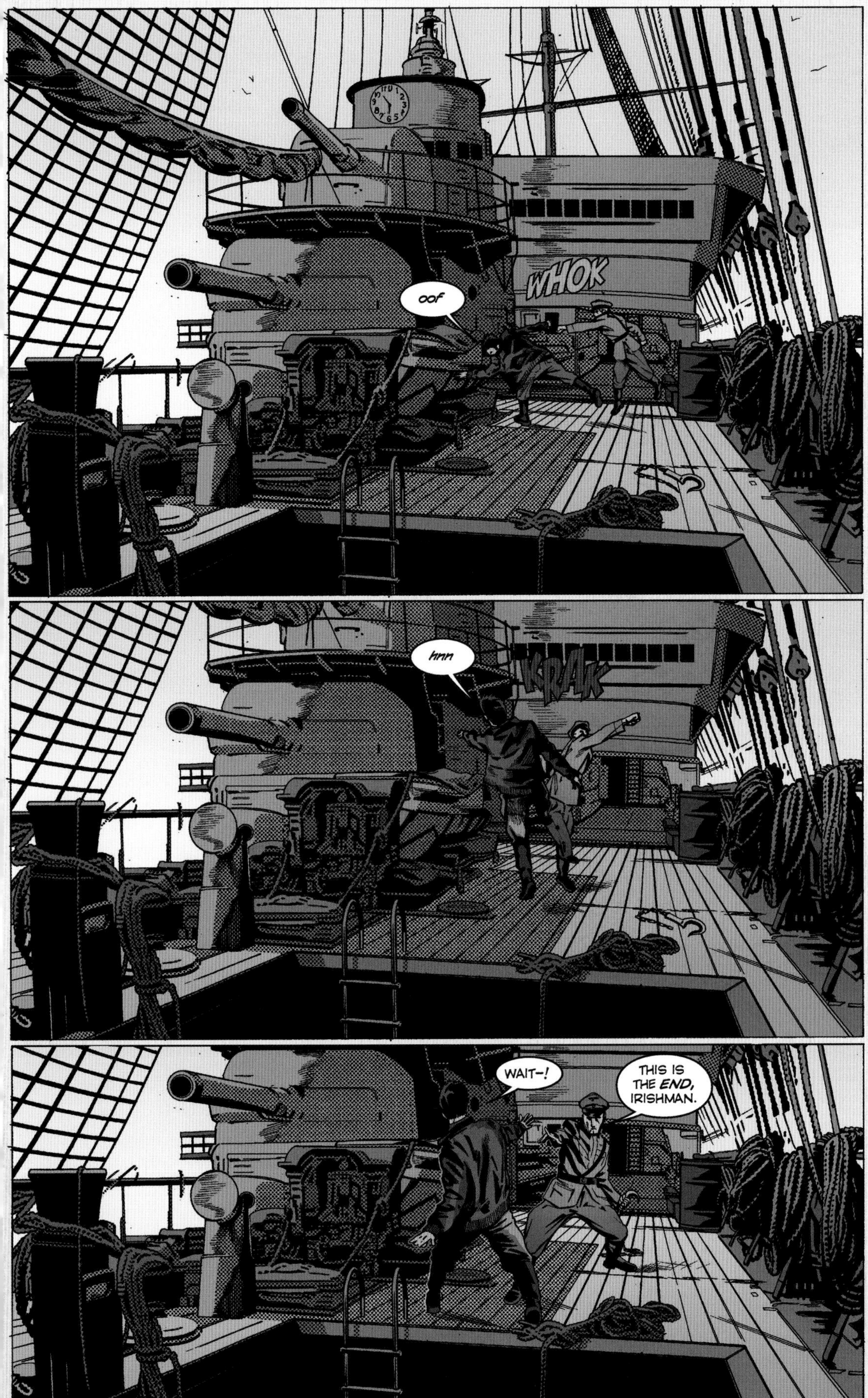
WHOK
oof
hnn
KRAK
WAIT-!
THIS IS THE END, IRISHMAN.

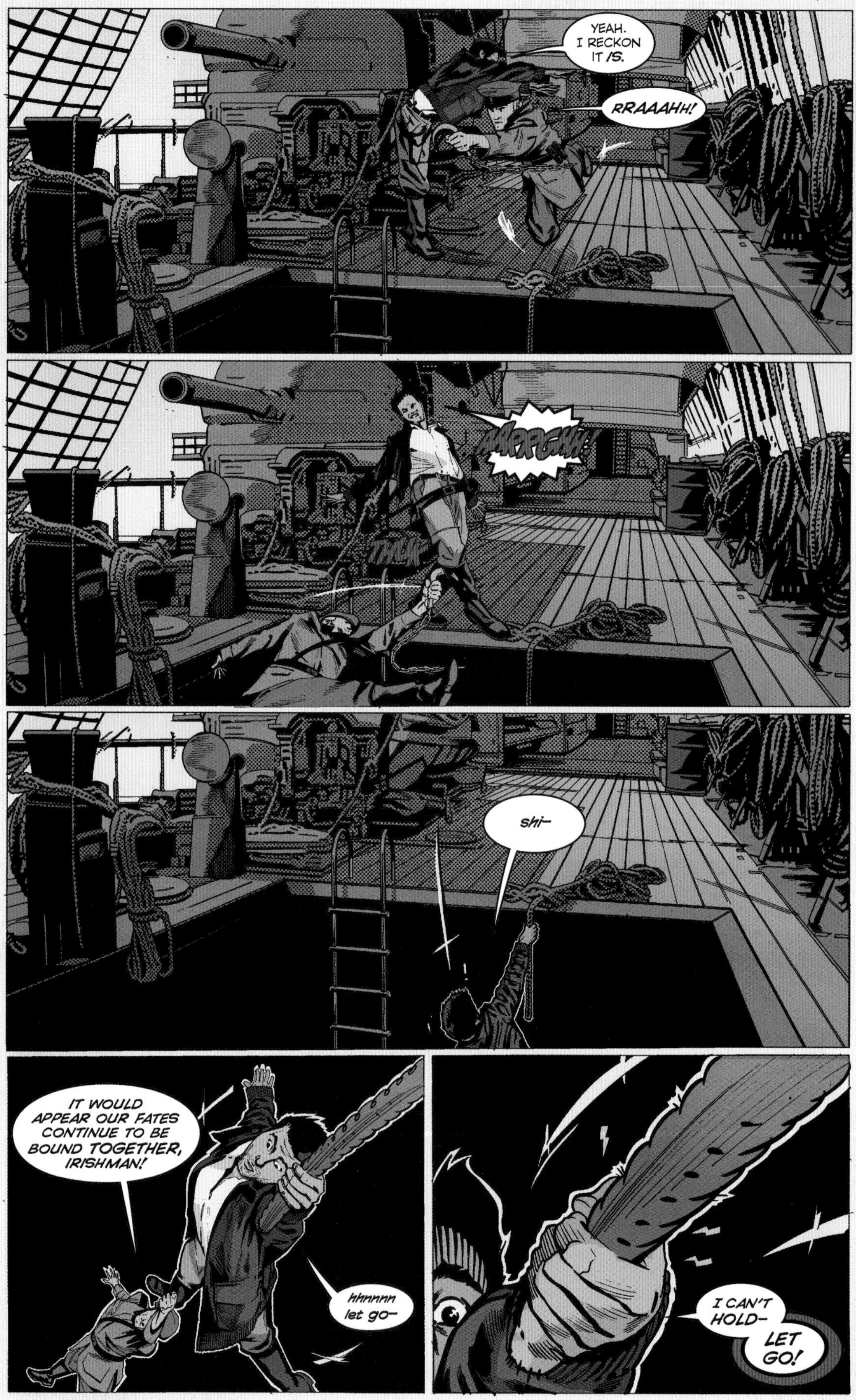
YEAH. I RECKON IT *IS.*
RRAAAHH!
AARRGHH!
THUK
shi–
IT WOULD APPEAR OUR FATES CONTINUE TO BE BOUND TOGETHER, IRISHMAN!
hhnnnn let go–
I CAN'T HOLD–
LET GO!

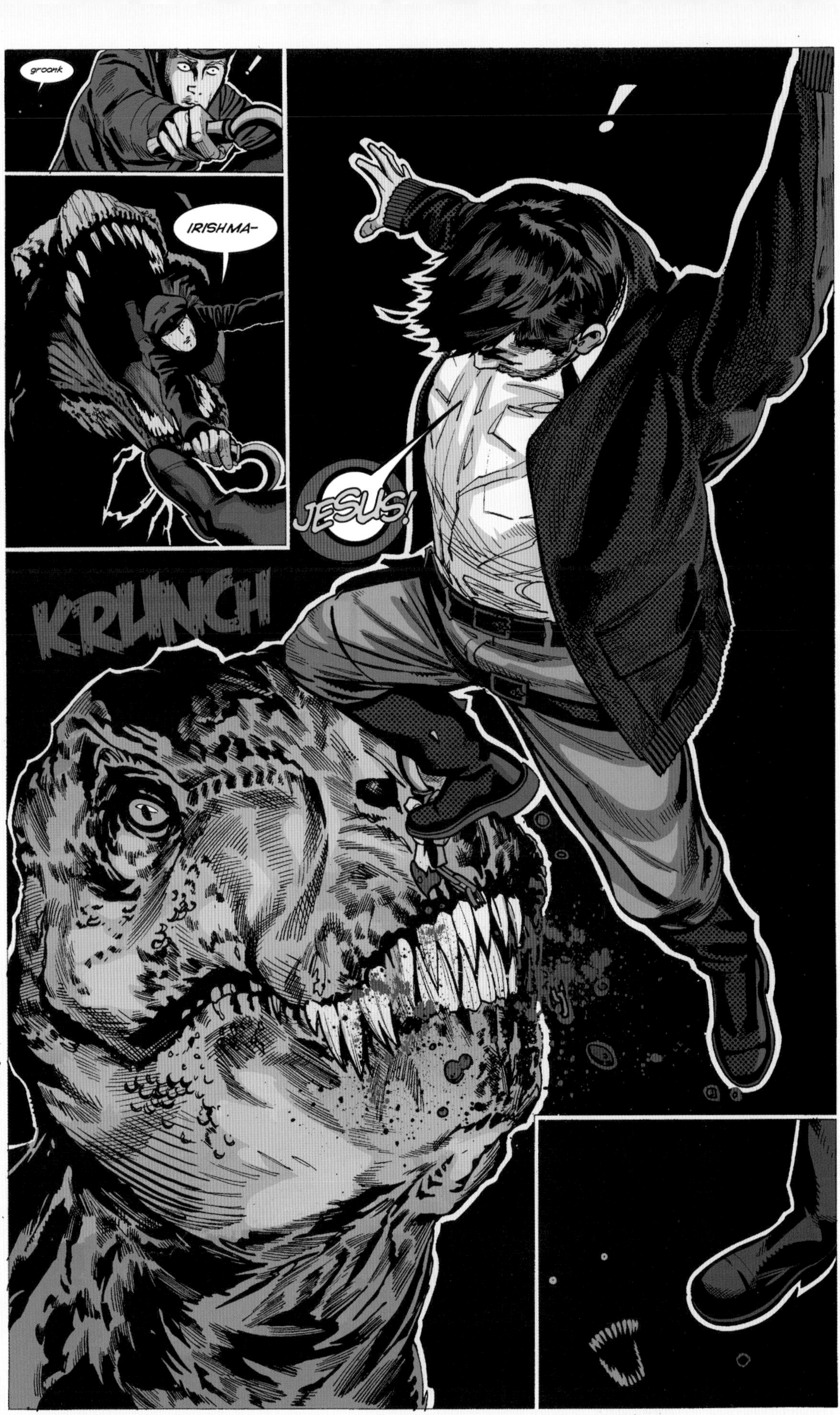
groonk
!
IRISHMA-
!
JESUS!
K'RUNCH

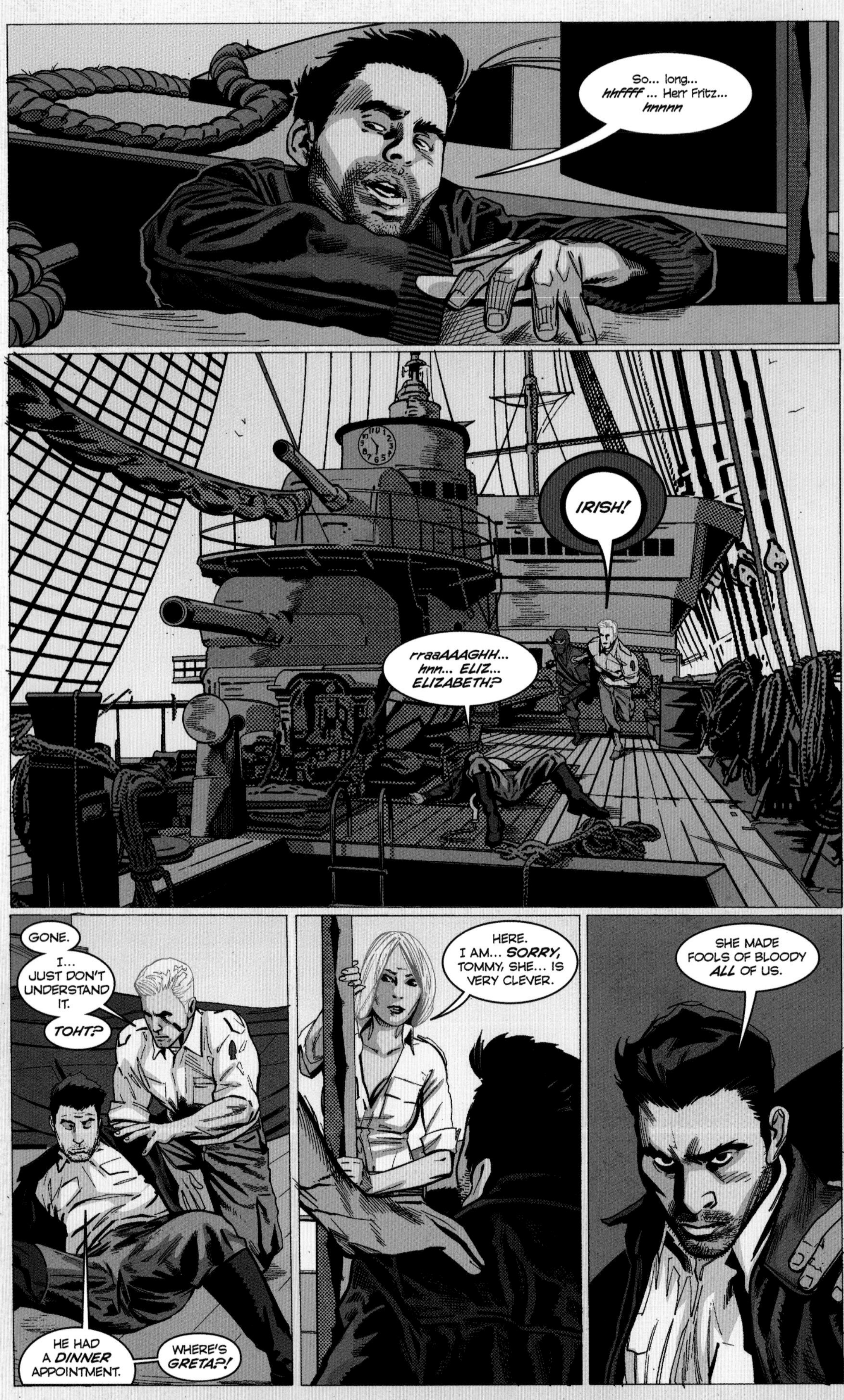
So... long... hhffff ... Herr Fritz... hnnnn
IRISH!
rraaAAAGHH... hnn... ELIZ... ELIZABETH?
GONE.
I... JUST DON'T UNDERSTAND IT.
TOHT?
HE HAD A DINNER APPOINTMENT.
WHERE'S GRETA?!
HERE. I AM... SORRY, TOMMY, SHE... IS VERY CLEVER.
SHE MADE FOOLS OF BLOODY ALL OF US.

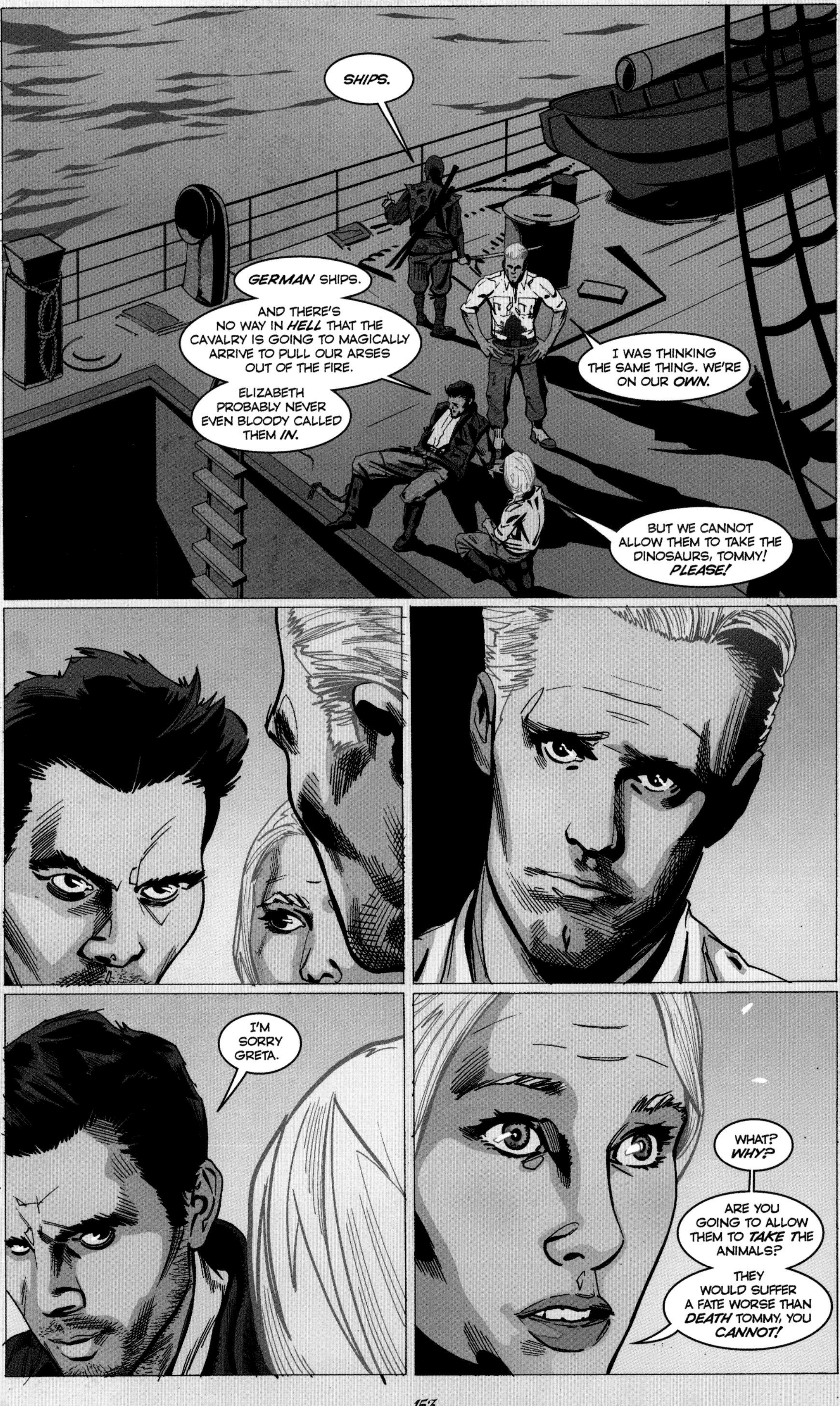
SHIPS.
GERMAN SHIPS.
AND THERE'S NO WAY IN HELL THAT THE CAVALRY IS GOING TO MAGICALLY ARRIVE TO PULL OUR ARSES OUT OF THE FIRE.
ELIZABETH PROBABLY NEVER EVEN BLOODY CALLED THEM IN.
I WAS THINKING THE SAME THING. WE'RE ON OUR OWN.
BUT WE CANNOT ALLOW THEM TO TAKE THE DINOSAURS, TOMMY! PLEASE!
I'M SORRY GRETA.
WHAT? WHY?
ARE YOU GOING TO ALLOW THEM TO TAKE THE ANIMALS?
THEY WOULD SUFFER A FATE WORSE THAN DEATH TOMMY, YOU CANNOT!

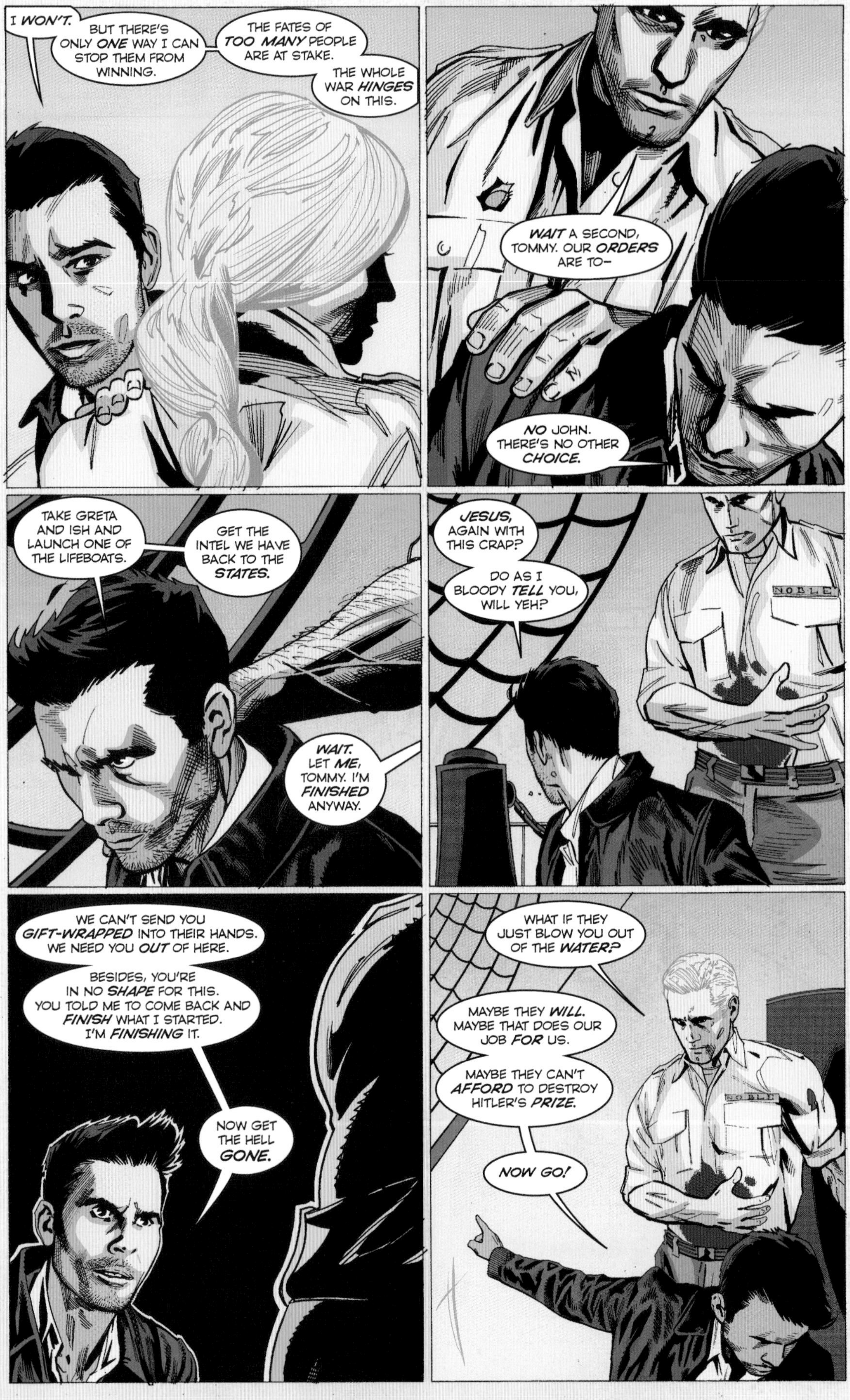
I WON'T.
BUT THERE'S ONLY ONE WAY I CAN STOP THEM FROM WINNING.
THE FATES OF TOO MANY PEOPLE ARE AT STAKE.
THE WHOLE WAR HINGES ON THIS.
WAIT A SECOND, TOMMY. OUR ORDERS ARE TO–
NO JOHN. THERE'S NO OTHER CHOICE.
TAKE GRETA AND ISH AND LAUNCH ONE OF THE LIFEBOATS.
GET THE INTEL WE HAVE BACK TO THE STATES.
WAIT. LET ME, TOMMY. I'M FINISHED ANYWAY.
JESUS, AGAIN WITH THIS CRAP?
DO AS I BLOODY TELL YOU, WILL YEH?
NOBLE
WE CAN'T SEND YOU GIFT-WRAPPED INTO THEIR HANDS. WE NEED YOU OUT OF HERE.
BESIDES, YOU'RE IN NO SHAPE FOR THIS. YOU TOLD ME TO COME BACK AND FINISH WHAT I STARTED. I'M FINISHING IT.
NOW GET THE HELL GONE.
WHAT IF THEY JUST BLOW YOU OUT OF THE WATER?
MAYBE THEY WILL. MAYBE THAT DOES OUR JOB FOR US.
MAYBE THEY CAN'T AFFORD TO DESTROY HITLER'S PRIZE.
NOW GO!

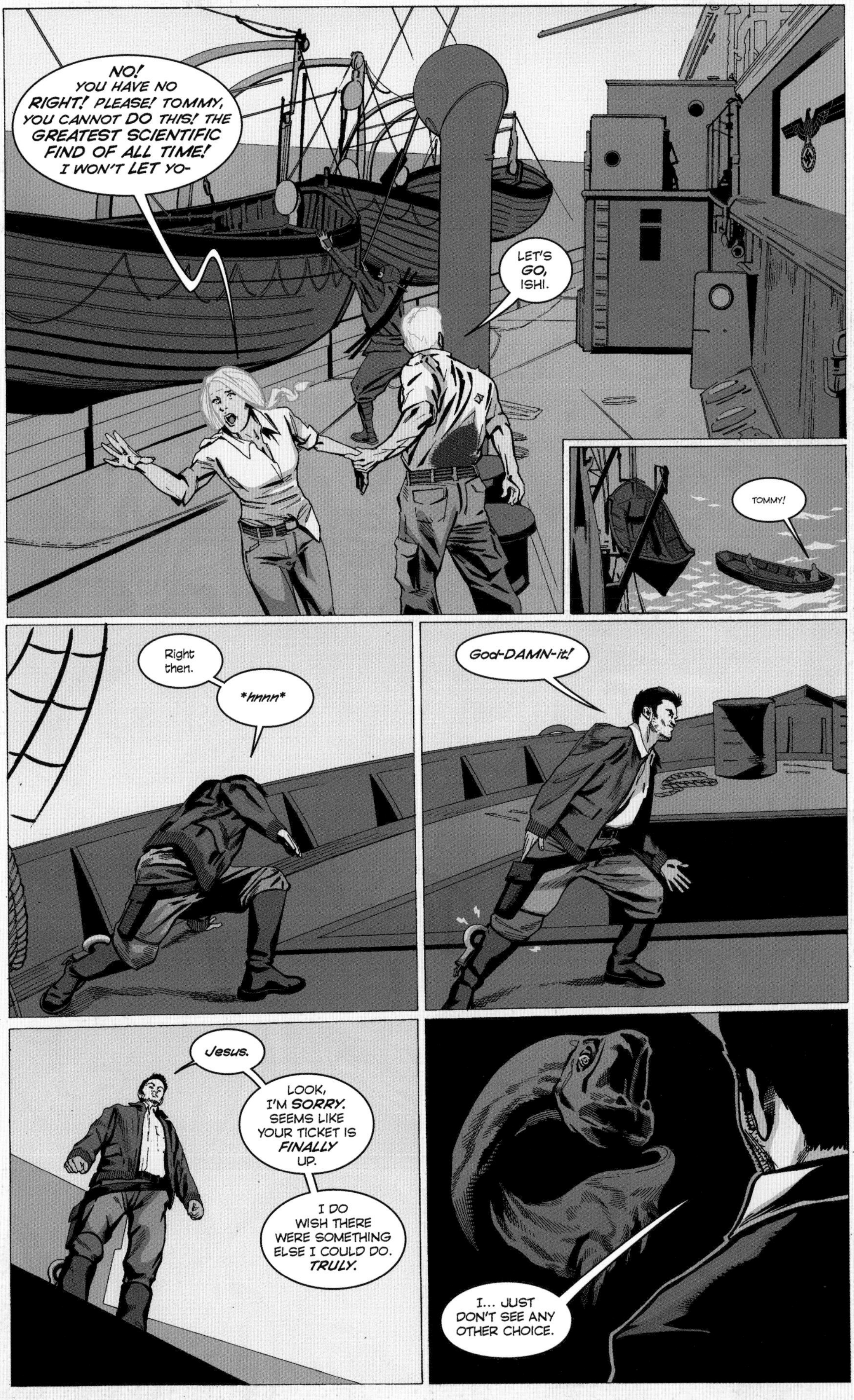
NO! YOU HAVE NO RIGHT! PLEASE! TOMMY, YOU CANNOT DO THIS! THE GREATEST SCIENTIFIC FIND OF ALL TIME! I WON'T LET YO-
LET'S GO, ISHI.
TOMMY!
Right then.
hnnn
God-DAMN-it!
Jesus.
LOOK, I'M SORRY. SEEMS LIKE YOUR TICKET IS FINALLY UP.
I DO WISH THERE WERE SOMETHING ELSE I COULD DO. TRULY.
I... JUST DON'T SEE ANY OTHER CHOICE.

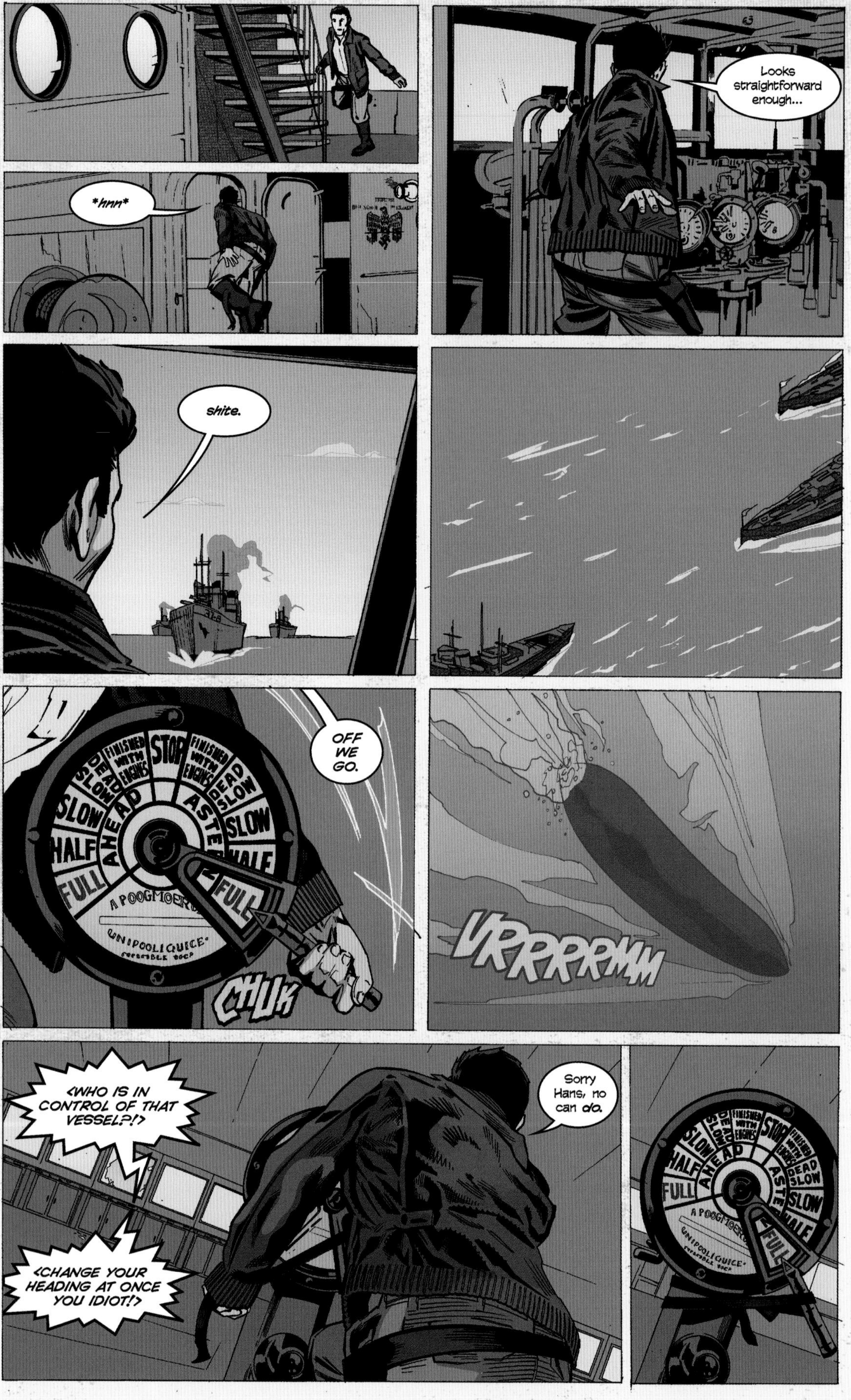
Looks straightforward enough...
hnn
shite.
OFF WE GO.
CHUK
VRRRRMM
<WHO IS IN CONTROL OF THAT VESSEL?!>
<CHANGE YOUR HEADING AT ONCE YOU IDIOT!>
Sorry Hans, no can do.

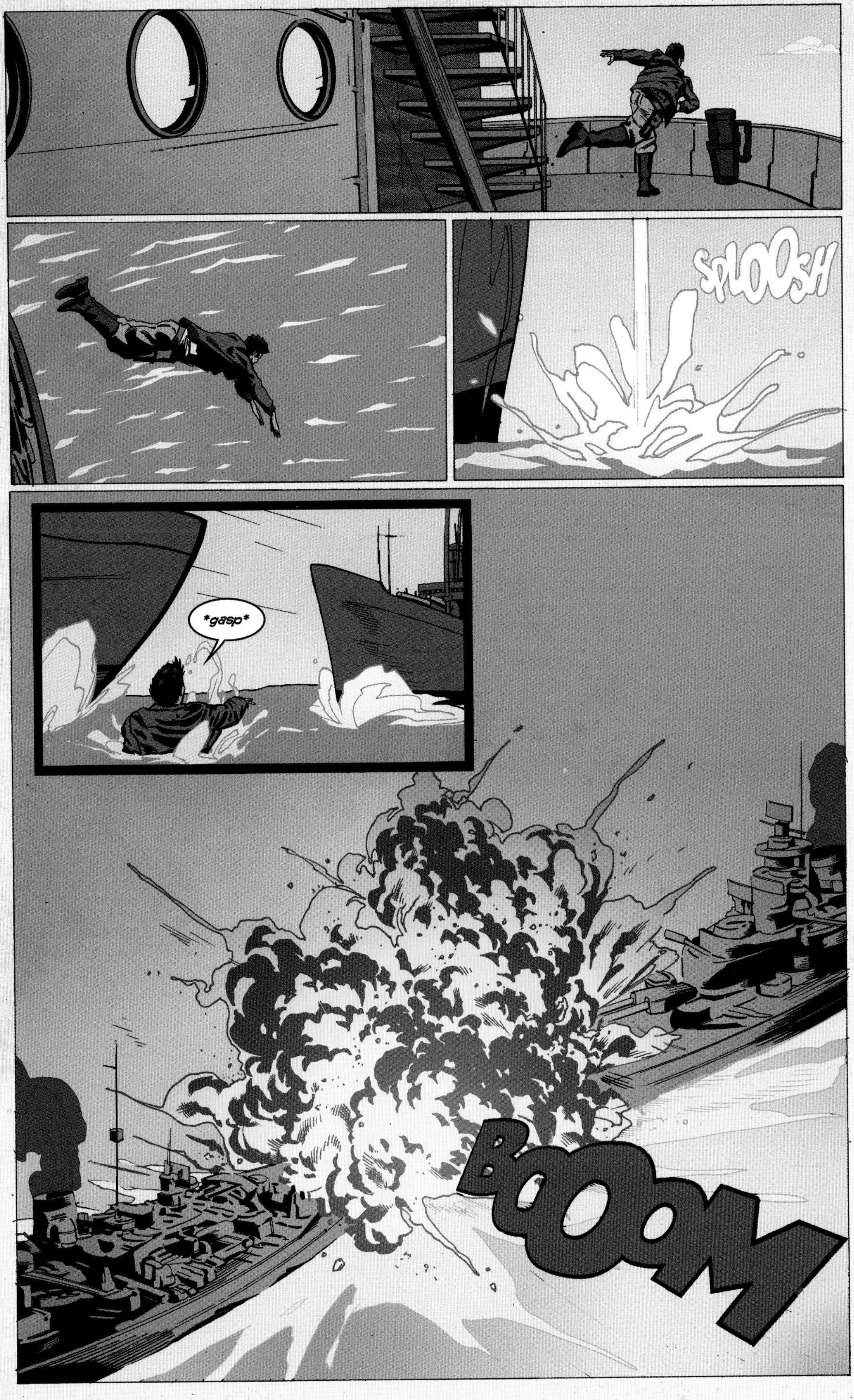
SPLOOSH
gasp
BOOOM

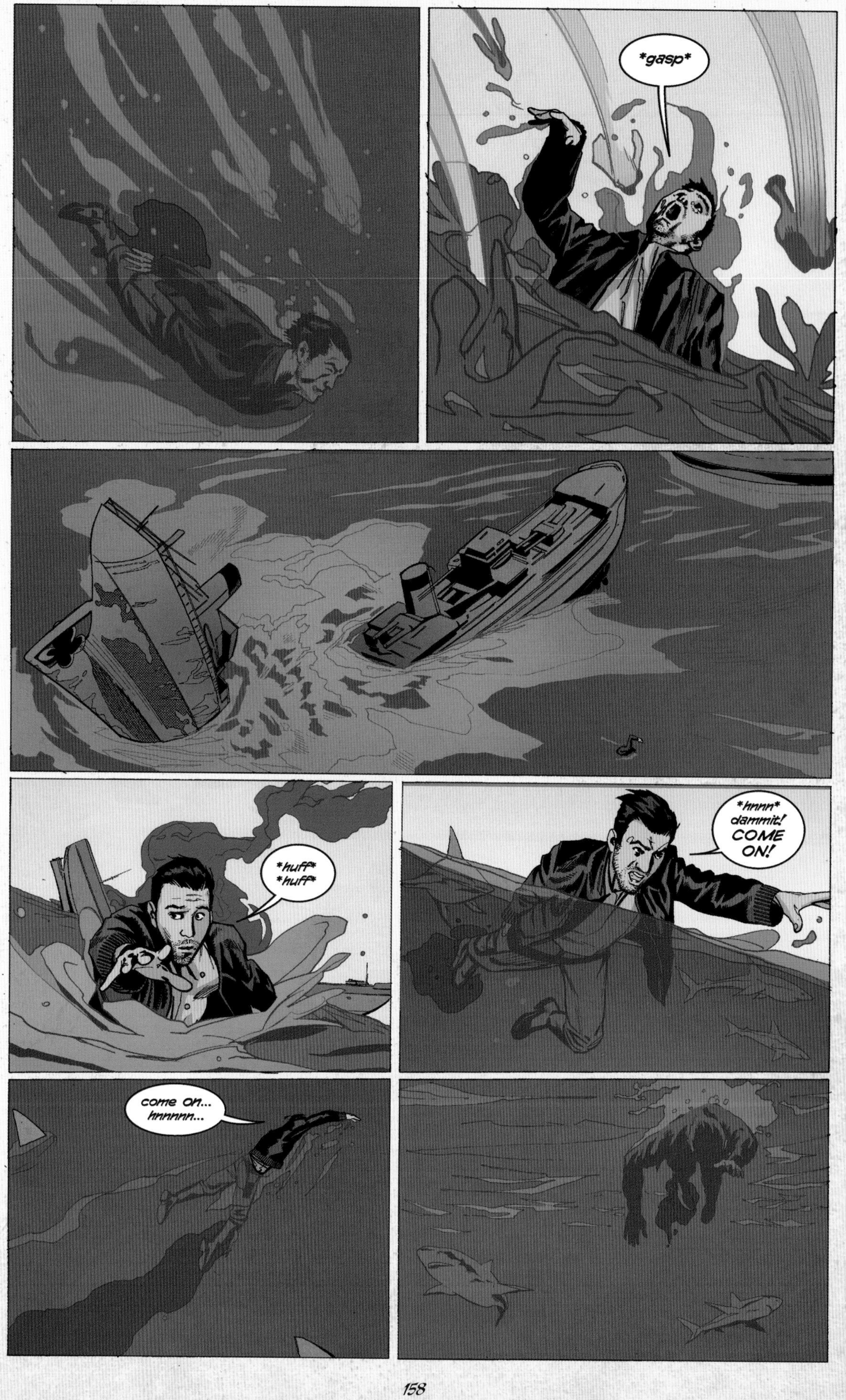
gasp
huff
huff
hnnn
dammit!
COME
ON!
come on...
hnnnnn...

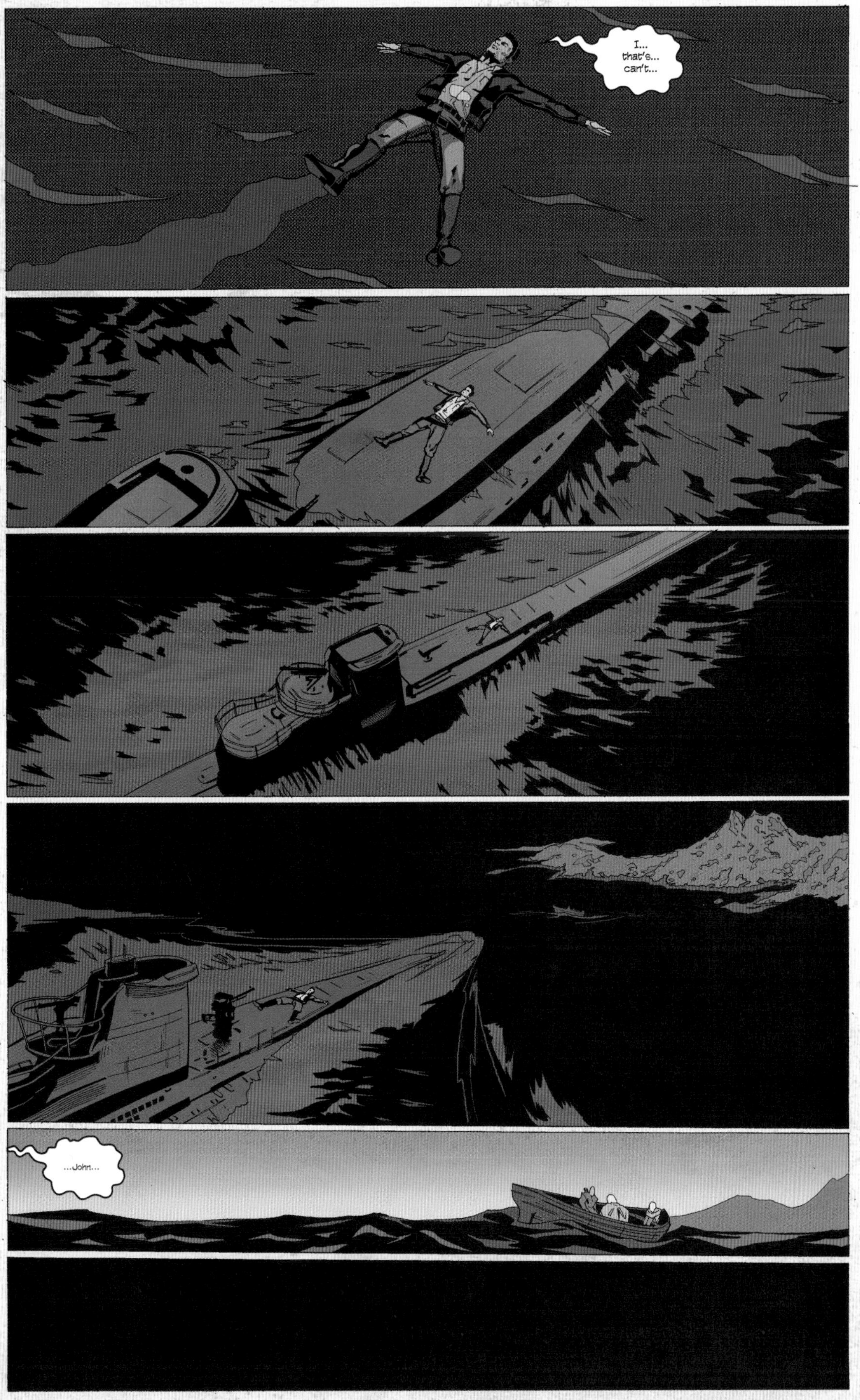
I... that's... can't...
...John...

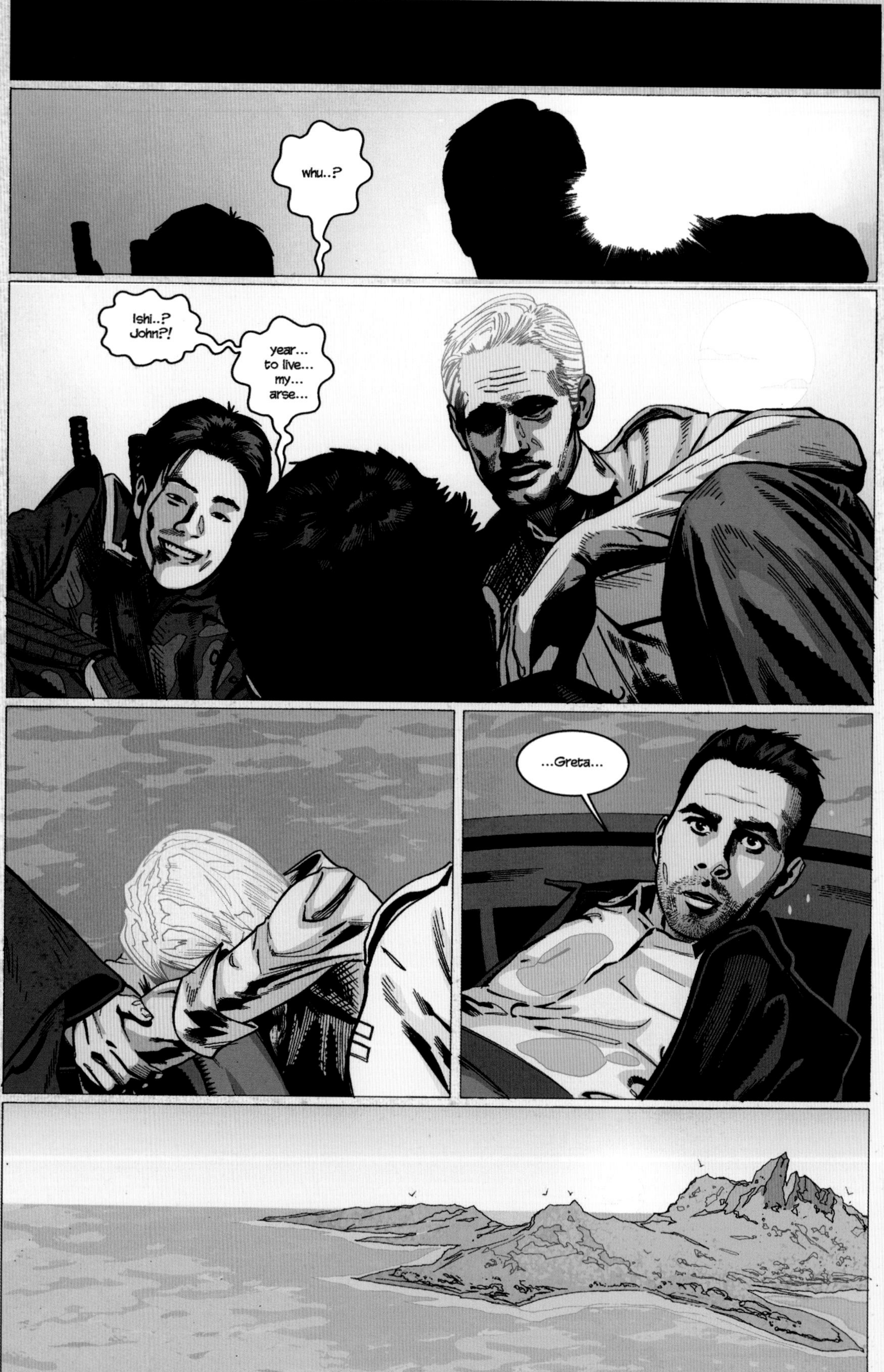
whu..?
Ishi..? John?!
year... to live... my... arse...
...Greta...

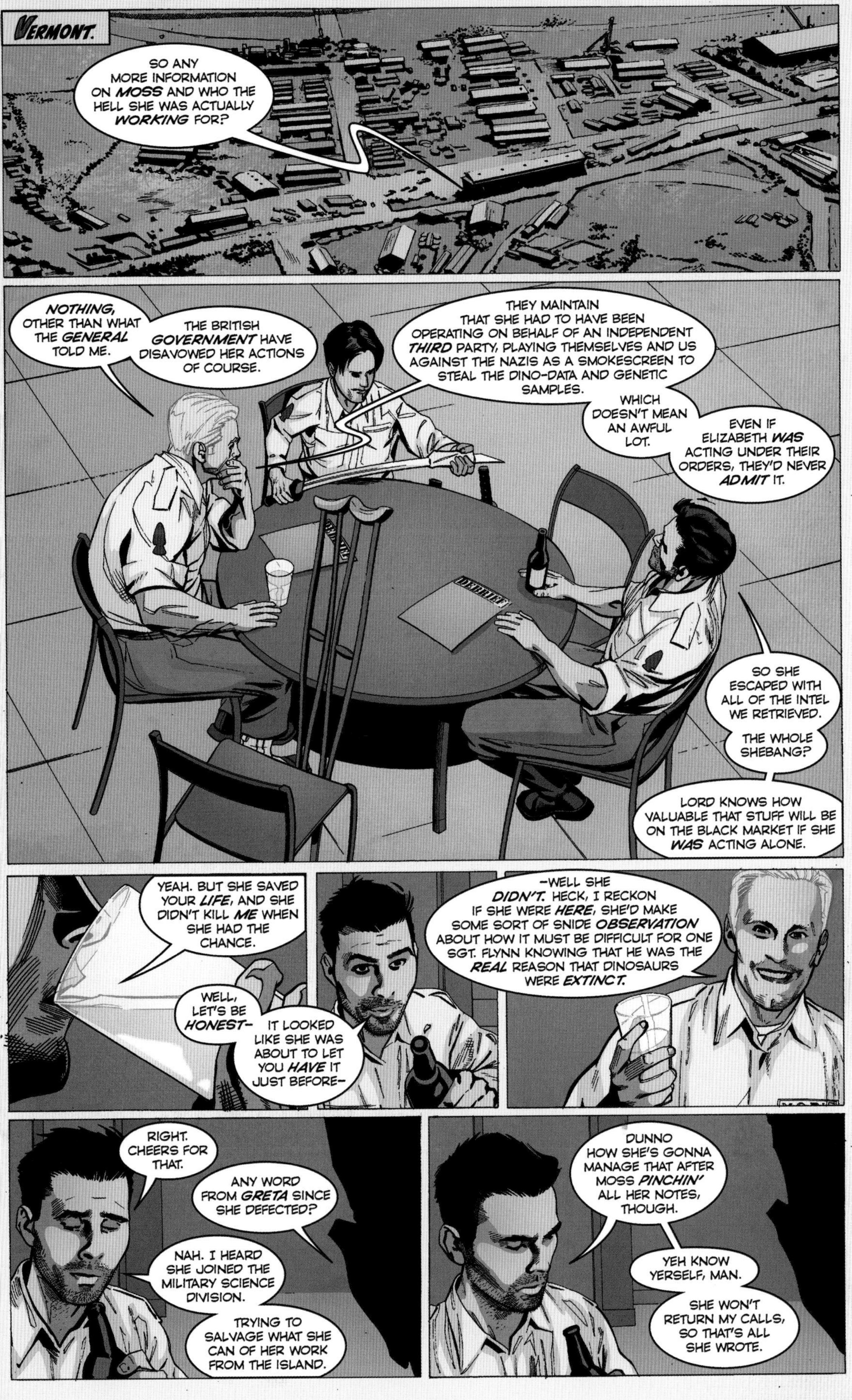
VERMONT.
SO ANY MORE INFORMATION ON MOSS AND WHO THE HELL SHE WAS ACTUALLY WORKING FOR?
NOTHING, OTHER THAN WHAT THE GENERAL TOLD ME.
THE BRITISH GOVERNMENT HAVE DISAVOWED HER ACTIONS OF COURSE.
THEY MAINTAIN THAT SHE HAD TO HAVE BEEN OPERATING ON BEHALF OF AN INDEPENDENT THIRD PARTY, PLAYING THEMSELVES AND US AGAINST THE NAZIS AS A SMOKESCREEN TO STEAL THE DINO-DATA AND GENETIC SAMPLES.
WHICH DOESN'T MEAN AN AWFUL LOT.
EVEN IF ELIZABETH WAS ACTING UNDER THEIR ORDERS, THEY'D NEVER ADMIT IT.
SO SHE ESCAPED WITH ALL OF THE INTEL WE RETRIEVED.
THE WHOLE SHEBANG?
LORD KNOWS HOW VALUABLE THAT STUFF WILL BE ON THE BLACK MARKET IF SHE WAS ACTING ALONE.
YEAH. BUT SHE SAVED YOUR LIFE, AND SHE DIDN'T KILL ME WHEN SHE HAD THE CHANCE.
WELL, LET'S BE HONEST-
IT LOOKED LIKE SHE WAS ABOUT TO LET YOU HAVE IT JUST BEFORE-
-WELL SHE DIDN'T. HECK, I RECKON IF SHE WERE HERE, SHE'D MAKE SOME SORT OF SNIDE OBSERVATION ABOUT HOW IT MUST BE DIFFICULT FOR ONE SGT. FLYNN KNOWING THAT HE WAS THE REAL REASON THAT DINOSAURS WERE EXTINCT.
RIGHT. CHEERS FOR THAT.
ANY WORD FROM GRETA SINCE SHE DEFECTED?
NAH. I HEARD SHE JOINED THE MILITARY SCIENCE DIVISION.
TRYING TO SALVAGE WHAT SHE CAN OF HER WORK FROM THE ISLAND.
DUNNO HOW SHE'S GONNA MANAGE THAT AFTER MOSS PINCHIN' ALL HER NOTES, THOUGH.
YEH KNOW YERSELF, MAN.
SHE WON'T RETURN MY CALLS, SO THAT'S ALL SHE WROTE.

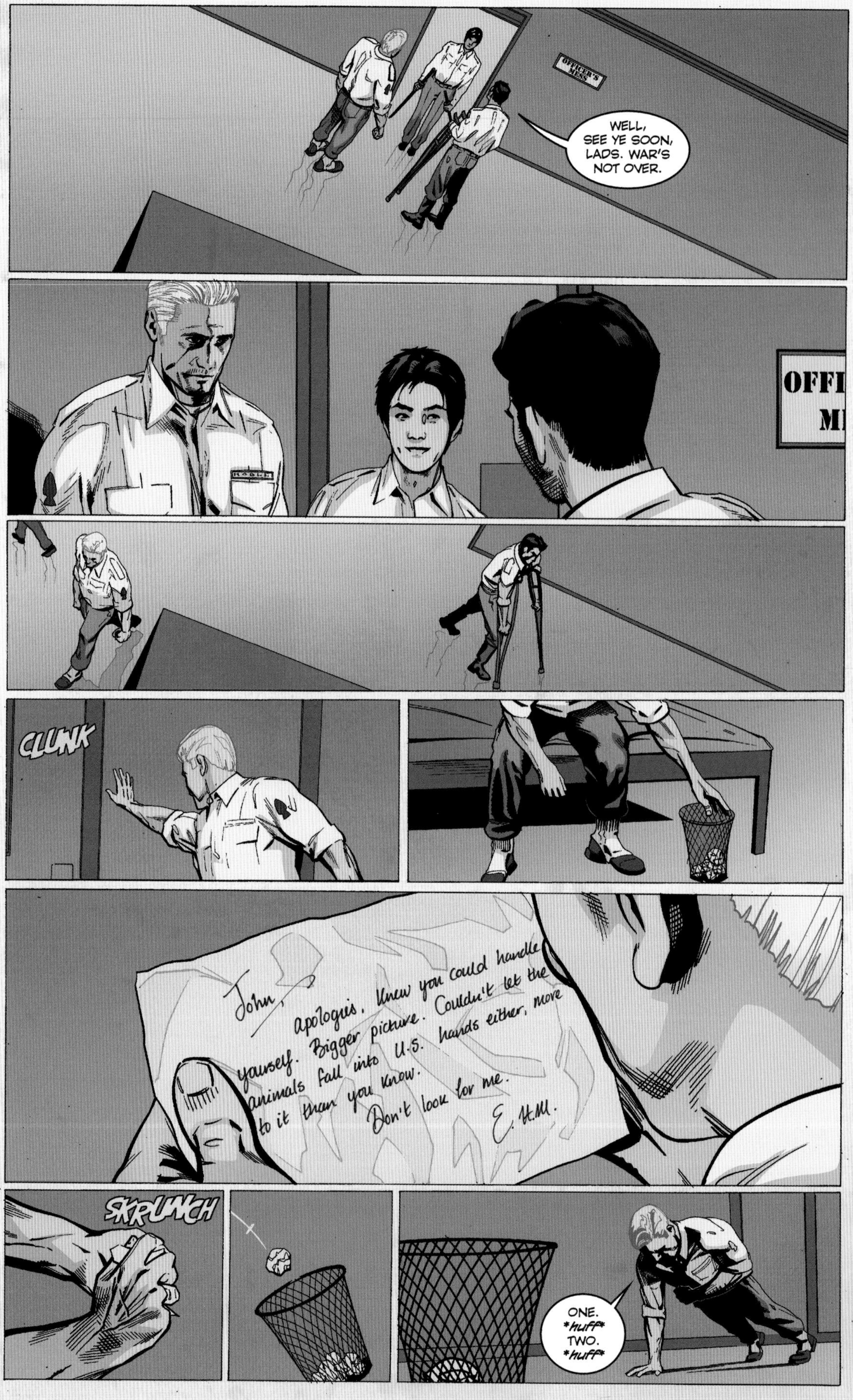
OFFICER'S MESS
WELL, SEE YE SOON, LADS. WAR'S NOT OVER.
CLUNK
John,
apologies, knew you could handle yourself. Bigger picture. Couldn't let the animals fall into U.S. hands either, more to it than you know.
Don't look for me.
E.H.M.
SKRUNCH
ONE. *huff* TWO. *huff*

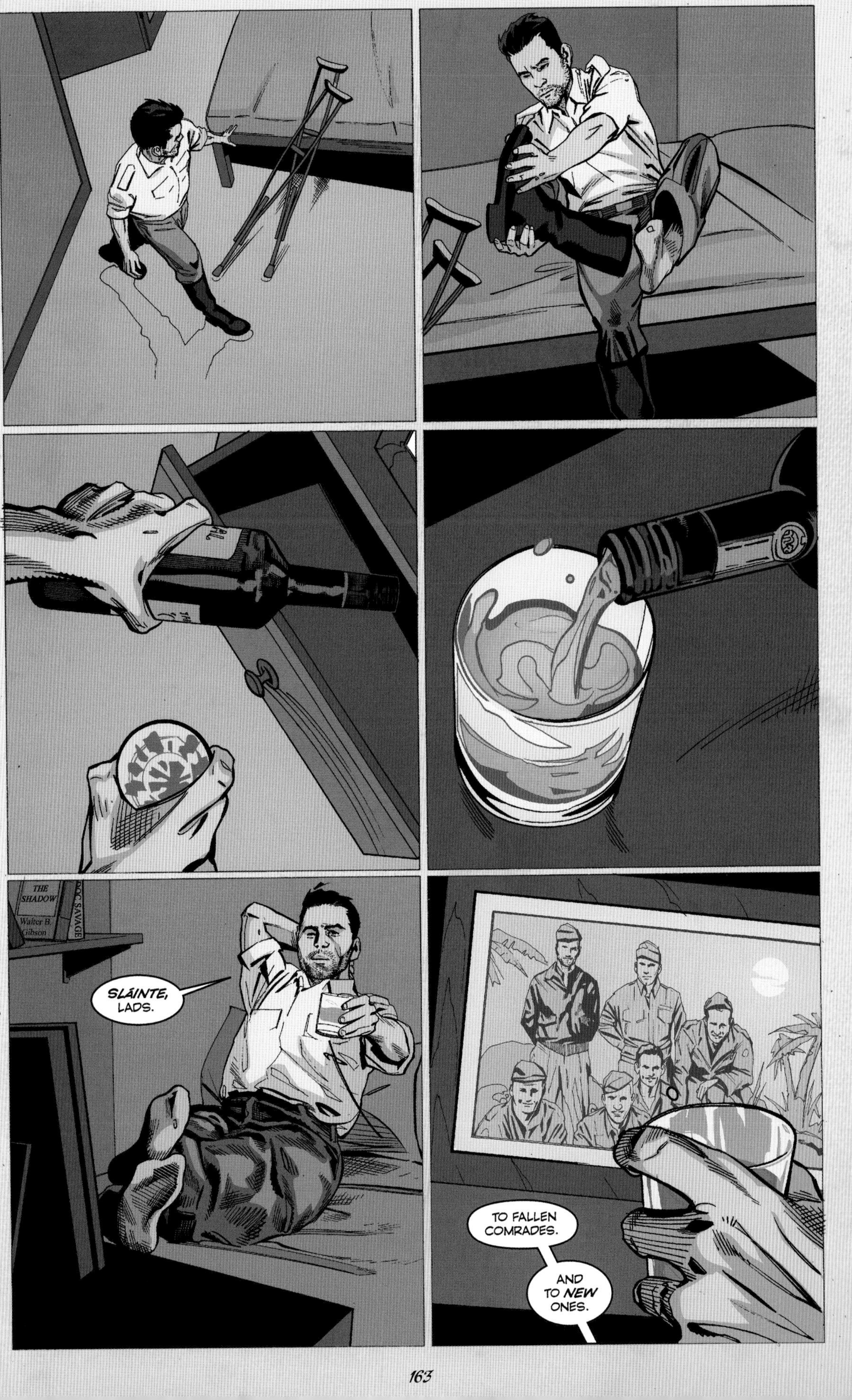
THE SHADOW
Walter B. Gibson
DOC SAVAGE
SLÁINTE, LADS.
TO FALLEN COMRADES.
AND TO NEW ONES.

IDW PUBLISHING
PRESENTS

HALF PAST DANGER

Dames. Dinosaurs. Danger.

Created, Written, and Drawn by
STEPHEN MOONEY

Colours by JORDIE 'RAVENWOOD' BELLAIRE

Edited by CHRIS RYALL and CHRIS SCHRAFF

Proof Reading by DECLAN SHALVEY,
NICK ROCHE, and SCOTT TIPTON

Huge Thanks to Variant Cover Artists
TOMMY LEE EDWARDS, DEC SHALVEY, LEE BERMEJO,
NICK RUNGE, NICK ROCHE and REBEKAH ISAACS.

Special Thanks to my fellow Eclectic Micks:
BOB BYRNE, STEPHEN 'TOMMY' THOMPSON
WILL SLINEY, TOMM 'OSCAR-BAIT' MOORE, PJ HOLDEN,
NICK 'NICKLEBACK' ROCHE, LEN O'GRADY
and DEC 'ARTISTE' SHALVEY
for their constant feedback, heckling and belittlement.

Extra Special Thanks in Even Bigger More Deserving Font
to my parents, MAURA MOONEY and DERMOT MOONEY,
for their constant encouragement and financial bail-outs,
and in equally as big and deserving font to my lovely wife,
JACINTHA 'HUNTINGTON-MOSS' O'REILLY-MOONEY.

The End

IDW PUBLISHING   BOLDY DIGITAL   MoonPie

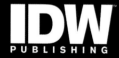

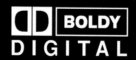

Half Past DANGER

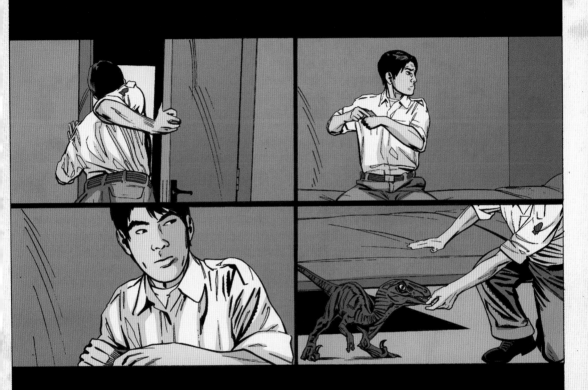

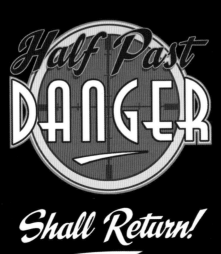

Shall Return!

FULLY PAST DANGER.

AN AFTERWORD

This is a strange thing for me to write. It's like tying a bow on a project I worked on... but it's not really my project. *Half Past Danger* is something I've been involved with for about two years now, without really being involved with it.

Stephen Mooney (or Handsome Stephen Mooney, as I like to call him. Also: Mooney) mentioned to me that he had a project he wanted to write and draw a while ago. He was working on various licensed comic books, one of which was *Angel*; a gig I was very much jealous of. Mooney had been working professionally in American comics for quite a while and had built a great reputation for being talented, dependable, and reliable.

Again, I was jealous. Unfortunately, what's little reported is that reliable artists can sometimes find themselves pigeon-holed; the real workhorses can end up working on books that need to be in NOW rather than should just be in on a reasonable deadline. As I started working for Marvel Comics a few years ago, I was a little concerned that was happening to my friend Mooney. And it was.

Where Mooney succeeded and others have failed, however, is that he took the brave decision, now or never, to do that ONE book. That dream project that has been in the drawer for years (we all have them). He took the risk and invested in HIMSELF for once.

And now, thanks to his own determination and dedication (as well as the unwavering support of his smart, practical, and beautiful wife Jacintha), his respected reputation with IDW Chief Chris Ryall, and some help from trusted friends (including Flame-haired stunner Jordie Bellaire on colours, Tommy Lee Edwards on that first spectacular variant cover and uh... ME, for Twitter or something), we have this gorgeous hardcover volume of Mooney's action-packed, atmospheric, fun adventure spectacular that's an ode to all of Mooney's loves and influences. And Dinosaurs. Jordie once described it as 'Spielbergian' and I think it really fits.

With both Mooney and myself hailing from Ireland, I also have to reflect on what the series means to our little island. As *Half Past Danger* hit, the Irish comics community got a real shot in the arm. The support for the book and others like it was tremendous and it seems to me that *Half Past Danger* is a shining example of what the Irish can contribute to comics. Mooney has showed by example, forging an entertaining story with excellent craftsmanship and top quality storytelling.

So anyway, the book is done and it's been amazing to see it take off from the initial idea, to seeing the first artwork, seeing first colours, Jordie coming onboard, the variant covers coming in one by one, the first issue release party and now, the hardcover collection. It's been a tale nearly as epic as *Half Past Danger* and, once again, I find myself jealous of Stephen Mooney.

Long may it continue.

Declan Shalvey

Dublin,

November 2014

Author's Commentary

It seems like an awfully long time ago now that I started *Half Past Danger*.
The main thing I remember is wanting strongly to do something that was my own;
a story that felt like only *I* could have produced it. Whether I succeeded or not is anybody's guess.
Come with me now, as I take a leisurely mental stroll to a place I like to call:
'Well, *that* took a long time.'

Issue 1:

I do love me a good establishing shot.
The very first image on the first page of the book illustrates the approach to the mysterious island the beasties call home. I wanted the opening shot of each issue to be a very cinematic introduction to the scene at hand, as well as serving as chapter headings.
I first saw this 'letterbox' technique employed by Tom Raney and Warren Ellis in their legendary *Stormwatch* run, and then later in Mark Millar and Brian Hitch's *Ultimates* book.
I shamelessly nicked it, and would do so again. It served my purpose nicely, and I think lends a lovely, sweeping, filmic sense to the opening of the book.
As we go on it'll become more apparent that I employed many 'Hollywood' techniques to the storytelling throughout the book, but my style just gravitates towards that stuff.
It's a direct result of emersing myself in all of the Saturday afternoon serials and matinee movies that heavily influenced *HPD*.

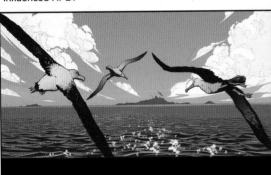

Chapter One
BITE THE BULLET

It was intentional on my part that it took a full four pages to arrive at the reveal of the main character. I love long, luxurious intros that drip with atmosphere and completely set up the world that the given characters inhabit.
The lack of dialogue until page three is by design also. Frankly, I would've gone a bit longer before hearing chatter if I hadn't been worried readers might start to get bored.
As the book progresses, you'll see that I'm a huge proponent of the 'less is more' school, especially when it comes to dialogue. For me, most characters talk too much in comics. Nobody describes their actions as they perform them in real life. Show, don't tell, baby.

The whole opening sequence was heavily influenced by the initial scene in *Raiders of The Lost Ark*, where the tension builds over the opening to ultimately reveal our hero at the pivotal moment. Hence why we only see Irish partially and from behind to begin with, as his squad crack wise about his previous exploits, and hopefully build the anticipation to be introduced to the character.

HA!, AIN'T NEVER BEEN A DRINK INVENTED HE CAN'T SOURCE.
ALRIGHT, ENOUGH ALREADY. KEEP YER *VOICES* DOWN.
AN' BESIDES, IT WAS *BRANDY,* NOT WHISKEY. STOLE IT FROM THE MAJOR.
GET YER *FACTS*--

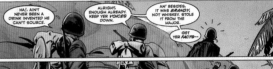

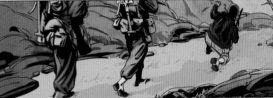

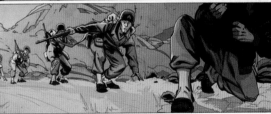

I felt that I needed to make the initial T-Rex attack really sing, since it was the major inciting incident for everything that was to follow, and let's face it, you promise dinosaurs on the front cover then this was the time to deliver.
It was a tricky one, though. I put a lot of thought at the start into how exactly I should represent my dinosaurs. Do I go with the classics I was raised with: *Jurassic Park*, *Xenozoic Tales*, even *One Million Years BC*? Or do I try and take a more modernist approach, and deal with the newer theories of feather-clad dinos which were much closer to the birds we have today rather than the old-school 'Thunder Lizard' interpretations?
Wasn't really a tough call at the end of the day. The traditional versions just looked *cooler,* and more importantly, they were the versions represented in my mind's eye when the mental movie played out. The versions I grew up with. And this book was all about what I grew up with.

THAT'S NO BEAR.

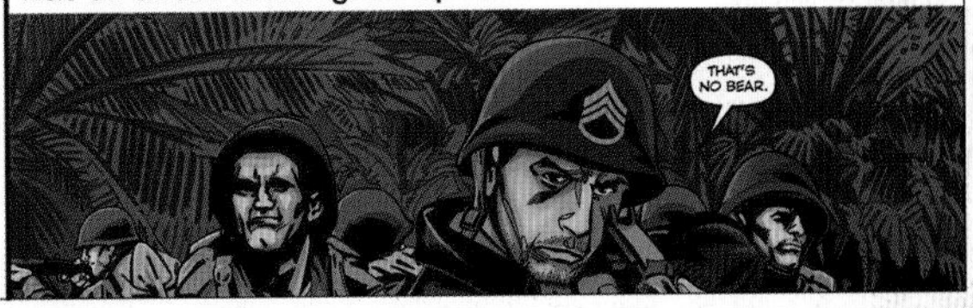

So I did my best to show my hand right out of the gate on the T-Rex front, and people seemed to be onboard from the off, thankfully. Once I'd gotten that page drawn and looking like I wanted it to, I felt much more relaxed about the whole thing, and knew I was on the right track.

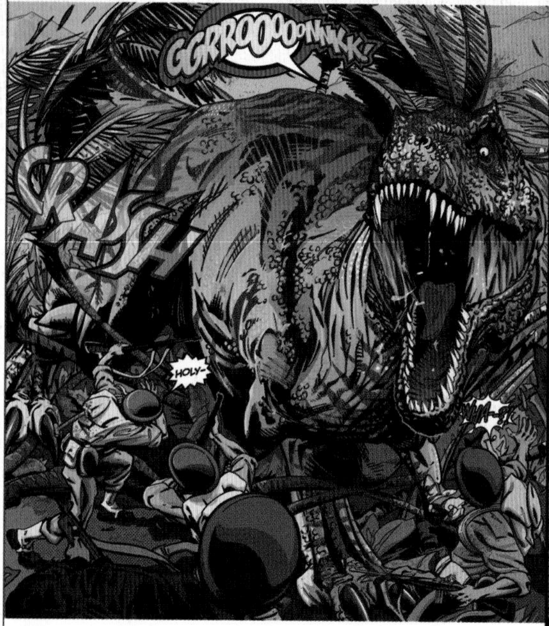
GGRROOOOONNKKK!
HOLY-

Another establishing shot I was really happy with. Those panels just do so much to anchor the story if executed correctly, and I enjoy drawing them, so win-win. This one was particularly fun to do, as it established the grimey 'Noo Yawk' of 1943 which I'd seen in so many classic movies through the years.

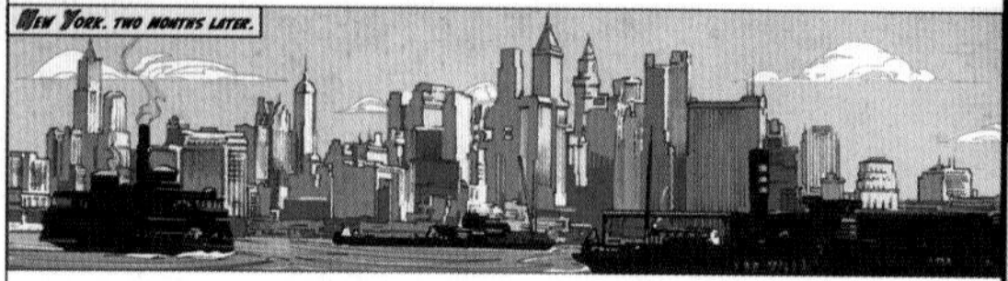
NEW YORK. TWO MONTHS LATER.

Here's a thing: I spent ages drawing the bottle of whiskey that Irish is drinking from at the bar. I love those old-fashioned Jack Daniels print ads that are lovely, simple black and white ink drawings. I wanted to replicate that style a little, so I painstakingly copied one of them and replaced the logo with 'Dack Janiels.' "Ho-ho!" I chortled, "aren't I the clever one?" Nope, yer the dope who spent two hours drawing a bottle nobody noticed.

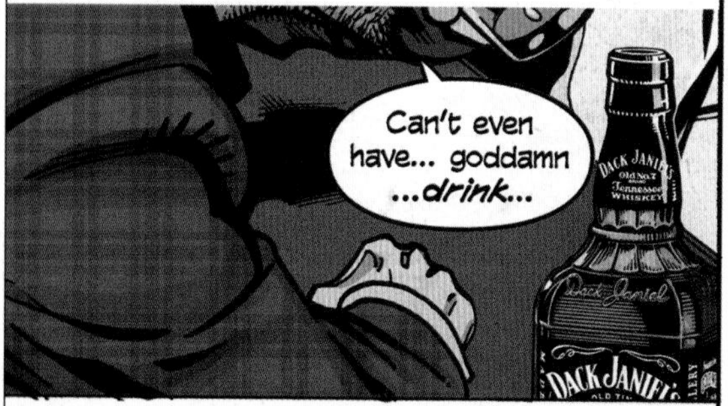
Can't even have... goddamn ...drink...
DACK JANIEL'S
Old No. 7
Tennessee WHISKEY
DACK JANIEL'S

The 132nd was the designation of my Scout troop in Dublin.

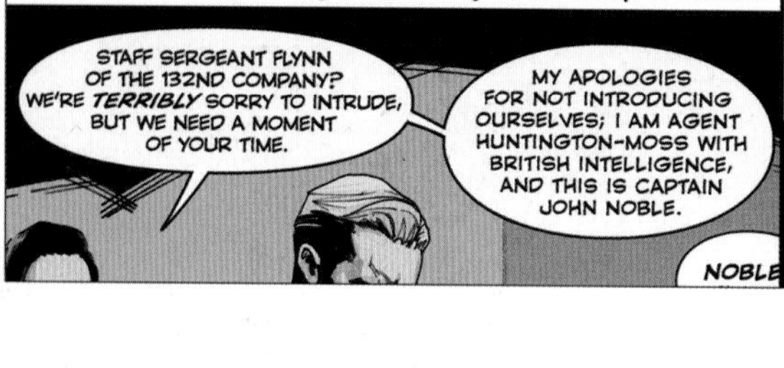
STAFF SERGEANT FLYNN OF THE 132ND COMPANY? WE'RE TERRIBLY SORRY TO INTRUDE, BUT WE NEED A MOMENT OF YOUR TIME.
MY APOLOGIES FOR NOT INTRODUCING OURSELVES; I AM AGENT HUNTINGTON-MOSS WITH BRITISH INTELLIGENCE, AND THIS IS CAPTAIN JOHN NOBLE.
NOBLE

I think the little sequence where Irish (uninvited) takes a drag from the bum's cigarette does a lot to establish his character. He's not the best-mannered chap in the world, but will always have a go.

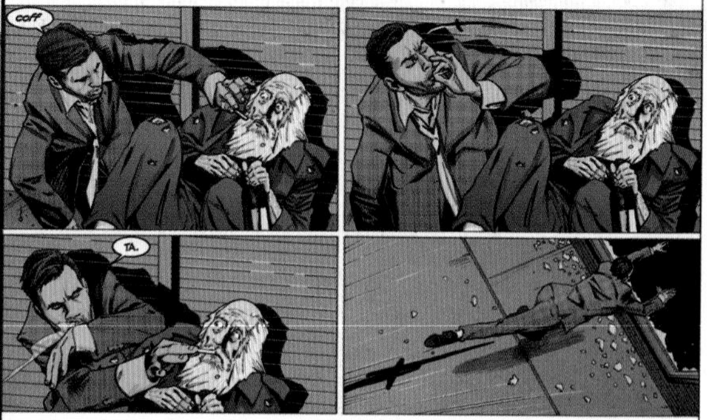
coff
TA.

Likewise, this panel really sets Elizabeth up nicely. Happy to let the silly boys thrash things out while she orchestrates and relaxes in the wings. I've never actually tasted Pimms...

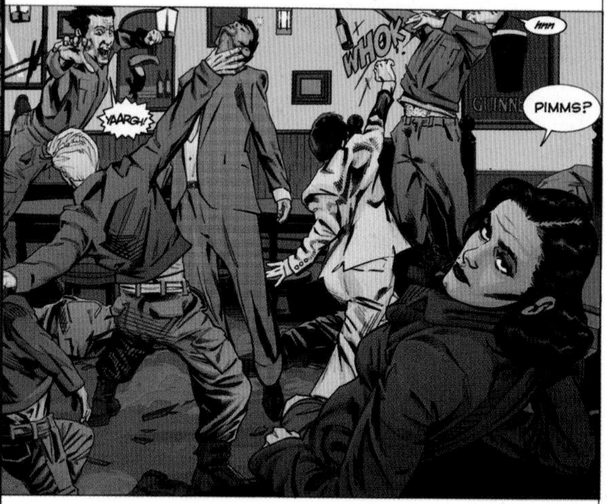
YAARGH!
WHOK!
hnn
PIMMS?

I hugely enjoyed laying out and drawing the whole bar brawl sequence. Like the T-Rex attack, it was a set-piece that I'd had in my mind's eye for a long time, and was almost a cathartic relief to finally get it out there. I figured if each issue was an act of the story, then two major set-pieces per issue/act would be the way to go. It's a template I stuck with pretty rigidly as the series progressed.

Issue 2:

So the big change with issue 2 was the addition of my good buddy, Ms. Jordie Bellaire, on colours.

I'd been utterly determined at the outset to control every aspect of the series myself, and at the beginning I'd managed that. I wrote, pencilled, inked, coloured and lettered issue 1. But it simply took too long. I spent something like three solid months on that first issue, and that wasn't a viable schedule if I wanted the series to see the light of day any time soon. When Jordie saw me flailing around in an anguished state she took pity on me, and offered to jump onboard and help me out.

At first (if you can believe it) I was a little reluctant to accept her ridiculously generous offer of help, becuase I'm such a bloody control freak, and giving up that (or any) aspect of the book terrified me. I also knew that Jordie's services were constantly in huge demand, and that *HPD* would have to be somewhat of a side-project for her. In the end though, I saw reason, and Jordie was IN.

IN LIKE FLYNN.

The very first image that Jordie coloured as a test for HPD was page four of issue 2. And I mean, she NAILED it.
Right off the bat she knew exactly what I was shooting for, tone-wise. It was so seamless it was ridiculous. Jordie took the palette and feel I'd established in issue 1, and refined and improved it while still remaining entirely consistent with what had come before.
I was bloody ecstatic. She was familiar with all of the same movies and books that I was, and was just as big a fan of much of the material. The transition was as smooth as silk, and we were in business.

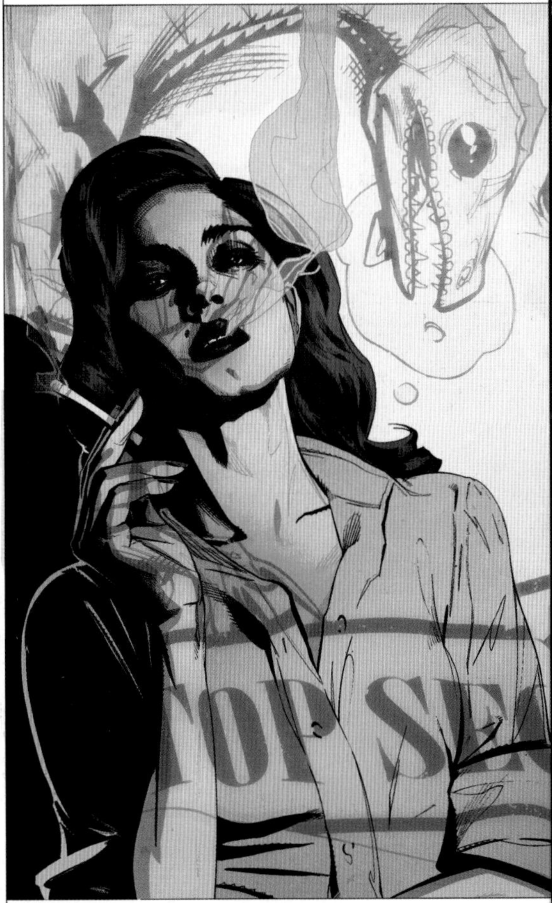

The 'Black Devils'; the special forces outfit based in Vermont that John and Ishi are part of were a real unit. They were officially called the '1st Special Service force' and were made up of U.S. and Canadian servicemen.
This outfiit was the beginnings of todays U.S. Special forces, and responsible for many a derring do in the second world war. Researching all of this stuff was almost as much fun as writing and drawing it.

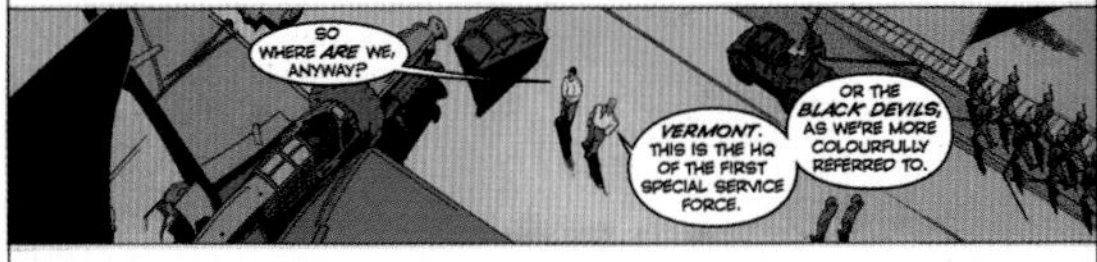
SO WHERE *ARE* WE, ANYWAY?
VERMONT. THIS IS THE HQ OF THE FIRST SPECIAL SERVICE FORCE.
OR THE *BLACK DEVILS*, AS WE'RE MORE COLOURFULLY REFERRED TO.

Every good yarn needs a good villain, and Oberleutnant Toht was my bad guy. Named after the rodent-like German from *Raiders of The Lost Ark* (yep, that again), he was one of my favourite characters to qrite. He was so far ahead of Irish and co. at every turn that I used to make myself giggle when coming up with his savage put-downs, constantly aimed Tommy's way.
The trick, I suppose, is to make the villain genuinely formidable, so as to place a real seed of doubt in the reader's mind that they know for sure exactly how everything will play out in the end. I mean, we know the hero is gonna prevail, but how so? We also know we won't be happy unless a T-rex eats the arch-villain at the end.
That's just science.

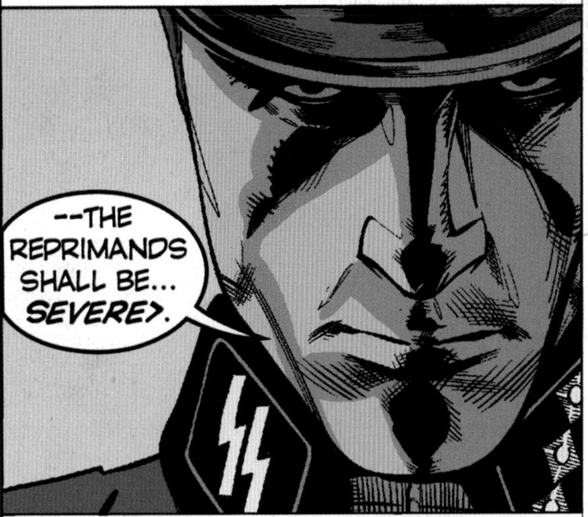
--THE REPRIMANDS SHALL BE... *SEVERE*>.

This one is pretty self-explanatory... Shameless, I know.

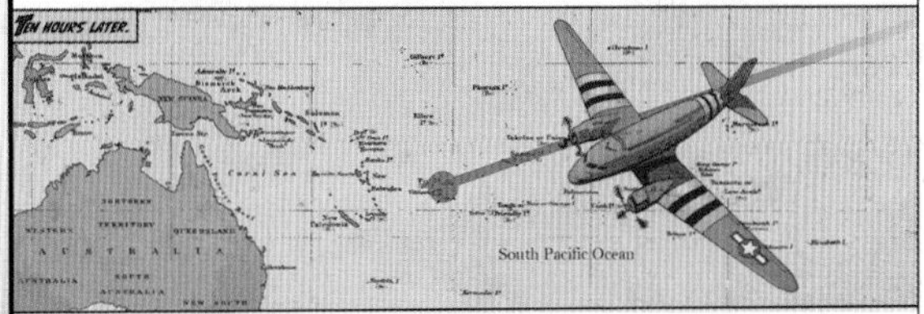
TEN HOURS LATER.
South Pacific Ocean

Yes, that is dino-shite in a jar. Jordie was also very proud of her speckled eggs. The ones in the panel, not her ovaries.

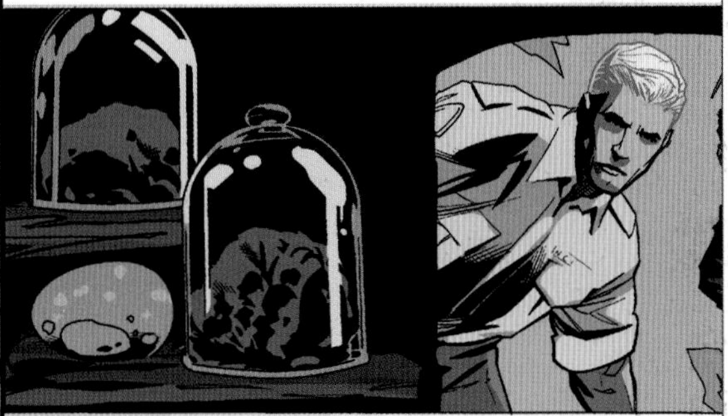

I went with the Deinonychus over the more ubiquitous Velociraptor, because I figured those had been done to death and in any case the Deinonychi were bigger and meaner.
Also, I got far too much enjoyment out of the 'Deinonychus? **Who** don't like us?' line. Thank you, Mr. Nick Roche.

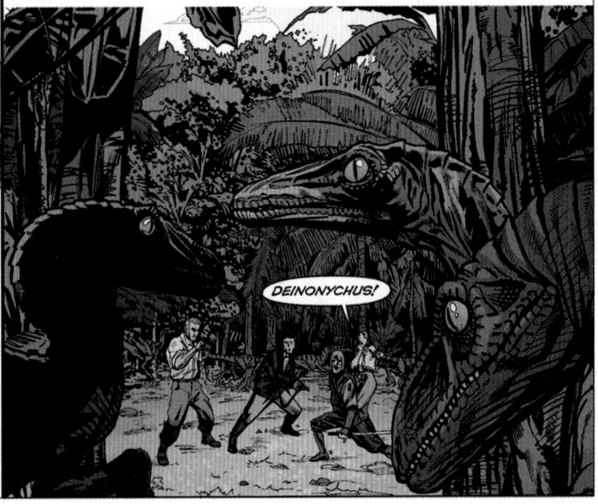
DEINONYCHUS!

I love Greta as a character. She's a nice counter-point to Agent Moss' severity, and happily cuts through Tommy's bullshit at any given opportunity. Her intelligence frequently exposes Irish for the nitwit he can often be. Plus, she's great fun to draw. The ladies are generally my favourite to work on overall. *cough.*

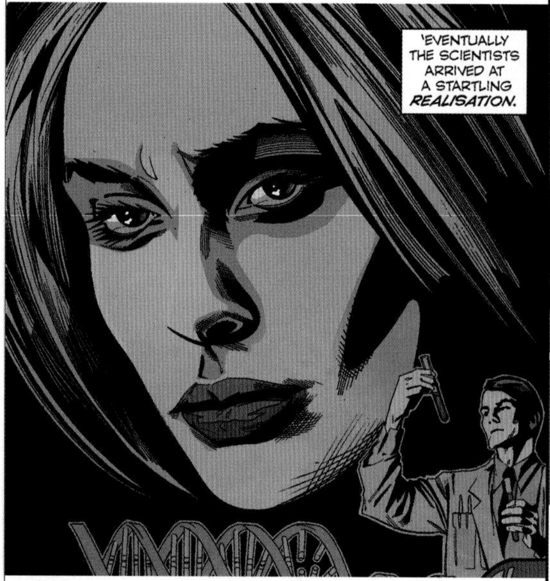
'EVENTUALLY THE SCIENTISTS ARRIVED AT A STARTLING *REALISATION.*

Plus, my comic book has Hitler in it. Does yours?

Issue 3:

I adore working with John, too, while I'm at it. He's obviously greatly inspired by the Steve Rogers/Doc Samson character archetype, but that doesn't make it any less enjoyable to play around with his back story and limitations. If I ever got my hands on a Marvel book, *Captain America* would be the one I'd love to try my hand at most. That stoic soldier-out-of-time material is right up my proverbial alley.

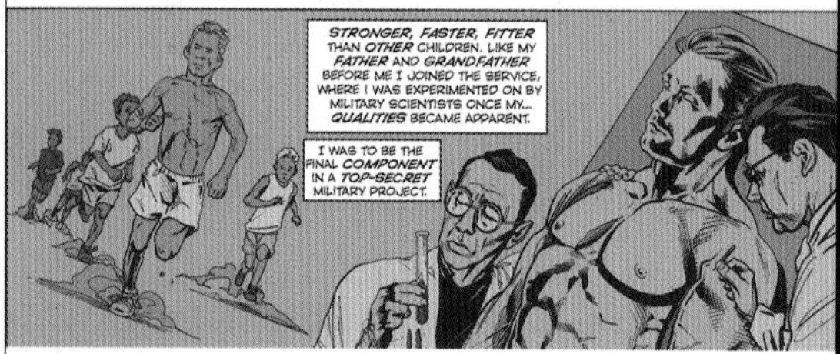
STRONGER, FASTER, FITTER THAN *OTHER* CHILDREN. LIKE MY *FATHER* AND *GRANDFATHER* BEFORE ME I JOINED THE SERVICE, WHERE I WAS EXPERIMENTED ON BY MILITARY SCIENTISTS ONCE MY... *QUALITIES* BECAME APPARENT.
I WAS TO BE THE FINAL *COMPONENT* IN A *TOP-SECRET* MILITARY PROJECT.

I wasn't as shy about portraying actual Jameson bottles when it came to the whiskey Irish favours, for some reason. I changed the name on the Jack Daniels bottle, but ploughed straight ahead with the Jemmy on about four separate occasions. Maybe it's because it's my own tipple of choice (I find the American stuff a tad too sweet). I guess in my wildest dreams I thought there might be an advertising tie-in opportunity down the line.
Hell, I'd take a free case.

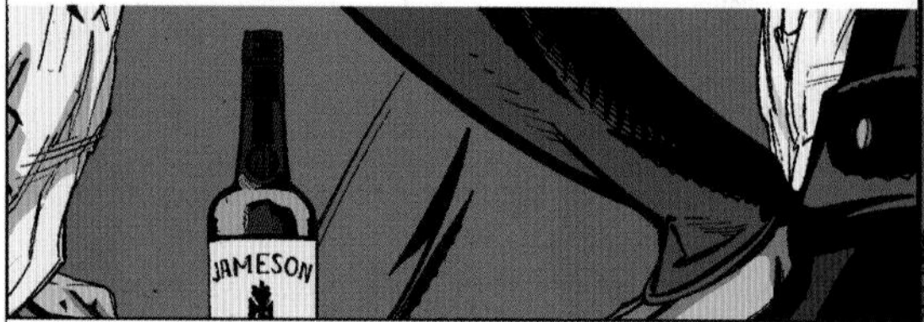
JAMESON

Page 11 of issue 3 is a good example of how I like to draw comics. These kind of sight gags really tickle me, and if paced and executed correctly, can really elicit an audible laugh from the reader. Tough to do, but oh-so rewarding when pulled off. I'd consider myself unsuccesful if i didn't manage at least one of these in each issue. Again, I enjoy full sequences with no dialogue whatsoever, since this happens all of the time in real life. I'm not a fan of narrative captions, either.

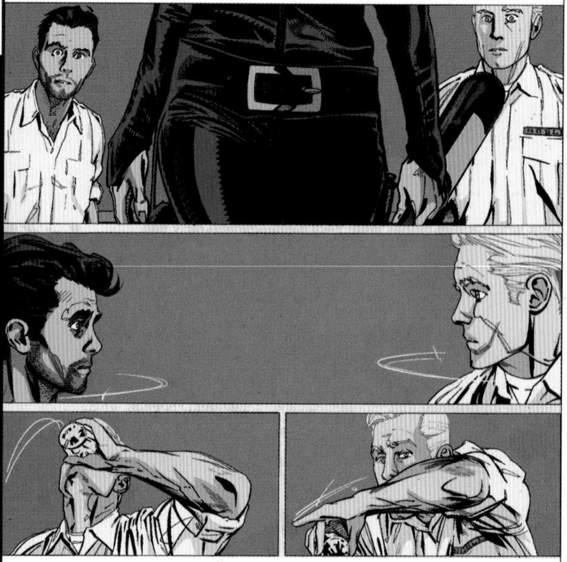

Just as much fun is getting to show Agent Huntington-Moss being a badass. I wish I could've fit more stuff like this into the first series, and plan on giving Elizabeth much more on-screen action in the sequel, assuming she's, y'know, *in* it (she is).
I'd actually love to do an Agent Moss one-shot, where she's off on a solo mission for MI6, but who knows if that'll happen as yet.

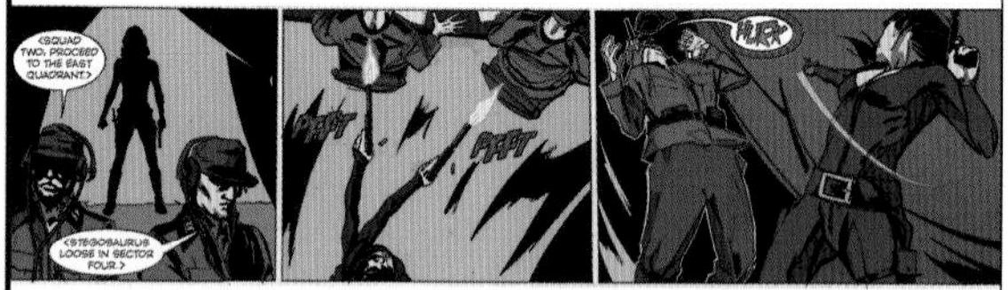
<SQUAD TWO: PROCEED TO THE EAST QUADRANT.>
<STEGOSAURUS LOOSE IN SECTOR FOUR.>

This one panel really illustrates the original premise for the book: Nazis versus Dinosaurs. That was my original high concept way back when, and the sentence that the whole thing spun out of. As much fun to work on as you'd imagine.

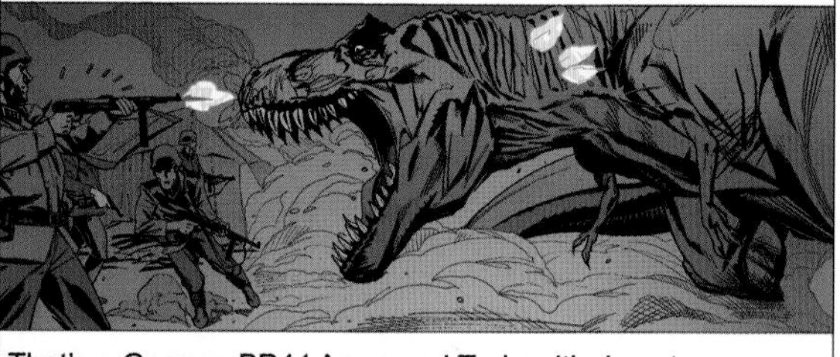

That's a German BP44 Armoured Train with desert camo. Those things actually existed. The Nazis had their downsides, sure, but you can't really fault their design sense.

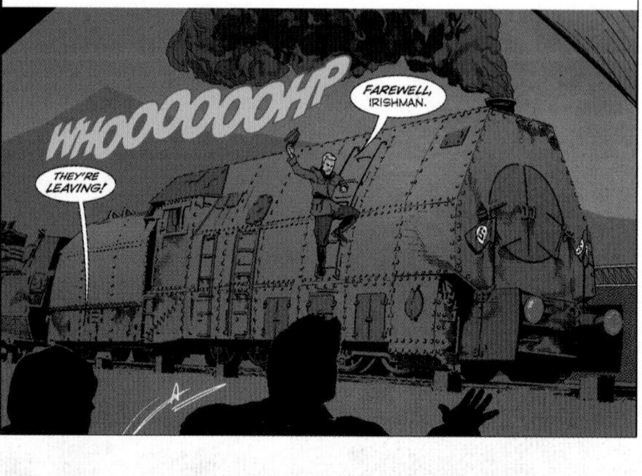
WHOOOOOOOHP
FAREWELL, IRISHMAN.
THEY'RE LEAVING!

Issue 4:

Yep, that's the Mercedes-Benz LG3000 truck from the famous chase scene in *Raiders of The Lost Ark*. See a pattern forming here?

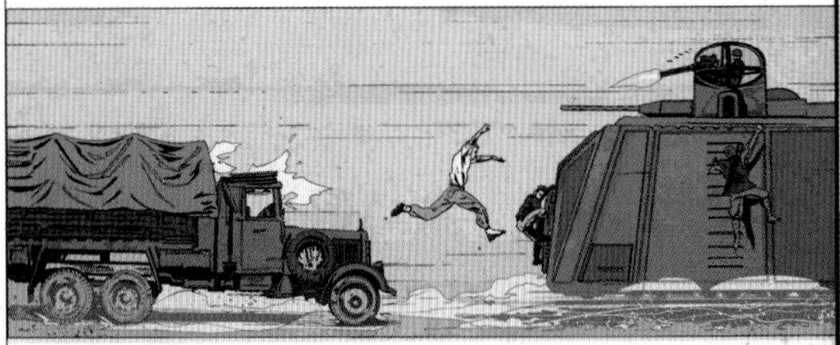

This is one of my absolute favourite panels in the book, and one of the very few that looks exactly as it had in my mind's eye for the past couple of years. An Irish bloke facing down two T-Rexes. Not the most groundbreaking narrative of all time, granted. But undeniably cool, or at least I hoped so.

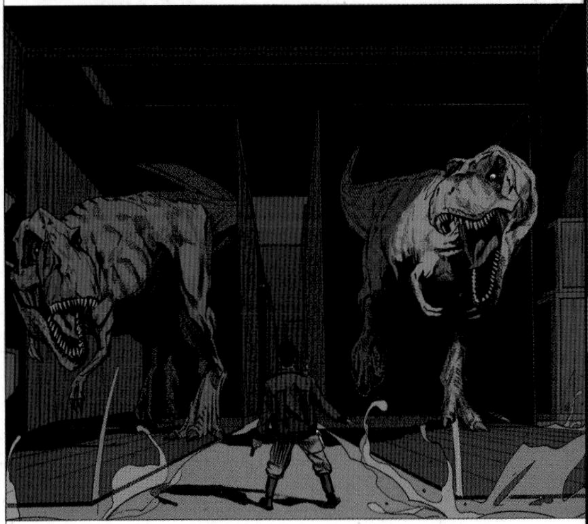

Issue 5:

I adore what Jordie did with the colours in the U-Boat sequence. I literally asked "can we make the sub interiors all red or green-lit depending on the alert level," and she came back with probably my favourite colour palette in the entire series. Here's to you, Bellaire.

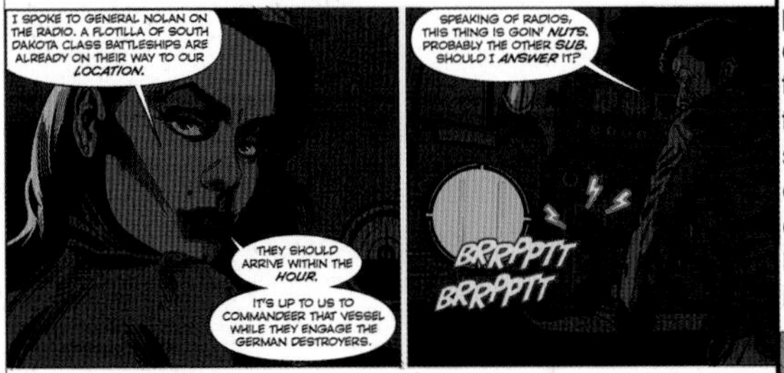
I SPOKE TO GENERAL NOLAN ON THE RADIO. A FLOTILLA OF SOUTH DAKOTA CLASS BATTLESHIPS ARE ALREADY ON THEIR WAY TO OUR *LOCATION.*
THEY SHOULD ARRIVE WITHIN THE *HOUR.*
IT'S UP TO US TO COMMANDEER THAT VESSEL WHILE THEY ENGAGE THE GERMAN DESTROYERS.
SPEAKING OF RADIOS, THIS THING IS GOIN' *NUTS.* PROBABLY THE OTHER *SUB.* SHOULD I *ANSWER* IT?
BRRPPTT
BRRPPTT

I've always wanted to draw an underwater sub vs. sub sequence. This is yet another set-piece that I've had in my mind's eye for a long while now. All of these various action scenes formed the nucleus of what would become *HPD*, once I could figure out how to write a pesky *story*.

One of my biggest concerns going into the writing of the book was that I was very aware that a bunch of cool action set-pieces do not an engaging narrative make. It's all very well and good having some cool visual ideas, but if you simply mash that all up and throw it at the wall to see what sticks, you're on a hiding to nothing. I've read too many action-oriented comics over the years where the 'storyline' was simply a vehicle to move the characters from one contrived fight scene to another.

This was the device I wanted to avoid more than any other, as I knew that *Half Past Danger* would live or die by its writing, not its art. I was relatively confident going in that I could deliver on the visual side of things to a reasonable extent, but it was squeeky bum-time when it came to the writing. Therein lay the terror sweat. At the end of the day though, by all accounts the storyline has been very well received, and people seem to be really digging where it's going. Which is hugely gratifying. I also have to say, sitting down and writing the script was one of the more enjoyable aspects to the whole venture.

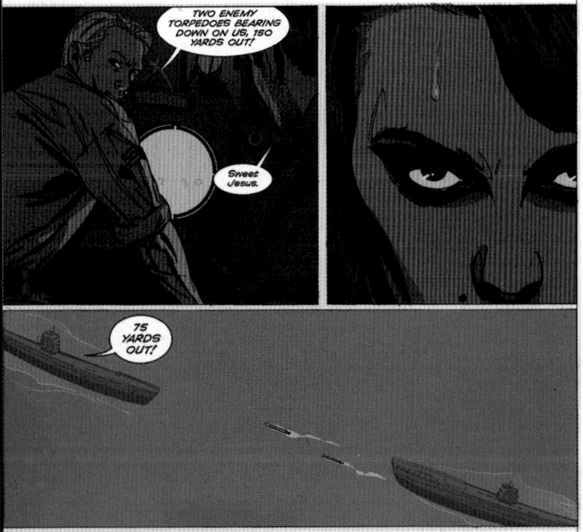
TWO ENEMY TORPEDOES BEARING DOWN ON US, 150 YARDS OUT!
Sweet Jesus.
75 YARDS OUT!

My favourite line of John's in the whole book. Yeah, baby!

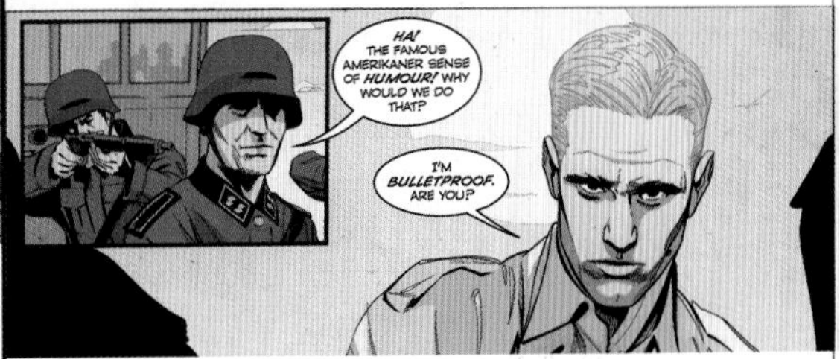
HA! THE FAMOUS AMERIKANER SENSE OF *HUMOUR!* WHY WOULD WE DO THAT?
I'M *BULLETPROOF.* ARE YOU?

Issue 6:

This, to me, was the big reveal as much as the Moss twist; that the Nazis were after John all along. I'm glad that not too many people guessed this aspect, so there was at least one element of surprise there. Moreso than the Femme Fatale character turning on her allies anyway, which is pretty much a staple of the genre by this point. To me, the twist with Elizabeth is that she *still* isn't all that she seems, and there's far more to come on that front. She's probably my favourite character, and I certainly wouldn't want her to be that one-note and clichéd. Let's just say that Elizabeth's true employers possibly haven't made the team's acquaintance yet.

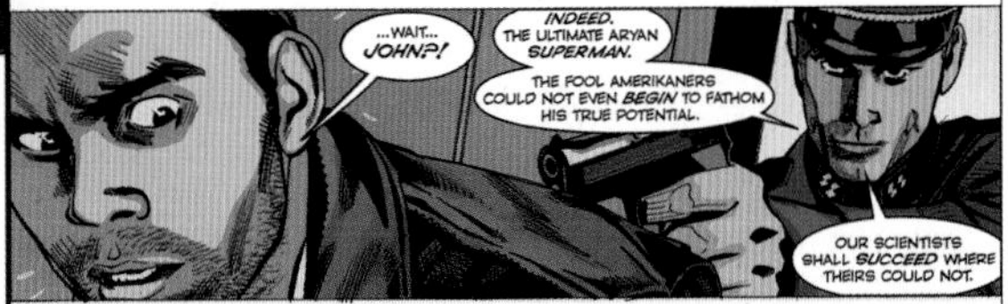
...WAIT... *JOHN?!*
INDEED. THE ULTIMATE ARYAN *SUPERMAN.*
THE FOOL AMERIKANERS COULD NOT EVEN *BEGIN* TO FATHOM HIS TRUE POTENTIAL.
OUR SCIENTISTS SHALL *SUCCEED* WHERE THEIRS COULD NOT.

So, in the end, Irish kills hundreds of innocent and incredibly rare animals. This isn't something I decided on lightly, but the question he faced was what's best for the human race, and that was the only viable answer. This isn't the last Tommy will be hearing about it, though. Stay tuned.

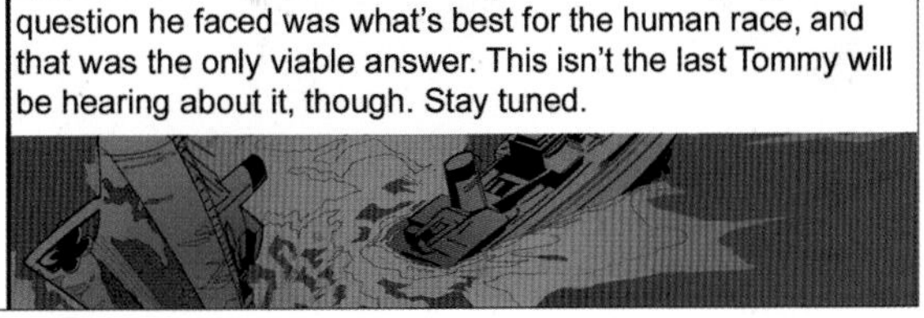

SERIES TEASER

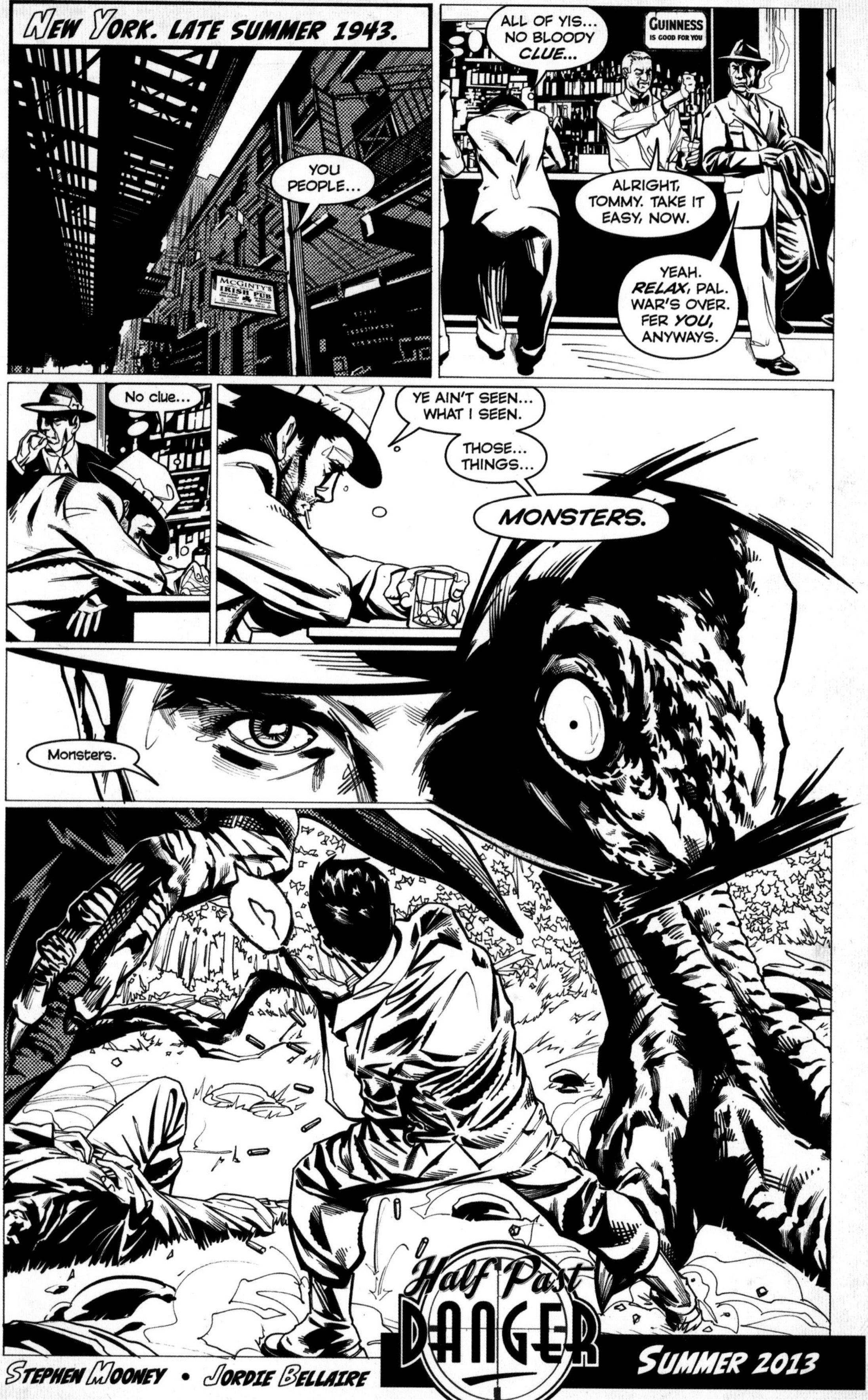
NEW YORK. LATE SUMMER 1943.
McGINTY'S
IRISH PUB
YOU PEOPLE...
ALL OF YIS... NO BLOODY CLUE...
GUINNESS IS GOOD FOR YOU
ALRIGHT, TOMMY. TAKE IT EASY, NOW.
YEAH. RELAX, PAL. WAR'S OVER. FER YOU, ANYWAYS.
No clue...
YE AIN'T SEEN... WHAT I SEEN.
THOSE... THINGS...
MONSTERS.
Monsters.
Half Past
DANGER

STEPHEN MOONEY • JORDIE BELLAIRE

SUMMER 2013

CHARACTER DESIGNS

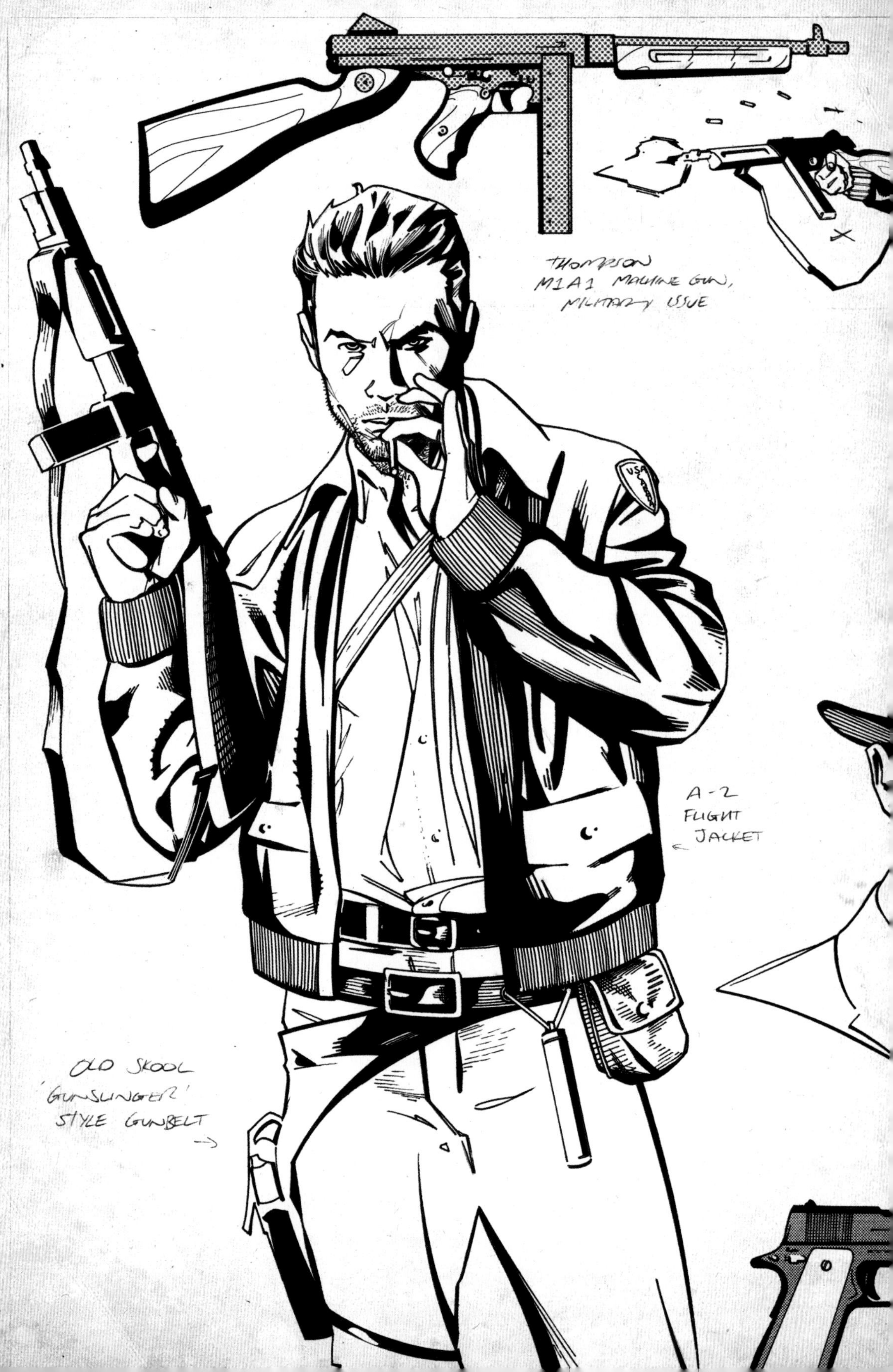
THOMPSON
M1A1 MACHINE GUN,
MILITARY ISSUE
A-2
FLIGHT
JACKET
OLD SKOOL
'GUNSLINGER'
STYLE GUNBELT

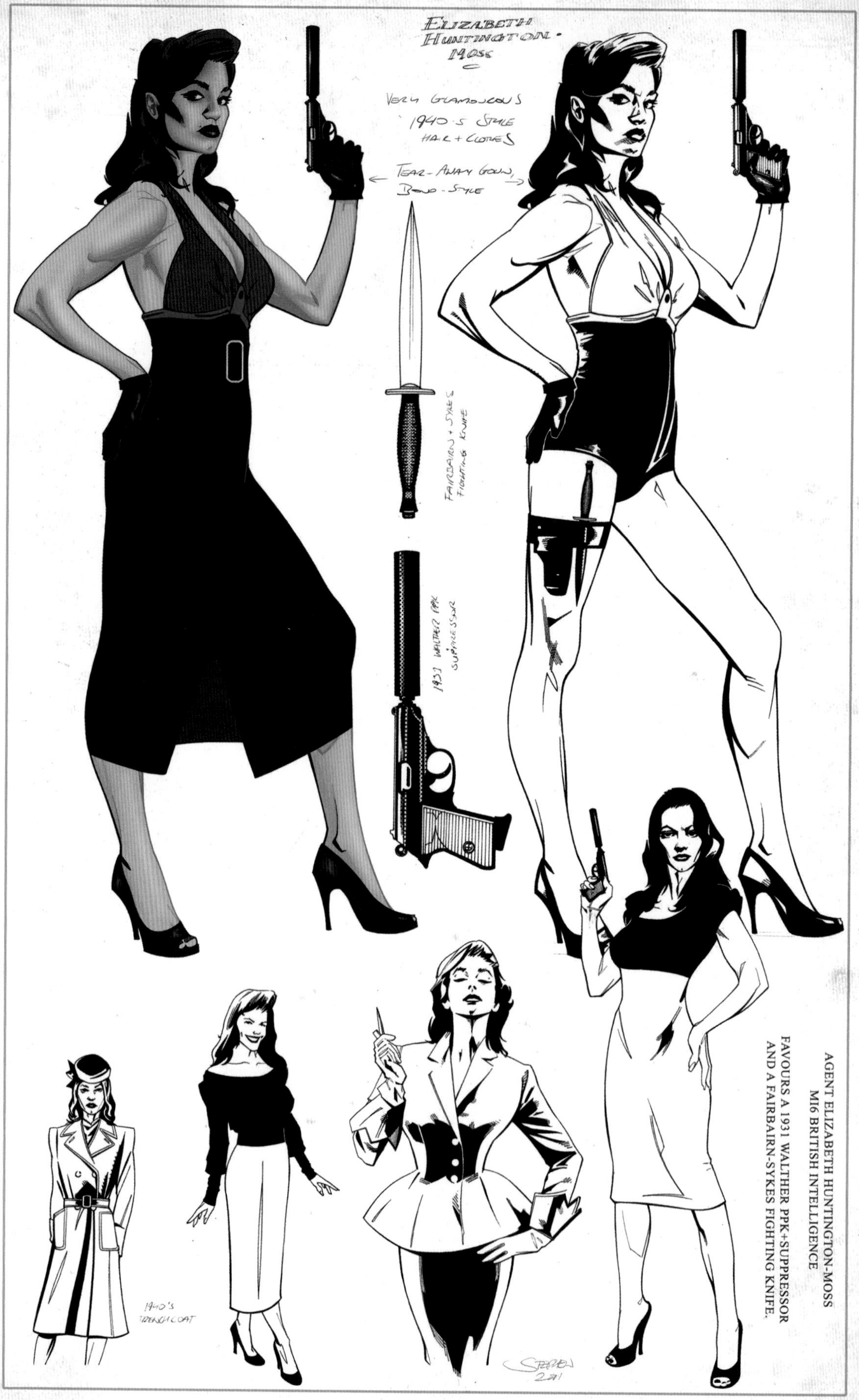

ELIZABETH HUNTINGTON-MOSS
VERY GLAMOROUS 1940'S STYLE HAIR + CLOTHES
TEAR-AWAY GOWN, BOND-STYLE
FAIRBAIRN + SYKES FIGHTING KNIFE
1931 WALTHER PPK SUPPRESSOR
1940'S TRENCH COAT
AGENT ELIZABETH HUNTINGTON-MOSS
MI6 BRITISH INTELLIGENCE
FAVOURS A 1931 WALTHER PPK+SUPPRESSOR
AND A FAIRBAIRN-SYKES FIGHTING KNIFE.

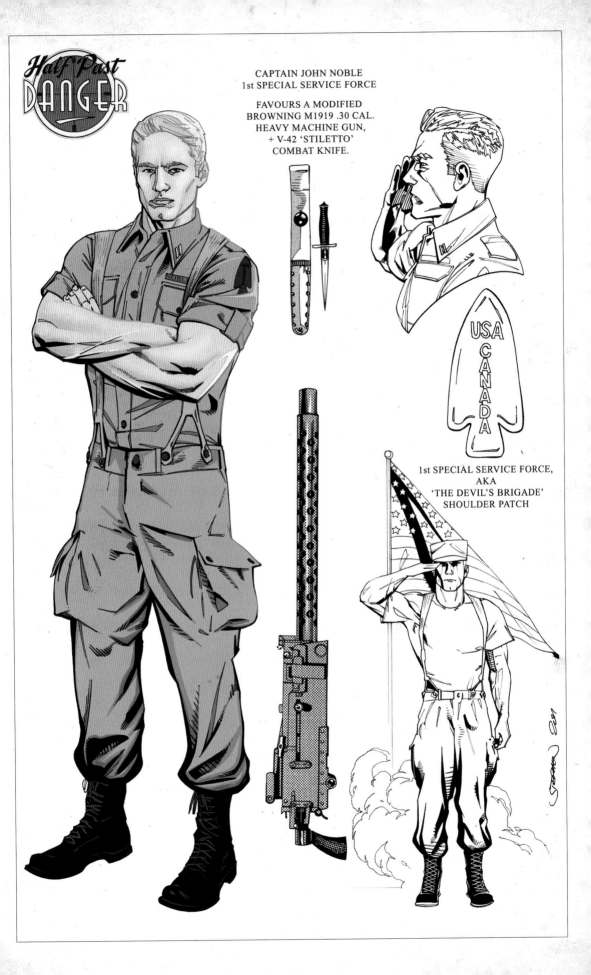

Half Past DANGER

CAPTAIN JOHN NOBLE
1st SPECIAL SERVICE FORCE

FAVOURS A MODIFIED
BROWNING M1919 .30 CAL.
HEAVY MACHINE GUN,
+ V-42 'STILETTO'
COMBAT KNIFE.

USA
CANADA

1st SPECIAL SERVICE FORCE,
AKA
'THE DEVIL'S BRIGADE'
SHOULDER PATCH

ISHIKAWA MINAMOTO
EX- JAPANESE SPECIAL NAVAL
LANDING FORCES (SNLF)

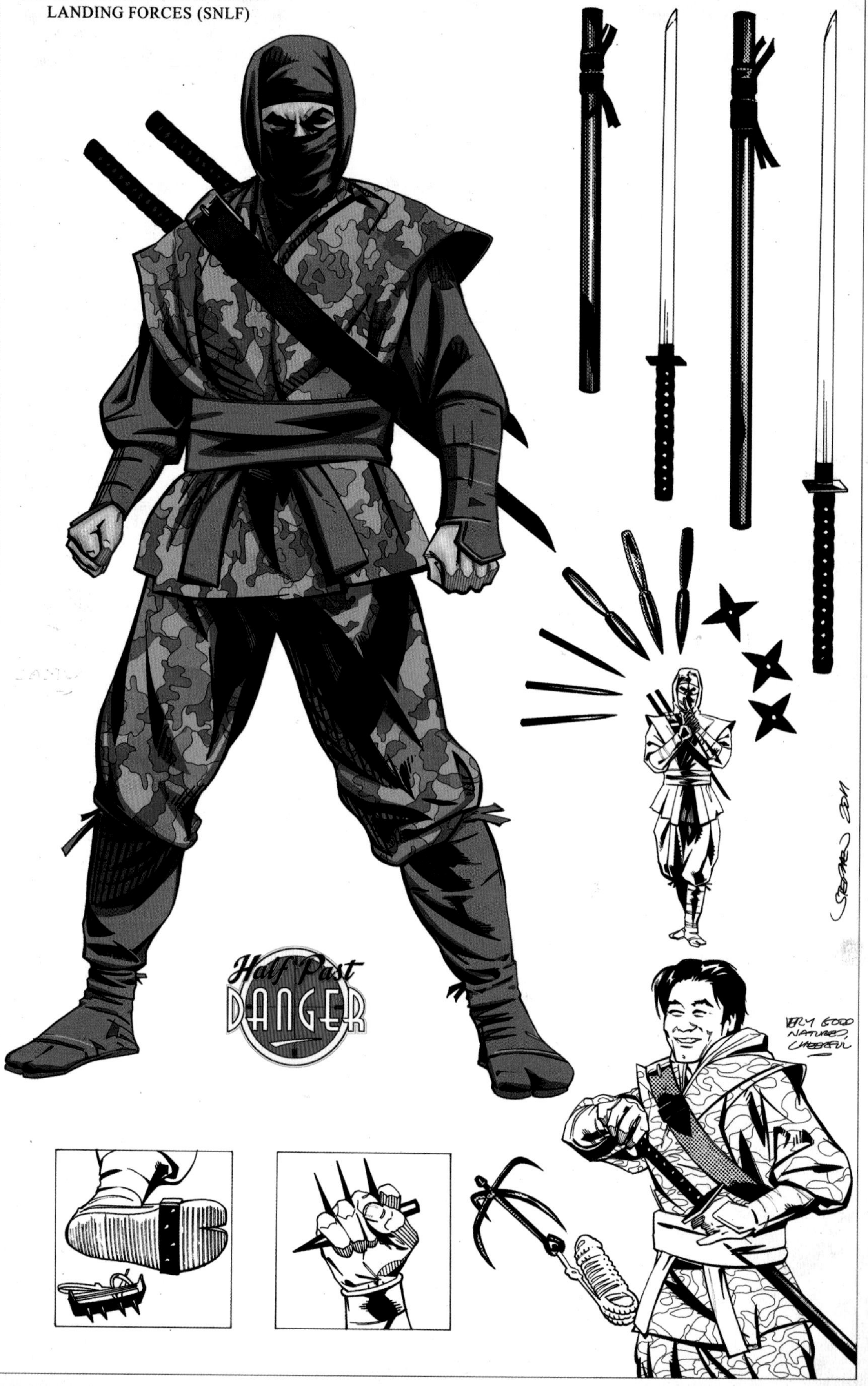
Half Past DANGER
VERY GOOD NATURED, CHEERFUL

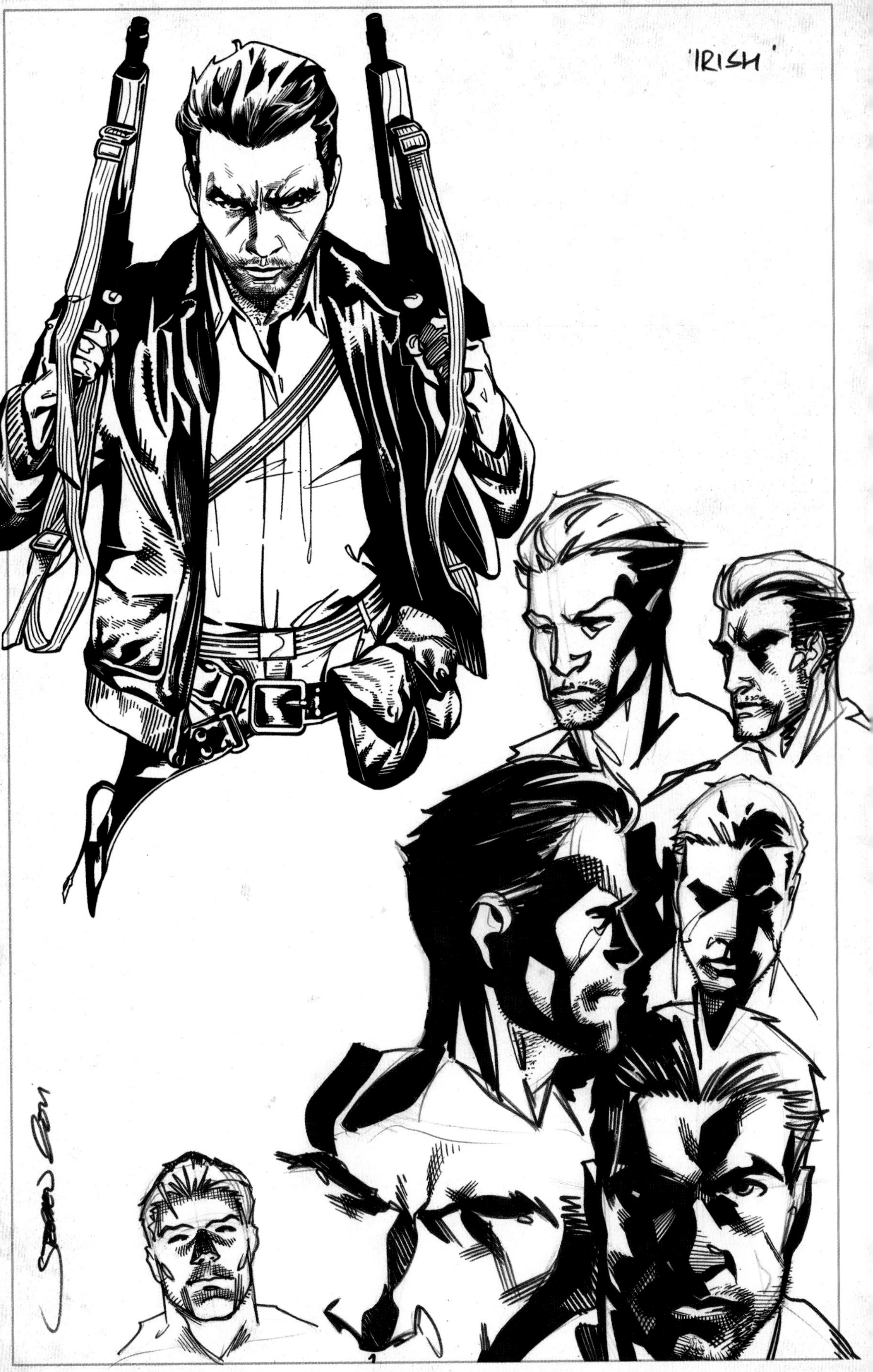
'IRISH'

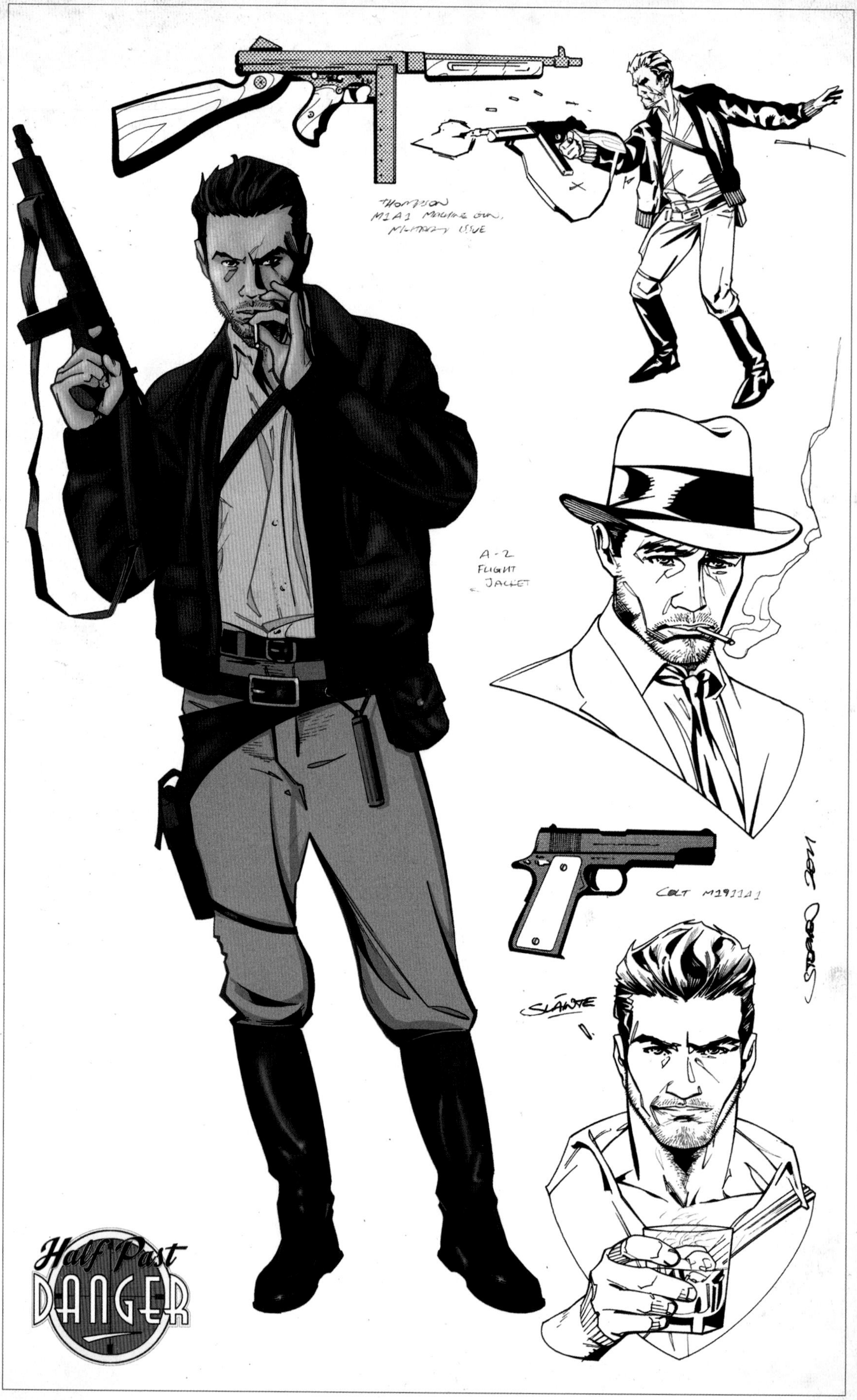

THOMPSON M1A1 MACHINE GUN, MILITARY ISSUE
A-2 FLIGHT JACKET
COLT M1911A1
SLÁINTE !
Half Past DANGER

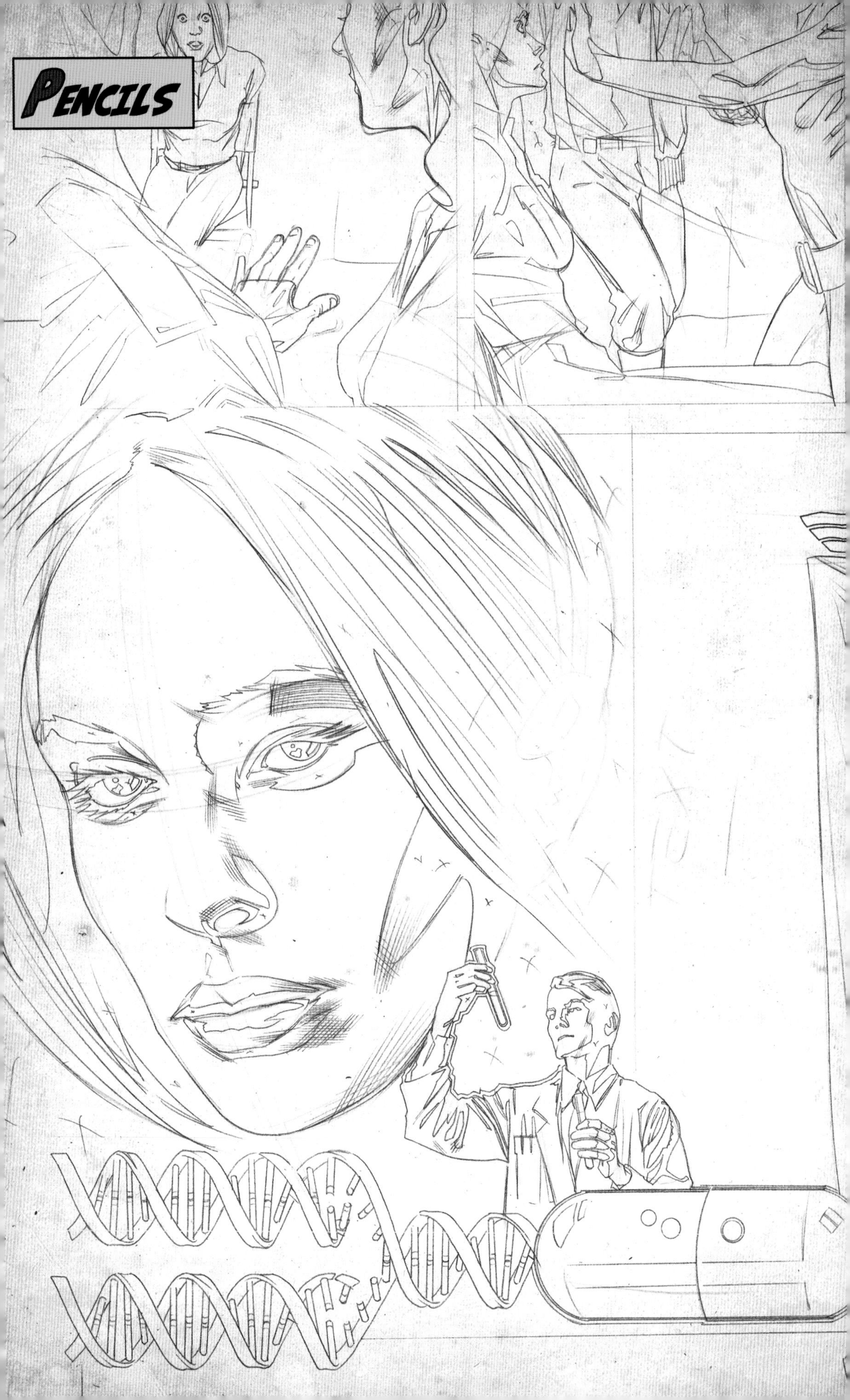
PENCILS

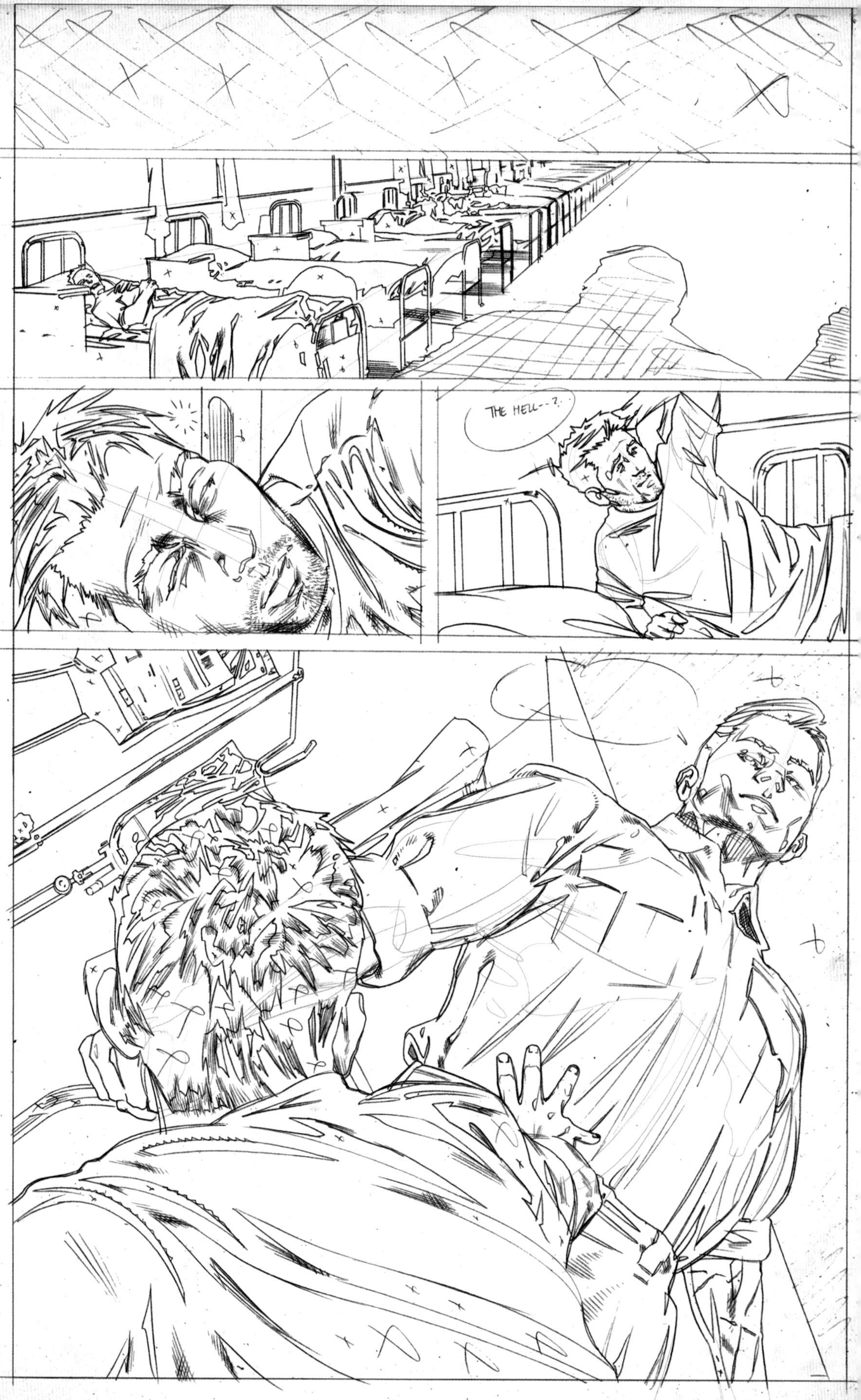
THE HELL--?

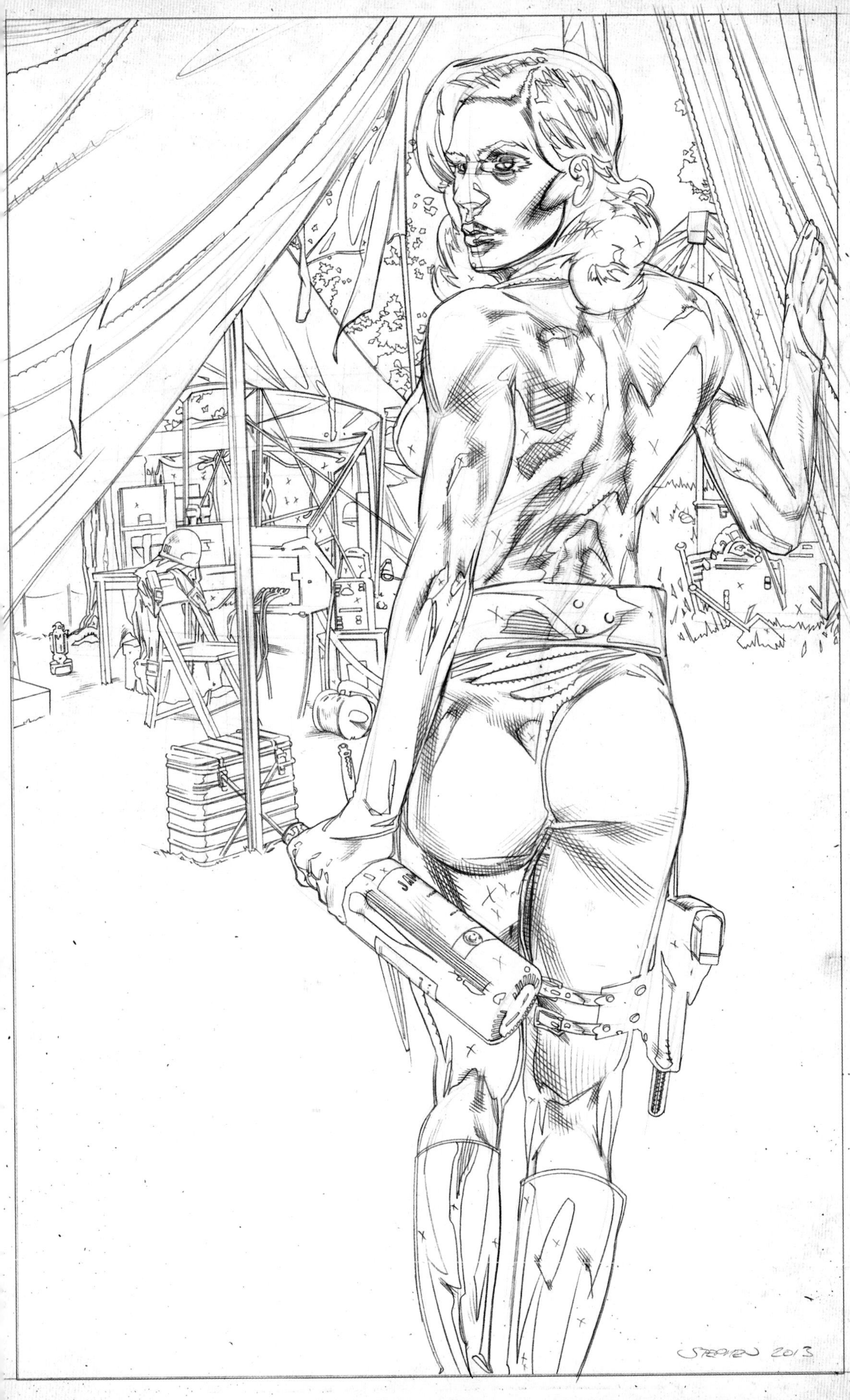
STEPHEN 2013

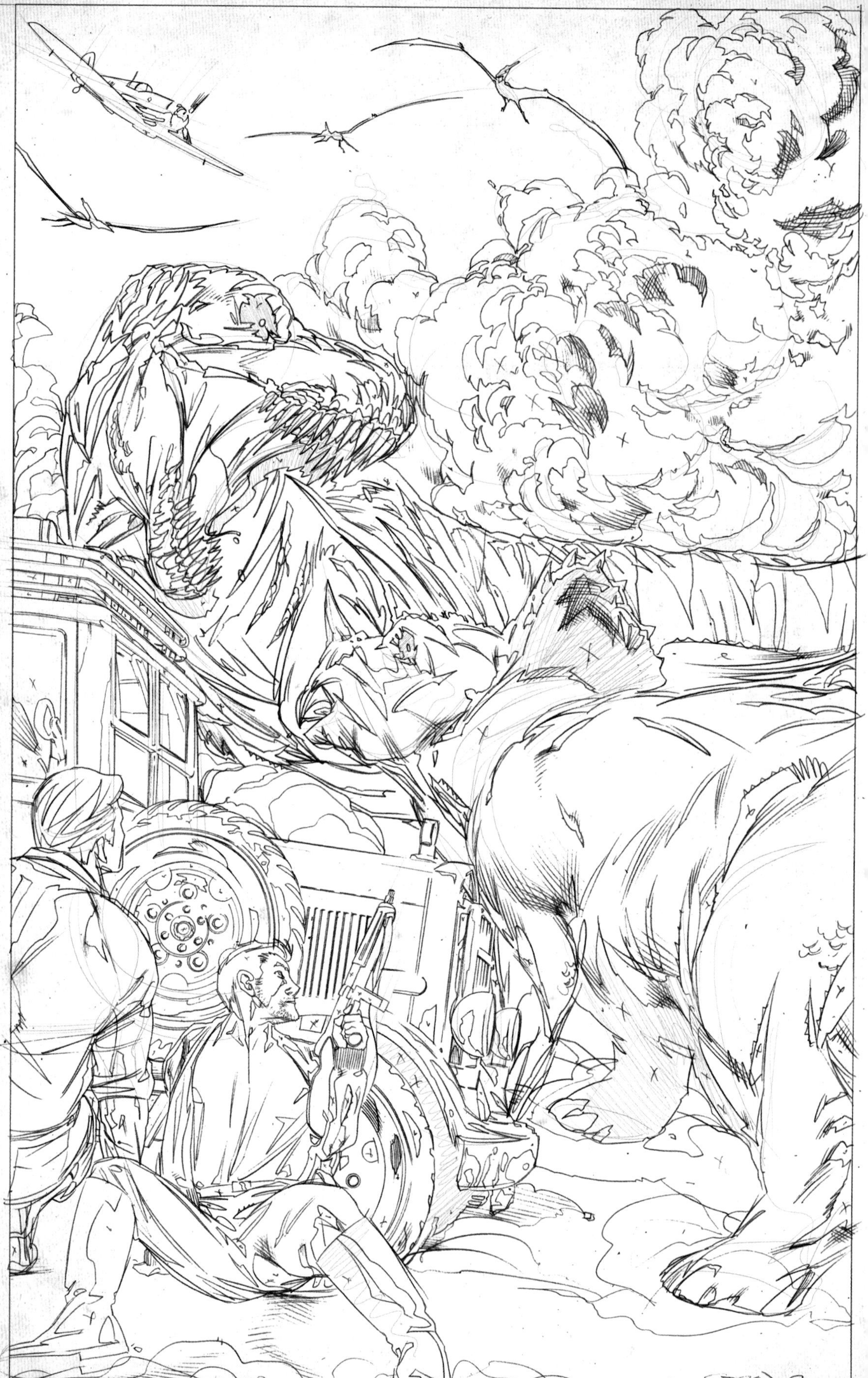

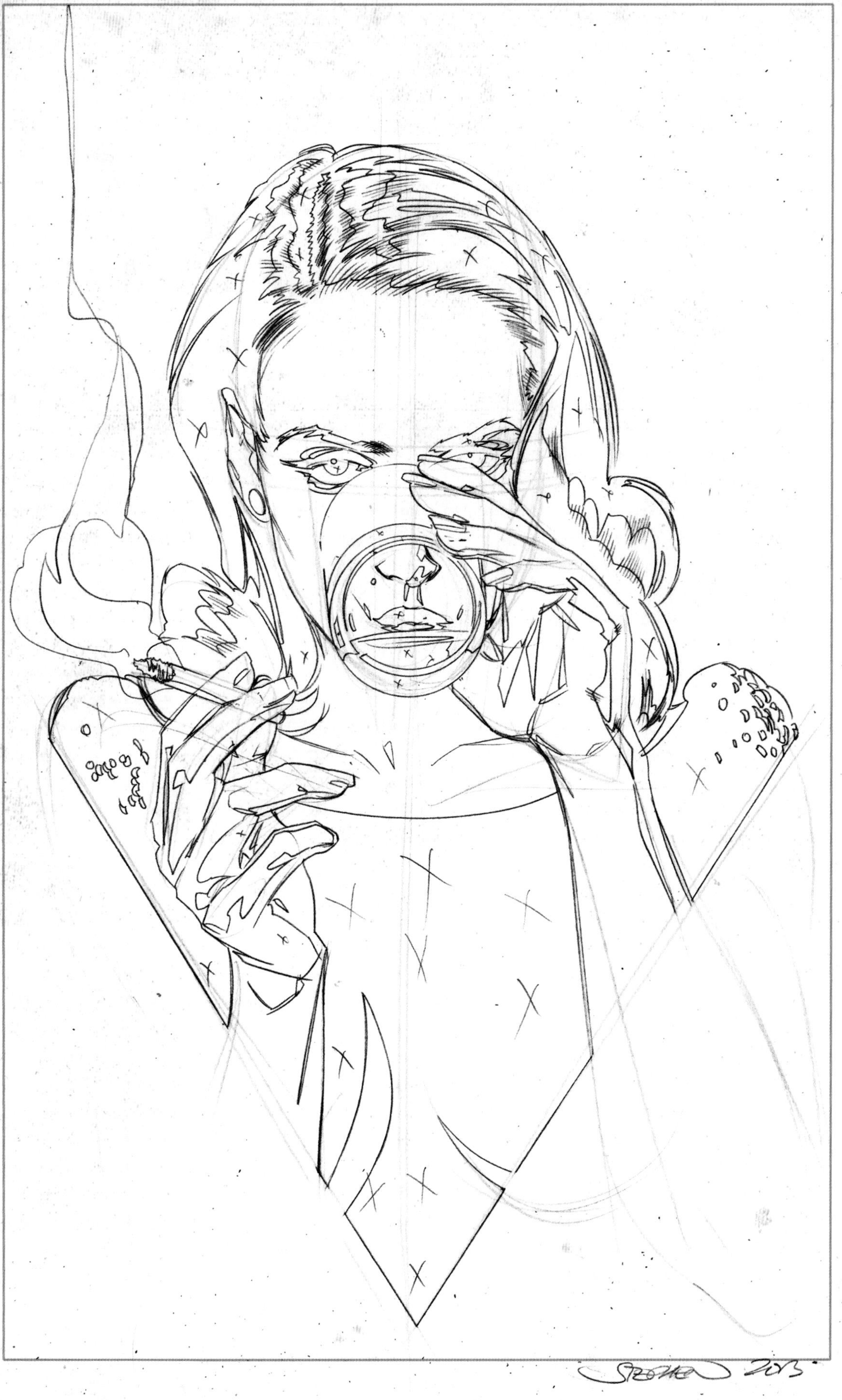

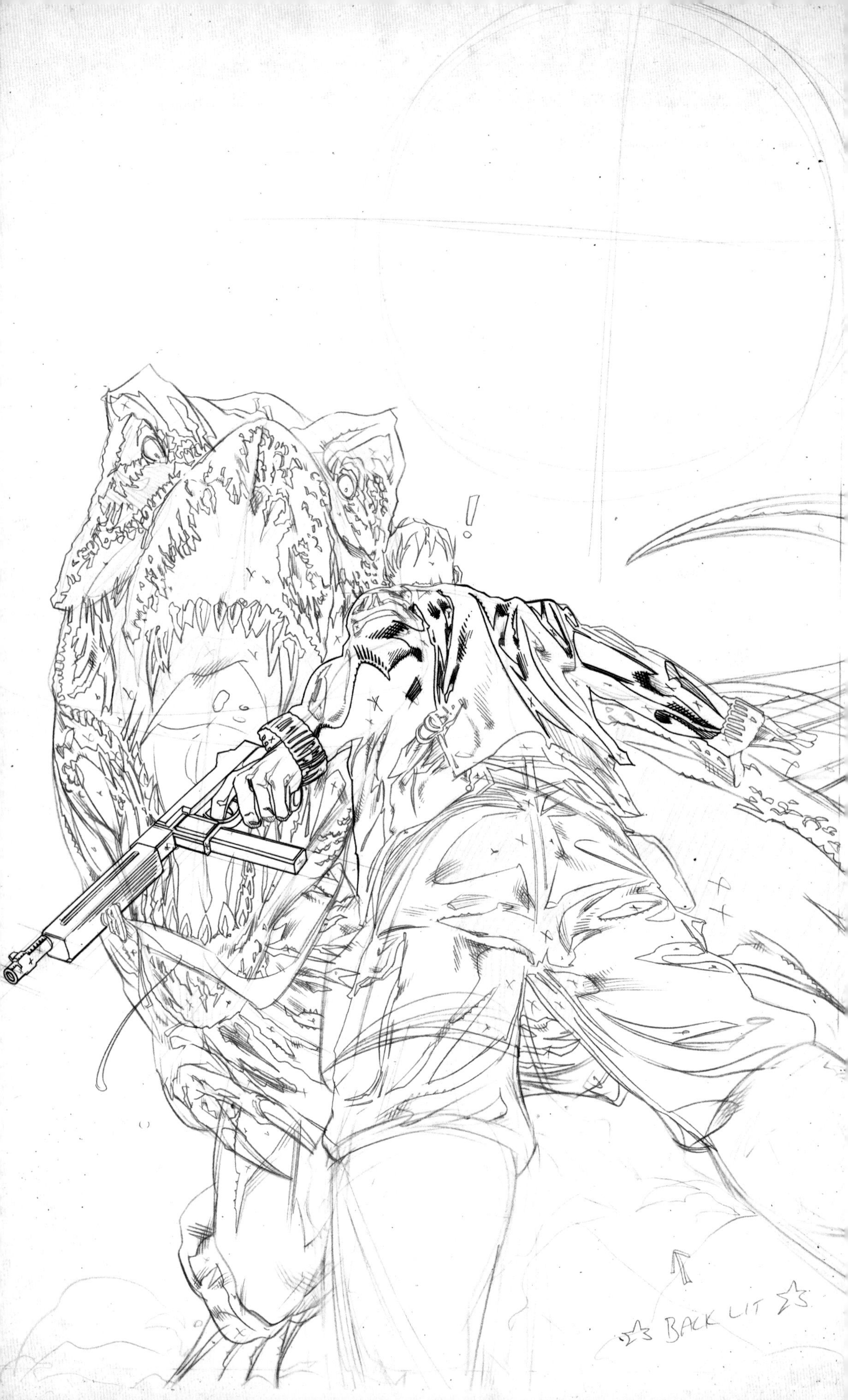
!
BACK LIT

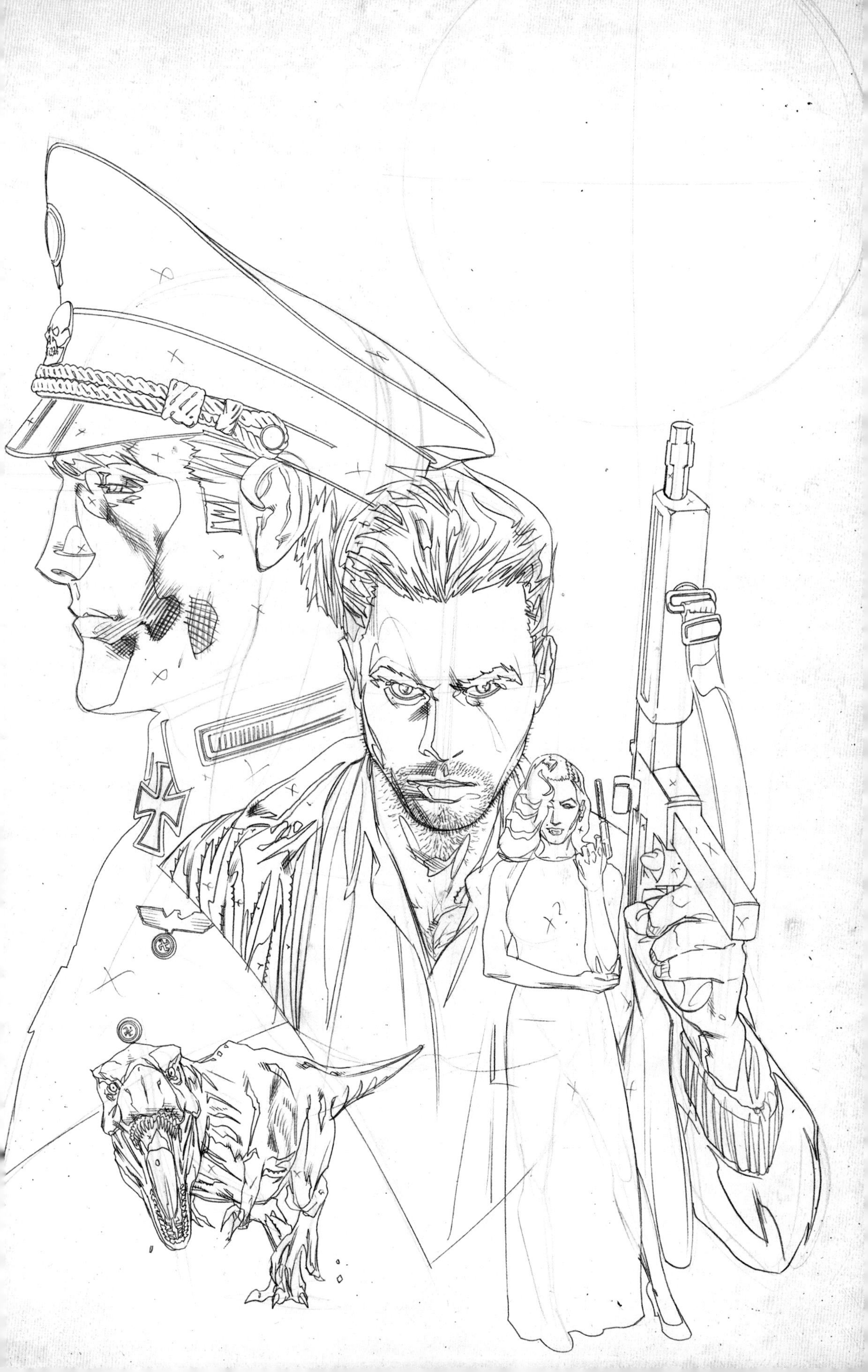

PIN-UPS

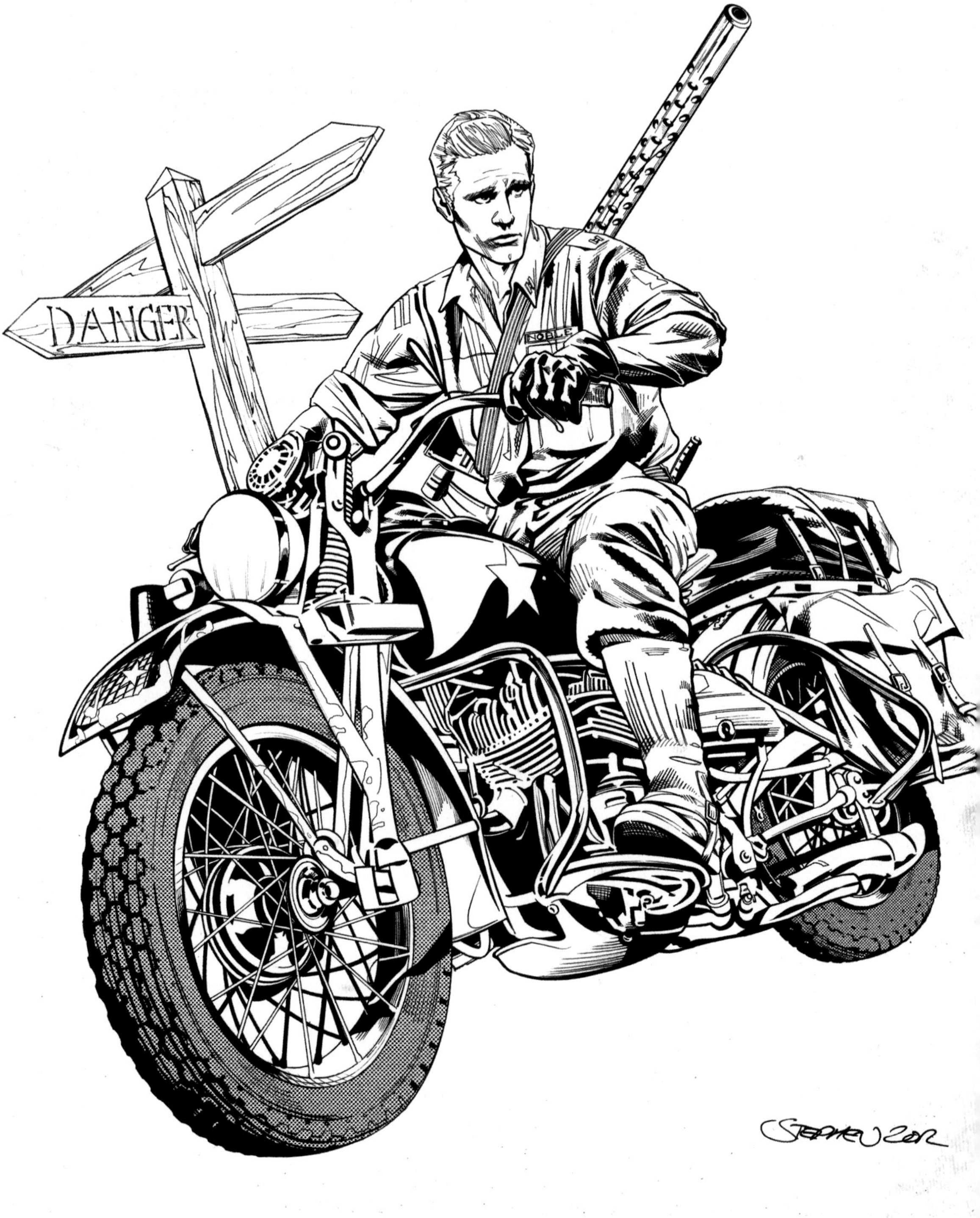
DANGER
NOBLE
STEPHEN 2012

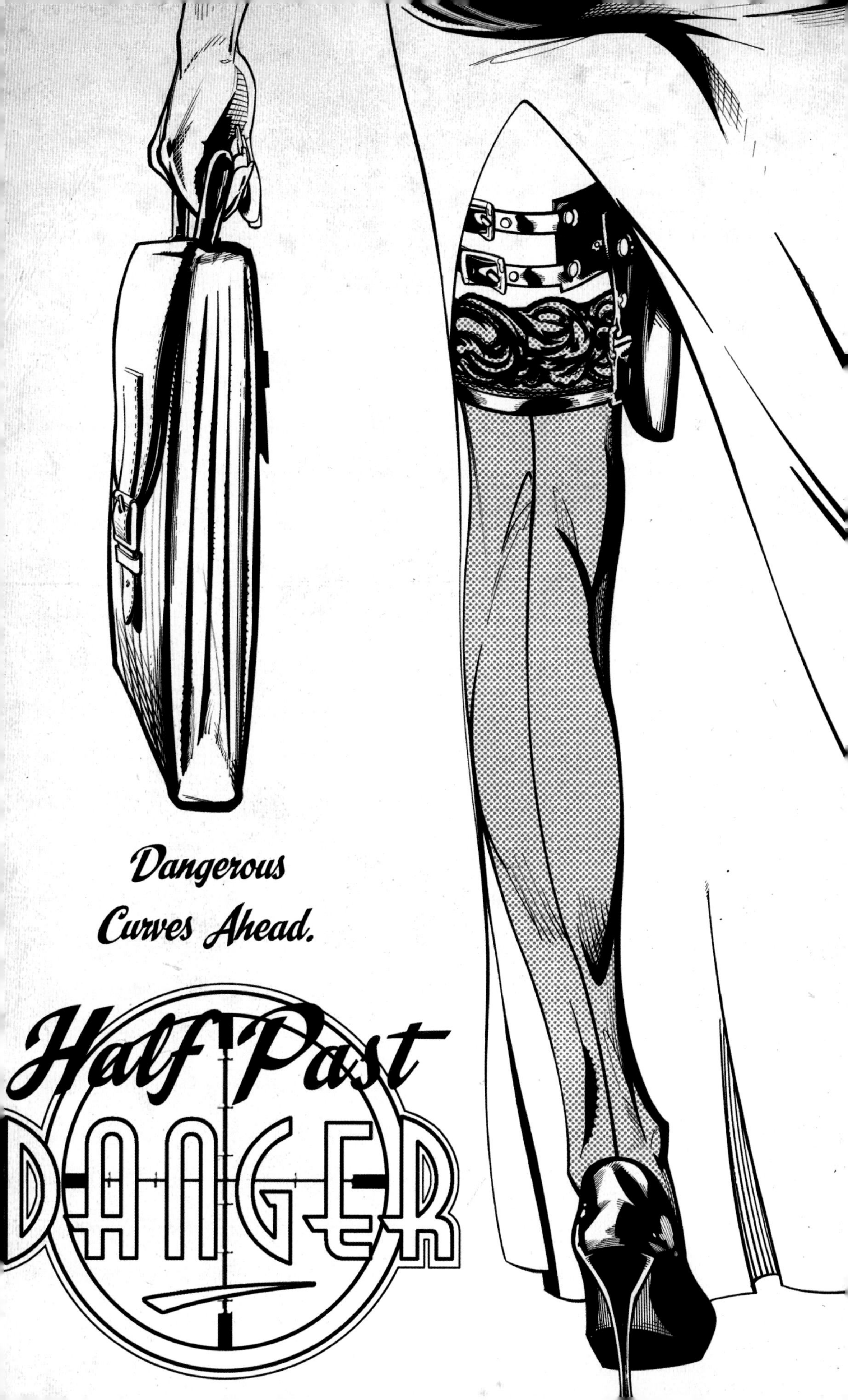
Dangerous
Curves Ahead.
Half Past
DANGER

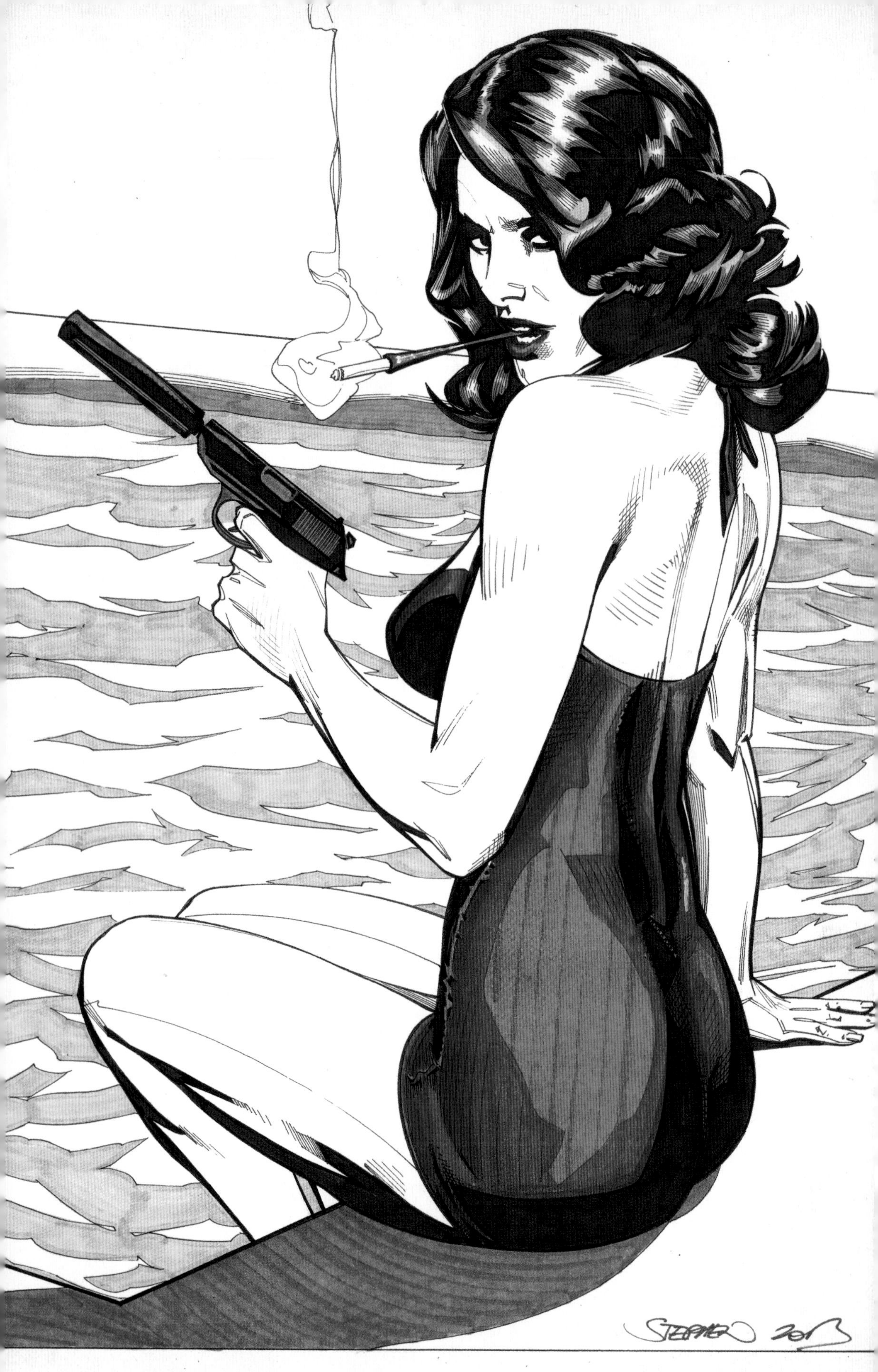
STEPHEN 2013

AGENT MOSS

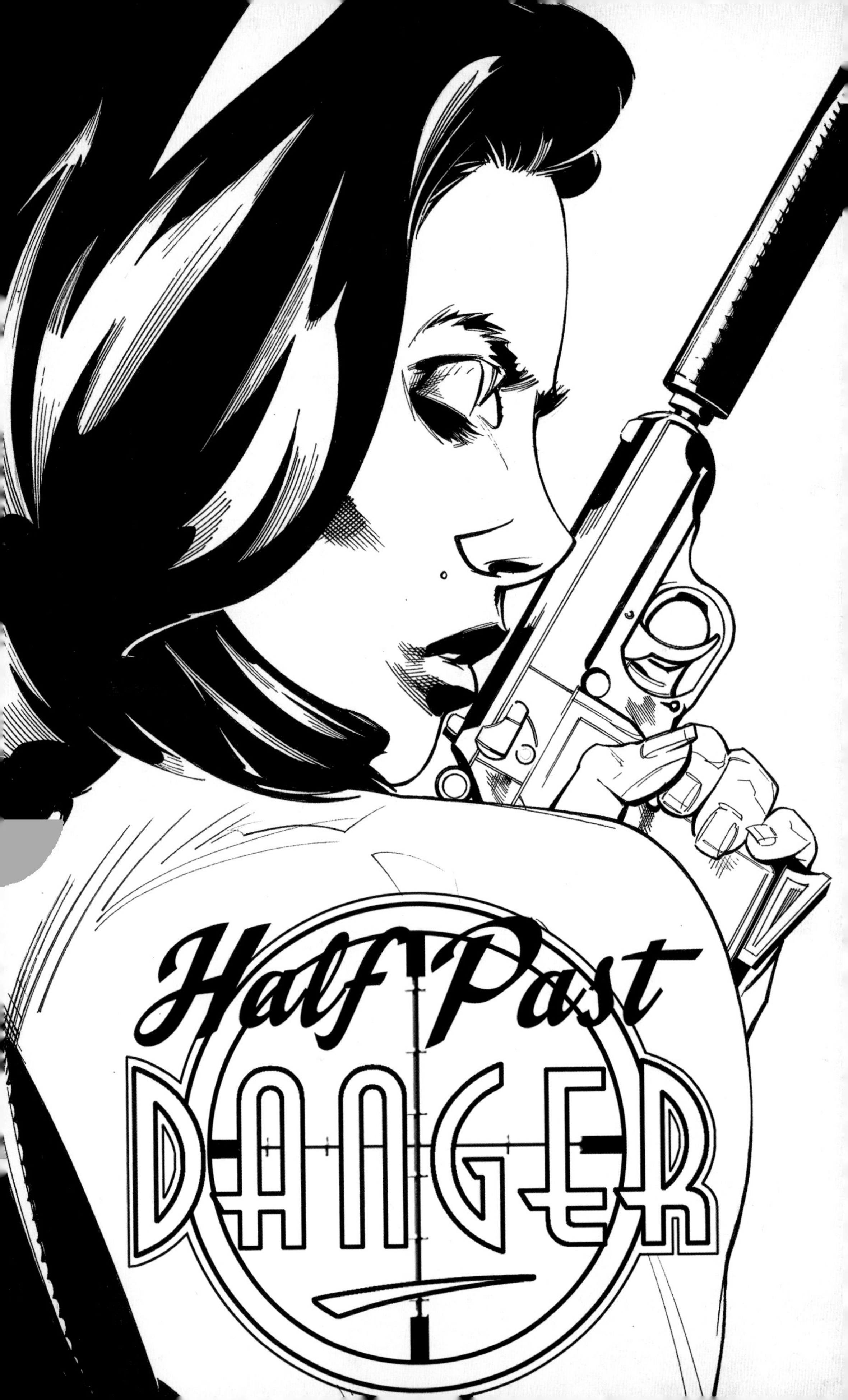
Half Past
DANGER

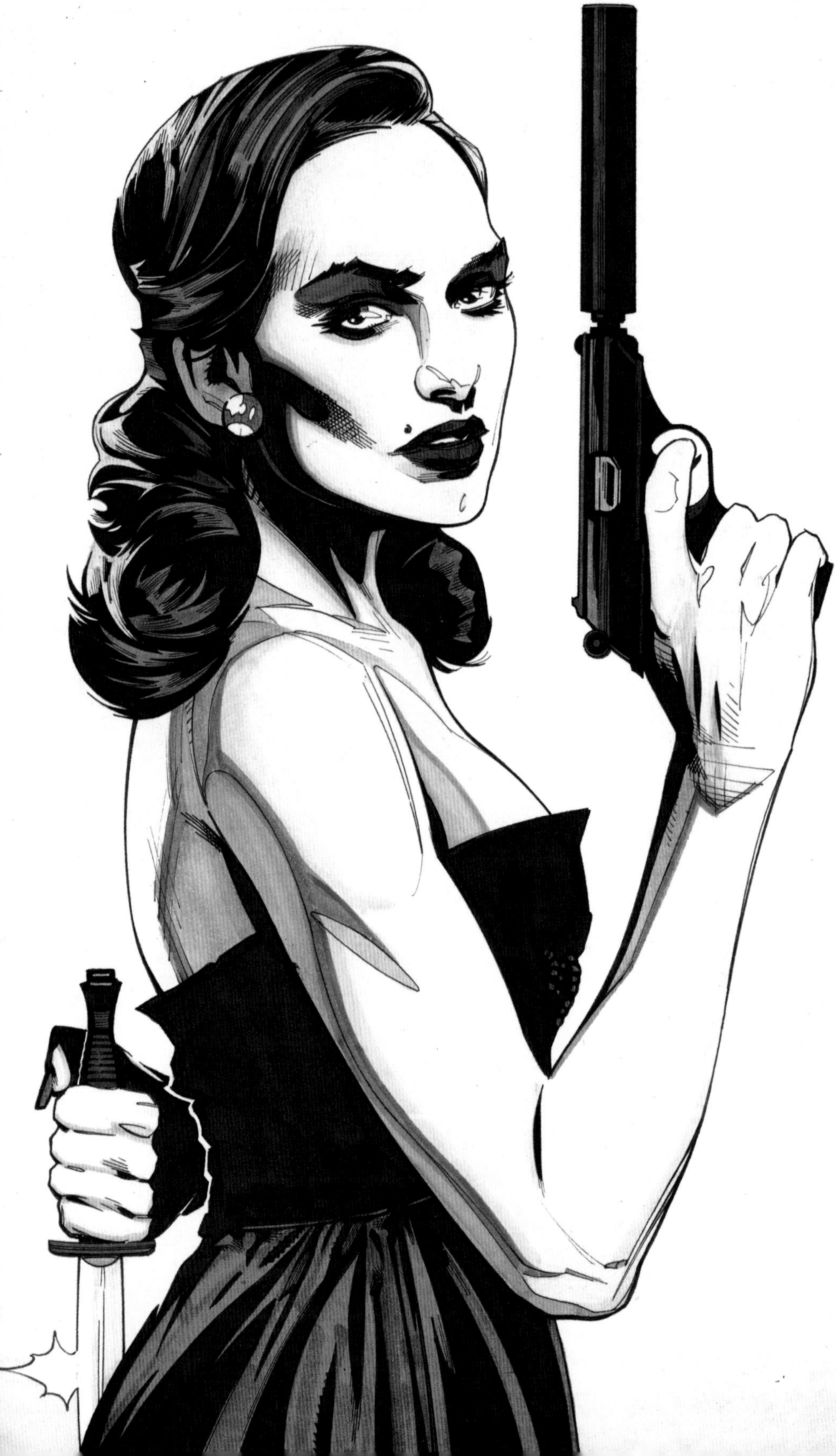

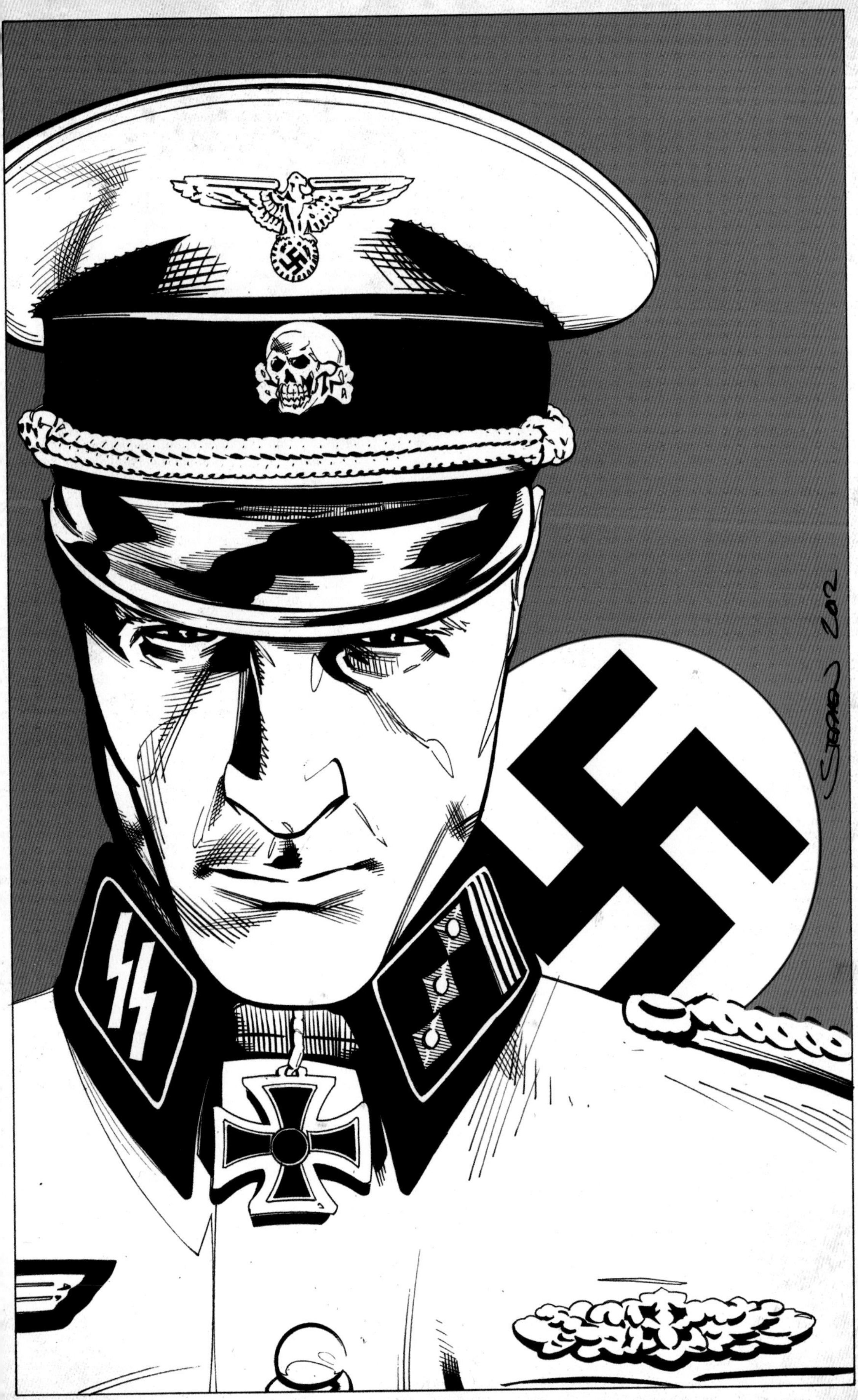

Jordie's various versions of our first collaboration for the series. When I saw these I knew this thing was in the safest possible hands.

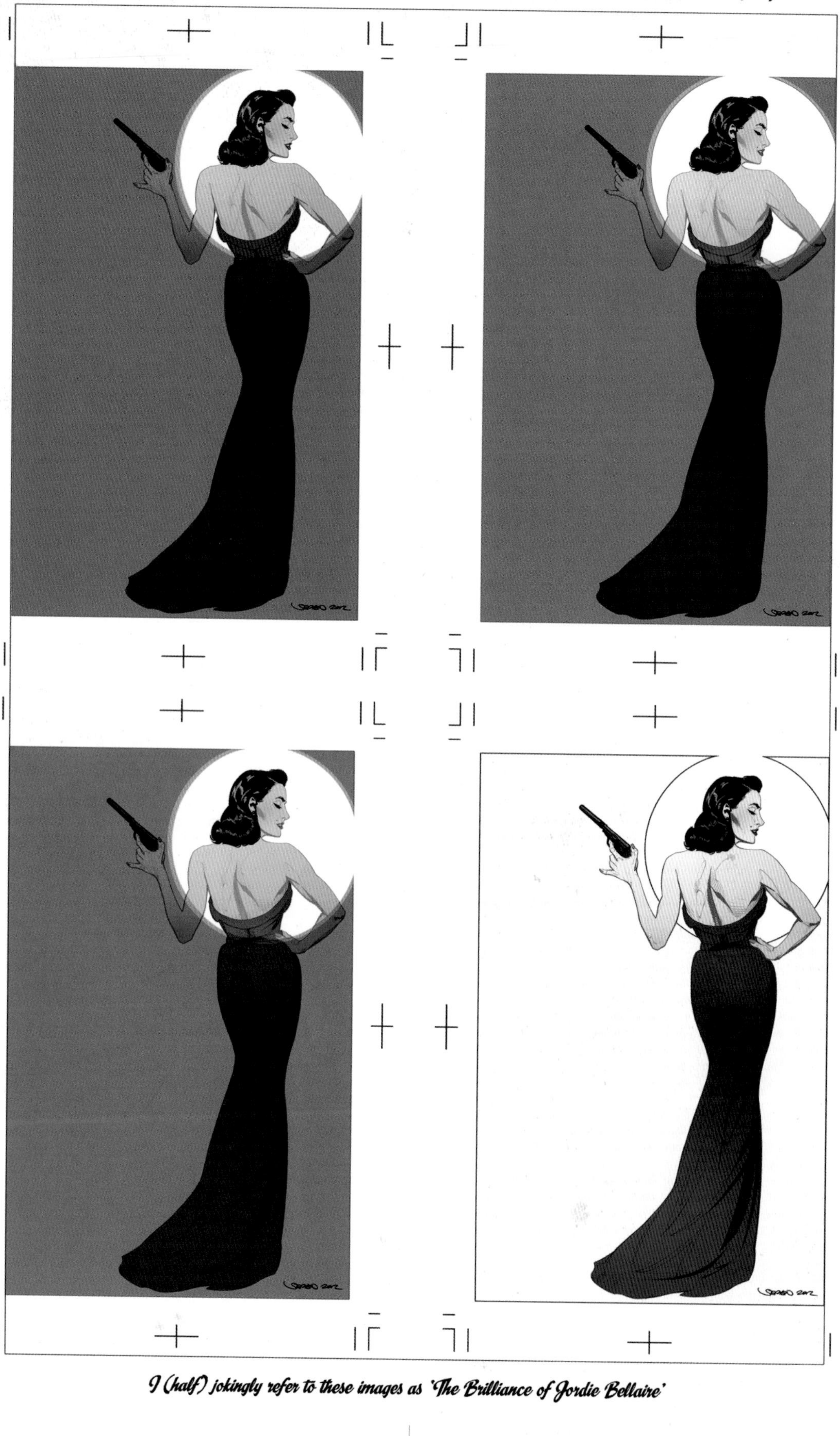

I (half) jokingly refer to these images as 'The Brilliance of Jordie Bellaire'

Cover gallery

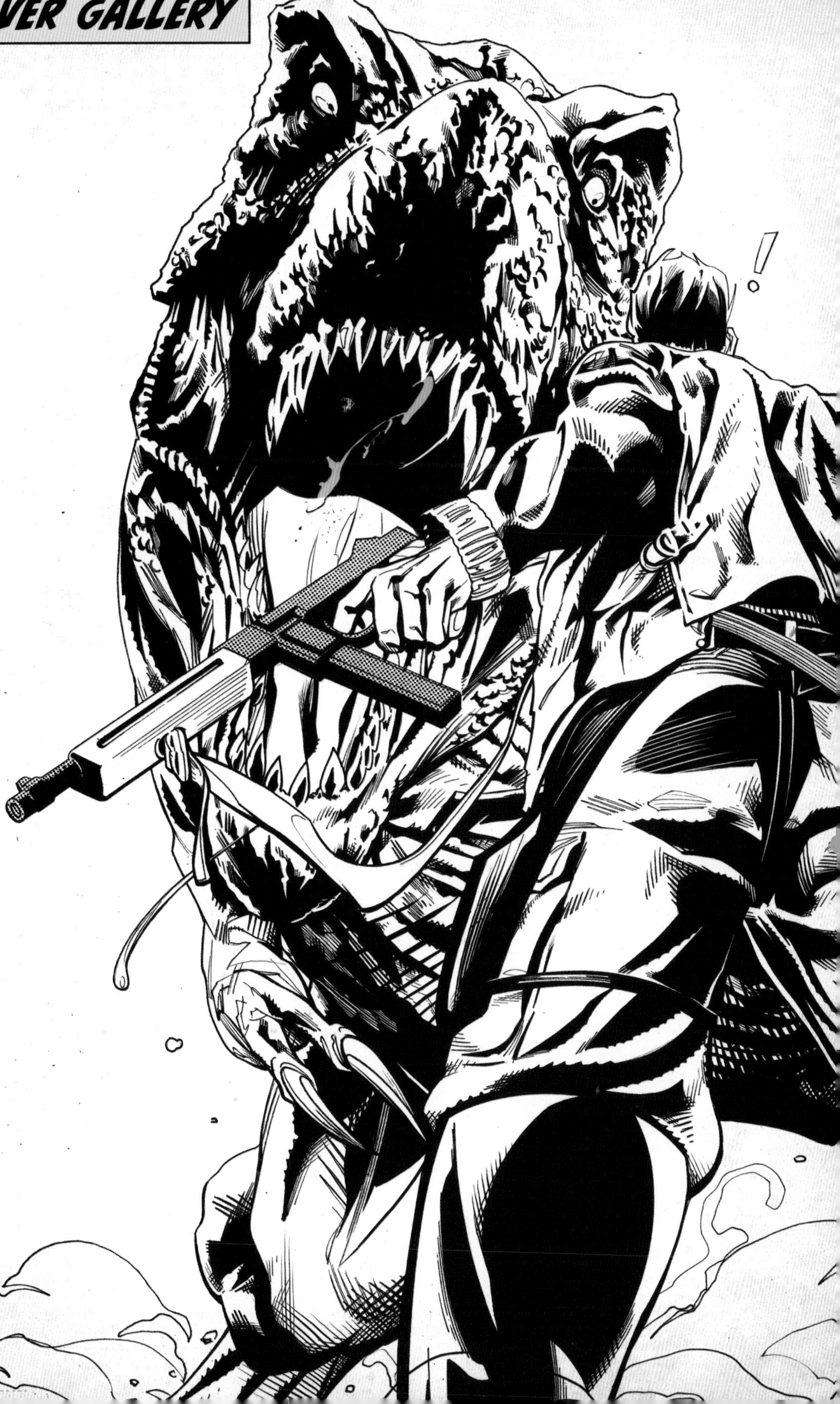
!

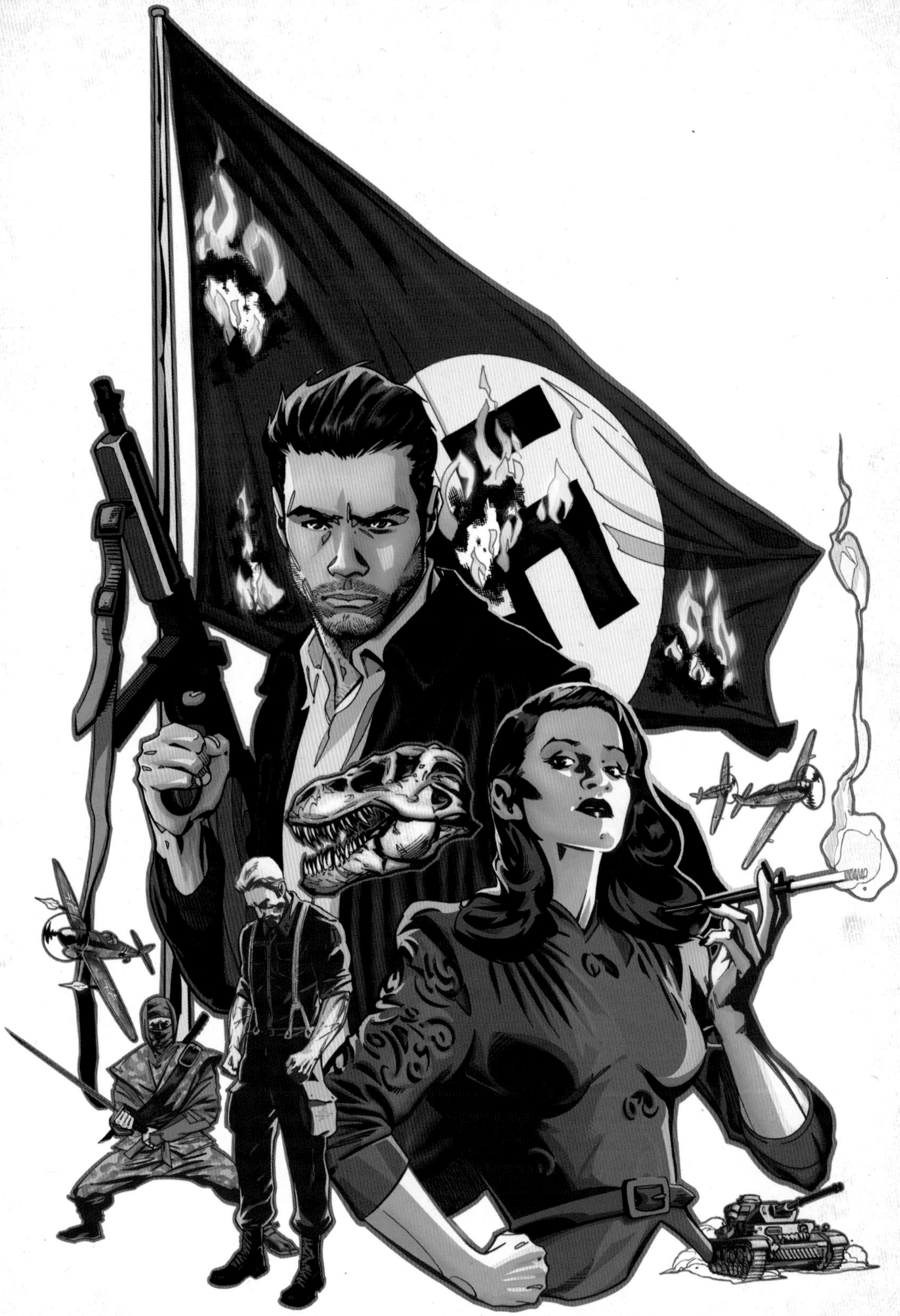

Art by Stephen Mooney

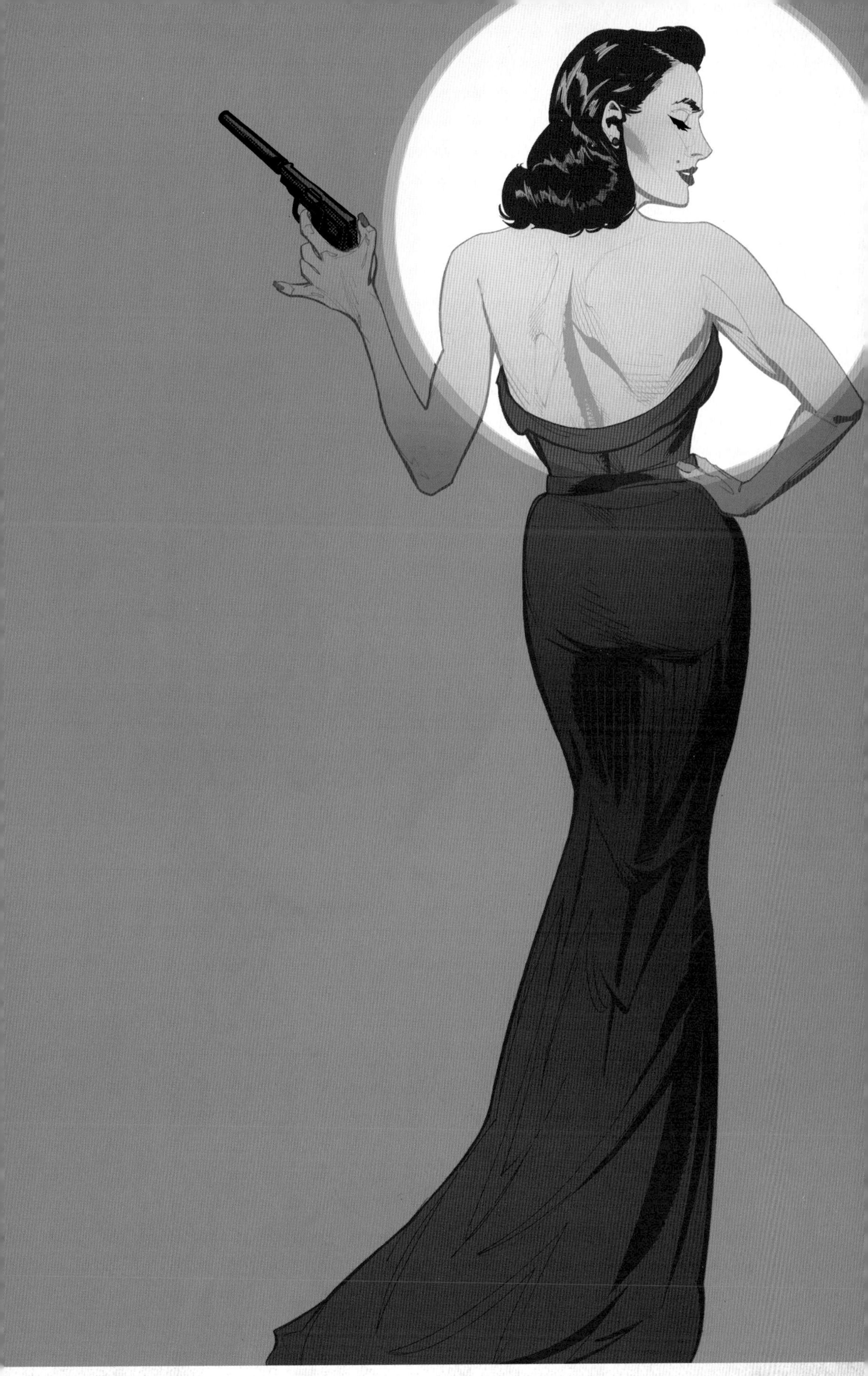

Art by Stephen Mooney • Colors by Jordie Bellaire

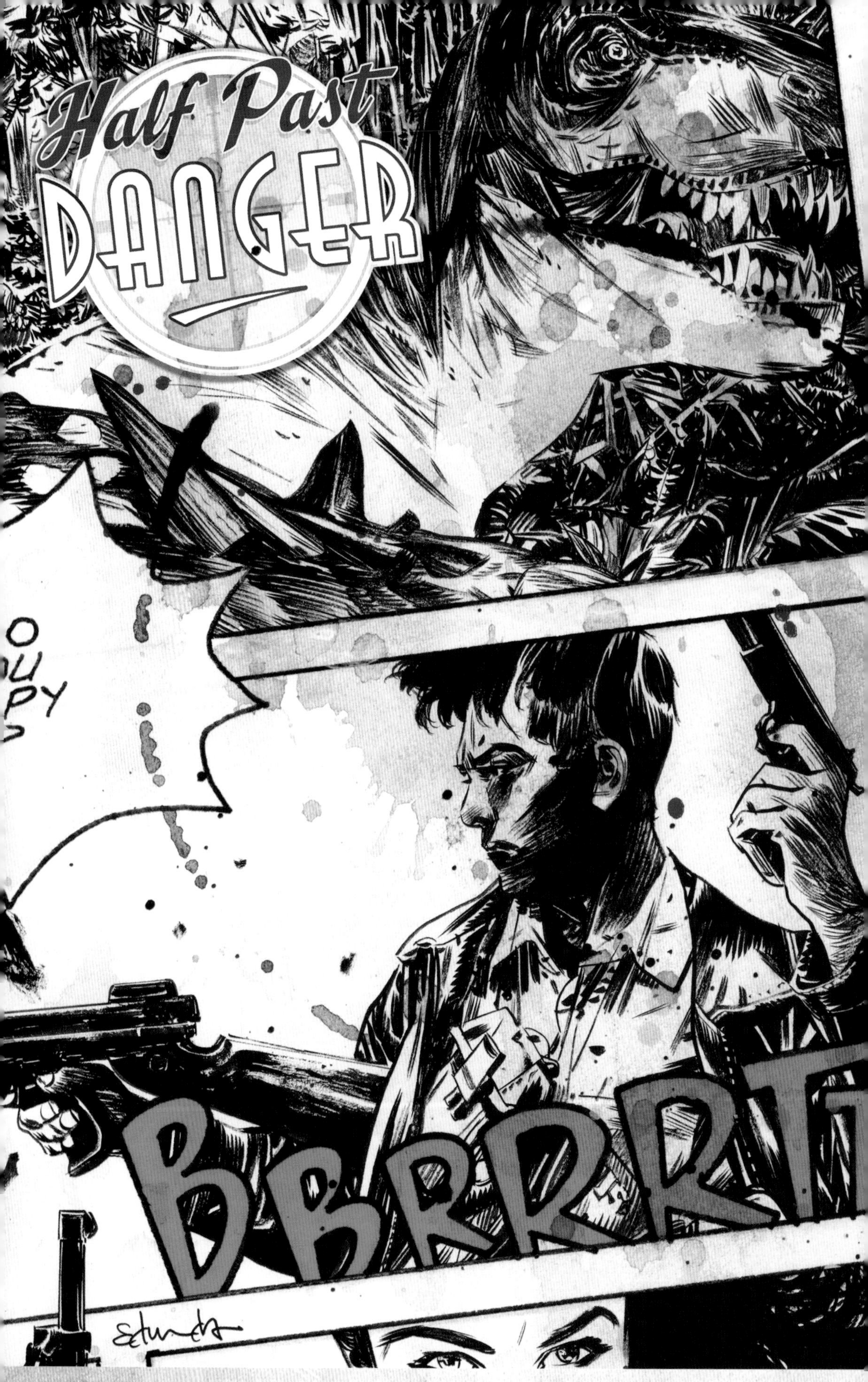
Half Past
DANGER
BBRRRT

Art by Tommy Lee Edwards

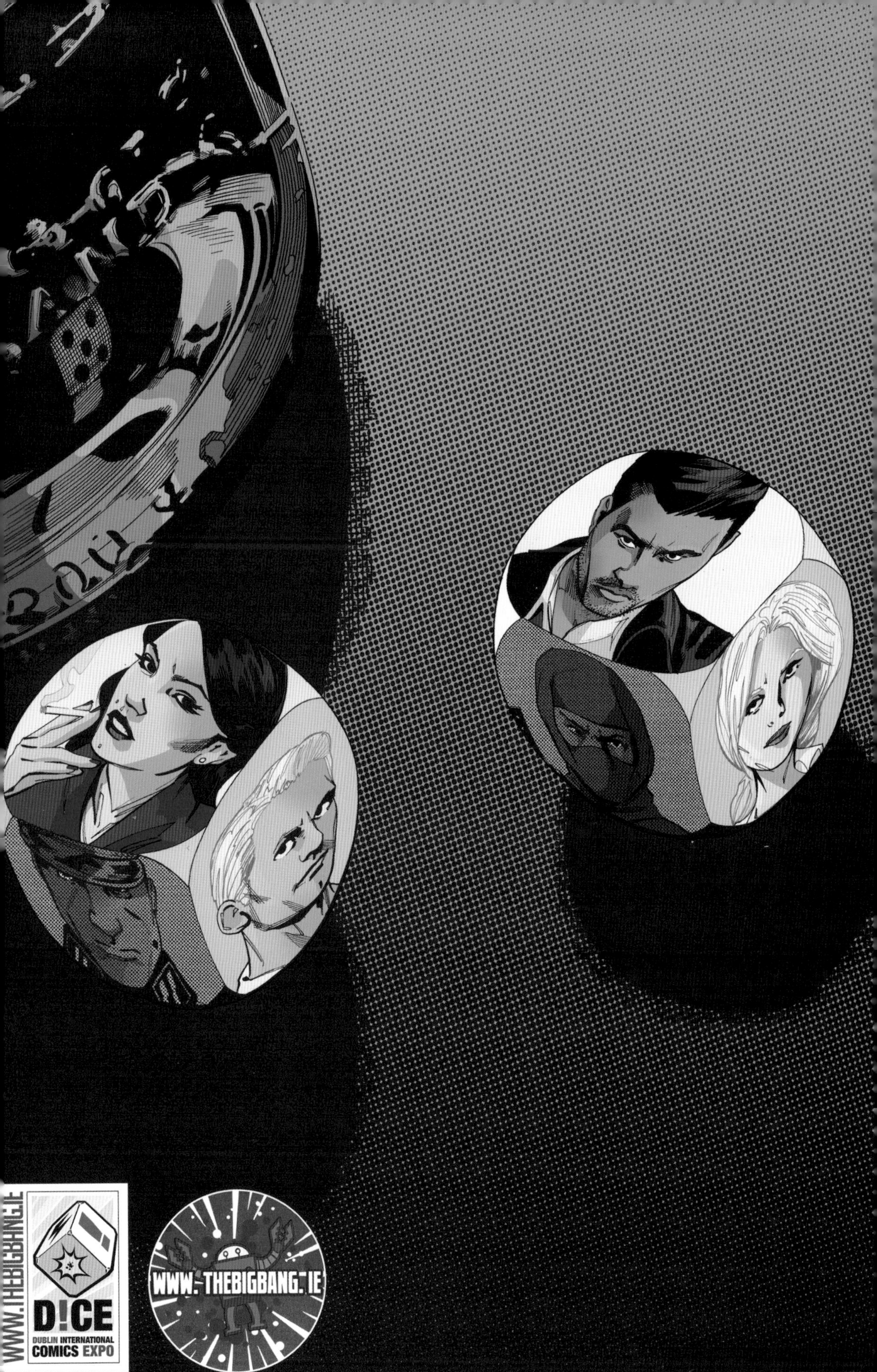
WWW.THEBIGBANG.IE
D!CE
DUBLIN INTERNATIONAL
COMICS EXPO
WWW.-THEBIGBANG.-IE

Art by Stephen Mooney • Colors by Ruth Redmond

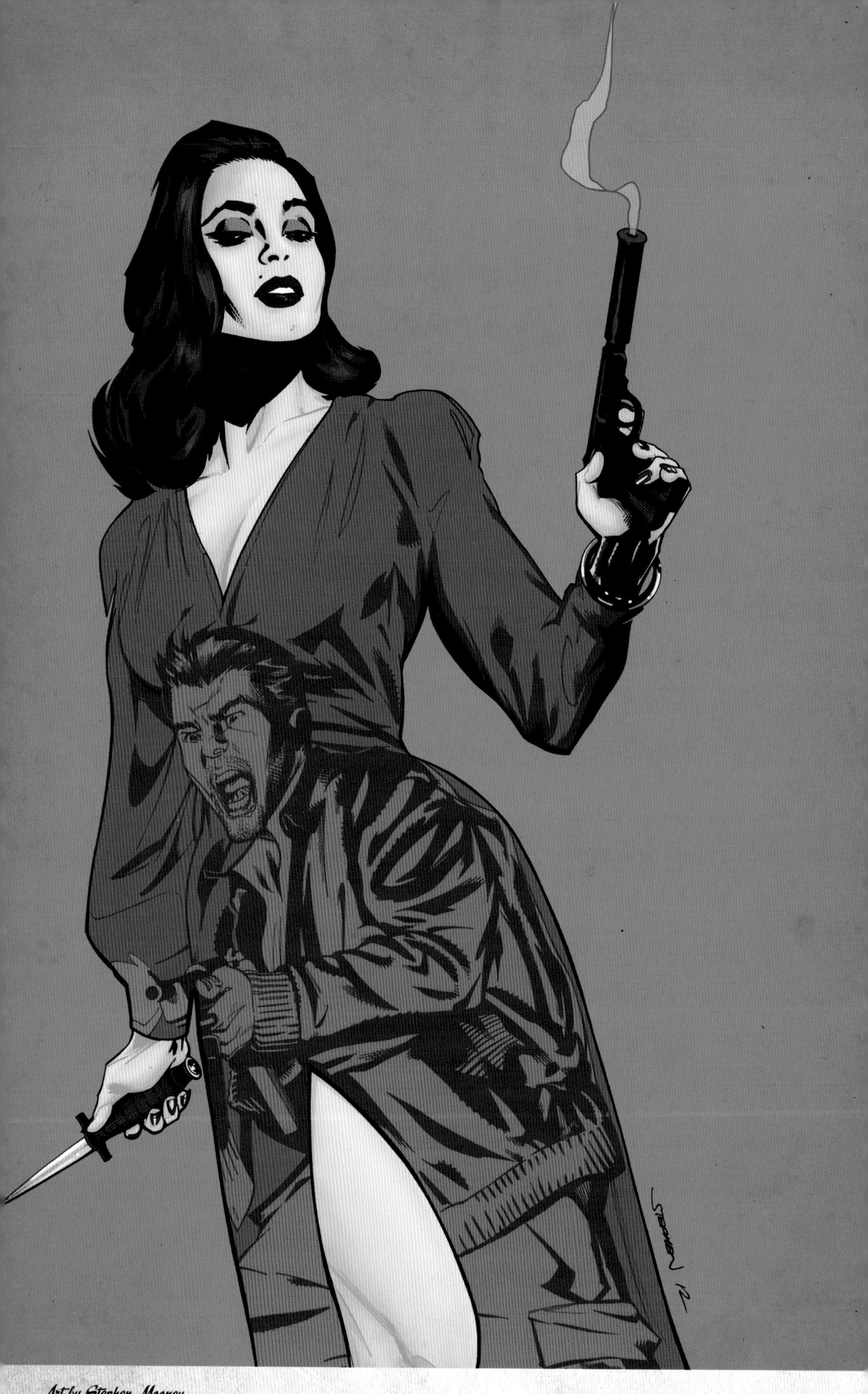

Art by Stephen Mooney

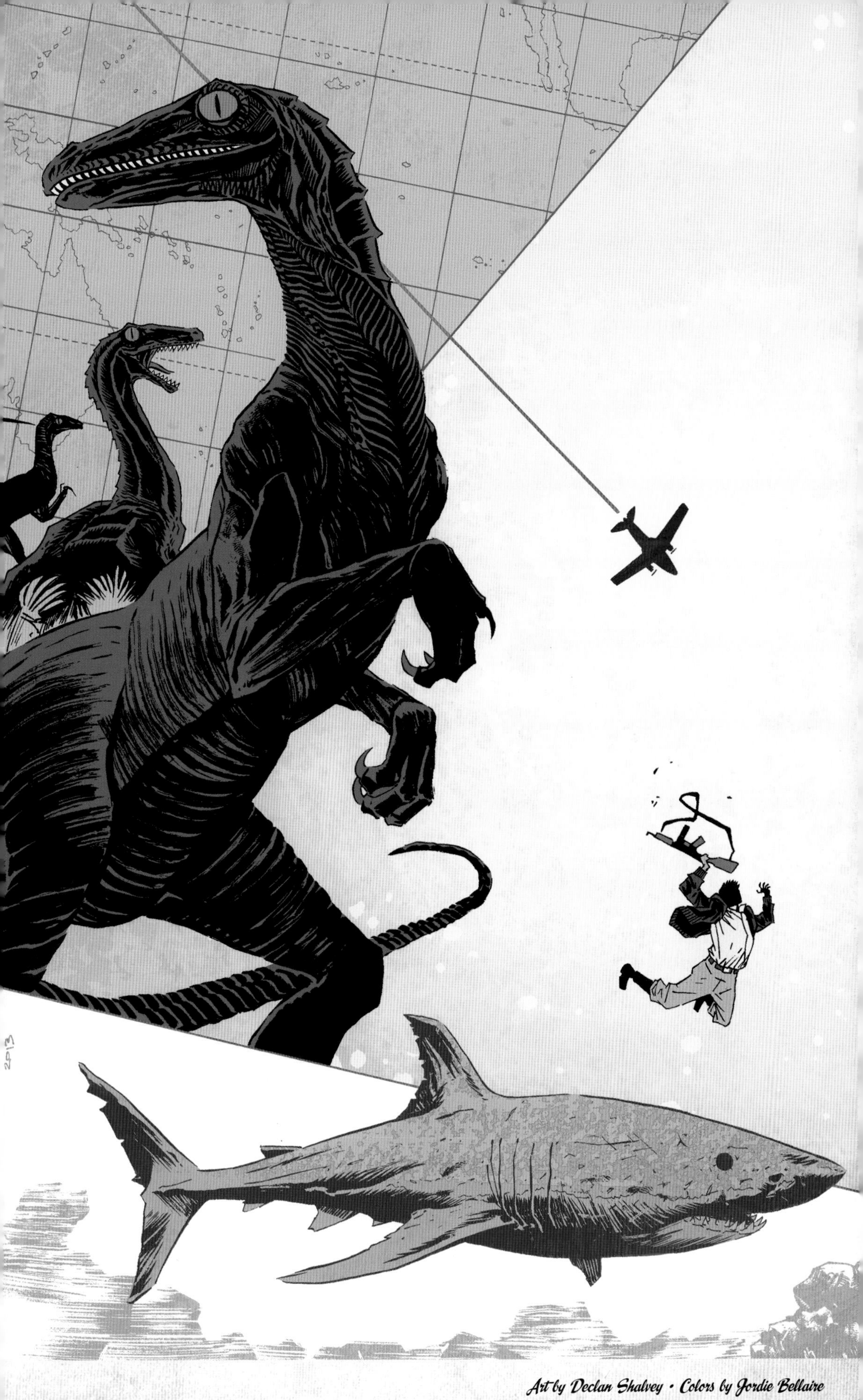

Art by Declan Shalvey • Colors by Jordie Bellaire

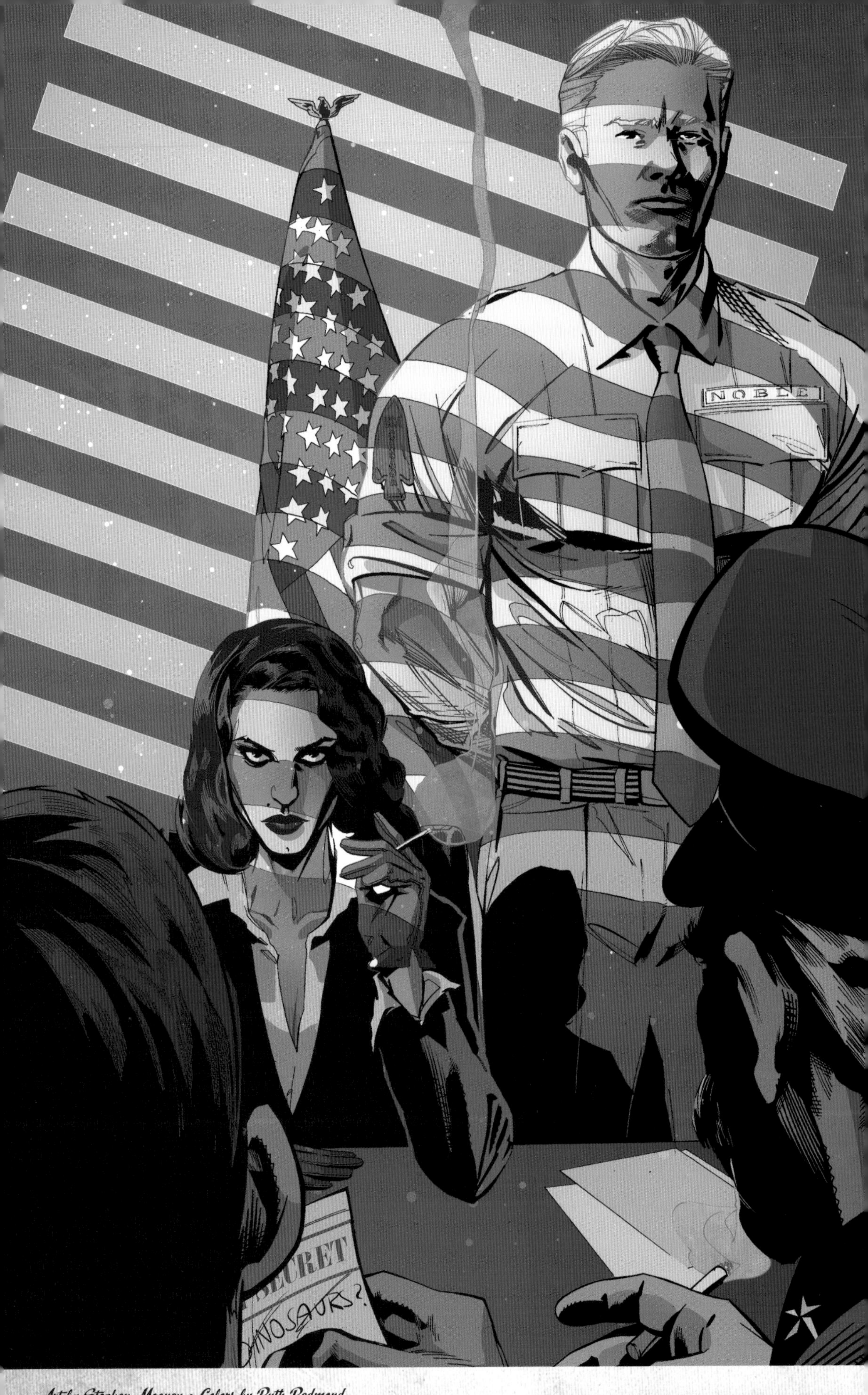
NOBLE
SECRET
DINOSAURS?

Art by Stephen Mooney • Colors by Ruth Redmond

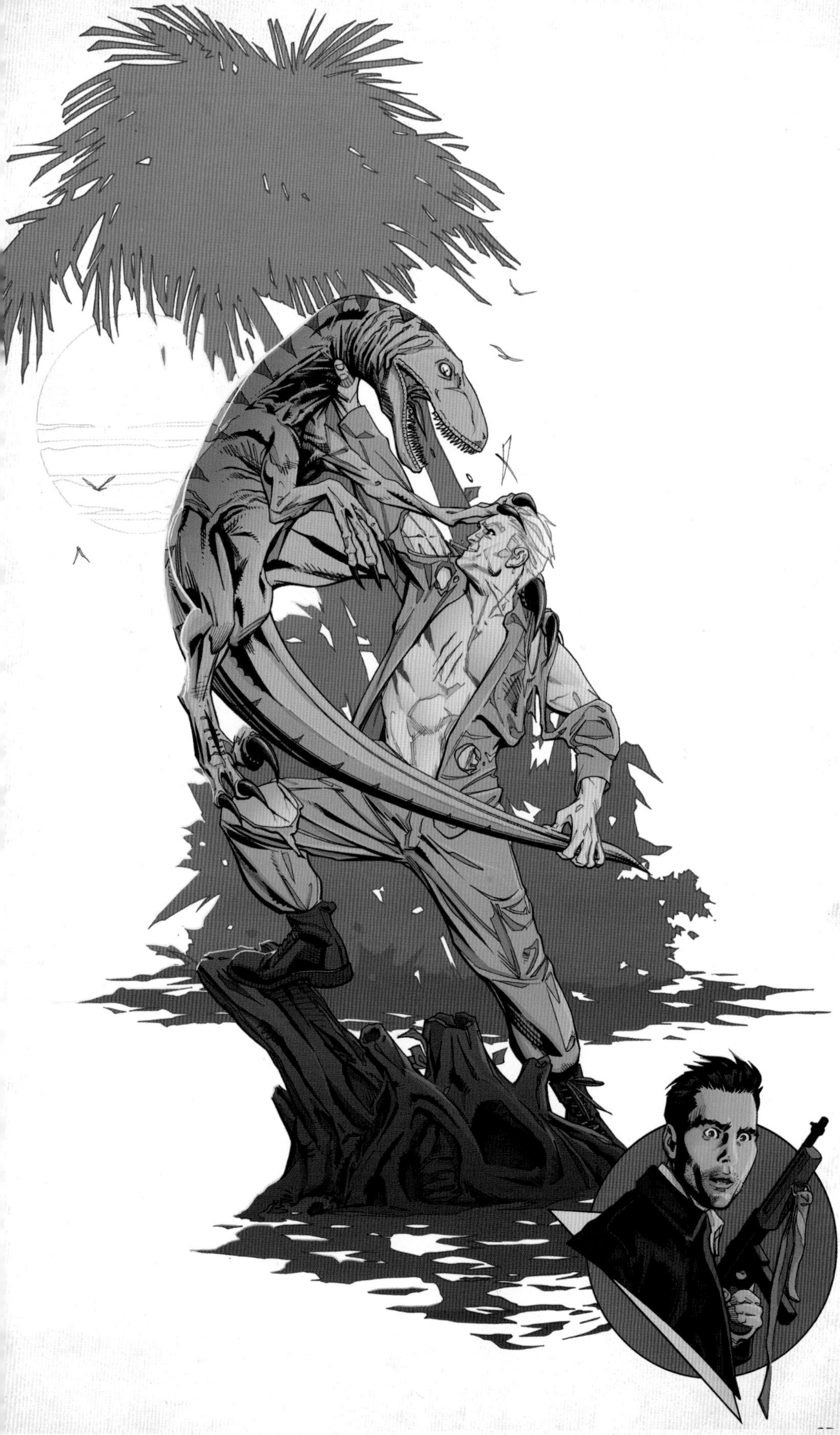

Art by Stephen Mooney

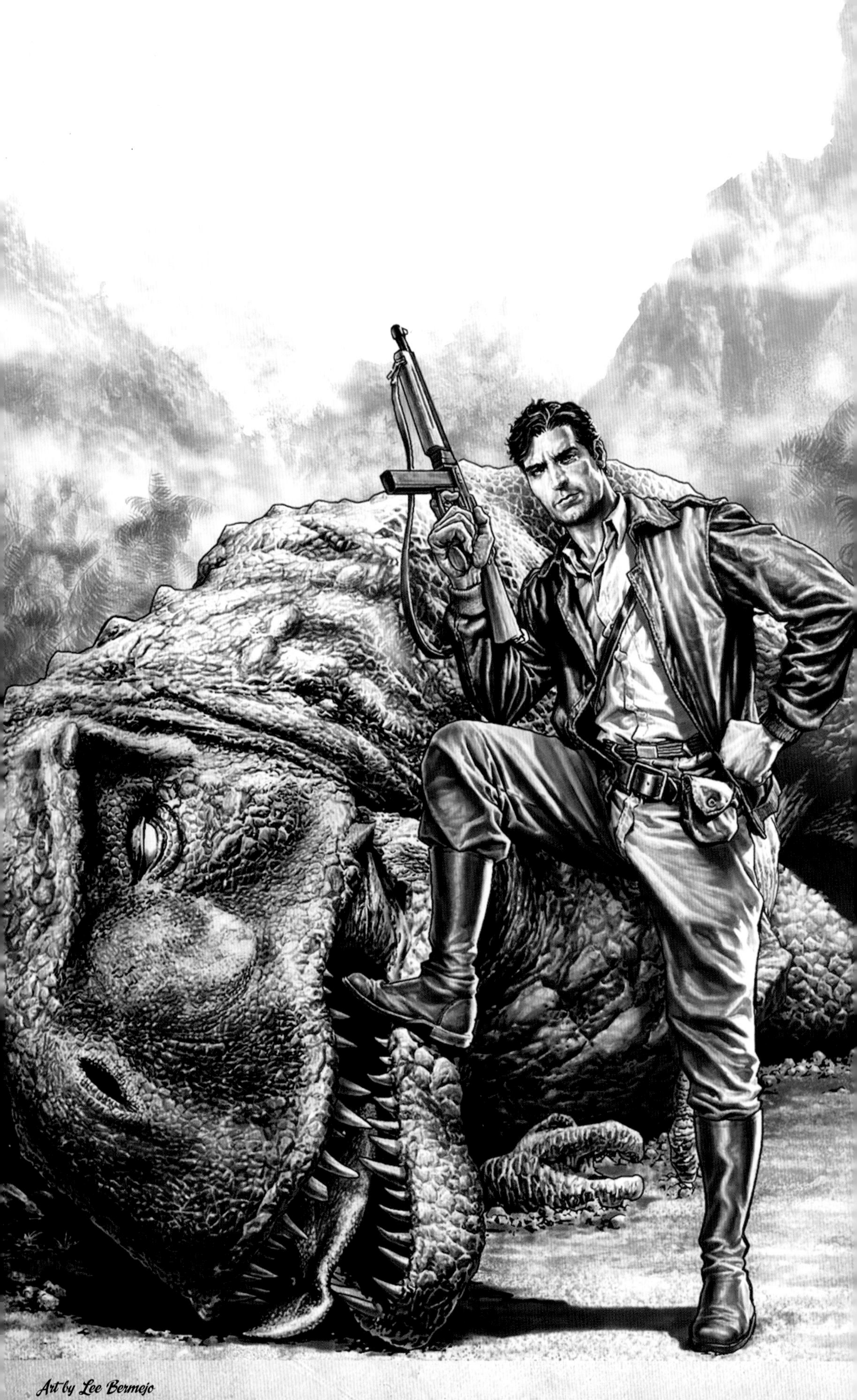
Art by Lee Bermejo

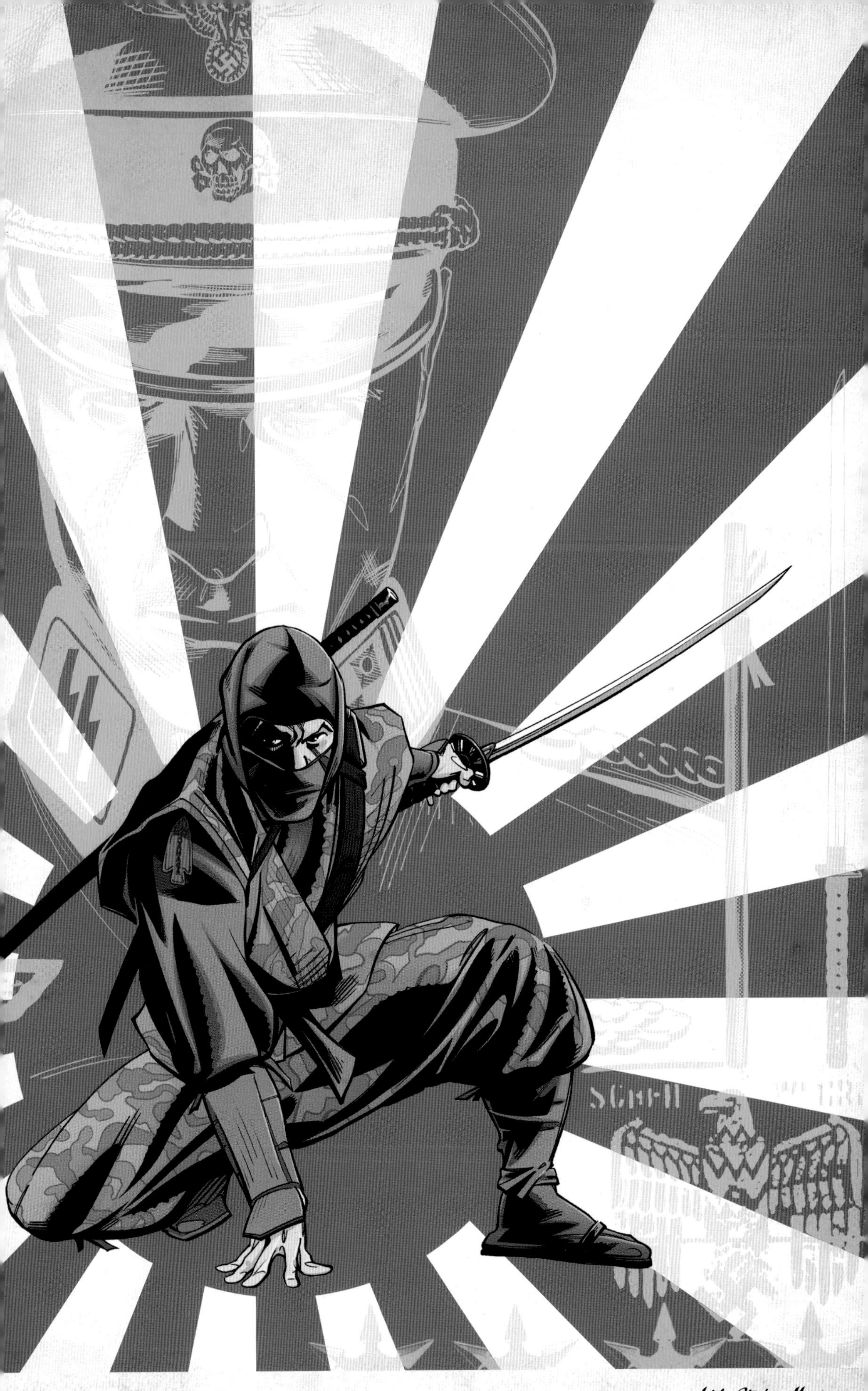

Art by Stephen Mooney

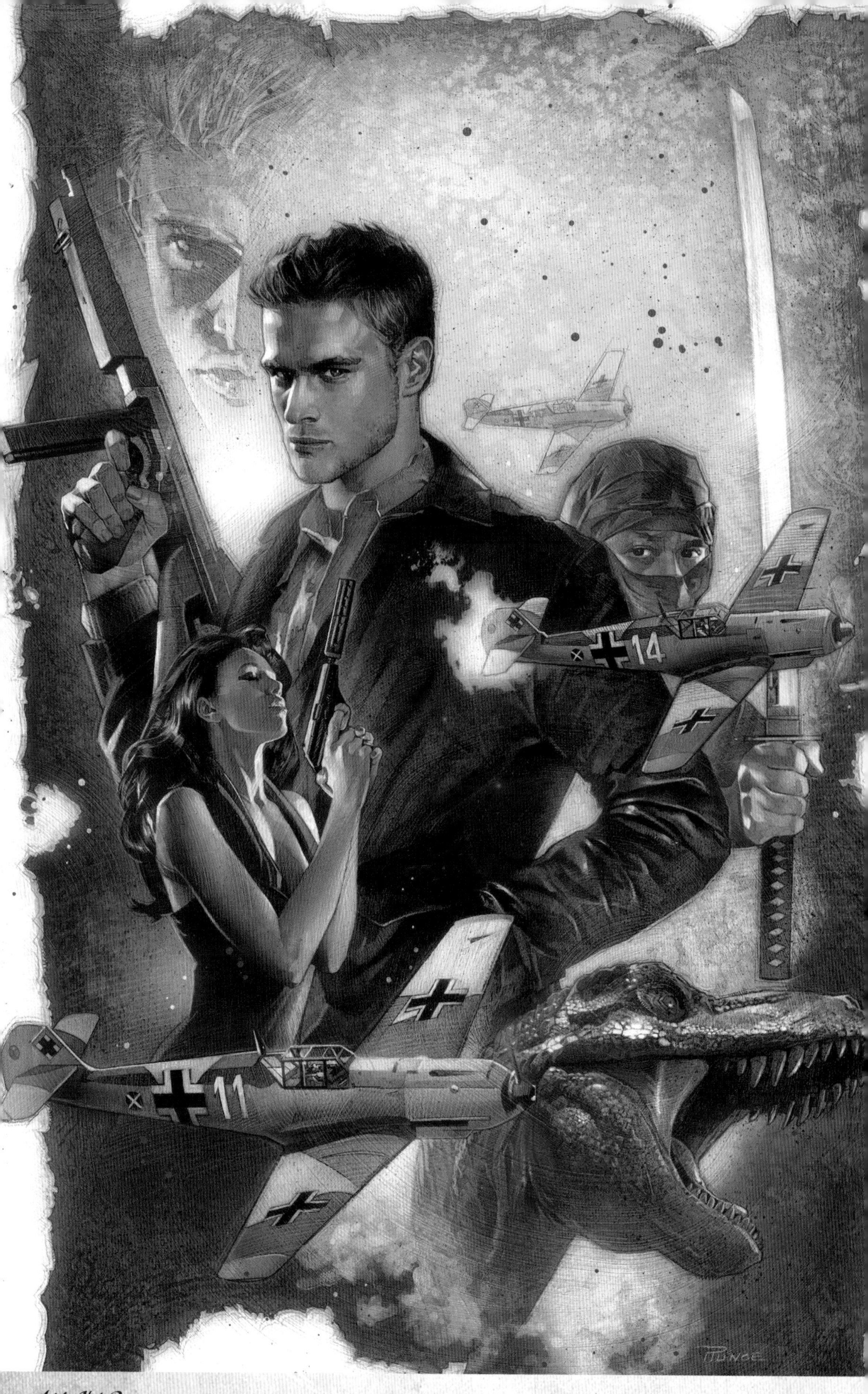
14
11
RUNGE

Art by Nick Runge

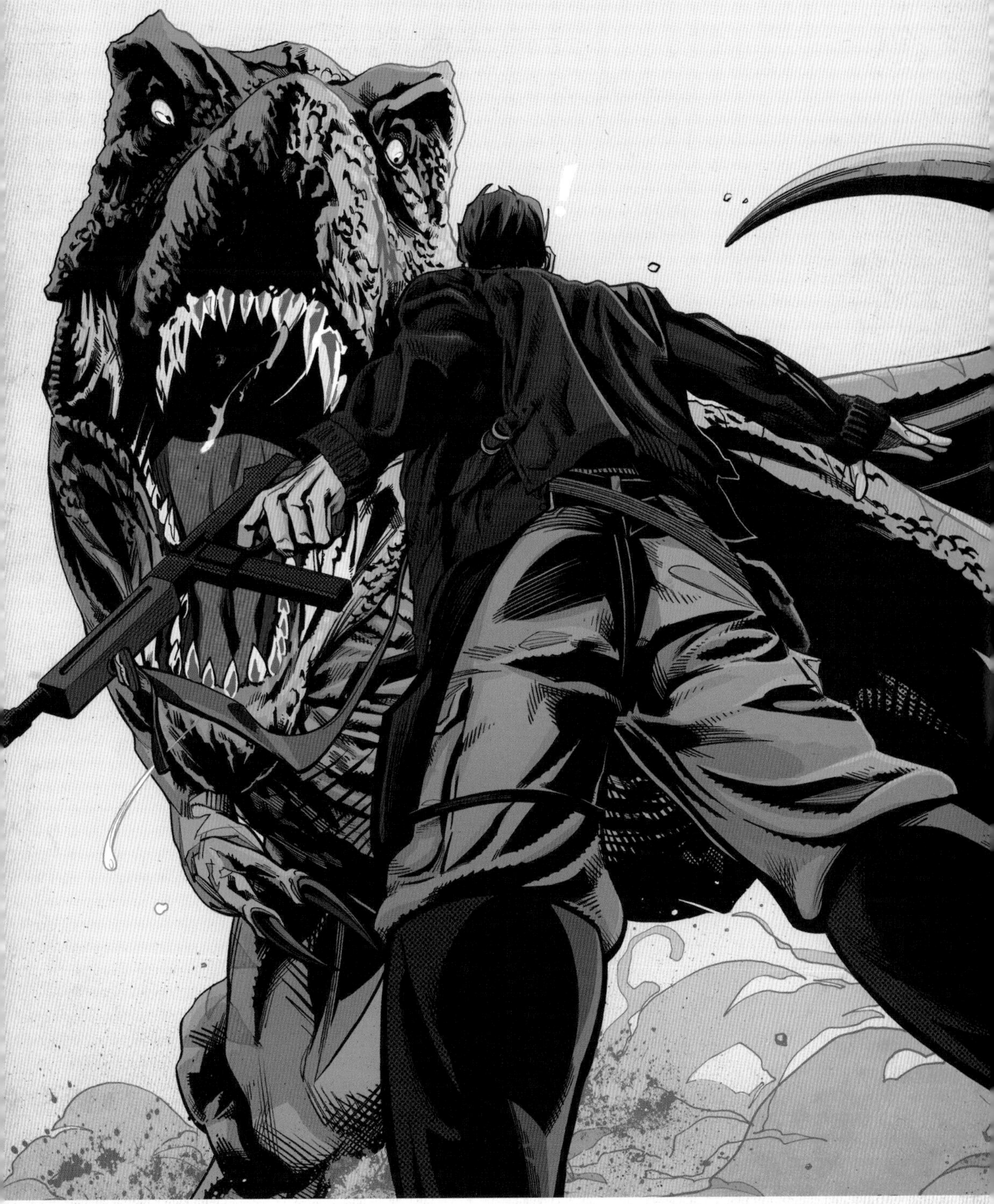
!

Art by Stephen Mooney

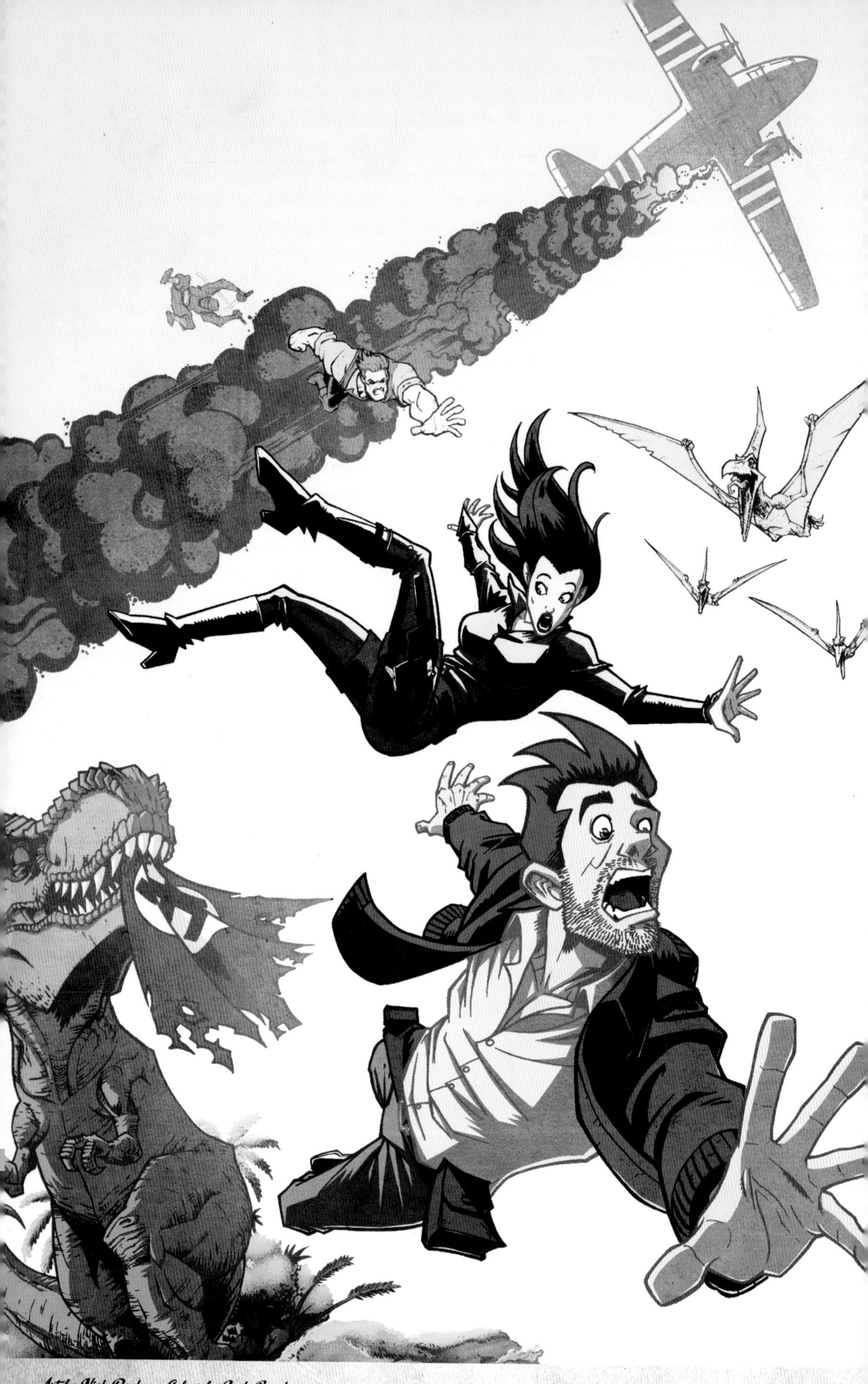

Art by Nick Roche • Colors by Josh Burcham

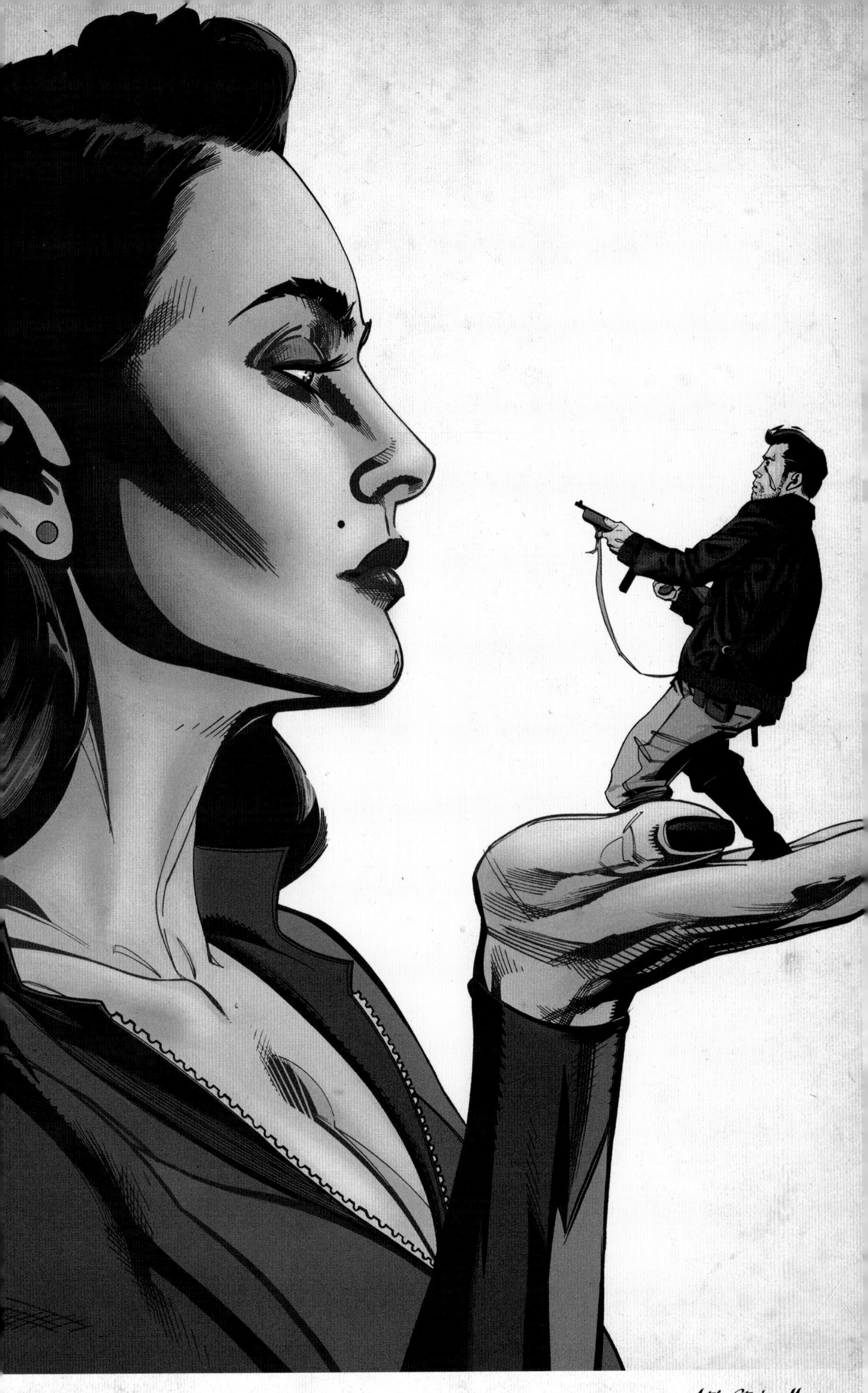

Art by Stephen Mooney

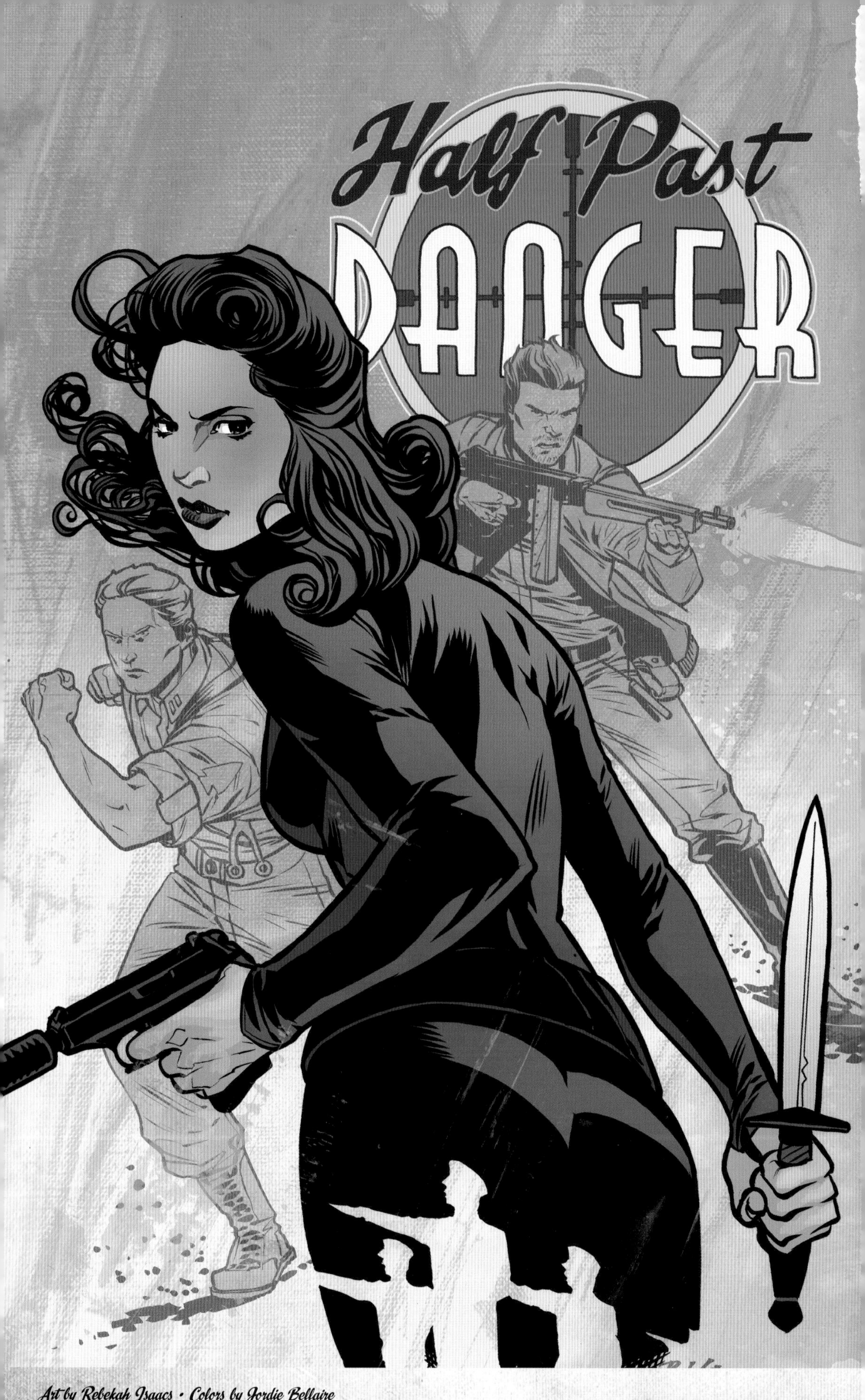
Half Past
DANGER

Art by Rebekah Isaacs • Colors by Jordie Bellaire

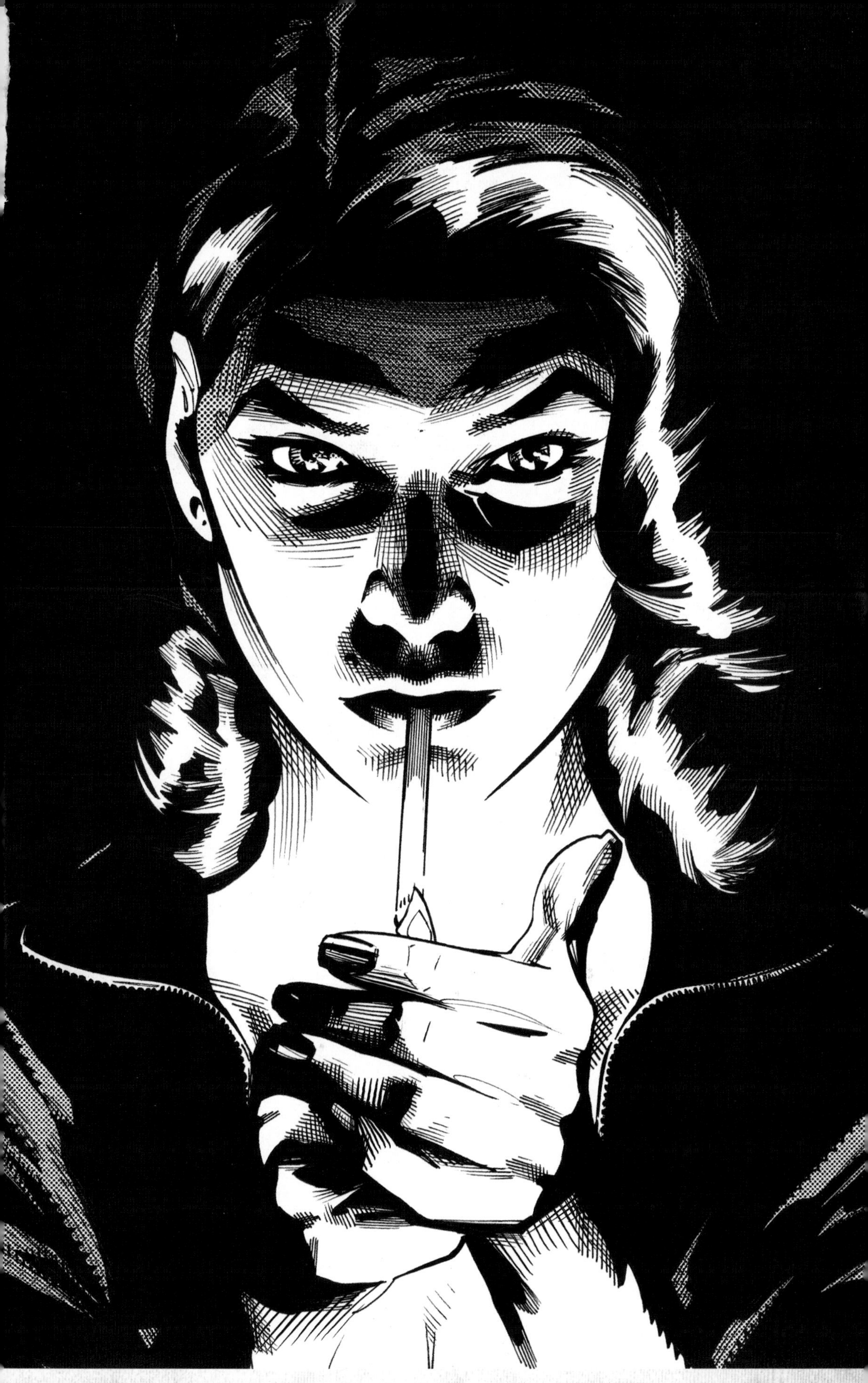

Art by Stephen Mooney

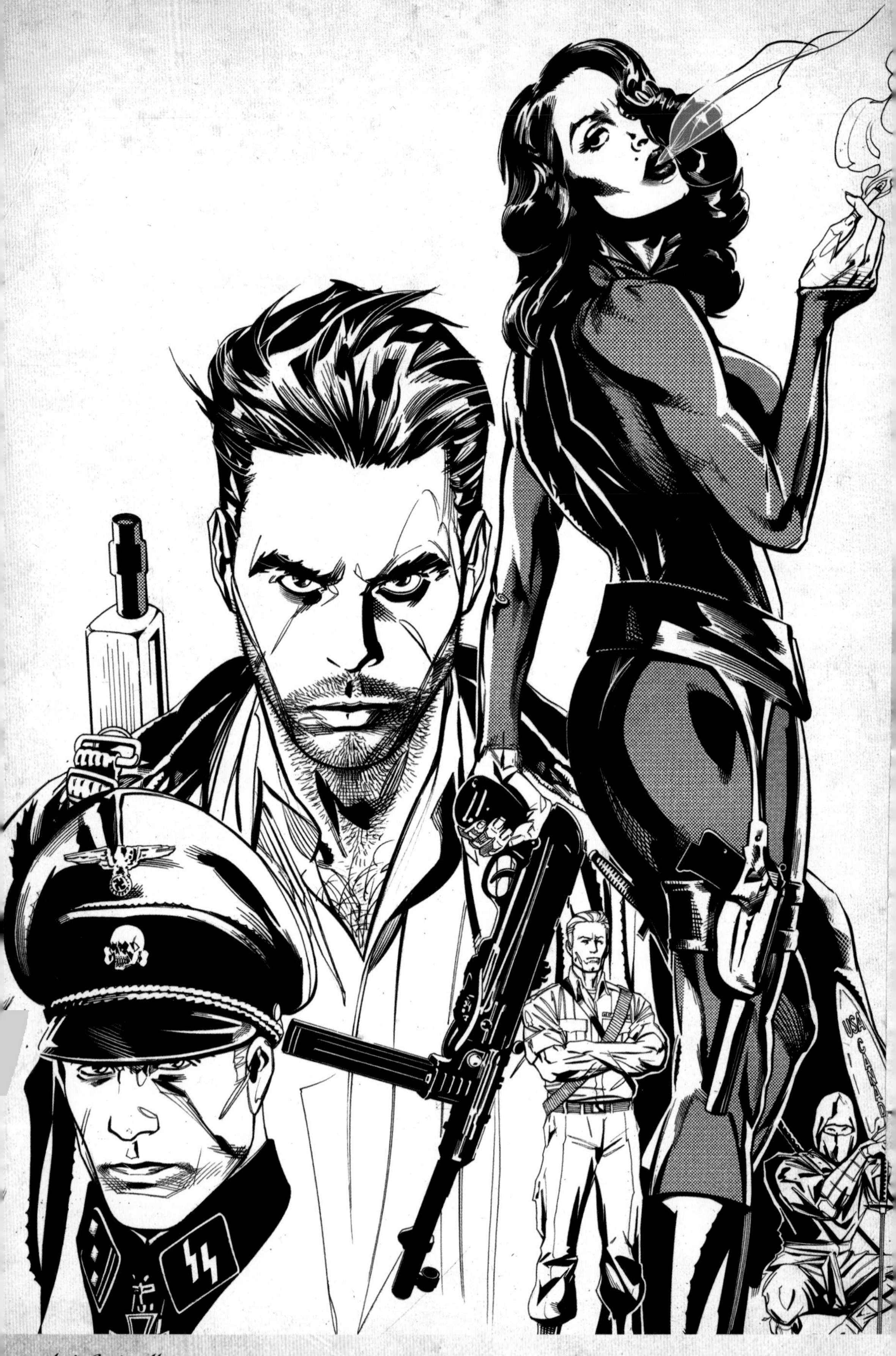
USA

Art by Stephen Mooney

Acknowlegdements

Massive thanks first and foremost to everybody at IDW, one of the very best publishing houses in the business. To my editor Chris Ryall and his assistant editor Chris Schraff (Chris 2: The Sequel). To the amazing design gurus also: Shawn Lee for making the issues sing, and Justin Eisinger for overseeing the production of this beautiful hardcover volume.

Huge thanks to all of my fellow Eclectic Micks and the other heads in the Irish scene, the amazing array of variant cover artists, the boys at Big Bang Comics in Dublin, to Ruth Redmond for her invaluable colouring assists, to my parents, brothers, and wife; thanks so much for all of the invaluable help.

Lastly, special thanks to comics' favourite couple, Dec Shalvey and Jordie Bellaire, who went above and beyond at every turn to help me make *HPD* a reality.

You guys complete me.
Wait.
You guys complete my comics.

About the Author

Stephen Mooney lives and works in his beloved Ireland. He's been working in comics for ten years, mostly at IDW Publishing. *Half Past Danger* is his first creator-owned work, and therefore closest to his heart.

Assuming he has one.

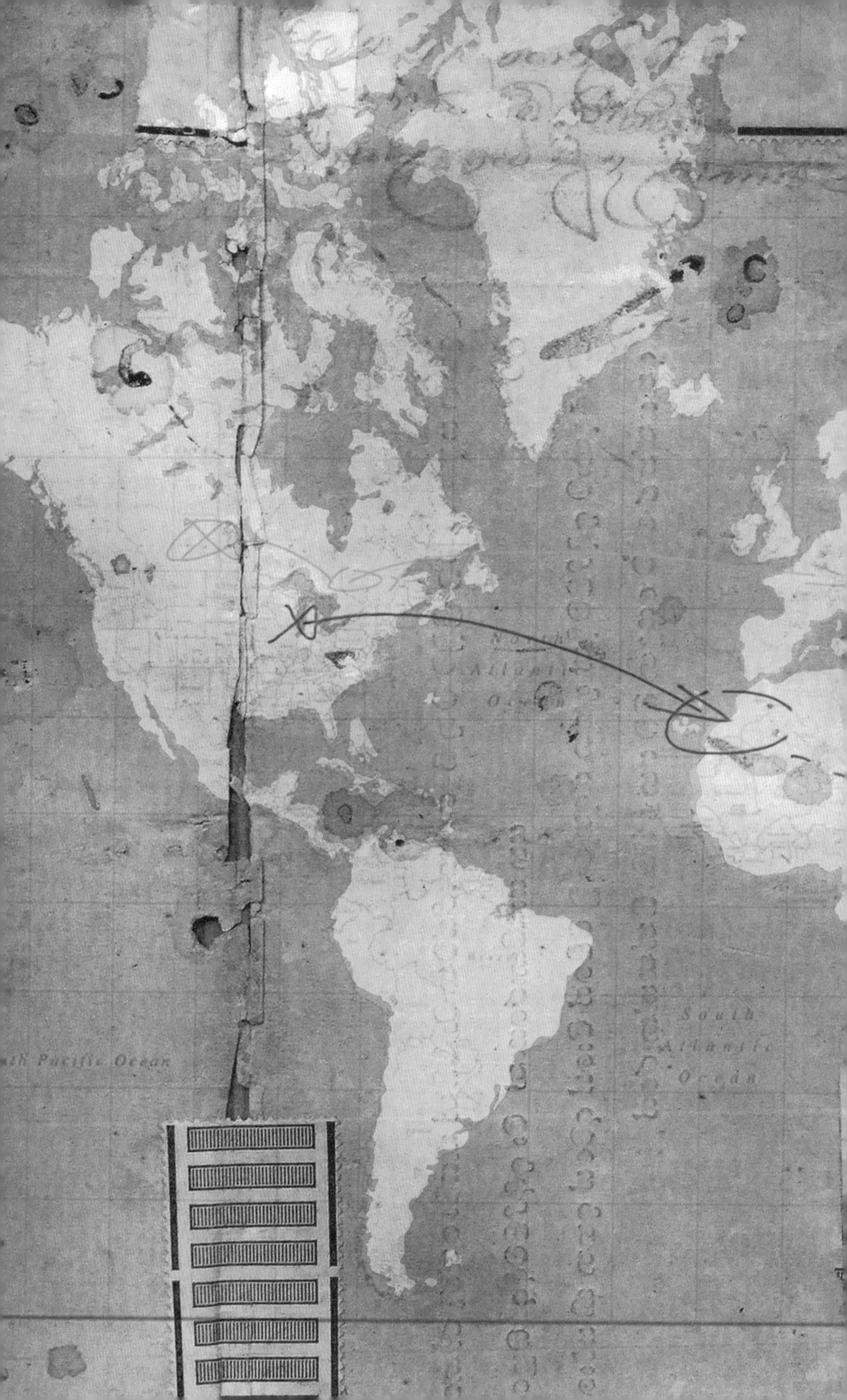
North Atlantic Ocean
South Atlantic Ocean
th Pacific Ocean